Human Conception
In Vitro

Boury Hall

1981

Human Conception
In Vitro

Proceedings of the first Bourn Hall meeting

edited by

R. G. EDWARDS
*Bourn Hall, Cambridge, Reader in Physiology, Cambridge
University and Fellow of Churchill College, Cambridge*

and

JEAN M. PURDY
*Bourn Hall, Cambridge and Physiological Laboratory,
University of Cambridge*

ACADEMIC PRESS, INC.
(Harcourt Brace Jovanovich, Publishers)
London   Orlando   San Diego   New York
Toronto   Montreal   Sydney   Tokyo

ACADEMIC PRESS INC. (LONDON) LTD.
24/28 Oval Road
London NW 1

United States Edition published by
ACADEMIC PRESS, INC.
Orlando, Florida 32887

British Library Cataloguing in Publication Data

Human conception in vitro.
1. Fertilization in vitro, Human — Congresses
I. Edwards, R. G.   II. Purdy, J. M.
618   RG135

ISBN 0-12-232740-3
LCCCN 82-71006

PRINTED IN THE UNITED STATES OF AMERICA

84 85 86 87   9 8 7 6 5 4 3

List of Participants

Basel	Dr. Angelo Conti, Universitats-Frauenklinik, CH 4031 Basel, Kantonspital Basel, Switzerland.
Bourn Hall	Dr. Robert G. Edwards, Physiological Laboratory, Cambridge University and Bourn Hall, Bourn, Cambridgeshire.
	Dr. Simon B. Fishel, Physiological Laboratory, Cambridge University and Bourn Hall, Bourn, Cambridgeshire.
	Miss Jean M. Purdy, Physiological Laboratory, Cambridge University and Bourn Hall, Bourn, Cambridgeshire.
	Mr. Patrick C. Steptoe, Bourn Hall, Bourn, Cambridgeshire.
	Mr. John Webster, Bourn Hall, Bourn, Cambridgeshire.
Gothenburg	Dr. Lars Hamberger, Department of Obstetrics and Gynaecology, University of Göteborg, Sahlgrenska Sjukhuset, S-413 45 Göteborg, Sweden.
	Dr. Torbjörn Hillensjö, Department of Physiology, University of Göteborg, Sahlgrenska Sjukhuset, S-413 45 Göteborg, Sweden.
	Dr. Lennart Nilsson, Department of Obstetrics and Gynaecology, University of Göteborg, Sahlgrenska Sjukhuset, S-413 45 Göteborg, Sweden.
Kiel	Dr. Vera Baukloh, Klinikum der Christian-Albrechts, Universitat Kiel, D-2300 Kiel 1, Hegewischstrasse 4, W. Germany.
	Dr. Lilo Mettler, Klinikum der Christian-Albrechts, Universitat Kiel, D-2300 Kiel 1, Hegewischstrasse 4, W. Germany.
Manchester	Mr. Philip Dyer, St. Mary's Hospital, Whitworth Park, Manchester, M13 0JH.
	Dr. Brian A. Lieberman, St. Mary's Hospital, Whitworth Park, Manchester, M13 0JH.

Melbourne— **Monash**	Professor John F. Leeton, Department of Obstetrics and Gynaecology, Monash University, The Queen Victoria Memorial Hospital, Melbourne, Australia 3000. Dr. Alan O. Trounson, Department of Obstetrics and Gynaecology, Monash University, The Queen Victoria Memorial Hospital, Melbourne, Australia 3000.
Melbourne— **Royal Women's** **Hospital**	Dr. Ian W. H. Johnston, Department of Obstetrics and Gynaecology, Royal Women's Hospital, University of Melbourne, Parkville, Victoria 3052, Australia. Dr. Alex Lopata, Department of Obstetrics and Gynaecology, Royal Women's Hospital, University of Melbourne, Parkville, Victoria 3052, Australia. Dr. Alec I. Speirs, Department of Obstetrics and Gynaecology, Royal Women's Hospital, University of Melbourne, Parkville, Victoria 3052, Australia.
Norfolk	Dr. Georgeanna S. Jones, Department of Obstetrics and Gynecology, Eastern Virginia Medical School, 603 Medical Tower, Norfolk, Virginia 23507, U.S.A. Dr. Howard W. Jones, Department of Obstetrics and Gynecology, Eastern Virginia Medical School, 603 Medical Tower, Norfolk, Virginia 23507, U.S.A.
Paris— **Clamart**	Dr. Rene Frydman, Service de Gynecologie-Obstetrique, Hôpital Antoine Beclere, 157, Rue de la Porte de Trivaux, 92140 Clamart, France. Dr. Jacques Testart, Service de Gynecologie-Obstetrique, Hôpital Antoine Beclere, 157, Rue de la Porte de Trivaux, 92140 Clamart, France.
Paris— **Sèvres**	Dr. Jean Cohen, Service de Gynaecologie Obstetrique, Hôpital de Sèvres, 92300 Sèvres, France. Dr. Michelle Plachot, Service de Gynaecologie Obstetrique, Hôpital de Sèvres, 92300 Sèvres, France.
Vienna	Dr. Wilfred Feichtinger, IInd Department of Obstetrics and Gynaecology, Medical School, University of Vienna, Spitalgasse 23, 1090 Vienna, Austria. Dr. Stephan Szalay, IInd Department of Obstetrics and Gynaecology, Medical School, University of Vienna, Spitalgasse 23, 1090 Vienna, Austria.

Preface

Many groups of investigators are now accepting the need to fertilize human oocytes *in vitro* and then replace cleaving embryos into the mother for the cure of various forms of infertility. The increasing number of reports of procedures, results, pregnancies and births attest to the widespread acceptance of these methods in clinical practice.

The current situation is a far cry from the time 12 years ago when we, in collaboration with Patrick Steptoe, began the lonely and frustrating pathway that ultimately led to the joy of the birth of Louise Brown. There were no funds freely available, nor any encouragement to begin or continue the work, while a chorus of criticism accompanied every advance in our attempts to introduce the methods.

Indeed, in retrospect we are astonished ourselves that so much was accomplished on a shoestring and at the distance of 180 miles separating us from Oldham. The control of ovulation, the fundamentals of follicle growth and aspiration of preovulatory oocytes, fertilization and cleavage to the hatched blastocyst *in vitro*, embryo replacements in stimulated and natural cycles, the first attempts at freezing and thawing human oocytes and embryos; all these were accomplished in our one-bed allowance in the tiny Kershaw's Hospital, with a minimum of laboratory space and equipment bought from our limited research grants at Cambridge University — and all of these discoveries were made before Louise and the other two babies were born.

It was accordingly with a sense of pride that we invited several groups of our colleagues to Bourn Hall where we have resumed our work after an interval of two years. We welcome the input of so many people into the field now, with their ideas on new treatments and methods. There is so much more to discover of scientific and clinical value about human reproductive physiology and embryology. Who can doubt that the observations presented in this book are still merely the first steps to greatly improved methods and approaches in clinical work, and perhaps to new forms of medicine on reproduction, embryo screening and other fields of endeavour.

We have attempted to retain the freshness of the debates at the meeting, together with the authoritative manuscripts and opinions submitted by the contributors. The topics chosen were intended to cover the full breadth of discussion of the field, yet at the same time to be of value in helping new groups to introduce these methods into their own hospitals. We hope that the inclusion of much fine detail, in addition to the consideration of many matters of principle from science to ethics will stimulate many of our readers into adopting these methods, or at least in understanding them better.

We have to thank so many people for their help. The staff at Bourn Hall and Churchill College did everything possible to make the conference memorable. Financial support came from Clin Path, Mercia Brocades, Academic Press and Savory and Moore, but mostly from our own funds in Cambridge University and Bourn Hall. We thank the authors and discussants for returning their contributions so promptly. And last but not least we are indebted to Barbara Rankin and Caroline Dawkin for their excellent secretarial work.

Robert G. Edwards
Jean M. Purdy
January, 1982

Contents

PART 2

Laparoscopy of the
Preovulatory Follicle

PART 3

Fertilization and
Preimplantation Growth
In Vitro

PART 4

The Luteal Phase Uterus
And
Replacement of Embryos

PART 5

Essential Topics

APPENDIX

Group Reports on
Methods and Results

Part 1

ENDOCRINOLOGY OF THE
NATURAL AND STIMULATED CYCLE

Endocrinology of the Menstrual Cycle with Reference to Fertilization *in vitro*

J. Cohen,[1] C. Debache,[1] J. Mandelbaum,[2] F. Pigeau[1] and M. Plachot[2]

An understanding of the hormonal events which control the ovulatory process during the menstrual cycle is essential to appreciate the physiologic basis for the recovery of human oocytes to achieve in-vitro fertilization.

The duration of the menstrual cycle in women is generally of 28 days and may be divided into three phases. The follicular phase lasts for 12 days approximately, the ovulatory phase for two days, and lastly there is a luteal phase of 14 days. The collection of oocytes for fertilization *in vitro* is primarily concerned with the two first phases.

Secretion of Gonadotrophins and Steroids During the Menstrual Cycle

Follicular Phase

This phase extends from the first day of menstruation until the day before the LH peak (Fig. 1). During this period, the rise in FSH continues; it had begun during the late preceding luteal phase. The rising levels of FSH initiated the increase in size and development of a cohort of follicles, from which the ovulatory follicle will be chosen. This elevation of FSH is not essential for the continuation of the ovulatory cycle. In monkeys, a period of 12 to 14 days is necessary for the recruitment and preparation of a new preovulatory follicle after the removal of the dominant follicle (di Zerega & Hodgen, 1980a, b; di Zerega *et al.*, 1980); these processes occur even if there is no elevation of FSH during the follicular phase of the cycle following the ablation of the follicle.

[1] Hôpital de Sèvres, 2 et 4 rue du Parc Cheviron, Sèvres 92.
[2] Hôpital Necker, 149–161 rue de Sèvres, 75730 Paris.

Levels of LH begin to rise 1 or 2 days after the increase in FSH. The secretion of ovarian steroids (oestrogens, androgens, progestins) is relatively constant and low during this period and they are released in a pulsatile manner. Theca cells and granulosa cells interact in producing androgens, oestrogens and progestins, under the influence of gonadotrophins (Fig. 2).

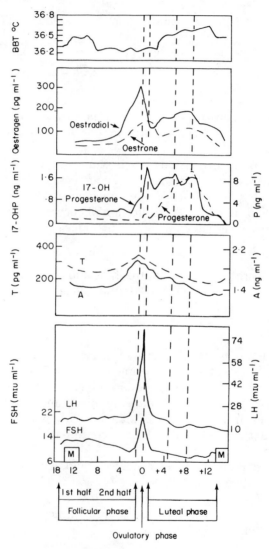

FIG. 1. Basal body temperature (BBT), steroids and gonadotrophins during the human menstrual cycle.

Theca cells possess FSH and LH receptors, whereas granulosa cells have only FSH receptors. During the second half of the follicular phase (7 to 8 days before the LH surge), there is an increased secretion of oestrogens by the ovary. The role played by the proliferation of the two types of follicular cells is well known (Yen & Jaffe, 1978).

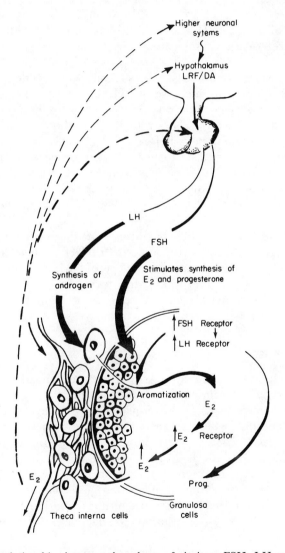

FIG. 2. Interrelationships between the release of pituitary FSH, LH and the ovarian steroids (Yen & Jaffe, 1978).

Androgens, e.g. androstenedione and testosterone, are produced under the influence of LH. They are secreted by theca cells then transformed into oestradiol-17β by granulosa cells. This conversion requires an enzymatic system. The aromatase activity needed is not present during the initial follicular phase. It is stimulated by FSH and by oestradiol-17β itself, and the capacity of follicles for aromatization increases as ovulation approaches. FSH influences both the growth of granulosa cells and its oestrogenic activity, while the production of oestradiol-17β increases concomitantly with the number of FSH receptors and the responses of the ovary to this gonado-trophin.

The elevation of plasma oestrogens is followed by a decrease of FSH and a small but definite increase in LH. This divergence between the two gonadotrophins may be due either to the preferential inhibitory action of oestrogens on FSH, or to the secretion of inhibin by the growing follicle. A few days before the LH peak, plasma androgens (D$_4$-androstenedione and testosterone) and progestins (17-hydroxy-progesterone and 20-dihydroprogesterone) start to rise, reaching their maximal levels at the time of the LH peak (MacIntosh *et al.*, 1980; Pauerstein *et al.*, 1978; Roger *et al.*, 1980; Schmidt-Gollwitzer *et al.*, 1978).

Twelve hours before the beginning of the peak, progesterone secretion increases and during the rise in LH its level is increased three-fold. Progesterone may be the steroid which triggers the LH surge and ovulation, after the rising levels in oestradiol-17β have prepared the hypophysial cells by sensitizing them to the action of LH-RH.

Ovulatory Phase

During this phase a dramatic six-fold increase in LH is observed, accompanied by a simultaneous two-fold rise in FSH. Repeated studies have led to controversial conclusions on plasma levels of oestradiol-17β. Most authors believe there is a decrease in oestradiol secretion during the rise of LH. Nevertheless, Hoff & Quingley (1980) have shown that oestradiol levels do not decrease before the LH peak. The follicle continues its secretion of oestrogens until the rise in LH is well started. Hence, the elevation of plasma progesterone before the peak of LH seems to be the major factor triggering ovulation. It is only after the peak of LH, that oestradiol-17β decreases and progesterone increases drastically.

The literature is controversial about the time of ovulation in relation to the LH surge. According to some estimates, ovulation would appear to occur 16–18 hours after the LH peak, or between 16 and 40 hours after the beginning of the LH rise (Croxatto *et al.*, 1980; Lunenfeld *et al.*, 1978, World Health Organization, 1981). Such estimates are highly imprecise because they rely on parameters such as the histological dating of the follicle or corpus luteum, or assessing ovulation from changing levels of steroid hormones in plasma.

Large variations are observed between the baseline levels of LH in different patients and also in a given patient from hour to hour. These fluctuations are explained by the pulsatile release of LH by the hypophysis, with a frequency of about one pulse per hour.

The Oocyte at Ovulation

During the development of graafian follicles, FSH promotes follicular growth and LH triggers the resumption of meiosis in the resting oocyte as well as the ovulatory mechanisms. Meiosis progresses through the first meiotic division, culminating in the extrusion of the first polar body, and progression of the second meiotic division up to metaphase, where it is physiologically arrested once again (Edwards, 1973). At this stage, which is typically the stage at which it is released from the follicle, the oocyte is characterized by the presence in the perivitelline space of the first polar body (Fig. 3), a minicell containing double-stranded chromosomes. Lying in the cortical area of the ooplasm, close to the location of the first polar body in the perivitelline space, is the second maturation spindle with the chromosomes lined up on the equatorial plate (metaphase-II). The properties of the cumulus cells are also modified, including their increase in number and mucification.

The nuclear changes characterizing a mature oocyte in its cumulus mass must be defined precisely, because in-vitro fertilization can only be achieved when oocytes have completed their maturation *in vivo* or *in vitro*.

Strategies to recover fertilizable oocytes depend upon the appreciation of the endocrinological factors leading to oocyte maturation. Such an approach has been attempted either by sequential oestrogen assays, or by precise determination of the LH surge.

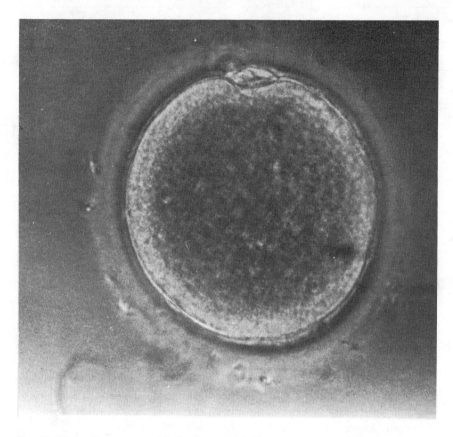

FIG. 3. Living human egg with the first polar body and the zona pellucida. (Courtesy of J. M. Purdy & R. G. Edwards.)

Strategies for Oocyte Recovery

Oestrogen Assays

The preovulatory peak of oestradiol-17β has been observed by several authors to occur 24–28 hours prior to the LH peak (Mishell *et al.*, 1971; Corker *et al.*, 1969). The plasma levels of oestrogens during the cycle are given in Table 1 and Figs 4 and 5, where day 0 is the day of the LH peak (Castanier *et al.*, 1969).

The timing of ovulation has been studied daily during the periovular period in 19 women attending artificial insemination during 24 menstrual cycles, using β-mode ultrasound examination and

Table 1
Levels of gonadotrophins and steroids (mean and range) during the human menstrual cycle (Castanier et al., 1980)*

Phase of cycle	Day of cycle	FSH ($IU\,l^{-1}$)	LH ($IU\,l^{-1}$)	E_1 ($pmol\,l^{-1}$)	E_2 ($pmol\,l^{-1}$)	P ($nmol\,l^{-1}$)	17-OHP ($nmol\,l^{-1}$)
Follicular phase	-14 to -8	3.8 2.3–6.0 n = 95	2.3 1.1–4.6 n = 94	144 37–318 n = 61	202 70–345 n = 77	1.1 <0.2–4.1 n = 76	1.6 0.9–2.4 n = 78
	-7 to -2	2.9 1.7–4.6 n = 157	3.0 1.4–5.1 n = 158	263 107–436 n = 100	496 209–955 n = 126	0.64 <0.2–1.6 n = 129	1.9 0.9–3.3 n = 127
Ovulatory phase	*	7.3 4.4–11 n = 44	22.0 11–36 n = 43	473 163–1002 n = 31	940 367–1524 n = 38	3.5 1.3–8.9 n = 36	6.4 4.2–9.4 n = 34
Luteal phase	+4 to +9	2.2 0.9–4.2 n = 123	2.4 0.7–5.8 n = 123	300 137–573 n = 69	532 235–826 n = 98	44.5 15.9–79.5 n = 99	10.0 5.1–15.7 n = 92

* For LH, FSH, P and 17-OHP = day 0; for E_1 and E_2 = day -1 or 0.

measurements of plasma oestradiol (Robertson, 1979). The maximum diameters of the ovarian follicles and the peak plasma oestradiol determinations all occurred within two days prior to and including the day of ovulation, as determined by conventional means, in the 12 normal cycles studied. The average values on the day prior to ovulation (day −1) for maximum follicle size and peak oestradiol determination were 2.5 cm and 1660 pmol I^{-1} respectively.

Assays for urinary oestrogens have been applied for the detection and timing of ovulation. The preovulatory peak of urinary oestrogens ranges between 40 and 100 μg 24 h^{-1}. The mean interval between the first observable rise and the oestrogen peak is 5.5 days. The day after the oestrogen peak (often the day of the LH surge) is believed to be the day of maximal fertility.

Rapid radioimmunoassays for serum oestradiol-17β or urinary oestrogens are available. Recently a direct radioimmunoassay, measuring ovarian oestrogens in small aliquots of urine, has been evaluated. Several authors including Denari *et al.* (1981) and Hedon *et al.* (1980) have shown that the first morning sample of urine gives a good correlation with the 24-hour collection. A daily survey of plasma oestradiol-17β or urinary oestrogens may therefore be carried out very easily. But, as shown by several authors, periovular levels of oestradiol or urinary oestrogens show considerable interpatient and intrapatient fluctuations, and may be considered as less efficient than LH determinations for the precise monitoring of ovulation in women.

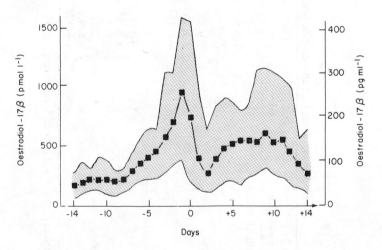

FIG. 4. Detailed changes in plasma oestradiol-17β during the menstrual cycle (Castanier *et al.*, 1980).

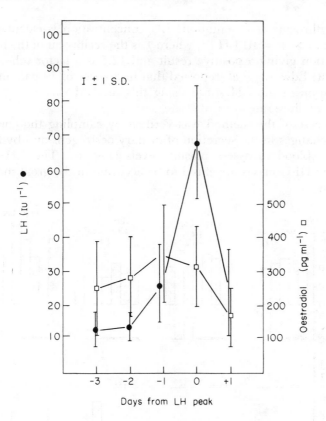

FIG. 5. Periovular concentrations of serum LH (routine assay, $n = 29$), and serum oestradiol (routine assay, $n = 28$) (Broom *et al.*, 1979).

LH Assays

The preovulatory changes in cervical mucus, levels of oestrogens and ultrasonic estimates of follicular growth are imprecise. Only the measurement of LH allows an exact prediction of ovulation.

In their first reported series, Edwards *et al.* (1980) indicated that an immunological test for assaying urinary LH (Hi-Gonavis, Mochida Pharmaceutical Co., Ltd., Tokyo, Japan) was suitable for assessing the onset of the LH surge. Using this test, results can be obtained after two hours in a series of urine dilutions. The test is based on the binding of LH (or HCG) to erythrocytes sensitized against HCG, leading to haemagglutination. A positive reaction is read as a smooth mat of erythrocytes at the bottom of the test tube, while a negative reaction, i.e. where there is no haemagglutination, is read as a ring formation due to erythrocyte sedimentation. LH concentration is calculated as follows: $12.5 \times T = IU\ LH\ l^{-1}$, where T is the reciprocal of the highest urine dilution giving a positive result and 12.5 is a factor inherent to the reagent. Edwards *et al.* reported that in a series of 79 patients, the determination of the LH surge using this method was wrong in 11 cases, i.e. a failure rate of 13.8%.

The success of the method was verified by sampling the complete profile of changes in the secretion of urinary oestrogens and by taking samples of blood to assess plasma levels (Fig. 6). The LH surge detected by Hi-Gonavis appeared to be accurate in the great majority of patients.

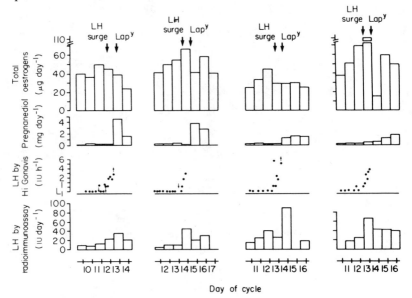

FIG. 6. Determination of the LH surge in urine. Levels of total oestrogens, pregnanediol, LH as determined by Hi-Gonavis and LH as determined by radioimmunoassay are shown (Edwards *et al.*, 1980).

A distinct diurnal rhythm was noted in the timing of the beginning of the LH surge. It began in most patients between 0600 and 1200 hours, especially during winter months (Fig. 7).

According to the information on the beginning of the LH surge, oocyte recovery was attempted at various intervals after the initial rise. Previous experience had shown that the optimum time to aspirate the follicle was approximately 32 to 34 hours after the injection of HCG. The optimal interval for aspirating oocytes after the LH surge began

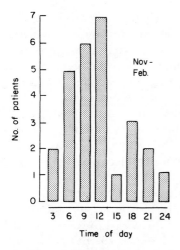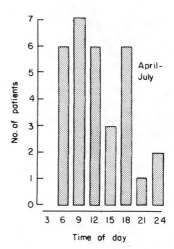

FIG. 7. Diurnal rhythm in the beginning of the LH surge in women during the natural cycle during winter and summer. It was assessed by analyses of urinary LH using Hi-Gonavis (Edwards *et al.*, 1980).

during the natural cycle was assumed to be slightly less, allowing for the time needed for the surge of plasma LH to accumulate in urine before it could be detected by assay (Saxena *et al.*, 1977). Accordingly, attempts to aspirate preovulatory oocytes were spread over a period of time from 15 to 35 hours after the beginning of the LH surge was detected in urine. Oocytes could be aspirated with a high rate of success between 15 and 24 hours after the surge of LH began, but results became progressively worse after this time (Table 2).

Table 2
Aspiration of preovulatory oocytes at various intervals after the beginning of the LH surge during the menstrual cycle (Edwards et al., 1980)

Interval LH surge-laparoscopy (hours)	No. of patients	No. with ovulatory eggs	Eggs not aspirated
15–17½	9	7	2
18–20½	12	9	3
21–23½	14	12	2
24–26½	19	14	5
27–29½	5	2	3
30–35	6	1	5
	65	45	20

Using the same Hi-Gonavis test, we carried out a qualitative test every six hours on whole undiluted urine samples, by assaying in each case for a positive result at 100 or 200 IU of LH. When the test was positive at 200 IU we proceeded to laparoscopy between 12 and 14 hours later. Twenty-two patients were monitored during 25 cycles. Fourteen oocytes were recovered. The maturation stage of the oocytes was very variable, because four oocytes had a germinal vesicle, three were in metaphase-I, three were in metaphase-II, and four were atretic. Only two of the oocytes were fertilized. No cleavage was observed. The distribution of stages according to the occurrence of LH-positive tests in urine shows no obvious correlation (Fig. 8).

Monitoring of urinary LH by the Hi-Gonavis method in our hands has therefore given very variable results and numerous failures. This result is not in accordance with that obtained by Edwards *et al.* (1980) who recognized the LH peak in 68 cases out of 79. But these authors

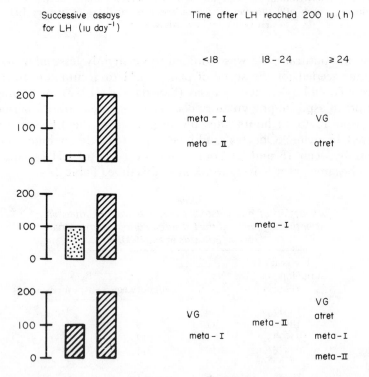

FIG. 8. Biological monitoring of oocyte growth and ovulation by the urinary LH assay (Hi-Gonavis test). Meta I = metaphase of the first meiotic division. Meta II = metaphase of the second meiotic division. V.G. = germinal vesicle. Atret = atretic.

used a 3-hourly assay, and each third or fourth sample of urine was examined, the previous sample being used as controls. The levels reported by Edwards *et al.* were expressed in IU h^{-1} and their peak was around 6 IU. This led us to believe that in our work a positive result at 100 IU day^{-1} would have been sufficient for accurate estimations.

In our experience, doubts about positive tests were very frequent. This may have been due to the fact that we simultaneously carried out repeated ultrasonic examinations of the follicles. The patients were drinking a lot and some of the samples of urine were very diluted. Our poor results may also be due to the fact that we assayed the samples only for a positive result at 100 and 200 IU during each 6 hours. In a few cases when we could compare the quantitative levels of LH in urine with the radioimmunological levels of plasma LH in the same patient, we observed a great variability in the appearance of the urinary LH peak which may precede, be contemporaneous with, or follow the plasma peak by 5 to 14 hours.

A method for assessing the LH rise based on the interpretation of plasma LH assays has recently been described (Testart *et al.*, 1980, 1981). Analysis of these assays (4 assays per day) permitted a clear determination of the onset of the LH surge. The threshold value of plasma LH (LH surge initiating rise = LH S.I.R.) is determined for each cycle as a function of the average baseline level of the previous day. Any level equal to or exceeding 180% of the mean value for the preceding four assays indicates the onset of the LH surge. The chronology of follicle and oocyte maturation after LH S.I.R. is similar to that which follows the administration of HCG: none of the 20 patients examined 30–35 hours after the LH S.I.R. had ovulated, whereas 2 out of 10 ovulated 36–38 hours afterwards. They also found that fertilization *in vitro* occurred in 1 out of 3, 9 out of 14 and 5 out of 5 patients when oocytes were collected 30–32, 33–35 and 36–38 hours after the LH S.I.R. respectively. Thus the oocyte can be collected 34–35 hours after the LH S.I.R., when ovulation has not occurred, and the oocyte is capable of being fertilized.

Since 1980, we have tested this method in 31 cases (Table 3). We confirm that 34–35 hours after the LH S.I.R. seems to be the best time for oocyte collection. But we observed a corpus luteum in four patients before 34 hours. Our rate of oocyte recovery is still inferior to the one obtained by other teams. Venous puncture four times a day to gain information on the patients does not seem to stress them.

Table 3

Relationship between hours after LH S.I.R., oocyte recovery and fertilization in vitro

Hours after LH S.I.R.	21	32	33	34	35	36	37	38	42	45
Patients with no oocyte		2	1	2	1	1	2	1	0	0
Patients where an oocyte was aspirated	1^C*		1^C, 1^N	2^C, 1^F+R	1^C, 1^VG	1^C, 1^F, 1^F+R	2^C		1^C	
No. of patients with a corpus luteum			3	1			3	1	1	1
Total no.	1	2	6	6	3	4	6	1	1	1

*C = control, N = not fertilized, F = fertilized, R = replaced in the mother.

Conclusion

The preovulatory changes in cervical mucus, oestrogen levels and ultrasound determination of follicular diameters is insufficient to assess the exact hour for the recovery of human oocytes for in-vitro fertilization. Only the measurement of LH suffices for an exact prediction of ovulation.

The LH surge may be detected in urine 15 to 24 hours before ovulation. This method requires good cooperation from the patients for water restriction, sampling of urine, and dilution. It is a simple and easy method of monitoring.

The LH surge may be detected in plasma. The method of the LH S.I.R. determination described by Testart *et al.* (1981) allows a 34-hour delay before laparoscopy, but needs a specialized laboratory.

References

Broom, T. J., Matthews, C. D., Raniolo, E. & Crawshaw, K. M. 1979. A comparison of serum estradiol and LH levels by rapid and routine assay for the recognition of human ovulation. *Infertility* **2**, 29–38.

Castanier, M., Roger, M., Papiernik, E., Frydman, R., Netter, A. & Scholler, R. 1980. Taux des gonadotrophines et des steroids chez la femme normale. In: *Hormonologie de la Stérilité*, p. 165. Ed. Sepe, Paris.

Corker, C. S., Naftolin, F. & Exler, D. 1969. Interrelationship between plasma luteinising hormone and oestradiol in the human menstrual cycle. *Nature*, **222**, 1063.

Croxatto, H. D., Ortiz, M. E. & Croxatto, H. B. 1980. Correlation between histologic dating of human corpus luteum and the luteinizing hormone peak-biopsy interval. *American Journal of Obstetrics and Gynecology*, **136**, 667.

Denari, J. H., Farinati, L., Casas, P. R. F. & Oliva, A. 1981. Monitoring ovarian function. *Obstetrics and Gynecology*, **58**, 5–9.

Di Zerega, G. S. & Hodgen, G. O. 1980a. The primate ovarian cycle: suppression of human menopausal gonadotrophin-induced follicular growth in the presence of the dominant follicle. *Journal of Clinical Endocrinology and Metabolism*, **50**, 819.

Di Zerega, G. S. & Hodgen, G. O. 1980b. Cessation of folliculo-genesis during the primate luteal phase. *Journal of Clinical Endocrinology and Metabolism*, **51**, 158.

Di Zerega, G. S., Nixon, W. E. & Hodgen, G. O. 1980. Inter-cycle serum FSH elevations: significance in recruitment and selection of the dominant follicle and assessment of corpus luteum normality. *Journal of Clinical Endocrinology and Metabolism*, **50**, 1046.

Edwards, R. G. 1973. Studies on human conception. *American Journal of Obstetrics and Gynecology*, **117**, 587.

Edwards, R. G., Steptoe, P. C. & Purdy, J. M. 1980. Establishing full term human pregnancies using cleaving embryos grown *in vitro*. *British Journal of Obstetrics and Gynaecology*, **87**, 737.

Hedon, B., Thuile, N., Gelis, M. T., Deschamps, F., Cristol, P., Descomps, B.,

Viala, J. L. & Durand, G. 1980. Apport de l'échotomographie au monitorage de l'ovulation. *Ultrasons*, **1**, 225–231.

Hoff, I. & Quingley, M. E. 1980. Hormonal changes associated with the midcycle LH surge: a multiphasic rise in progesterone. The Endocrine Society, Washington, June 1980. Abstract no. 622.

Lunenfeld, B., Ben-Aderet, N., Ben-Michael, R., Grunstein, S., Kraiem, Z., Potashnik, G., Rofeh, C., Shalit, A. & Tikotsky, D. T. 1978. Temporal relationships between hormonal profile and ovarian morphology during the periovulatory period in human. In: *Endocrinology of the Ovary*, p. 187. Ed. R. Scholler. Sepe, Paris.

MacIntosh, J. E., Matthews, C. D., Crocker, J. M., Broom, T . J. & Cox, L. W. 1980. Predicting the LH surge. *Fertility and Sterility*, **34**, 125.

Mishell, D. R., Nakamura, R. M., Crosgnani, P. G., Stone, S., Kharma, K., Nagata, Y. & Thorneycroft, I. H. 1971. Serum gonadotropin and steroid patterns during the normal menstrual cycle. *American Journal of Obstetrics and Gynecology*, **111**, 60.

Pauerstein, C. J, Eddy, C. A., Croxatto, H. D., Hess, R., Siler-Khodr, T. M. & Croxatto, H. B. 1978. Temporal relationship of estrogen, progesterone and luteinizing hormone levels to ovulation in women and infrahuman primates. *American Journal of Obstetrics and Gynecology*, **130**, 876.

Robertson, R. D., Picker, R., Wilson, T. C. & Saunders, D. M. 1979. Assessment of ovulation by ultrasound and plasma estradiol determination. *Obstetrics and Gynecology*, **54**, 686–690.

Roger, M., Grenier, J., Houlbert, C., Castanier, M., Feinstein, M. C. & Scholler, R. 1980. Rapid radioimmunoassays of plasma LH and estradiol-17β for the prediction of ovulation. *Journal of Steroid Biochemistry*, **12**, 403.

Saxena, B. B., Saito, T., Said, N. & Landesman, R. 1977. Radioreceptor assay of luteinizing hormone-human chorionic gonadotrophin in urine: detection of the luteinizing hormone surge and pregnancy. *Fertility and Sterility*, **28**, 163–167.

Schmidt-Gollwitzer, M., Eiletz, J., Sackmann, U. & Nevinny-Stickel, J. 1978. Detection of ovulation by radioreceptor assay for human LH. *Journal of Clinical Endocrinology and Metabolism*, **46**, 902.

Testart, J., Thebault, A. & Frydman, R. 1980. Human oocyte maturity and in-vitro fertilization. In: *World Congress on Embryo Transfer, in-vitro Fertilization and Instrumentation*. Kiel, September 1980 (in press).

Testart, J., Frydman, R., Feinstein, M. C., Thebault, A., Roger, M. & Scholler, R. 1981. Interpretation of LH assay for the collection of mature oocytes. *Fertility and Sterility*, **36**, 50–54.

World Health Organization. 1981. Task force on methods for the determination of the fertile period. *American Journal of Obstetrics and Gynecology*, **139**, 886.

Yen, S. S. C. & Jaffe, R. B. 1978. *Reproductive Endocrinology*, pp. 126–151. W. B. Saunders, Philadelphia.

Rapid Assay of Urinary LH in Women using a Simplified Method of Hi-Gonavis

R. G. Edwards, G. Anderson, J. Pickering and J. M. Purdy

We would like to describe our experiments with the kit Hi-Gonavis (Mochida Pharmaceuticals), for the determination of levels of luteinizing hormone (LH) and human chorionic gonadotrophin (HCG) in human urine. We have used this semiquantitative system extensively to detect the onset of the LH surge, both in patients examined during the natural cycle, and in those given clomiphene. We have found that the system is simple, rapid, and accurate, and have miniaturized it to make it even cheaper and more acceptable. We will describe first the method for collecting samples of urine during the follicular phase, then describe the value of Hi-Gonavis using the method described by the makers, and finally give details of our modifications.

Collection of Urine Samples

The timing of urine samples is carefully controlled. Samples are collected at intervals of 2, 3, or 4 hours from the time the patients are admitted to the clinic, and continued until the LH surge is positively identified just before laparoscopy for oocyte recovery. Patients are asked to pass samples of urine at specific times throughout the day and night. Water intake is regulated, but is adequate, and the total volume of urine passed on each occasion is measured accurately.

An aliquot from each urine sample is taken to assess levels of LH by Hi-Gonavis. The remainder of the urine sample is placed in a container, to obtain 24-hour samples for estimating urinary oestrogens. A combination of LH assays every few hours by Hi-Gonavis, and 24-hour samples of oestrogens is sufficient to assess the

Physiological Laboratory, Cambridge University, and Bourn Hall, Cambridge, U.K.

growth of follicles and the onset of ovulation (Edwards *et al.*, 1980). The LH levels in successive samples of urine is converted to output per hour, and a pattern can be kept, graphically if necessary, of the changing levels of LH throughout successive days of the menstrual cycle for each patient.

The Kit Hi-Gonavis as Produced by the Manufacturer: the Standard Tube Method

The kit contains all the requisite materials: vials of phosphate-buffered saline, lyophilized bovine serum albumin and ampoules containing lyophilized sheep erythrocytes coated with antiserum against HCG. The whole assay can be assembled on a stand, which provides two rows for tubes. The rear row is used for the dilutions of urine, while the front row is designed to hold the ampoules containing the sensitized erythrocytes (Fig. 1).

The method of assay, although very simple, is still unnecessarily cumbersome. First, serial dilutions of the urine are made in phosphate-buffered saline containing 1 mg ml^{-1} albumin. Next, standards of aliquots of phosphate-buffered saline are pipetted into the ampoules containing the lyophilized erythrocytes in order to suspend them. Finally, a small amount (0.1 ml) of each diluted urine is added to its corresponding ampoule of suspended erythrocytes. The assay is now complete, and can be read two hours later. The cost of the assay is fairly high, because at least three ampoules must be used, each one costing approximately £1.50.

The assay essentially involves a step-wise dilution of neat urine. The makers recommend doubling dilutions of urine which are satisfactory for pregnancy tests. The principle of the assay is based on haem-agglutination, and is similar to methods used by immunologists for measuring small amounts of protein. If there is sufficient HCG or LH in the urine dilution being tested, the sheep erythrocytes are agglutinated, and this modifies their sedimentation pattern in the ampoules. Consequently, a positive reaction is seen as a smooth mass of cells at the bottom of the ampoule, in two hours. If there is insufficient HCG or LH in the urine sample, the erythrocytes do not agglutinate, and they sediment rapidly to give a negative result, seen as a distinct ring at the base of the ampoule. Intermediate readings ($\pm$) can be scored between positive and negative.

The assay can obviously be read quickly, and involves no more manipulations once it is set up. The principle is simple, the range of values in urine samples is read rapidly, and the ease of operation is a great advantage (Table 1, Fig. 2). The assay is sensitive to 12.5 IU LH or 5.0 IU HCG, according to the maker, which is much more sensitive than other forms of agglutination tests. Its problems are cost, the necessity for step-wise readings, and its inapplicability to serum.

Steps 1 and 2 (rear tubes)

1. Add 0.3 ml phosphate-buffered saline containing 1 mg ml^{-1} albumin to each tube

2. Make urine dilutions by serially transferring 0.3 ml

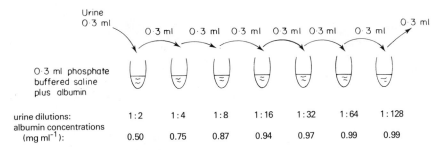

urine dilutions:	1:2	1:4	1:8	1:16	1:32	1:64	1:128
albumin concentrations (mg ml^{-1}):	0.50	0.75	0.87	0.94	0.97	0.99	0.99

Steps 3 and 4 (ampoules in front row)

3. Add 0.4 ml phosphate-buffered saline to each ampoule of erythrocytes

4. Transfer 0.1 ml of each dilution of urine from the rear tube to the corresponding ampoule

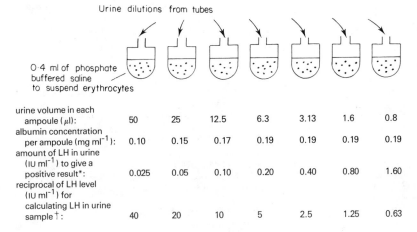

urine volume in each ampoule (μl):	50	25	12.5	6.3	3.13	1.6	0.8
albumin concentration per ampoule (mg ml^{-1}):	0.10	0.15	0.17	0.19	0.19	0.19	0.19
amount of LH in urine (IU ml^{-1}) to give a positive result*:	0.025	0.05	0.10	0.20	0.40	0.80	1.60
reciprocal of LH level (IU ml^{-1}) for calculating LH in urine sample†:	40	20	10	5	2.5	1.25	0.63

*Each ampoule of coated erythrocytes reacts with 0.00125 IU LH (Mochida).
† Example: if the urine sample of 200 ml is positive to 1:8, the total amount of LH in it = 200/10 = 20 IU. If this is a 3-hour sample, the LH output is 20/3 = 6.7 IU h^{-1}.

FIG. 1. The standard tube method of Hi-Gonavis

Table 1
Testing the standard tube method of Hi-Gonavis against standard amounts of HCG

A. Comparison with standard solution

Conc. of HCG in test solution (IU 100 ml^{-1})	1:2	1:4	1:8	1:16	1:32	1:64	1:128	Calculated conc of HCG (IU ml^{-1})*
			Urine dilution in the tube test					
20			+	+	±	−		26.7–<40
10		+	+	−				10–<13.3
5	+	+	−					5–<6.7
2.5	+	−	−					2.5–<3.3
1.25	±	−						<2.5

B. Effects of increasing dilution of standard solution

Volume of PBS used for dilution (ml)	1:2	1:4	1:8	1:16	1:32	1:64	1:128	1:256	Calculated conc of HCG (IU ml^{-1})
				Urine dilution in tube test					
i. Diluting 2.5 IU HCG[+]									
50	+	+	−						2.5–<3.3
100	+	−							2.5–<3.3
200	±	−							<5
400	−								<10
ii. Diluting 10 IU HCG[++]									
50			+	+	−				10–<13.3
100		+	+	−					10–<13.3
200	+	+	−						10–<13.3
400	+	±	−						10–13.3
iii. Diluting 50 IU HCG[++]									
50					+	+	±	−	40–53
100				+	+	−			40–<53.3
200			+	+	±	−			53–<80
400			+	±	−				53–<80

*Ranges calculated as follows:
Assay in top row: 1:16+ = 100/5 = 20 IU; 1:32± = 100/3.75 = 26.7 IU; 1:40- = <100/2.5 = <40 IU.
Assay in second row: 1:8+ = 100/10 = 10 IU; 1:16 was not ±, hence = <100/7.5 = <13.3 IU.
Assay in third row: 1:4+ = 100/20 = 5 IU; 1:8 was not ±, hence = <100/15 = <6.7 IU.
Assay in fourth row: 1:2+ = 100/40 = 2.5 IU; 1:4 was not ±, hence = <100/30 = <3.3 IU.
Assay in fifth row: 1:2± = <100/40 = <2.5 IU.
[+] Levels typical of tonic and surge levels during the menstrual cycle.
[++] Levels typical of pregnancy urine soon after implantation.

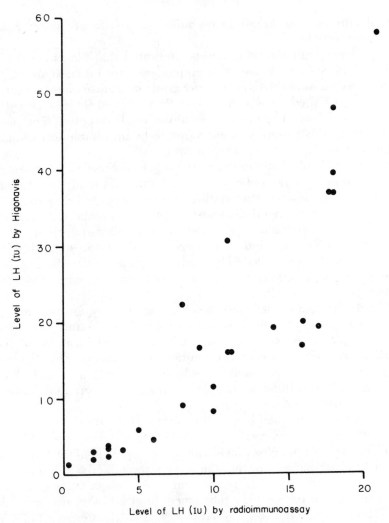

FIG. 2 Comparison of the standard tube method of Hi-Gonavis and radioimmuno-assay of urinary LH. The relationship is curvilinear, Hi-Gonavis being more sensitive with increasing concentrations of LH.

The Modified System: The Microtitre Method

We decided that three improvements were needed. First, the volume of erythrocytes used for each individual test had to be reduced, and a total volume of 0.1 ml, i.e. one-quarter of the quantity recommended by the manufacturers, was found to be sufficient to identify positive and negative reactions.

Experience with the tube method indicated that plates containing wells would be easier to use than ampoules. After initial analyses, the plates selected were the tissue-culture grade microtitre plates produced by Sterilin Limited, U.K. These have 96 U-shaped wells, each with a capacity of 200 μl. The non-tissue culture grade of polystyrene plates produced by this Company were found to be unsuitable, occasionally giving rise to non-specific positive assays.

Lastly, a simple automation of the whole process could make the assay even more rapid and easier to carry out, and reduce the amount of pipetting necessary. After testing various pieces of equipment, the Compu-Pet 200 (General Diagnostics, Warner-Lambert, U.K.) was selected. This microdilutor permits a controlled microvolume of medium to be drawn into a tubing, and the same or a different microamount to be expelled. These advantages permitted the establishment of urine dilutions in one step, without the time-consuming method of repetitive dilutions.

The doubling dilutions were not fully satisfactory for assaying the slight changes in the range of urinary LH levels found during the follicular phase. A ratio of 1.625 : 1.0 of urine : diluent in a serial dilution greatly improved the resolution of the assay. This dilution, approximately 62% per well, gave a finer control in assessing the amounts of LH in different samples of urine. More gradual dilutions could have been used if necessary.

The microtitre method is now very simple (Fig. 3). The Compu-Pet microdilutor is primed with a phosphate-buffered saline, provided by Mochida. It is set to deliver 65 μl and to pick up 40 μl of medium. The initial 40 μl are picked up from the urine sample, and 65 μl, including this 40 μl, are delivered to the second well. The mixture is stirred, using the end of the delivery tube, then 40 μl is withdrawn from the well, leaving 25 μl in it (Fig. 3). Next 65 μl are delivered into the third well, and 40 μl withdrawn, etc. As a result, 25 μl of successive urine dilutions are established, in serial dilutions of 1.6 : 2.6. If necessary, the first well can be used for 25 μl of neat urine, in case the titres of LH in the sample are very low or if the volume of the urine is very high (Fig. 3).

The sensitized erythrocytes are then added. The ampoules of erythrocytes provided by Mochida are reconstituted in 0.4 ml of phosphate-buffered saline containing 0.2 mg ml^{-1} of bovine serum albumin (also provided by Mochida). A sample of 100 μl of the erythrocytes are simply delivered into each well, by Compu-Pet or dropper,

Steps 1 and 2

1. Load CompuPet with phosphate-buffered saline, and pick up 40 μl urine
2. Serially deliver 65 μl, stir, and pick up 40 μl at each successive well

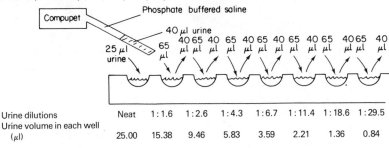

Urine dilutions	Neat	1 : 1.6	1 : 2.6	1 : 4.3	1 : 6.7	1 : 11.4	1 : 18.6	1 : 29.5
Urine volume in each well (μl)	25.00	15.38	9.46	5.83	3.59	2.21	1.36	0.84

Step 3

3. Add 100 μl erythrocytes suspended in phosphate-buffered saline containing 0.2 mg ml^{-1} albumin to each well, using CompuPet or dropper

albumin concentration per well (mg ml^{-1})	0.16	0.16	0.16	0.16	0.16	0.16	0.16	0.16
amount of LH in urine (IU ml^{-1}) to give a positive result*	0.012	0.020	0.033	0.054	0.087	0.142	0.230	0.374
reciprocal of LH (IU ml^{-1}) for calculating LH in urine sample^{+}	80.0	49.2	30.3	18.6	11.5	7.1	4.3	2.7

*Each well contains coated erythrocytes reacting with 0.003125 IU LH
$^{+}$ Example: if the urine sample of 200 ml is positive to 1 : 2.6, the total amount of LH in it = 200/30.3 = 6.60 IU. If this is a 3-hour sample, the LH output = 6.60/3 = 2.20 IU h^{-1}.

FIG. 3. The microtitre method for assaying urinary LH by Hi-Gonavis.

and the whole tray is gently shaken. This completes one assay. One row of wells can be used for a standard control with a ''zero'' well at the end to identify non-specific positive agglutination. Eleven assays can then be carried out in one tray (Fig. 4). Results can be read easily in 2 hours, and graded as + , ± , and –.

The method is reliable (Table 2, Fig. 5). A typical protocol is shown in Table 3 and Fig. 6. The microtitre method has proved invaluable in detecting the onset of the LH surge in many of our patients (Table 4), and in following daily rhythms in the tonic levels of urinary LH (Fig. 7).

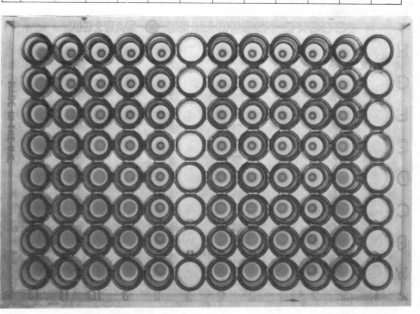

Name	80	50	30	19	11	7	4·5	2·5	Time	Vol.	LH (i.u.)
1	+	+	+	+	+	+	+	+	12.00	115	32·9
2	+	+	+	+	**+**	**−**	−	−	″	220	20·0
3	+	+	**+**	+	**−**	−	−	−	″	70	3·7
4	+	**+**	±	−	−	−	−	−	″	100	2·5
5	−	−	−	−	−	−	−	−	″	100	<1·25
6	+	+	±	−	−	−	−	−	″	150	3·75
7	+	+	±	−	−	−	−	−	″	90	2·25
8	**+**	**+**	−	−	−	−	−	−	″	200	4·0
9	−	−	−	−	−	−	−	−	″	125	<1·6
Standard	+	+	+	+	**−**	−	−	−	−	100	5·2

FIG. 4. Example of the microtitre method for assaying LH. (a) Nine urine samples, and a standard were assayed, as shown in the plate. (b) The results are given in relation to the volume of urine and the calculated amounts of LH in each sample. With experience, only the dilutions indicated in bold type need to be tested. There is no necessity to assess positive or negative values distant from the end point of each assay.

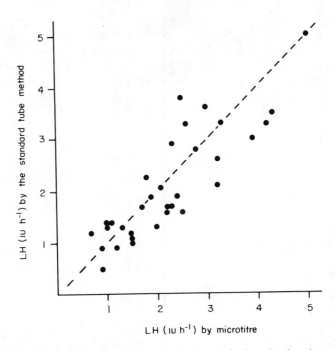

FIG. 5. Comparison between the standard tube method and microtitre method of Hi-Gonavis for assaying urinary LH.

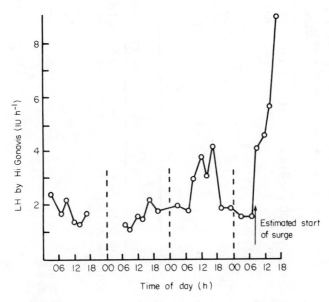

FIG. 6. Graphical representation of data in Table 3.

Table 2
Testing the microtitre method of Hi-Gonavis against standard amounts of HCG

A. Comparison with standard solutions

Conc. of HCG in test soln. (IU 100 ml⁻¹)	Urine dilutions in microtitre method								Calculated conc. of HCG (IU 100 ml⁻¹)*
	1:1 80.0	1:1.6 49.2	1:2.6 30.3	1:4.2 18.6	1:6.9 11.5	1:11.1 7.1	1:18.6 4.3	1:29.5 2.7	
20					+	+	+	−	23.2–<28.6
10				+	+	±	−		10.7–<14.1
5			+	+	−				5.4–<6.6
2.5		+	±	−					2.5–<3.3
1.25	+	−							1.25–<1.5
0.625	−	−							<1.25
0.313	−	−							<1.25

B. Effect of increasing dilution of standard solution

i. Diluting 2.5 IU HCG

Volume of PBS used for dilution (ml)	1:1 80.0	1:1.6 49.2	1:2.6 30.3	1:4.2 18.6	1:6.9 11.5	1:11.1 7.1	1:18.1 4.3	1:29.5 2.7	Calculated conc. of HCG (IU ml⁻¹)
50			+	+	−				2.7–<3.3
100		+	±	−					2.5–<3.3
200	+	−							2.5–<3.1

ii. Diluting 10 IU HCG

Volume of PBS used for dilution (ml)	1:1 80.0	1:1.6 49.2	1:2.6 30.3	1:4.2 18.6	1:6.9 11.5	1:11.1 7.1	1:18.1 4.3	1:29.5 2.7	Calculated conc. of HCG (IU ml⁻¹)
50					+	+	+	−	11.6–<14.3
100				+	+	±	−		10.8–<14.1
200			+	+	−				10.8–<13.3
400		+	±	−					10.1–<13.2

iii. Diluting 50 IU HCG

	1:4.2	1:6.9	1:11.1	1:18.6	1:29.5	1:47.9	1:77.8	1:126.4	
	18.6	11.5	7.1	4.3	2.7	1.6	1.0	0.6	
40				+	+	+	+	−	50– <62.5
100			+	+	+	±	−		46.5– <62.5
200		+	+	+	−				46.5– <56.1
400	+	+	+	−					43.0– <56.3

*Ranges calculated as follows:

1:18.6 + = 100/4.3 = 23.2 IU.
1:11.1 ± = 100/9.3 = 10.7 IU.
1:4.2 + = 100/18.6 = 5.4 IU.
1:2.6 ± = 100/39.75 = 2.5 IU.
1:1 + = 100/80 = 1.25 IU.
1:1 − = < 100/80 = <1.25 IU.

1:29.5 was not ± = < 100/3.5 = <28.6 IU.
1:11.1 was not + = < 100/7.1 = <14.1 IU.
1:6.9 was not ± = < 100/11.5 = <6.6 IU.
1:2.6 ± = < 100/30.3 = <3.3 IU.
1:1.6 was not ± = < 100/64.6 = <1.5 IU.

Table 3
Protocol for the excretion rate of LH (IU hr⁻¹) by a patient for 4 days*

Date	Time sample passed	Volume of sample (ml)	Dilutions of urine sample								Total IU LH in sample	Minimum IU LH per hour
			1:1 80.0	1:1.6 49.2	1:2.6 30.3	1:4.2 18.6	1:6.9 11.5	1:11.1 7.1	1:18.1 4.3	1:29.5 2.7		
3/3	0300	180			+	+					9.7	2.4
	0700	80				+	+	−	−		6.9	1.7
	0900	80			+	+	−				4.3	2.2
	1200	325	+	−							4.1	1.4
	1400	125		+	−	−					2.5	1.3
	1630	125		+	+	−					4.1	1.7
	1930	180										
	2300	295										
4/3	0300	300										
	0700	95			+	+	−				5.1	1.3
	0900	65			+	−	−				2.1	1.1
	1200	145		+	+	−		−			4.6	1.6
	1400	90			+	−	−				3.0	1.5
	1630	170		+	+	−					5.6	2.2
	1930	215		+	±	−					4.4–5.4	1.5–1.8
	2300											
5/3	0300	400	+	+	−						8.1	2.0
	0700	85				+	+	−			7.4	1.8
	0900	70					+	−			6.1	3.0
	1200	210			+	+	−				11.3	3.8
	1400	150			+	±	−				5.0–6.1	2.5–3.1
	1630	195			+	+	−				10.5	4.2
	1930	285		+	−	−					5.8	1.9
	2300	545	+	−	−						6.8	1.9

6/3								
0300	320	+			−		6.5	1.6
0700	120			+	+	−	6.5	1.6
0900	95	+	+	+	−	−	8.3	4.1
1200	340		±	−	+	−	11.2–13.9	3.7–4.6
1400	130		+	+	+	+	11.3	5.7
1630	100			+	+	−	23.3	9.3

*Laparoscopy timed for 1000 hr, i.e. 25 hr after estimated start of LH surge between tonic level at 0700 and raised level at 0900 hr. Notice the daily fluctuation in tonic levels on 5/3.

Table 4
Results of the microtitre system during the first six months of use. (Fifty successive patients examined on three different occasions in 1981)

Patients	Feb./Mar.	May	July
Total number	50	50	50
Surge identified	40	42	44
Surge missed	2?*	3	1?*
Discharged			
Surge under way on admission to clinic	3	1	1
Other causes †	5	4	4
Success in identifying surge (%)	95.2	93.3	97.8

*Surge very weak in three of these cases

† Patients discharged before LH surge began because of breast abcess, husband had infected semen, anovulatory as assessed by progesterone assays, follicles growing in ovary occluded by adhesions, etc.

Advantages of the Microtitre Method

Several advantages accrue from this method:

(i) The serial dilutions are narrower than with the original method. Accordingly there is a greater precision in the assays.

(ii) The method is much simpler. It requires fewer movements by the operator, because the Compu-Pet method can be simply adjusted to cope with the necessary dilutions and additions.

(iii) The method is much cheaper — approximately one-quarter the cost of that described by the makers.

(iv) The method is more reliable, in as much as the concentration of albumin is constant in all wells in the microtitre method, whereas it varies considerably in the standard tube method (compare Figs. 1 and 3). The concentration of albumin will presumably modify the sedimentation patterns of erythrocytes, hence it is essential to keep it constant.

(v) The method saves greatly in space, and numerous assays can be carried out in one small tray.

(vi) Neat urine can be tested if necessary, extending the range of the method because the phosphate-buffered saline containing albumin is added directly to the erythrocytes (compare Figs. 1 and 3).

(vii) The method can be used as a rapid pregnancy test.

(viii) The stepwise method of assay is not as accurate or quantitative as radioimmunoassay, but is sufficient for perhaps the great majority of assays needed for clinical and scientific work.

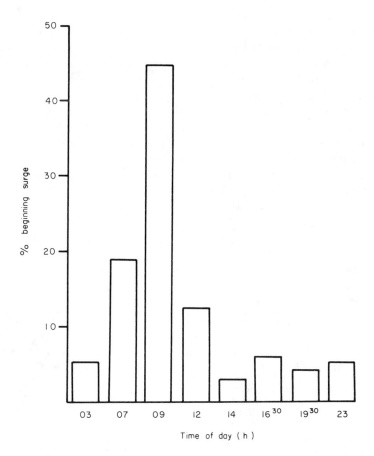

FIG. 7. Diurnal rhythm in the onset of the urinary surge of LH in women in Bourn Hall. The time shows the initial rise in levels of urinary LH which was followed by a sustained rise (Edwards, 1981). Reprinted by permission of *Nature*.

Comments

Radioimmunoassays are the most widely used method for assaying samples of urine and serum. They have been modified to give results within two hours approximately, the same time as with Hi-Gonavis, but in comparison they are complicated and difficult. Immunoassays involve incubations, the disadvantages of using tracers and centrifugation. Radioimmunoassay kits must be used before the ^{125}I decays, which may be a matter of days. Scintillation counting is even more tedious.

The standard tube method of Hi-Gonavis described by the manufacturer is a considerable simplification, yet it is sensitive enough for assaying the range of LH in urine during the follicular phase of the cycle. Its sensitivity is not much lower than radioimmunoassay. Even so, the tube method is now outdated by the microtitre method if large numbers of urine samples have to be assayed for LH. .

The microtitre method has proved its value in our work as a semi-quantitative assay. One person can carry out 100 assays per day without difficulty. With it, we have assayed tonic and surge levels of LH in over 400 patients, and there have been virtually no mistakes in predicting ovulation long before it occurred. Daily rhythms in the tonic and surge output of LH have been identified. If necessary, occasional samples of urine can be assayed quickly and simply. In one sense, the assay has been restricted by the need to use the kit supplied by Mochida for the tube test, and new forms of packaging are needed to suit the microtitre method.

The microtitre method has proved suitable for assaying LH in urine. It could also be adapted to assay other urinary hormones, especially the pituitary hormones. Improvements in titre and specificity of the antibody used to coat the erythrocytes, e.g. by using monoclonal antibodies, could enlarge the value of the method considerably. The principle may then be extended to the analysis of protein hormones in plasma, and perhaps to urinary and plasma steroid hormones.

References

Edwards, R. G. 1981. Test-tube babies 1981. *Nature*, **293**, 253–256.
Edwards, R. G., Steptoe, P. C. & Purdy, J. M. 1980. Establishing full term human pregnancies using cleaving embryos grown *in vitro. British Journal of Obstetrics and Gynaecology*, **87**, 737–756.

Discussion on the Natural Cycle

Assaying LH in Plasma and Urine

Trounson: We have not used natural cycles for a long time now. It is very important to collect the egg at the right stage of maturation, and I have doubts about assaying LH every six hours. This would introduce an error of about 10 hours and it seems a long interval for the precision that is needed to time oocyte collection. There also seem to be difficulties in oocyte collection itself, and this may arise from the same problem.

Edwards: I agree that six hours is too wide an interval for the precision of oocyte collection. If the interpretations of the LH surge get too close to the time of ovulation, then it is too hurried and difficult for everyone concerned, especially the surgeon who must organize his team quickly.

We analyse samples of urine for LH in patients given clomiphene and in their natural cycle. The intervals between samples are two hours during some periods of the day, especially in the morning, which we have found to be a critical time. We feel this is especially important at 7 a.m. and 9 a.m., when most patients are beginning to discharge their LH surge. We have a 3-hour interval for most of the rest of the day and 4-hour intervals overnight.

We are more convinced than ever that Hi-Gonavis is a marvellous test for assaying urinary LH. Collecting urine does not stress the patients, and we can predict in the great majority of them the moment when the LH surge begins. We have confirmed that daily rhythms occur, especially during the winter, with the majority of patients discharging their LH surge early in the morning (Edwards *et al.*, 1980). This has proved to be a wonderful bonus for us, because most laparoscopies can be carried out 26 hours later, which is on the morning of the following day, usually from 8 a.m. to noon. We feel these daily rhythms are less marked during the summer, but we must confirm these data.

We have miniaturized the Hi-Gonavis test, without losing its

35

reliability. We can carry out twelve tests on a small plate, and obtain the results within two hours, or even less if they are needed urgently.

Johnston: Our greatest problem with Hi-Gonavis was the variation in the amount and quality of the urine samples presented. They seemed to vary according to the patient's fluid intake, and partly due to the time she was admitted to hospital. There seems to be a natural diuresis when the patient goes to bed, lasting approximately 24 hours. The increased urine output creates problems of dilution, so the patients are warned to reduce their output, then many of them stop drinking altogether and produce a concentrated urine.

We find the patients take at least one cycle to get the message and to adjust their intake properly. We always have a lot of debate as to what constitutes a significant rise in urinary LH as judged by Hi-Gonavis, and we do not know if it should be an arbitrary figure, or two standard deviations above the mean. Sometimes we found a rise was not sustained; it declined, only to rise again several hours later. So it is easy to detect rises and falls, but decisions about the actual beginning of the LH surge in urine can present major problems.

Edwards: I would like to comment on the use of Hi-Gonavis. When our patients enter the clinic, our nurses must do a marvellous job, because within 2–3 hours the patients understand that they must restrict their water intake to a certain level, and produce urine samples with our desired volume. We do not want vast amounts in each sample—merely about 200 ml which assist greatly with the Hi-Gonavis test. It is remarkable how quickly patients adapt to this system in our clinic. Even so, we always treat the first sample with great circumspection.

We treat every patient individually. Some of them secrete large amounts of tonic LH, whereas others secrete minor amounts. We do not put any arbitrary figure on the amount of LH to be discharged, judging levels in each individual patient. We collect urine almost until the time of laparoscopy, to make absolutely sure that any rise in LH is sustained. The only patients who give us trouble are those with a modest LH surge, where it is possible to mistake this for a daily rhythm using the Hi-Gonavis test. We can even detect LH changes in patients who have a long follicular phase associated with very low levels of gonadotrophins.

I would like to stress that the patterns of LH discharge are similar to the natural cycle in most patients given clomiphene and exactly the same care is needed with them, even if only to decide when HCG can be safely given before the endogenous LH surge has started.

Lopata: We have had some difficulty with the use of Hi-Gonavis to predict human ovulation. Our experience is that ovulation may begin at any time between 26 and 36 hours after the beginning of the LH surge. The approach of ovulation has been measured accurately using ultrasound and, in some cases, we have actually observed ovulation occurring *in vivo*. We believe there is a 10-hour variation during the time in which ovulation may occur in different patients. When you predict ovulation, do you refer to an individual patient or do you refer to the average patient?

Edwards: We deal with individual patients. We have a very high success rate in predicting the time of laparoscopy in order to aspirate a fully ripe egg, and the mistakes are remarkably few—hardly any at all. We are very disappointed if we find the patient has ovulated, and some of these errors have not been ours. One of our patients, for example, had a fasting day, which we were unaware of, and this happened to coincide with the beginning of her LH surge. The resulting chaos in her LH output completely misled me, and we found she had ovulated when we did the laparoscopy.

There are difficulties in interpretation—it is sometimes not easy when there are daily tonic rises which sometimes turn into a surge. Each patient must be assessed very carefully and critically. We are very disappointed if we do not collect a preovulatory oocyte from our patients, provided that the ovaries are accessible. There have been one or two near misses, including one case where we had to pluck the preovulatory oocyte from the surface of a newly-ruptured follicle. In some doubtful cases, we may inject 500 IU of HCG to sustain a modest rise in urinary LH, but these conditions are rare. We hope that this part of the technique is largely solved. There may be a small penalty that, on occasions, some eggs may be slightly unripe, but both here and in Kershaw's Hospital we followed the practice of incubating these oocytes for 2 or 3 hours before insemination so that they could complete their maturation *in vitro*.

I would like to stress that we time the beginning of the LH surge from the first rising assay, not from a point intermediate between the last tonic recording and the first rise, which is perhaps more accurate.

Feichtinger: I think there is some confusion over the point taken by various investigators to identify the beginning of the LH surge. Edwards takes his from the first rising assay. We date ours from the last tonic assay, so we have a slightly longer base line, i.e. 28½–30 hours, before we perform laparoscopy. Another method would be to take the midpoint between the two estimations, the last tonic assay and the first rising assay. We have combined ultrasound with the analysis of LH in LH in urine during the natural cycle, and have shown that our interval is very suitable for the collection of preovulatory oocytes.

Steptoe: I think we must make a very important point about using these tests. This is that we are attempting to recover the preovulatory oocyte from our patients. Timing must be precise, because if laparoscopy takes too long then it is more difficult to collect the egg. A difference in timing of 3 or 4 hours can be very vital: if the egg is slightly immature it can be incubated to complete its maturation. But, if it is over-ripe, then it can cause difficulties during aspiration owing to increased viscosity.

Maturation of Oocytes in Culture
After Their Collection During the Natural Cycle

Cohen: If an oocyte is immature when collected, it must be cultured *in vitro* for some time. How long do you incubate the oocyte for to ensure that the maturation is advanced before you inseminate it?

Edwards: We assume that an oocyte collected 26 hours after the LH surge begins requires a further 6–8 hours to complete its maturation. Depending on its appearance, we incubate it for 2–3 hours or, if we feel it is less than ripe when judged by its cumulus cells, we may incubate it for between 4 and 5 hours. We have no difficulty in the immediate fertilization of ripe eggs, or on an insemination 4–5 hours later if the egg is slightly unripe.

Mettler: Is the oocyte mature if it is collected between 24 and 26 hours after the rise in LH? We cannot judge from the cumulus cells whether the oocyte is in metaphase-I or metaphase-II at this time, and we would like to have guidelines. Can the oocyte be matured in a suitable medium for 5–6 hours *in vitro* after collection, or does it have to be matured *in vivo* before it is collected?

Edwards: By 26 hours after the LH rise, the cumulus is fairly viscous in most of our oocytes. Sometimes the oocyte and its cumulus mass is ½ cm across, and can easily be seen with the naked eye. The closer to ovulation, the more viscous the cumulus becomes, and at 26 hours we incubate most eggs for perhaps two hours because they appear to be so ripe. It is interesting that the data of Testart and his colleagues presented later in this discussion on the timing of ovulation in women accords exactly with our earlier findings that 37 hours was the time when ovulation began in the great majority of patients after an injection of HCG (Edwards & Steptoe, 1975; Edwards, 1980).

Trounson: Data from animals (Moor & Warnes, 1978; Trounson *et al.*, 1981) has shown that the oocyte must be matured for some length of time in the follicle, but then its maturation can be completed *in vitro* to sustain fertilization and normal embryonic growth.

Maturation can be completed *in vitro*, in the oviduct, or even in the uterus. If sperm are added to oocytes before they are fully mature, the completion of maturation is in some way prevented, and a normal embryo is not produced under these circumstances. Oocytes can remain *in vitro* for up to 12 hours before insemination and the resulting embryos may look normal. However, a long delay in fertilization may result in the embryo becoming asynchronous with the mother's luteal phase. All our pregnancies have come from inseminations which are delayed for at least four hours, the average time is for about six hours. The errors introduced by LH assays would mean an error of six hours in predicting the time of ovulation, and incubating the oocyte for six hours will ensure that the oocyte is fully mature when the spermatozoa are added.

Jones, G: Progesterone assays may enable us to decide whether to incubate the oocyte for 6 or 12 hours, depending on the level of progesterone in the plasma. On one occasion, we had to incubate an oocyte for 12 hours, yet this was fertilized and went on to produce an embryo. I am not concerned about asynchrony in oocyte collection, because this particular oocyte was apparently not ready to ovulate when it was collected.

Trounson: Aspirating the follicle in that way may have initiated luteinization, and twelve hours is perhaps the maximum in which the oocyte can be incubated before insemination. The difficulty is that incubations *in vitro* for a longer period may result in the embryo and the luteal phase of the mother being out of phase. If there is any delay in embryonic growth, the gap may be as much as 24 hours by the time the embryo is replaced.

Jones, H: We must remember that removal of the oocyte itself may trigger luteinization rather than the LH surge itself. If so, the beginning of luteinization would differ from the expected time, and this may influence the results of replacing the embryo. I suggest that it depends mostly on LH rather than the excision of the oocyte, hence the correlation must be with the LH surge.

Trounson: You may be correct if assessing the luteal phase by levels of progesterone. But when aspirating the follicle, many other compounds are removed besides steroids. Large amounts of prostaglandins, for example, and other hormones are removed, and I doubt that the rupture of the follicle can be considered merely an incidental change in the pattern of luteinization. It is a momentous event, releasing large amounts of various compounds into the body, including the withdrawal of an enormous amount of steroid. This could well have importance for the onset of the luteal phase.

Mettler: A report at a recent meeting in Holland showed that inhibin may be important, especially that present in follicular fluid. If the follicle is damaged, punctured, or treated in various ways, there is a great loss of inhibin from it, and it is possible that during various operations for the removal of adhesions or other treatments, that traumatization of the follicle exerts such effects on the woman.

Timing of Ovulation During the Natural Cycle

Jones, H: Edwards collects the oocytes regularly at 26 hours after the LH surge begins. This figure does not indicate when ovulation occurs; it merely tells us that this is the best time, or at least an optimal time, for collecting a ripe preovulatory oocyte.

Edwards: That is correct. All the patients we have studied have come to us for in-vitro fertilization. We cannot carry out studies on the time of ovulation on this group of patients, because as a consequence we may fail to collect an oocyte for fertilization. In our earlier work in Oldham, we regularly collected preovulatory oocytes between 32 and 34 hours post-HCG, and we knew that ovulation occurred about 37½ hours after the HCG injection. The state of the preovulatory oocytes we are collecting during the natural cycle corresponds to those collected 34 hours after the HCG injection following stimulation by HMG, and I would prophesy that ovulation occurs at around 30–32 hours after the rise in urinary LH, using our current methods for monitoring the natural cycle.

Testart: We have collected information on the timing of ovulation in relation to HCG or the rise in LH during the natural cycle. Using plasma assays, we get a very precise time in the rise of LH. We can even get intervals as close as one hour between estimated times of the beginning of the LH surge. We have had no ovulations in 22 patients after the rise in LH or an injection of HCG when they were examined up to 34 hours later. Between 34 hours and 36 hours, we obtained 3 ovulations in 89 patients. Between 37 and 39 hours, half of the patients had ovulated. In the three patients who had ovulated before 37 hours, we suspect that sonography may have induced an early ovulation, and so we are concerned about the use of this technique to predict ovulation (see pages 62 and 89).

Jones, H: Our data on the timing of ovulation has been gained after estimating serum LH on 4-hourly samples. I believe that such collections do not stress the patient. We find that the shape of the curve is such that it is difficult to use the peak of the LH surge in any meaningful way to predict ovulation. We have arbitrarily decided that 60 mIU is an arbitrary limit where the LH surge has begun, but even that is treacherous, because levels can rise up there and then drop below it again.

We have also collected some data on the formation of the corpus luteum in relation to the rising LH during the natural cycle. The first observed corpus luteum was 28½ hours after the LH surge. Collecting oocytes at 26 hours would therefore be prior to ovulation in our patients, using our methods. Ovulation appeared to occur at occasional times in different women after this period, and is by no means a constant thing.

Hamberger: So far, no one has described the use of serum assays for progesterone and 17-hydroxyprogesterone to predict ovulation. If both of these steroids are measured, there are indications that they may be superior to oestrogens in indicating the time of ovulation.

Jones, G: We have used assays of these two hormones retrospectively. The assays we use require too much time to give a good prediction for oocyte collection. The method may be useful to find out why an egg was immature, but it could not be used predictively at present.

Jones, H: Another trouble is that the changes in the levels of progesterone before ovulation are very modest. The rise may be from 0.4 to 1.2 pg ml^{-1}, and it is therefore difficult to place any confidence in the assay. But it appears to me that the precise indication of ovulation is not all that important. There appears to be considerable leeway in securing an egg which can be matured *in vitro* for some time if necessary, and then fertilized *in vitro*.

Testart: I am still concerned about the timing of ovulation. Jones showed a picture where ovulation occurred 28 hours after the beginning of the LH surge in plasma. This is surprising to us, because we never find ovulation 34 hours after the beginning of the LH rise, and this is in patients who have not been examined by sonography. So we cannot accept from our data that ovulation can take place before this time. The LH level when the surge begins differs in each patient; it is not common to all of them, and it is essential to be careful in interpretation. This is why it is important to check the values of LH well before the LH surge begins.

Edwards: Our observations agree with those of Testart. We have studied ovulation in various animal species, and in women. It is always highly regular after an injection of HCG, and almost certainly such regularity also occurs after the LH surge. We found a great constancy in oocytes maturing in the human ovary when examined at a common time after HCG, and ovulation began at 37 hours (Steptoe & Edwards, 1970).

I was especially impressed by Testart's data because the timing of ovulation after the natural LH rise in plasma is identical to that occurring after an injection of HCG. The endogenous LH discharge appears to resemble that in a patient injected with HCG. I would be somewhat sceptical of the methodology employed in reports that do not confirm this sort of evidence. We know of so much data in animals; mice, rabbits, rats, monkeys, showing that once HCG is given, the programme of ovulation is defined and rigid. It is almost impossible to vary it by an hour or two. I suspect that exactly the same thing occurs in women, and ovulation occurs at a definite time after the LH surge or an injection of HCG. In our work, we find we can explain the few exceptions by a failure of our monitoring system.

Conti: I would like to agree with the timing of ovulation presented by Testart. We have not seen ovulation in the natural cycle less than 34 hours after the beginning of the LH surge. This evidence encourages us to consider shifting the time of laparoscopy closer to 30 hours than 26 hours, in order to obtain oocytes during the final stages of ovulation.

Edwards: For my part, if we had the data of the type that Testart has described, we would treat the beginning of the LH surge as we do an injection of HCG. We routinely recover occytes between 32 and 34 hours after injection of HCG, and we have done for years. With such LH data from plasma, I would recommend doing the same in the natural cycle following the endogenous LH discharge. However, we prefer to measure LH in urine, and we will stick to 26 hours after the first rising urinary assay. This method works in our hands, and we have defined the rise in LH to our own satisfaction.

Johnston: We would agree with Edwards on the timing of ovulation after the injection of HCG. After carrying out 250 laparoscopies we have hardly seen an ovulation hence we have considerable belief in these methods. Even at 36 hours, it is rare to find a single follicle that has ovulated after an injection of HCG.

Daily and Seasonal Rhythms in Women

Jones, G: We are interested in daily rhythms and seasonal rhythms. It would be fascinating if the daily rhythm in the beginning of the LH surge was less pronounced during summer, because after many years of observations we believe that there are many more anovulatory cycles in women in the summer time. We believe that this has influenced our pregnancy rates in the treatment of various types of infertility; do you find you get lower pregnancy rates in the summer following in-vitro fertilization?

Edwards: We have only really resumed our work 9 months ago, and we are still in our first summer here in Bourn Hall. There were seasonal effects in our initial study in Oldham (Edwards *et al.*, 1980). At the present time, our feelings about seasonal disturbances in the LH discharge need to be corroborated. We will be keeping a close watch on our results during late summer and winter, although at present there are too many other variables interfering with our success rates to be able to attribute changing rates of implantation to a seasonal difference. At least, this is my opinion at the moment; time will tell if there are such effects.

We would like to carry many more studies on the effect of long days on human reproduction. One method would be to examine urinary and plasma hormones in men and women who are exposed to the full length of the Arctic summer, i.e. who slept out of doors, so that they received the full amount of light during that period. This could be done very easily now that we have simple methods such as Hi-Gonavis for assaying the LH surge, and we could get some very meaningful data. There have been other reports of seasonal variations in the fertility of human beings during the long, light summers (Parkes, 1976), but the significance of the data is still obscure. We have often wondered if the Australians have seasonal variations in their data, although their day length will vary much less than ours because of their geographical position.

Trounson: I am convinced that there is no daily rhythm in the timing of the LH surge in our patients in Australia who are examined during the natural cycle or following stimulation by clomiphene. I want to stress that other clinics studying the natural LH surge may not find a daily rhythm either. Our lack or failure to detect may be due to our method of assay, but I doubt it because we use basically the same method. Our rhythm in Melbourne is quite random.

Edwards: I am very surprised indeed at what I hear about the lack of daily rhythms in Australia, both in the surge of LH and in the tonic levels during the day. We find distinct daily variations in the tonic levels of LH in urine, and a remarkable similarity in different women in the time of the beginning of the LH surge. Both of these rhythms appear to be tied to the adrenal rhythm (Fig. 1).

We want to know if such daily rhythms are due to changes in the pulsatile discharge of LH, either by an increasing amplitude per pulse, or through a larger number of pulses per hour. Plasma assays would be necessary for these studies. We find that many of the short-term rises in the levels of urinary LH referred to by Johnston and others are due

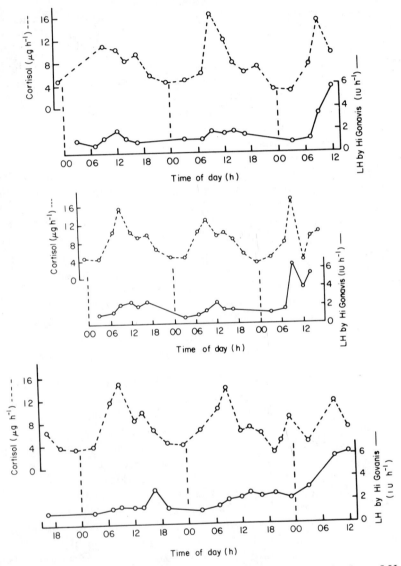

FIG. 1. Correlation between diurnal rhythms in urinary cortisol and urinary LH in three patients as they approached their LH surge during a natural menstrual cycle

to this daily rhythm, and we have learnt to recognize it. The daily rhythm is often most pronounced in most patients on the day before the LH surge begins (Fig. 2) and it can be an excellent marker of an impending LH surge in the patient.

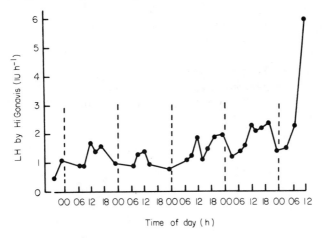

Time of day (h)

FIG. 2. Diurnal variations in the levels of urinary LH in women during the menstrual cycle. "Tonic" levels rise each morning, then decline. The LH surge began during the morning in this patient (Edwards, 1981). Reprinted from *Nature* with permission.

We have examined people coming to our clinic from distant countries, who have come from different time zones. Most of our patients who fly in from America are still on American time, and they discharge their LH six hours or more after the British patients (Fig. 3). Similarly, those coming from the East are usually more advanced in discharging their LH, as compared to British patients. We have also noticed that one or two of these patients who have remained in Britain after their first treatment have shifted to British time within three cycles, so their original cycle does not freewheel for longer than this period.

Some British patients have proved to be exceptions to the usual rhythm. We have examined these patients for their discharge of cortisol, and found their peak of cortisol secretion also occurred during the afternoon, or there was a secondary peak, coincident with the beginning of the LH surge (Fig. 3). We therefore believe at the present time that the LH rhythm is probably coincident with the adrenal rhythm which, as is well known, usually shows a rise in the morning, but can show a secondary rise in the afternoon.

Steptoe: I believe that many people here are working in a hospital environment. We do not have our patients in bed; they are fully ambulent, and they are encouraged to walk around the grounds and the village.

Johnston: At the Women's Hospital in Melbourne, our data does show a diurnal variation in the beginning of the LH surge. I cannot remember if it is seasonal, but there is certainly a diurnal rhythm.

Lopata: Yes, we have recently constructed histograms like those first published by Edwards *et al.* There appears to be a popular time when the LH surge begins. There are very few discharges beginning between 11 p.m. and 3 a.m., and there is a massive increase during the day. If this is a diurnal rhythm, then we can confirm its existence in our patients in Melbourne.

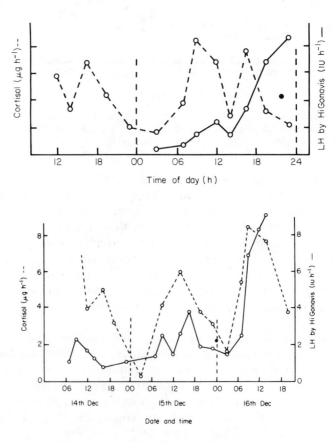

FIG. 3. Relationship between diurnal rhythms in urinary cortisol and urinary LH in two patients beginning the LH surge during the afternoon in their natural cycle.

Testart: In spring, many of our patients have the onset of their LH surge at 3 o'clock in the night.

Jones, H: In our hands, we sometimes find that the natural surge appeared to be postponed. The only solution we could suggest was that this was due to stress. Has this been overcome in your surroundings at Bourn Hall?

Edwards: We believe the environment has certainly seemed to be effective, because the great majority of our patients appear to start their cycle early in the morning. If ever we get a "wrong" cycle, i.e. of unusual length, it is the follicular phase that varies and the luteal phase that appears to be remarkably constant except in patients who have a short luteal phase. We can sometimes recognize such patients by their low levels of gonadotrophins in the follicular phase. Perhaps it is the quiet surroundings here that help to establish a regular cycle.

Effects of Stress During the Collection of Blood or Urine

Conti: One of the reasons why Edwards, Purdy and Steptoe introduced urinary assays was to remove the stress from patients for repeated blood sampling. We put an intravenous catheter on a peripheral vein 48–72 hours before the LH surge is expected, and we can make collections of blood or urine at various intervals, at 1-hour intervals or at 6-hour intervals as we choose. If we use a vein in the back of the hand, we can collect samples throughout the night or day as we desire, and this does not disturb that patient in any way. Moreover, the rise of LH in blood is very rapid, and so we believe that it is very useful, although taking blood every six hours is not sufficiently precise. I would suggest that 2-hour intervals are more satisfactory.

Jones, H: We found some of our patients were having a very delayed interval to the beginning of the LH surge. Before coming to our hospital, they would have normal 28-day cycles, but on their arrival in our clinic their hormones would show no sign of movement until much later than expected.

Edwards: I believe you use plasma hormones to measure LH in your patients. Each time a needle is inserted into a patient to collect blood, there is a risk of stress. Taking blood is needless in our circumstances, because our urinary assays are perfectly satisfactory. If we can get results in urine, we prefer to use it and avoid taking blood. We should first do the simple things to relieve stress, and using urine is one simple method of avoiding it. Obviously, many other things could stress a patient besides blood-taking, but at least we can avoid this particular source of it.

Trounson: In general, I fully agree with those remarks. It is very difficult to collect blood from some women, and it may be possible to collect from them once a day. But to expect a nurse in a general ward to take repeated samples of blood without stressing the patient seems to me to be asking too much.

Jones, G: Another good reason for using urine is that one sees the whole spectrum of the day, pooled in urine collections. A plasma sample gives a single point in time, and it can be misleading if there is any pulsatile release.

Edwards: Urinary oestrogens can be assayed very quickly and easily and the procedures are not difficult. Moreover, if there is any doubt about a result a sub-sample of three hours can be taken for additional assay, which will still give an excellent reading. Assays of urinary LH are readily available in two hours, which is excellent for our purposes. We only need urine to follow the follicular phase and the LH surge — we do not need blood.

Szalay: We have studied the effects of anaesthesia on levels of cortisol, regarding it as a stress hormone. We have a distinct increase in the secretion of cortisol after various types of general anaesthesia. We assay the patient for up to 12 hours or longer after the anaesthesia was given, especially after 120 minutes, which is the post-operative period (see paper by Szalay *et al.*, in Part 2, page 105).

Frydman: We have noticed that many of our patients were stressed during the first cycle they come into hospital, since they demonstrated delayed ovulation. More recently, we find that they are less stressed, so perhaps the habits of the team doing the investigations are important. Perhaps the team was stressed too in the beginning! We have compared urine and plasma samples taken every three hours, and sometimes there has been difficulty in providing urine samples at a required time. Many patients preferred blood rather than urine collection.

References

Edwards, R. G. 1981. Test-tube babies 1981. *Nature*, **293**, 253–256.

Edwards, R. G. & Steptoe, P. C. 1975. Induction of follicular growth, ovulation and luteinization in the human ovary. *Journal of Reproduction and Fertility*, Supplement 22, 121–163.

Edwards, R. G., Steptoe, P. C. & Purdy, J. M. 1980. Establishing full-term human pregnancies using cleaving embryos grown *in vitro*. *British Journal of Obstetrics and Gynaecology*, **87**, 737–756.

Moor, R. M. & Warnes, G. M. 1978. Regulation of oocyte maturation in mammals. In: *Control of Ovulation*, pp.159–176. Eds. D. B. Crighton, G. R. Foxcroft, N. B. Haynes & G. E. Lamming. Butterworths, London.

Parkes, A. S. 1976. *Patterns of Sexuality and Reproduction*. Oxford University Press, London.

Trounson, A. O., Leeton, J. F. & Wood, C. 1981. In-vitro fertilization and embryo transfer in the human. In: *Follicular Maturation and Ovulation*. IVth Reinier de Graaf Symposium. Excerpta Medica, Amsterdam.

Steptoe, P. C. & Edwards, P. G. 1970. Laparoscopic recovery of preovulatory human oocytes after priming of ovaries with gonadotrophins. *Lancet*, **i**, 683–689.

The Endocrinology of Clomiphene Stimulation

A. O. Trounson and J. F. Leeton

Introduction

The continued investigation of stimulated ovulatory cycles, by the group at Monash University following the report by Edwards *et al.* (1980) of successful in-vitro fertilization in the natural or spontaneous ovulatory cycle, was based on animal reproductive experience which depends to a large extent on superovulation to provide sufficient numbers of embryos to work with. Furthermore, limitations of resources such as staff and an available operating theatre meant that fertilization *in vitro* during the natural cycle could only be attempted periodically. Although the group had attempted in-vitro fertilization by stimulation with clomiphene previously (Lopata *et al.*, 1978) a preliminary study was initiated in 1979 (Trounson *et al.*, 1980a) to re-evaluate the technique.

As a consequence of encouraging results with a modified procedure of Clomid and HCG a controlled trial was carried out in 1980 to compare the natural ovulatory cycle with clomiphene and HCG and with clomiphene and natural LH release for in-vitro fertilization in 50 patients with tubal infertility. The result of this study (Trounson *et al.*, 1981b) was the demonstration that pregnancies could be established with clomiphene and HCG or clomiphene and natural LH release. This was the first demonstration that normal pregnancy (Wood *et al.*, 1981) could be established with a procedure that controlled the time of laparoscopy and hence a more efficient use could be made of the available resources. Furthermore, the birth of twins established the possibility of multifetal pregnancy by in-vitro fertilization, a concept attractive to some patients but presenting the clinic with an increased possibility of obstetric complication.

Department of Obstetrics and Gynaecology, Monash University, Queen Victoria Medical Centre, Melbourne, Australia.

51

Endocrine Response to Clomiphene

The procedure established after preliminary experiments was to provide Clomid on days 5 to 9 at a dose of 150 mg day^{-1}, taken as three 50 mg tablets spaced equally throughout each 24-hour period. The initial response to clomiphene is an increased pulsatile release of LH and moderate (often undetectable) increase in basal FSH levels in peripheral plasma. The exact action of clomiphene is still unresolved. However, it is generally considered that the negative feed-back control of pituitary gonadotrophins is interrupted, resulting in increased pituitary gonadotrophin secretion.

Increased LH and FSH may result in multiple follicles continuing in the growth and maturation phase instead of entering atresia. This is probably a consequence of the increased availability of LH and FSH for binding to ovarian thecal cells, the stimulation of thecal androgen secretion for conversion by granulosa to oestradiol-17β, and continued maturation of all follicular elements. However, as there is only one antral follicle capable of responding to gonadotrophin, even continued treatment with clomiphene will not induce superovulation as the single follicle will ovulate before the small follicles responding later to clomiphene can reach preovulatory proportions.

The very properties of clomiphene which impart the mild superovulatory properties of the drug, i.e. its anti-oestrogenic characteristics, may reduce the effectiveness of clomiphene if there is a genuine effect on the uterine endometrium. Garcia et al. (1977) reported that uterine biopsies in almost 50% of anovulatory patients treated with clomiphene were not histologically compatible with the presumed postovulatory stage. This was corrected with HCG and progesterone suppositories. This situation may reduce the implantation rate of developing embryos. It is difficult to be sure that this is the case in ovulatory women treated with clomiphene. In a series of our patients, treatment with progesterone or hydroxyprogesterone hexanoate had no effect on improving the pregnancy rate after embryo transfer (Trounson et al., 1981b).

As a consequence of the possible antifertility effects of clomiphene we are investigating three types of superovulatory schedules; clomiphene alone, clomiphene and HMG, and HMG alone. These schedules are being evaluated by pregnancy rates of transferred embryos and it will be some time before any conclusions can be drawn.

Detailed studies have been made of steroid secretion during the luteal phase after clomiphene and HCG were given to patients for treatment by fertilization in vitro (Trounson et al., Kerin et al., Brown *et al.*, unpublished data). No difference has been found between those patients in which follicles were aspirated and those where the follicles ovulated normally. Progesterone and oestrogen values in the luteal phase were higher than in non-treated patients, and in the majority of cases the luteal phases were of normal length. Given this information, it is difficult to argue in favour of luteal phase support. However, there may be subtle differences, not detected by daily blood sampling, which may prevent some patients from becoming pregnant.

Clomiphene Schedules

In a trial investigating various schedules and dose rates of clomiphene (Trounson, 1982) we found:

(a) 50 mg clomiphene per day did not result in multiple ovulation and only single oocytes were recovered,

(b) Clomiphene given on days 2–6 or 3–7 was not as effective as days 5–9 for multiple follicular development,

(c) Prolonged treatment with clomiphene (days 5–12) prolonged the anti-oestrogenic effects on cervical mucus and did not improve the rate of oocyte collection.

The normal schedule of 150 mg/day, from days 5–9 (Trounson *et al.*, 1981) is now used as a routine procedure.

Monitoring of Clomiphene-treated Cycles

The present criteria used for monitoring of clomiphene-treated patients is described by Trounson, Leeton and Wood (1981a).

Daily assays of plasma oestradiol-17β (E_2) are begun on day 9 of the menstrual cycle and an ultrasonic scan of the ovaries is performed when plasma E_2 begins to rise above 400–500 pg ml^{-1}. Depending on the number and size of follicles present, the patient is admitted to hospital. As a general rule we believe each follicle of 1.7 cm or larger will produce a maximum of about 500 pg ml^{-1} of oestradiol-17β. The patient is admitted to hospital if E_2 values are rising rapidly or if a single large follicle on ultrasound shows E_2 approaching 400–500 pg ml^{-1}. When in hospital, urine is collected every 3 hours and assayed by radioimmunoassay twice daily (Trounson *et al.*, 1980b). Daily cervical mucus scoring is also recorded. If a spontaneous LH rise occurs before injection with HCG, laparoscopy is carried out 26–27 hours after the midpoint in time of the first elevated sample. However, most patients (>90%) are given HCG when:

(a) E_2 levels approach a value of about 400 × the number of large follicles (>1.7 cm) in pg ml^{-1}, or exceed 1 to 1.5 ng ml^{-1}.

(b) There is no endogenous LH surge.

(c) Cervical mucus ferning is ovulatory.

Ultrasound reports of follicular size are no longer used as a primary criterion for HCG injection because of the errors involved (Trounson, 1982). Laparoscopy is carried out 36–37 hours after the HCG injection. Occasionally (approx. 10% of cases) a single large follicle may have ruptured at this time, however, it is rare that there is no other preovulatory follicle present and on some occasions the oocyte may be recovered from the Pouch of Douglas or the ovulated follicle.

Anomalies of Clomiphene Stimulation

In a small proportion of patients there may be an abnormal ovulatory response to clomiphene which is usually not repeated on the next occasion of clomiphene stimulation. These may include:

(a) The occurrence of a single large atretic (sometimes termed cystic) follicle which expands to 3 cm or larger in diameter. These follicles do not contain normal granulosa nor a normal oocyte and do not produce any significant quantity of oestrogen. They always regress and are not seen in the next ovulatory cycle.

(b) Ovulation before the completion of clomiphene treatment may occur in women with regularly short menstrual cycles.

(c) Multiple follicular development may not occur in some women even with 150 mg Clomid per day. In the case of repeated failure to superovulate, HMG may be given alone or in combination with clomiphene. Usually the next cycle of clomiphene treatment will result in superovulation.

(d) Menstrual cycles of clomiphene treatment may be longer than usual because of an increased follicular phase. This has no apparent effect on conception rate.

We have not encountered overstimulation of patients with clomiphene nor any significant increase in shortened luteal phases following treatment with clomiphene. The 12 babies born to date in our programme have all resulted from clomiphene treatment as have the majority of the pregnancies (>40). We believe that clomiphene stimulation of ovarian response and HCG to control of the time of ovulation is an extremely useful procedure for in-vitro fertilization of human eggs and may be used to establish the technique as a routine clinical procedure.

References

Edwards, R. G., Steptoe, P. C. & Purdy, J. M. 1980. Establishing full-term human pregnancies using cleaving embryos grown *in vitro*. *British Journal of Obstetrics and Gynaecology*, **87**, 737–756.

Garcia, J., Jones, G. S. & Wentz, A. C. 1977. The use of clomiphene citrate. *Fertility and Sterility*, **28**, 707–717.

Lopata, A., Brown, J. B., Leeton, J. F., Talbot, J. Mc. & Wood, C. 1978. In-vitro fertilization of preovulatory oocytes and embryo transfer in infertile patients treated with clomiphene and human chorionic gonadotrophin. *Fertility and Sterility*, **30**, 27–35.

Trounson, A. 1982. In-vitro fertilization. In: *The Endocrinology of Pregnancy and Parturition*. Eds. L. Martin and V. James. Academic Press, New York.

Trounson, A. O., Leeton, J. F., Wood, C., Webb, J. & Kovacs, G. 1980a. The investigation of idiopathic infertility by in-vitro fertilization. *Fertility and Sterility*, **34**, 431–438.

Trounson, A. O., Herreros, M., Burger, H. & Clarke, I. 1980b. *Proceedings of the Endocrine Society of Australia*, **23**, 73.

Trounson, A. O., Leeton, J. F. & Wood, C. 1981a. In-vitro fertilization and embryo transfer in the human. In: *Proceedings of the Van der Graaf Symposium*, Nijmegen 1981. Excerpta Medica, Amsterdam.

Trounson, A. O., Leeton, J. F., Wood, C., Webb, J. & Wood, J. 1981b. Pregnancies in humans by fertilization *in vitro* and embryo transfer in the controlled ovulatory cycle. *Science*, **212**, 681–682.

Wood, C., Trounson, A. O., Leeton, J., Talbot, J. Mc., Buttery, B., Webb, J. & Jessup, D. 1981. A clinical assessment of nine pregnancies obtained by in-vitro fertilization and embryo transfer. *Fertility and Sterility*, **35**, 502–508.

Discussion on Clomiphene Stimulation

Mode of Action of Clomiphene

Edwards: There must be certain assumptions about the use of clomiphene. Once the drug is taken, it can have effects on the central nervous system or the pituitary gland, which may need careful consideration. For example, it may stimulate follicular growth in such a way that follicles will grow but the patients may be unable to discharge their LH surge. We have to stand by, ready with HCG, to be injected at the most appropriate moment. The mode of action of clomiphene is an oestrogen agonist and, as far as I can see from the various observations on oestrogen-sensitive cells *in vitro*, and from studies in animals, it appears to internalise oestrogen receptors, so that the tissue may no longer be responsive to the steroid for several days (Baudendistel *et al.*, 1978; Katzellenbogen *et al.*, 1975; Watson *et al.*, 1981). Accordingly, patients given clomiphene may produce large amounts of oestrogens from the ovary, but the pituitary cannot respond, and there can be no LH surge.

Some of our patients have shown rising oestrogen levels which have indicated multifolliculation and good follicles, yet they had no LH surge, and their oestrogen levels gradually declined after a very high peak (Fig. 1) (Edwards, 1981). Some similar reports have come from animal studies (Adashi *et al.*, 1981). As the oestrogens turned down, we injected HCG in the hope of triggering ovulation in the follicles. But the follicles had become cystic by the time the laparoscopy was performed, and there were no pre-ovulatory oocytes to be obtained. We have also had some patients with low or moderate levels of oestrogens who failed to have an LH surge (Fig. 1), and this is also a difficult situation because it is essential to know when to inject the HCG before the follicles become atretic.

We have an arbitrarily defined level of oestrogens to serve as a guide. When our patients reach 120 μg of urinary oestrogens per day, we inject HCG late that evening. This is a highly arbitrary level. Some of our patients given clomiphene who can discharge their own LH, do so, with levels of 120–130 μg day^{-1}, others at 75 μg day^{-1}. In each individual patient, we will not know what that level really means in terms of follicle growth, even if we knew the numbers of follicles that were growing. It will be impossible to detect if some follicles are becoming atretic, or whatever. It is not easy choosing the exact time to inject HCG, although we are very successful with our regime and recover at least one preovulatory oocyte from 90% or more of our patients if there are no abdominal complications (see the description by Steptoe and Webster in Part 2).

We have found many non-ovulatory follicles in some of our patients given clomiphene and HCG. They have had 5 or 6 follicles at laparoscopy, but only one or perhaps two were preovulatory. As a result, only one of the five oocytes were fertilized. Deciding when to inject HCG is not easy, although it is very convenient to induce

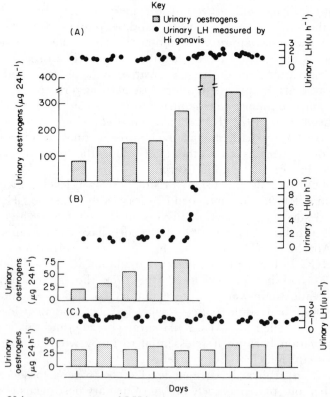

FIG. 1. Urinary oestrogens and LH in women treated with clomiphene. Reprinted by courtesy of *Nature*.

ovulation at a desired time of day. Does anyone know what happens to these follicles, this mixture of ovulatory and non-ovulatory follicles when we puncture them to aspirate the oocytes?

We would also like to know if clomiphene also internalizes oestrogen receptors in the reproductive tract. This could be most important for our work, because it may give long-term stimulus to the secretory uterus, which could assist in implantation.

Trounson: It is well known that clomiphene will internalise oestrogen receptors. It is also true that clomiphene will persist for up to three months in the body tissues. It is not broken down, and has a long half-life, but levels decline rapidly after ingestion. I feel that the number of receptors that remain on the tissue is rapidly stabilized, so the tissue can respond to natural oestrogens. We have the same pregnancy rate in our patients whether we use HCG or not; there is no difference in the success of the treatment, although the use of HCG is very convenient for inducing ovulation at a particular time.

There has also been discussion about the antioestrogen effects of clomiphene. I believe these are not very well understood. A great deal of work was published soon after clomiphene was introduced, but there has not been much follow-up in recent years, except for treatment in anovulatory patients.

Regarding multiple follicles in the ovary at laparoscopy, we thought at one time that we should leave one follicle intact. The idea here was to allow the luteal phase to be established on the base of this follicle which would ovulate normally. The other follicles were aspirated, and may be damaged during the aspiration. We reasoned that the single intact follicle would therefore help with the luteal phase. But now we believe that this has no particular benefit and that we merely lost the oocyte we could otherwise have collected, and which was presumably ovulated into the abdominal cavity.

We have had one case of a woman who was pregnant with large numbers of luteal cysts, but she subsequently aborted. This case is the only one in which we have had difficulty in response to the use of clomiphene. We know that where a large cystic follicle develops during one cycle, it regresses and is gone by the next cycle, and it cannot be detected by ultrasound. On the base of these data, I do not have any doubts about stimulation with clomiphene, or even about adding HMG. At the present moment, we have many pregnancies and births, and we are happy with the way we are proceeding in this direction. There may be other systems which give equally good results.

Spiers: We have had many cycles where graafian follicles of different sizes have grown following the use of clomiphene stimulation.

The fertilization rate of oocytes recovered from these follicles does not seem to differ. So we have no doubts about the different-sized follicles, which will yield an egg that can be fertilized. We time the laparoscopy when the size of the largest follicles is approximately 2 cm, knowing that some smaller ones are present.

Lopata: We decide when to inject HCG on the basis of the rate of growth and size of the dominant follicle. We have compared fertilization rates of eggs from dominant follicles with fertilization rates of eggs from all other follicles, and have observed no differences in fertilization or cleavage rates in the two groups.

There is another method of analysing the data. In some patients treated with clomiphene, there is only one follicle and only one oocyte is recovered. Again, there is no difference in the fertilization rates of these single eggs as compared with the fertilization rates of eggs collected from patients with more than one follicle. We therefore suggest that there is no difference in the rates of fertilization and cleavage from the different-sized follicles induced in our patients with clomiphene.

Edwards: I believe that the reintroduction of clomiphene by the Australian group has helped considerably in the treatment of in-vitro fertilization. We had abandoned it in the early seventies because pregnancy rates in oligomenorrhoeic patients treated with it appeared to be too low (Edwards, 1973), but now it seems to me that it is an excellent treatment and we are using it and have many pregnancies. I am nevertheless concerned about monitoring the follicular phase using clomiphene. Once it is given, it is essential to monitor the patients very closely by the use of urinary oestrogens and LH in either urine or plasma because cervical mucus tests are unsatisfactory. It is so easy to "miss" an individual patient if these guidelines are not followed. It is a failure for us if her oestrogens turn down because her follicles may have become cystic, or if her LH surge is discharged before the HCG is given so that at laparoscopy she has ovulated. I would stress that it is impossible to rely on the simple use of clomiphene and HCG, combined with a parameter such as Spinnbarkeit or scanning. It is essential to follow oestrogens and LH.

Trounson: We would agree with those remarks. We get very high rates of egg recovery, and replace embryos into most of our patients now we are measuring plasma oestradiol, although occasionally we do find some patients have ovulated. Even here, one follicle may have ovulated, but another may still be intact and the oocyte can be collected. But this can only be done if the oestrogen is rapidly monitored, and we use a rapid immunoassay, in combination with ultrasound.

We feel that the levels of plasma or urinary oestrogens do not make a great deal of sense unless we know how many follicles are growing. If, at scanning, the number of follicles are there in the number and size we expect, then the patient is introduced into the programme. The patient then goes on 3-hourly urine collections, and we try to inject the HCG to fit in with the schedule in our busy hospital. We do monitor for LH, but we keep the monitoring down to as brief a time as possible. We could use an alternative system, taking a blood sample before the injection of HCG to find out levels of LH. If LH levels had risen, the patient could be sent home until the next cycle. In our clinic, if we find that there is a rise in urinary LH before the HCG is injected, then we simply bring the operation forward. A combination of ultrasound, oestrogens and LH is very satisfactory in the system.

Rising levels of oestrogen are very important, but we have stimulated preovulatory development of follicles with HCG when they were falling. Sometimes, levels of oestrogens do not rise satisfactorily, and the patient can go home. If there is an erratic rise, we may let the oestrogens go on rising until she has her own endogenous LH surge. Our treatment depends on each individual patient, and if, for example, a follicle has passed 3 cm, we decide it is cystic or atretic and the patient goes home. This condition is usually associated with a fall in oestrogens, and is a guide to an atretic follicle. Sometimes, however, levels of oestrogens fall before a natural LH surge, so one has to be very careful. Perhaps there are some other regulators besides oestrogens which are involved in discharging the endogenous LH, and inhibin may be one of them.

Jones, G: Levels of progesterone should be rising in the patients if follicles are growing strongly. There is an indication that progesterone rises at the time of the LH surge, and so it would be a good marker.

Trounson: We have measured progesterone at the required level to follow such small changes as occur before ovulation (Trounson *et al.*, 1980). It is a case of having rapid assays which are sufficiently sensitive.

Dosage of Clomiphene

Webster: Leeton is using 150 mg of clomiphene daily on days 5 and 9. In some cases, the treatment was extended between 3 and 10. Why was this?

Trounson: We were experimenting with clomiphene, trying to get the dose right. We were changing dose rates according to time, in order to get the best response in the patient. After all our efforts, we found that 150 mg between days 5 and 9 produced just as good a result as any other treatment. We wished to get a better response by varying the dose and time of administration of clomiphene, but in the end we found no differences.

We are trying to create a system for ourselves to make the treatment as simple as possible, so that there is no problem with variations between patients or circumstances. If one of our patients fails to respond satisfactorily between days 5 and 9, we will give her a small amount of HMG combined with clomiphene in the next cycle to improve her response. We make an arbitrary decision that if she did not respond in one cycle, we will give an extra stimulus in the next one. The slightly longer treatment did not stimulate the small follicles on day 9 and the small cysts sometimes formed, so we abandoned it and now use our standard method.

Jones, G: Our experience using clomiphene over the years with anovulatory patients is that an increase in treatment alters their secretion of LH. To get a more satisfactory response, it is important to increase the amount of clomiphene given early on in the course of treatment.

Conti: We believe that some of our patients with large cystic follicles during examination by ultrasound have been treated for a long time with clomiphene. They may have been on this treatment for some years. There appears to be a correlation between length of time and ovarian follicular response. We believe that some of these patients are now no longer suitable for treatment with clomiphene continuously, or for in-vitro fertilization.

Visualizing Follicle Growth and Ovulation by Ultrasound After Treatment with Clomiphene and HCG

Hamberger: In the stimulated cycles, Trounson observed 3, 4 or 5 follicles. My experience with these follicles is that they can ovulate over a period of time, perhaps over a 12-hour interval. It is obvious that some of the follicles are in advance of others, and it is interesting that Lopata obtained high rates of fertilization in follicles of all sizes. Is there any evidence that oocytes in the most advanced follicles are preferable to those of more retarded follicles?

Does anyone know what happens *in vivo*, whether there is a long series of ovulations following such treatment? We do not know from our own work that oocytes which are aspirated 12 hours after the oocyte of the leading follicle do not show signs of atresia. We have attempted to assess the proportion of follicles ovulating by means of repeated examination by ultrasound, and we have witnessed their successive collapse as one after the other underwent ovulation. We have checked these observations afterwards with laparoscopy. These patients were, of course, treated with clomiphene and HCG.

Steptoe: I am not sure about the easy identification of early corpora lutea versus late follicles. When a follicle is aspirated, there is an initial collapse, but the antrum is filled with blood within a few minutes.

Hamberger: Time-lapse techniques have revealed how a follicle collapses, and this can be seen ultrasonically over a period of a few minutes. It has been observed by us and already published by Robinson and co-workers (Hoult *et al.*, 1981).

Conti: In my opinion, provided the same operator is doing the scanning repeatedly on the same patient, it is possible to detect ovulation and follicular rupture. A follicle can be recognized on successive scans, to find out if it has changed in any way.

Hamberger: I believe that ultrasound is a safe method for distinguishing between follicles and corpora lutea. The experiences of Lauritzen, an experienced worker with ultrasonics, revealed that he could identify the follicle and corpus luteum ultrasonically with high precision.

Johnston: I know that Robinson has carried out repeated ultrasonic examinations to watch follicular growth and ovulation (see Hoult *et al.*, 1981). The examinations were made daily until ovulation approached, when they were very frequent. At the moment of ovulation, the patients were virtually under constant observation by ultrasound, and at the moment of ovulation the follicle would collapse for a period of 1–1½ minutes. It would then begin to fill up with blood within a period of 20 minutes, almost to its original volume, but then it had a different echo. In other words, it had the ''snowstorm'' appearance rather than the clear appearance of the earlier follicle. The fluid could be seen running behind the uterus, to form a pool in the Pouch of Douglas.

Trounson: I would accept that ovulation can be seen when patients are under constant observation. But I find it difficult to believe that women ovulate over a period of 12 hours after stimulation. It certainly is not the case in animals, for ovulation occurs over a much briefer time, even when they are hyperstimulated.

Lopata: In the study referred to by Johnston, two follicles were seen in one patient, and observed to ovulate simultaneously. These were observed during the natural cycle.

Cohen: I feel convinced that numerous ultrasound examinations made after the patient has been stimulated with hormones alter the physiological conditions in the ovary. I would be careful in interpreting results on constant sounding, especially in relation to what may happen normally (see discussion after Feichtinger's paper in Part 2). I would like to ask Trounson how he chooses the treatment each patient should receive. How do you make your mind up as to whether a patient should be given clomiphene or HCG, clomiphene alone, HMG alone, or some other treatment? Could you also indicate how frequently you carry out ultrasound in your patients, in order to study their follicular growth.

Trounson: In most patients we carry out only a single ultrasound examination to visualize the follicles. If, however, the follicles are small, i.e. if they are smaller than 1.4 cm, and oestrogens are rising we may do two closely successive examinations at a 2-day interval. We would also use two ultrasound examinations if we felt the first one was incorrect. They are incorrect on occasions.

We choose our patients quite arbitrarily. On the first cycle of treatment we use clomiphene and in the non-responders we give clomiphene and HMG. We have obtained pregnancies from both treatments. At the present time, we have a trial where some patients are given clomiphene and others receive only HMG. And perhaps there may be half-way treatment which combines the two, and placates Edwards's wishes not to internalize receptors! The patients understand before they come that they will be put into groups on a statistical basis, although we try to give them a treatment that will be successful.

Jones, H: I do not understand how people integrate levels of oestrogens within follicles seen by ultrasound. Ultrasound is sometimes very difficult to interpret if there is a cluster of follicles, when it is not easy to be sure if there are two or three. There are also other tissues in the pelvis which can give shadows resembling follicles. It must be very difficult to make decisions on the basis of steroid output per follicle, even though the levels of plasma steroids are known. It must be an art to interpret the two!

Spiers: Some of the small follicles, of 5 mm or smaller, will not be found by ultrasound. In stimulated cycles, there may be four or five of such follicles which can produce a lot of oestrogen. Nevertheless, the more parameters that are obtained the more useful the information.

Value of the Mucus Test

Edwards: Could I ask about the value of the mucus test? All that I have read has shown that this test, in whatever manner it is employed, gives a very variable result for the onset of ovulation. It is useful for predicting mid-cycle, but nowhere near precise enough for fertilization *in vitro*. In Berlin, Trounson and his colleagues stressed how they were simply using mucus and ultrasonics (Trounson *et al.*., 1981); now, they measure oestrogens and LH, as we did earlier in Oldham. Of what value is the mucus test when carefully measured levels of oestrogens and LH are available? Does it provide an advanced warning of ovulation?

Trounson: No, it does not. But if a patient is given clomiphene, nurses can detect the secretion of mucus which indicates mid-cycle. The examination of mucus only becomes useful when two of the other tests conflict. If oestrogens conflict with ultrasound, then the mucus test is very valuable; in these cases, it does provide a reserve for interpreting the cycle.

Edwards: Have you ever found a conflict between oestrogens and, for example, spinnbarkeit, and decided to rely on the spinnbarkeit as opposed to the oestrogens? Personally, I would always rely on an assay, but I wonder if other people would differ.

Trounson: I would use the oestrogen assay myself as often as I could. But there can be problems because assays can go wrong, whereas cervical mucus is a biological test, and we measure the response of an end organ. We do not use it much nowadays, but occasionally, in cases of doubt, we do employ it.

Steptoe: In our experience, clomiphene reduces the amount of cervical mucus, which becomes extremely scanty. This has been witnessed over the years, for clomiphene alone causes many difficulties in assessing cervical mucus. The addition of an HCG injection to the regime of clomiphene seemed to improve pregnancy rates for many doctors, but it seemed to have no relation whatsoever to the cervical mucus.

Trounson: Yes, that is quite right. Clomiphene does reduce cervical mucus. In our clinic, we place more reliance on ferning and colour, and these changes can be detected. It is much more difficult to take and to assay, but with experienced people it can be done.

Johnston: In our A.I.D. service, we correlated LH, oestrogens and changes in the mucus. There is an exact correlation between the rise in oestrogens and maximal cervical score, both occurring at the LH peak in the natural cycle. Occasionally, if there are problems we certainly take note of the cervical mucus, in order to assist with an assay for LH which might be giving difficulties. We have not done the same kind of thing on the in-vitro fertilization programme. It is more difficult to score mucus in clomiphene cycles.

Steptoe: But dealing with A.I.D. or A.I.H. presents a different situation. We are then trying to get sperm into the uterus before and again after ovulation to establish a pregnancy. There is lots of time to work and the intention is to obtain fertilization *in vivo* under those circumstances. We are looking for something much more precise for fertilization *in vitro*.

Jones, G: We are just evaluating the first six months of our work using HMG. We feel it is very important to monitor the patient's own biological responses. We measure both maturation index and the cervical mucus, but when measuring cervical mucus it is also essential to measure cervical dilation, the amount of mucus and the spinnbarkeit. These biological responses of the patient then correlate with her oestrogen response. In our cycles using Pergonal we believe we are getting a suppression of the patient's own LH, so that her response, as far as her oestrogen is concerned, is remarkably variable. It is possible to have low plasma oestrogens, yet have a biological response in the cervix. When we have accepted this point, we have been able to obtain preovulatory eggs that have been fertilized *in vitro*.

We are currently using gonadotrophins to stimulate follicle growth. We give between 6 and 8 or 9 ampoules of HMG, depending on the response of the patient. We then give HCG to induce ovulation. This is a satisfactory method of stimulating follicle growth and ovulation, and it has been used widely in the treatment of anovulatory patients, where it is very successful. It is an alternative method to the use of clomiphene, and avoids some of the snags of that treatment. We plan to continue using this method in the foreseeable future.

Edwards: The dose of HMG you are giving is relatively modest. Are you giving such a low dosage because you fear hyperstimulation in ovulatory women with greater amounts, and do you have any problems with the luteal phase? We felt that the short luteal phase was a major problem with HMG and HCG treatment in Oldham, although in most of our work we are giving less HMG that you are now giving (Edwards *et al.*, 1980).

Jones, G: We hope to obtain one or two extra follicles above the natural cycle, but to avoid multiple follicles. But we often get 7 or 8 follicles, even with the low dosage we use. I do not believe that pregnancy rates are improved by hyperstimulation even in anovulatory women. We are planning on adding pure FSH to the Pergonal in a series of older patients who we are now introducing to our clinic. The luteal phase is quite normal unless our patients show hyperstimulation. In this case, the luteal phase can be 10 days, provided she is not pregnant. If she is pregnant, the corpus luteum is rescued.

Trounson: Could we know your form of treatment and its success rate? It would be nice to know about the kind of system and what it gave in terms of collecting oocytes and obtaining fertilization.

Jones, H: We have used this method 31 times. We do not measure fertilization rates, only cleavage rates, and this has been rather poor. We obtain approximately 1.9 eggs per patient. Three of the transfers were multiple transfers, two of two embryos and one of three embryos, none of which became pregnant. We suspect that the injection of HMG depresses the levels of the patient's own LH. We have never yet seen an endogenous LH surge in our patients despite the high levels of oestrogens. We attempt to avoid the treatment of patients in successive cycles with HMG.

Cohen: In some cases, patients given HMG in successive cycles may have an advantage. The second cycle of treatment may benefit from the oestrogens released during the first cycle, and so pregnancy rates may be better although the level of oestradiol may be greater during the second cycle of treatment.

Do Continuous Superovulation Treatments Damage the Ovary?

Jones, H: We have examined levels of HCGβ in some of our patients given HCG to induce ovulation. The levels rise immediately except in rare patients, where there may be some delay. Perhaps the method of injection or absorption, or some other technical problem may be responsible for the weak uptake of HCG.

Hamberger: We believe that too much HCG may interfere with the luteal phase, but we also know that the succeeding cycles may be affected by such treatment. There is some delay in the beginning of the next cycle if too much HCG is given. This was found in studies involving the removal of follicles and the study of the succeeding cycle in women. We have now an average of 2.6 oocytes per patient, using 100 mg clomiphene and 4500 IU HCG, and we can fertilize approximately 50% of these.

I would like to comment on the induction of corpora lutea following hyperstimulation. The presence of several corpora lutea can damage surrounding small follicles, and this may cause long-term damage to the ovary. In some of our patients, we have been unable to stimulate them again two years after a heavy overstimulation with HMG and HCG. Some of our patients have even had no follicles left and have entered a premature menopause after such treatments.

Jones, G: But many of these patients treated in these circumstances were oligomenorrhoeic or amenorrhoeic, and might have been menopausal before the treatment was given. I do not believe 9,000 IU of HCG is excessive.

Hamberger: We believe that heavy superovulation damages the ovaries in many of our patients, and we prefer to avoid excessive stimulation.

Edwards: This point is very interesting. I think you must exclude all of the other possible causes of failure of ovarian response in your patients before you can attribute such damage to the hyperstimulation of the ovary. Have you done ultrasound of your patients to see if follicles are forming and growing, and can you exclude abnormal endocrine conditions which are preventing ovulation?

Hamberger: Similar studies have been carried in the rat, and they do not show an oestrous cycle after heavy hyperstimulation with gonadotrophins. Clinically, it is difficult to know how long an amenorrhoeic or otherwise hormonally-disturbed patient should continue to have ovulatory cycles. But some certainly stop having functional cycles soon after such hyperstimulation. Heavy luteinization can cause damage to the ovaries. Indeed, if we observe that our patients have several large follicles after stimulation, we may consider carrying out a laparoscopy prior to ovulation and aspirate all but one or two follicles from them, in order to avoid this hyperstimulation.

Jones, G: I believe that Hamberger's hyperstimulation is not necessarily caused by HCG. It is caused by the hyperstimulation by FSH, in the follicular phase. The data I know shows that a high dose of HCG can be given, without causing damage.

Hamberger: Yes, I agree. The treatment with HMG can give up to 8 or more follicles, and this may cause the damage. After injection of HCG, even 4,500 IU, there are heavily luteinized ovaries. In early days, the treatment with HMG was often too prolonged, especially with high doses, and this probably caused a great deal of damage to the patients. We believe that ultrasound is very important in these cases, perhaps more than determinations of oestrogens, in order to find out how many follicles are stimulated.

Trounson: I cannot accept the results Hamberger has just described. It is very different from our experience in cattle and with other species, where we reported superovulation every two months, carrying on for over 15 years. The ability of cows to respond bears no relationship at all to the corpora lutea they have had. Women have been repeatedly stimulated with HCG, e.g. by Leeton and Johnston, and there was no such difficulty.

Hamberger: I am referring to very heavy superstimulation of human ovaries. This is very different from a moderate stimulation in cattle.

Trounson: Again, I find it difficult to accept this conclusion. We have seen up to 100 corpora lutea in cattle, maybe even as many as 30 or 40 embryos. Yet, it does not prevent a successive response to PMS. Of course, in older animals, superovulatory responses are less, but this is well known. There is no physiological basis for your remarks on the human, unless there are limitations on the number of primordial follicles available in the patient.

Edwards: I cannot agree with some of the observations of Hamberger. We have repeatedly superovulated mice, and they were continually responding and ovulating large numbers of eggs. The human ovary works like any other ovary, and the number of follicles available declines with age following stimulation. The human ovary will be similar. Evidence must be produced to show that high levels of progesterone or the formation of many corpora lutea have prevented the dynamics of ovarian follicular growth. There can be so many other explanations: perhaps the exogenous gonadotrophins have induced a Stein–Leventhal syndrome, producing a series of cystic follicles. I find it difficult to evaluate his results on the basis of the present evidence.

Hamberger: There is a risk in the repeated treatment of women during successive cycles to induce a heavy hyperstimulation of the ovaries. We fear that the microcirculation of the ovary may be damaged and this causes destruction of neighbouring follicles. The circulatory disturbance can persist for two weeks, as is known in animals, and the rate of atresia and disappearance of oocytes may be influenced by such treatment. Having seen these ovaries by laparoscopy, they do sometimes look disturbed, and they may have large cysts and other pathological signs.

Testart: We observe that 25% of the oocytes collected in clomiphene-treated cycles were still in germinal vesicle or metaphase-I after two days in culture. We prepared the egg according to Thibault's method, and observed a nucleus sometimes, but many times we observed first meiotic phase without polar body formation.

After clomiphene treatment, we observe that oocytes from a third of the follicles appear abnormal. Their follicles have a very low level of progesterone, less than 5,000 mg ml^{-1}, a level never seen in a spontaneous cycle, plus high levels of androgens.

Edwards: I have hardly ever seen a human egg arrested in metaphase-I, to the best of my knowledge. In some circumstances, especially with certain animal species, a lot of arrest occurs in metaphase-I, but in species like human and cow, the oocytes always proceed to metaphase-II in our systems.

References

Adashi, E. Y., Hsueh, A. J. W. & Yen, S. S. C. 1980. Alterations induced by clomiphene in the concentrations of oestrogen receptors in the uterus, pituitary gland and hypothalamus of female rats. *Journal of Endocrinology*, **87**, 383-392.

Baudendistel, L. J., Ruh, M. F., Nadel, E. M. & Ruh, T. S. 1978. Cytoplasmic oestrogen receptor replenishment: oestrogens versus anti-oestrogens. *Acta Endocrinologica*, **89**, 599-611.

Edwards, R. G. 1973. Studies on human conception. *American Journal of Obstetrics and Gynecology*, **117**, 587.

Edwards, R. G. 1981. Test-tube babies 1981. *Nature*, **293**, 253-256.

Edwards, R. G., Steptoe, P. C. & Purdy, J. M. 1980. Establishing full-term human pregnancies using cleaving embryos grown *in vitro*. *British Journal of Obstetrics and Gynecology*, **87**, 737-756.

Hoult, I. J., deCrespigny, L. C., O'Herlihy, C., Speirs, A. L., Lopata, A., Kellow, G., Johnston, I. & Robinson, H. P. 1981. Ultrasound control of clomiphene/ human chorionic gonadotrophin stimulated cycles for oocyte recovery and in-vitro fertilization. *Fertility and Sterility*, **36**, 316-319.

Katzellenbogen, B. S. & Ferguson, E. R. 1975. Antioestrogen action in the uterus: biological ineffectiveness of nuclear bound estradiol after antiestrogen. *Endocrinology*, **97**, 1-12.

Trounson, A. O., Leeton, J. F., Wood, C., Webb, J. & Kovacs, G. 1980. The investigation of idiopathic infertility by in-vitro fertilization. *Fertility and Sterility*, **34**, 431-438.

Trounson, A. O., Wood, E. C., Leeton, J. F., Webb, J., Wood, J., Buttery, B., Mohr, L., McTalbot, J., Jessup, D. & Kovacs, G. 1981. A programme of successful in-vitro fertilization and embryo transfer in the controlled ovulatory cycle. In: *Third World Congress of Human Reproduction*, Berlin, 1981. Excerpta Medica, Amsterdam.

Watson, C. S., Medina, D. & Clark, J. H. 1981. Estrogenic effects of nafoxidine on ovarian-dependant and independent mammary tumour lines in the mouse. *Endocrinology*, **108**, 668-672.

Wood, C., Trounson, A., Leeton, J., McKenzie Talbot, J., Buttery, B., Webb, J., Wood, J. & Jessup, D. 1981. A clinical assessment of nine pregnancies obtained by in-vitro fertilization and embryo transfer. *Fertility and Sterility*, **35**, 502-508.

Part 2

LAPAROSCOPY OF THE PREOVULATORY FOLLICLE

The Preovulatory Follicle and Oocyte

W. Feichtinger, S. Szalay, P. Kemeter, A. Beck, Ch. Bieglmayer,
P. Riss, A. Kratochwil and H. Janisch

One of the basic problems for success in in-vitro fertilization is the acquisition of mature oocytes of good quality. This situation is highlighted by the uncertainty as to whether all embryos which cleave apparently regularly are sufficiently viable to establish pregnancy after their replacement. Such questions led us to embark on some work in this field, and in the following we wish to reveal the results of the consequent studies conducted by our group.

LH in Urine and Ultrasonic Monitoring of Growing Follicles

In view of the time sequence of intrafollicular maturation of the preovulatory oocyte we wish briefly to relate some of our experiences with the standard timing methods, predominantly ultrasound of the graafian follicles and the Hi-Gonavis tests for urinary LH. Unfortunately we are unable to give very exact estimations of the time intervals from the onset of the LH surge to laparoscopy, for the organizational constraints made it impossible to perform three-hourly LH assays. However, together with the ultrasonic monitoring, we often managed sufficient orientations from urines collected during spontaneous cycles.

Regular cleavage occurred when oocyte recovery was performed 24–30 hours after the start of the LH surge from the baseline, or 24–26 hours after the mid-point of the two LH estimations, whence the sequential LH increase began. In some cases we did not orientate from the mid-point because of a longer overnight interval between collections. These varying time intervals did not seem to significantly influence either the cleavage of eggs pathologically or their failure to cleave.

Second Department of Obstetrics and Gynecology, Medical School, University of Vienna, Austria.

A confident follicle diagnosis could not be given by ultrasound earlier than three days before ovulation in the natural cycles; we found it was generally of greatest use as the LH surge began. In one-quarter of all LH recordings a preliminary early peak was registered and disturbed estimates of the correct timing. Here, ultrasound was most helpful, as in the example shown in Fig. 1, where no follicle was seen by sonography at the first examination. After the initial rise in LH, there was a subsequent decrease and then a secondary rise. Following this later rise, a mature follicle was detected by ultrasound and a preovulatory egg was recovered at laparoscopy.

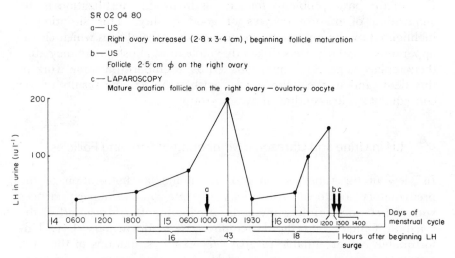

FIG. 1. Ultrasonic monitoring as a helpful means for the correct timing of oocyte recovery in a case with a preliminary early LH peak in urine.

However in about one-fifth of all cases, ultrasound failed due to misinterpretation of the scans in the presence of cystic structures or hydrosalpinx. When strong adhesions or gas-filled bowels were present, no diagnosis could be made.

The corresponding results using stimulated cycles were similar (Table 1), and total failures numbered approximately 20% of the patients examined. A truly correct diagnosis emerged in about two-thirds where all follicles present could be detected or none in cases with a poor stimulation effect. In the remaining cases, some follicles were measured and this was very helpful for timing the injection of HCG. In 13 patients,

Table 1
Results of ultrasonic follicle measurements in clomiphene-HCG controlled cycles

Total number of cases: 42

Absolutely correct diagnosis
  One follicle   8 ⎫
  Two follicles   14 ⎬ 26 (62%)
  Three follicles   4 ⎭
                             31 (74%)*
Partially correct diagnosis
  One of two   2   5
  Two of three   1
  One of three   1   5
  Two of four   1
                                     33 (78.5%)
Poor stimulation effect (small follicles
  only) correctly diagnosed   2
Failures (no follicle or wrong side described, wrong size, no help for
  timing the HCG injection)   9 (21.5%)

* Number of cases and percent when ultrasound most helpful in timing the HCG injection.

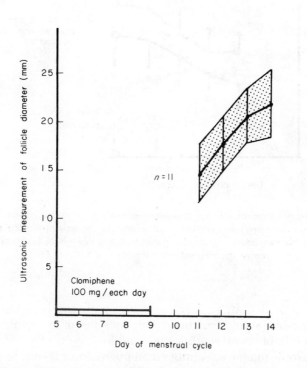

FIG. 2. Daily ultrasonic growth control of follicles (mean size mm ± SD) in 13 patients given clomiphene 100 mg from day 5–9 of their menstrual cycle.

daily ultrasound scans were performed when clomiphene was given and in most of these the follicle appeared for the first time on day 11.

The daily growth control of the follicles (Figs 2 and 3) show a good correlation with the mean diameters at laparoscopy, calculated from the volume of the aspirated fluid (Fig. 3). However, in some cases the aspirated volume was lower than that corresponding to the ultrasonic measurement one day before laparoscopy. This finding coincides well with those published already by O'Herlihy *et al.* (1980). It is interesting to note that in patients with a second follicle, this seemed to grow later than the first, for some of them were initially detected just after the HCG injection.

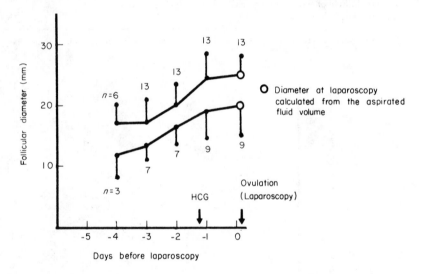

FIG. 3. Mean values of follicles measured by sonography on various days prior to ovulation (laparoscopy) and diameters of follicles at laparoscopy calculated from the volume of the aspirated fluid (13 patients, clomiphene-HCG controlled cycles, laparoscopy 36 hours after injection of 5,000 IU HCG).

Close to ovulation, in rare cases and with excellent equipment, a faint, cone-like solid structure sometimes becomes visible inside the follicle, probably representing the cumulus oviger (Fig. 4). We know that ultrasonic diagnosis cannot reach microscopic levels, but, as in this case, the cumulus cells and viscous fluid can provide sound increase and a good echo.

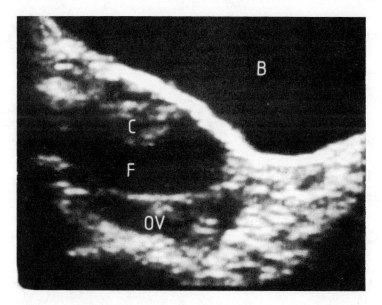

FIG. 4. Ultrasonographic demonstration of a single preovulatory follicle in a non-stimulated ovary, with evidence of a cumulus oviger. B = Bladder, OV = Ovary, F = Follicle, C = Cumulus (Kretz combison 200, Polaroid).

Cumulus, Follicular Fluid and Egg Measurements

After aspiration the viscous cumulus has a size from 2–5 mm and is helpful to us in identifying the oocyte quickly. On the other hand, in our opinion, the approximate size estimation of the cumulus could not serve as a maturity criterion of the egg. For instance, an egg embedded in a large amount of viscous fluid failed to fertilize and cleave, whereas another from the same patient recovered in a smaller cumulus cloud gave a normal embryo. However, the cumulus could be distorted and split into pieces at aspiration.

Measurements of the size of all recovered eggs revealed some interesting findings (Table 2). The first group lists eggs which were recovered from nonovulatory follicles and were classified as immature. Group two comprises of eggs which either could be fertilized, but failed to cleave or which showed pathological fertilization or cleavage. In the third group we put those oocytes which led to successful fertilization and regular cleavage. Of course there were almost no cumulus in the immature group and as the amount of follicular fluid was 2.17 ml, the eggs were significantly smaller (113 ± 12 μm) than in the other groups.

Table 2
Statistical comparison of the amount of follicular fluid, size of cumulus and size of
egg when oocytes were either classified to be immature, failed to cleave or showed
pathological cleavage, and when they cleaved regularly

Immature eggs (n = 6)		Eggs fertilized but failed to cleave. Eggs fertilized, cleaved irregularly (n = 9)		Eggs fertilized, cleaved regularly (n = 8)
		Follicular fluid (ml)		
2.17 ± 1.44		4.14 ± 1.55		5.13 ± 2.72
	$P < 0.05$		n.s.	
		$P < 0.05$		
		Size of cumulus (mm)		
0.75 ± 1.25		3.37 ± 1.09		3.38 ± 0.52
	$P < 0.001$		n.s.	
		$P < 0.001$		
		Size of egg (μm)		
113 ± 12		138.44 ± 10.4*		158.7 ± 5.8*
	$P < 0.001$		$P < 0.001$	
		$P < 0.001$		

*Eggs with polar body observed: 149 ± 12.2 (n = 10).

No difference could be found between the pathological and regular group in both the amount of follicular fluid and size of cumulus. However, the eggs which gave a regular embryo were significantly larger (158.7 ± 5.8 μm) than the others (138.44 ± 10.4 μm).

The size of the eggs was estimated by phase contrast microscopy at a magnification of 125 × either immediately following recovery or after removing the egg from the insemination medium, when the cumulus had already dispersed. Size seemed to be independent of the appearance of a polar body, because eggs with polar bodies were represented in both groups (although they were not seen in all classes) and therefore the mean size was also intermediate (149 ± 12.2 μm). Size estimation of the egg could well be a more valuable criterion for both egg maturity and quality compared to other factors. We are following up these observations and are now undertaking regular egg measurements which seem to serve as a valuable prognostic tool.

Endocrine Changes in Preovulatory Follicles

We have studied endocrine changes using a concept which has already been thoroughly tried in the investigation of steroid content and steroidogenesis in pre- and nonovulatory follicles by Fowler *et al.* (1977, 1978). In stimulated cycles especially, preovulatory follicles may be compared with those which are less mature (nonovulatory) and present concomitantly (Edwards *et al.*, 1980; Fowler *et al.*, 1977, 1978).

For our investigations, we selected substances in follicular fluid whose importance has not yet been definitively elucidated in the human. These are:

(1) β-Endorphin.
(2) Prostaglandins.
(3) Collagenolytic activity as an "ovulatory factor".

β-Endorphin-like Substances

β-Endorphin is an opiate-like peptide widely distributed in the brain and present in the cerebrospinal fluid. It evidently exerts an inhibitory action on the neuroendocrine factors regulating pulsatile LH secretion (Quigley *et al.*, 1980). This action seems to be reversed by morphine antagonists especially in the presence of high oestrogen and progesterone feedback as in the periovulatory phase (Quigley *et al.*, 1980; Ropert *et al.*, 1981).

Hence we were keen to know if β-endorphin also appears in follicular fluid, perhaps playing a role in intrafollicular hormone interactions. We estimated its levels in fluid by radioimmunoassay (New England Nuclear). Some preliminary results (Table 3) indicate that the concentration of immunoreactive material resembling β-endorphin seems to be low in follicular fluid. No difference was found between follicles.

Most of the values in fluids from both mature follicles (where eggs gave normal embryos), and nonovulatory follicles were within or just above the sensitivity range of our method.

Prostaglandins and Collagenolytic Activity

Prostaglandins seem to play an important role in the complex mechanism of ovulation (LeMaire *et al.*, 1979). Several animal studies e.g. in rats and rabbits, have shown that both E and F prostaglandins increase significantly in ovulatory follicles whereas they remain low in

Table 3
Preliminary evaluation of β-endorphin like substances
in human pre- and nonovulatory follicles

Patient	Follicle number	Ovulatory follicle	Non-ovulatory follicle
Z.E.	I	30	
	II		15
	III	30 (egg cleaved)	
T.H.	I	20 (egg cleaved)	
	II		20
K.I.	I	30 (egg cleaved)	
	II	30 (egg cleaved)	
S.I.		125	
M.R.	I		15
	II	30	
	III	30	
A.M.		50 (egg cleaved)	
K.M.			0

nonovulatory follicles (Yang *et al.*, 1974). The inhibitory effects of prostaglandin antagonists on ovulation are well known. Furthermore prostaglandins are known to activate enzymes from lysosomes by labilizing their membranes (Weiner & Kaley, 1972).

We directed our interest towards collagenase, which is supposed to be the ovulatory enzyme dissolving the large amount of collagen in the follicular wall (Edwards, 1980) and has been found in animal studies to be greatly increased close to ovulation (Espey, 1978). In a recently published work, Szalay *et al.* (1981) showed that PGE locally applied to the cervix of pregnant women at term significantly increased the collagenolytic activity measured in tissue biopsies, compared with a control group.

In the present study, prostaglandins were extracted from follicular fluid according to the methods described by Jaffe and Burman (1979) and chromatographed on silicagel columns by a modified procedure (Bieglmayer, 1981). PGE and PGF fractions were determined by radioimmunoassay kits purchased from "Clinical Assays" (Cambridge, Mass., U.S.A.). For the determination of PGE an alkaline dehydration was performed to convert PGE to PGB. Values were corrected for losses during extraction and column chromatography by the addition of standard amounts of tritiated PGE_1 and $PGF_{2\alpha}$.

Estimations of prostaglandins were carried out in the fluid of 20 pre- and nonovulatory follicles of 13 patients in whom the cycle was regulated by clomiphene and HCG. The follicles were aspirated 36 hours after the injection of HCG. After removal of the eggs, the fluids were centrifugated and immediately deep frozen for storage.

Collagenolytic activity was measured in 10 of the follicular fluids with C_{14}-labelled collagen as substrate by a modified procedure of Gisslow and McBride (1975). The Biorad dye-binding assay was used for protein determinations in the follicular fluids.

The few preliminary results indicate that no correlation existed between collagenolytic activity in the fluids and the levels of prostaglandins. Collagenolytic activity seems to be similar in pre- and nonovulatory follicles (Fig. 5). In contrast $PGF_{2\alpha}$ was significantly higher in ovulatory (11.53 ± 9.76 ng ml^{-1}, n = 11) than in nonovulatory follicles (0.86 ± 0.61 ng ml^{-1}, n = 6). PGE was higher in ovulatory follicles too; this difference was statistically not significant, hence $PGF_{2\alpha}$ was much lower in nonovulatory follicles than PGE. The highest prostaglandin levels could be observed in those follicles which yielded oocytes giving regular embryos (n = 5) (Fig. 5); evidently these follicles had reached optimal maturity.

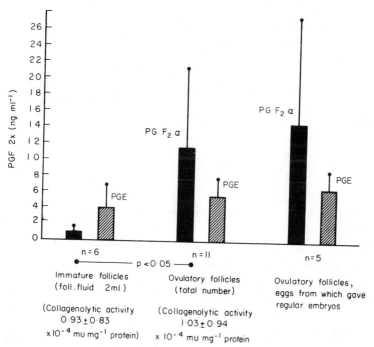

FIG. 5. Prostaglandins E and $F_{2\alpha}$ (mean ng ml^{-1} ± SD) in pre- and nonovulatory human follicles, as well as in follicles which yielded eggs giving regular embryos.

Additionally, we wish to discuss some single cases. In two patients large follicles of 7 and 8 ml and even 20 ml contents were present, but yielded almost no granulosa cells and no egg could be found. In these cases, prostaglandins were very low and did not correspond to follicular size. These findings support the suggestion that granulosa cells appear to be the major source of prostaglandins, since they have been shown to synthesize PGF and PGE in culture (Shutt & Lopata, 1981). In one patient, laparoscopy was performed too late and revealed two follicles which had already burst spontaneously. The fluid aspirated from the cul-du-sac contained large amounts of both $PGF_{2\alpha}$ (23.7 ng ml^{-1} and PGE (9.4 ng ml^{-1}). However, no collagenolytic activity could be detected in this fluid.

As shown in animal studies, we may conclude from our results that prostaglandins play a dominant role in the mechanisms of ovulation in the human. Their exact role in the ovulatory process remains a major unanswered question. It has been suggested that the final event in the follicular rupture involves an enzymatic process which weakens the follicular wall, and prostaglandins could be involved in the activation, release or synthesis of this "ovulatory enzyme" (LeMaire *et al.*, 1979). As far as conclusions could be drawn from our preliminary data, collagenolytic activity in human follicles does not seem to be enhanced by the presence of increased prostaglandins. Other proteolytic enzymes may play a role, together with the stimulation of ovarian smooth muscle by increasing follicular prostaglandin levels, which could promote the rupture of the follicular wall and the extrusion of the oocyte.

References

Bieglmayer, C. Manuscript in preparation. 1981.

Edwards, R. G. 1980. *Conception in the Human Female*, p. 324. Academic Press, London.

Edwards, R. G., Steptoe, P. C., Fowler, R. E. & Baillie, J. 1980. Observations on preovulatory human ovarian follicles and their aspirates. *British Journal of Obstetrics and Gynaecology*, **87**, 769–779.

Espey, L. L. 1978. Ovarian contractility and its relationship to ovulation: a review. *Biology of Reproduction*, **19**, 540.

Fowler, R. E., Chan, S. T. H., Walters, D. E., Edwards, R. G. & Steptoe, P. C. 1977. Steroidogenesis in human follicles approaching ovulation as judged from assays of follicular fluid. *Journal of Endocrinology*, **72**, 259.

Fowler, R. E., Edwards, R. G., Walters, D. E., Chan, S. T. H. & Steptoe, P. C. 1978. Steroidgenesis in preovulatory follicles of patients given human menopausal and chorionic gonadotrophins as judged by the radioimmunoassay of steroids in follicular fluid. *Journal of Endocrinology*, **77**, 161.

Gisslow, M. T. & McBride, B. C. 1975. *Annals of Biochemistry*, **68**, 70.

Jaffe, B. M. & Burman, H. R. 1979. *Methods of Hormone Radioimmunoassay*, p. 19. Ed. B. M. Jaffe and H. R. Burman. Academic Press, London & New York.

Le Maire, W. J., Clark, M. R. & Marsh, J. M. 1979. Biochemical mechanism of ovulation. In: *Human Ovulation*, p. 159. Ed. E. S. E. Hafez. Elsevier North Holland Biomedical Press, Amsterdam.

O'Herlihy, C., de Crespigny, L., Lopata, A., Johnston, I., Hoult, I. & Robinson, H. 1980. Preovulatory follicular size: a comparison of ultrasound and laparoscopic measurements. *Fertility and Sterility*, **34**, 24.

Quigley, M. E. & Yen, S. S. C. 1980. The role of endogenous opiates on LH secretion during the menstrual cycle. *Journal of Clinical Endocrinology and Metabolism*, **51**, 179.

Ropert, J. F., Quigley, M. E. & Yen, S. S. C. 1981. Endogenous opiates modulate pulsatile luteinizing hormone release in humans. *Journal of Clinical Endocrinology and Metabolism*, **52**, 583.

Shutt, D. A. & Lopata, A. 1981. The secretion of hormones during the culture of human preimplantation embryos with corona cells. *Fertility and Sterility*, **35**, 413.

Szalay, S., Husslein, P. & Grünberger, W. 1981. Local application of prostaglandin E_2 (PGE_2) and its influence on collagenolytic activity of cervical tissue. *Singapore Journal of Obstetrics and Gynaecology*, **12**, 15.

Weiner, R. & Kaley, G. 1972. Lysosomal fragility induced by prostaglandin $F_{2\alpha}$. *Nature*, **236**, 46.

Yang, N. S. T., Marsh, J. M. & Le Maire, W. J. 1974. Postovulatory changes in the concentrations of prostaglandins in rabbit graafian follicles. *Prostaglandins*, **6**, 37.

Discussion on the Preovulatory Follicle

Follicular Changes Before Ovulation

Johnston: I found the data on prostaglandins fascinating. $PGE_{2\alpha}$ is evidently involved in the mechanism of follicular rupture (i.e. Le Maire & Marsh, 1975; Wallach et al., 1975). The role of PGE is more uncertain, even though it is present in the preovulatory follicle. During our ultrasonic examinations, we had reports on the patients of pre-ovulatory pain (Mittelschmertz) and we found that it did not coincide with ovulation. It seems to precede the process of ovulation by at least 24 hours, and the pain has disappeared long before the actual process of ovulation begins. Perhaps the action of prostaglandins on the muscle may precede the actual event of ovulation.

Hamberger: We agree that the preovulatory pain precedes the moment of follicular rupture. We are also interested in collagenase activity that Feichtinger was measuring in follicular fluid. The major action of this enzyme could, of course, be also in the follicle, e.g. in the follicular wall. Have any attempts been made to excise follicle cells, and to examine the contribution of the different types of cell in the follicle towards the production of this enzyme?

Feichtinger: We have not assayed the tissues of the follicle. It is easy to estimate in follicular fluid. We felt this was very appropriate becuase the follicular wall is sometimes so thin, that the amount of enzymes in it would be too low to detect.

Hamberger: Our data on the analysis of follicular walls from preovulatory follicles involved incubations with tritiated proline or hydroxyproline, and we assayed the incorporation of the tracer into follicular cells. After two hours incubation, in the presence of $PGF_{2\alpha}$, or PGE_2, we found a reduction in the incorporation of hydroxyproline. There was no difference between the two prostaglandins in this effect. We are firmly convinced that prostaglandins are involved in decreasing collagen synthesis in the follicular wall prior to rupture.

Cohen: Has anyone observed any particular shape of the follicle as it approaches ovulation? We have noticed no change in shape from the day before ovulation until the moment of rupture, and scanning does not give enough precision to decide when aspiration should be performed.

Hamberger: We have made repeated ultrasonic examinations on the growth of follicles and corpora lutea. We have a very high success rate in following the growth of the leading follicle and the secondary follicle, and we can sometimes see the oocytes with their cumulus masses. We can visualize clear structures in certain follicles, and this can give us some idea of the type of follicle we are dealing with. We have not seen the detachment of the cumulus cells from the wall of the follicle. We have filmed animal follicles where this process can be seen, as the cumulus mass begins its movement before follicular rupture takes place.

Frydman: We have noticed that the picture of cumulus and the oocyte appears just before ovulation in spontaneous cycles, but can be seen one or two days before the LH surge or HCG administration in stimulated cycles.

Hamberger: We agree with those observations. We use the pictures of the cumulus cells and oocytes as an indication that a follicle is preovulatory and growing well.

Trounson: Some of these criteria are perhaps being made too difficult. We have a pregnancy from an egg that had no cumulus at all. There is a tremendous range in all the components of the follicle, and in the follicular fluid. We know that the levels of some compounds such as oestrogen and progesterone are very high indeed, and I was interested in Feichtinger's data on levels of prostaglandins of the follicle. They are very high, as high as we find in some corpora lutea. We also require a good marker to indicate the stage of oocyte maturation, but I think that we have not yet found the ideal component.

Mettler: We have watched the movement of the oocyte in rabbit follicles undergoing ovulation, but even though we could see a great deal of the follicle, we could never see the detachment of the cumulus mass from the wall of the follicle.

Aspirating the Preovulatory Follicle

Cohen: On some occasions we have found at laparoscopy that the follicle was ruptured, and there was a hole in the follicular wall. We have passed the needle through this hole, into the follicular space, and managed to collect the oocyte. How can this be explained?

Steptoe: We have occasionally found the oocyte on the surface of the follicle, just after rupture must have occurred. On other occasions, the oocyte was deep inside a follicle that had ruptured, as just described by Cohen. I believe that the oocyte does not necessarily lie just beneath the operculum, but may lie deeper within the follicle.

Edwards: The oocyte is perhaps anchored within the follicle or at least to the outer follicular wall by the viscous fluid. This was demonstrated in rabbits by Mastroianni and his colleagues some years ago, following fimbriectomy in rabbits (Mastroianni, 1977). The oocyte is then brushed from the ovarian surface by the gentle movements of the fimbria. If the human follicle ruptures, the egg may be retained within the follicle or on its surface, especially if there is no fimbria to remove it, and we found such a situation in a patient. I believe that oviductal hyaluronidase or some other enzyme gently dislodges the oocyte on the surface of the ovary, assisted by the movement of cilia in the fimbria.

Feichtinger: There is some evidence to suggest that if the oocyte is collected in the first aspirate, then it is lying free in the lumen and is probably ovulatory. If repeated washing is necessary, it is still attached to the wall of the follicle and is relatively immature.

Trounson: The data to which you are referring was published in a recent paper in *Fertility and Sterility* by our group (Wood *et al.*, 1981). We merely gave details of the first pregnancies, and described where the eggs had appeared during aspiration. But these data refer to the first nine pregnancies we have obtained, and were published to give an idea of factors which were not incompatible with pregnancy.

Webster: When aspirating the ripe follicle, are there not problems with the use of a very wide bore needle? If an operculum is developing, would you place a needle through it?

Jones, H: We use such needles, and in general there is no difficulty. Occasionally, they will tear, hence it is important to select carefully the position on the follicle where the puncture is made. We avoid areas that are paper-thin, and choose a thicker area in the follicular wall. Slight pressure is applied first, the follicle indents, and then the needle is gently turned and it will usually penetrate well. We have passed a needle through the operculum on some occasions and, although we have missed many oocytes, we have obtained some.

Edwards: With a finer needle, the entry of blood could cause a serious problem with clotting. We sometimes get blood clots in the needle which prevents the continuous aspiration of a follicle.

Trounson: We line the needle with Teflon, which has the lowest surface friction of any material known. The clot is simply drawn through the needle as it forms. Perhaps the clot may stick on to an edge, e.g. a burr on the needle, but provided the needle does not dry before washing, the blood does not stick to the Teflon lining, and it can be washed through very simply and effectively. If the internal surface of the Teflon-lined needle is compared with that of a stainless steel needle, the latter can be seen to have many burrs and protrusions, giving a very irregular surface. The Teflon is smooth and clean, and to insert it we simply draw the Teflon tube through the needle, stretch it, and cut it. It is moulded in place during sterilization by dry heat and it will always go back to its original shape after heating, so that the lining remains intact. There are several types of Teflon, and we use a thick-wall type, so that the internal diameter of our needle is 0.9 mm. When using Teflon with a thin wall, we found that it kinked considerably, but this problem was avoided by going to the thicker-wall variety.

The avoidance of clotting in the needle, or at least the withdrawal of the clot, allows the laparoscopist to remain in the follicle for the whole time of the aspiration. There is no need to withdraw the needle if a clot has formed because it is pulled through immediately by the aspiration pressure.

Steptoe: At one time we were using a needle with an internal diameter of 0.9 mm. Edwards thought there was some damage to the oocyte, but this was not lined with Teflon.

Trounson: We have not seen a damaged oocyte in the sense that it cannot be fertilized. We have had two examples with a ruptured zona pellucida, and this led to extreme polyspermy, but we doubt that these were damaged during passage through the needle. They probably were damaged during penetration of the follicle or during the initial withdrawal of the oocyte into the needle.

Edwards: I have been concerned about withdrawing a large cumulus mass into a narrower needle. Even with our needles, the cumulus mass is drawn into a sausage shape. There is a slight distortion of the cumulus, but its viscosity may protect the oocyte.

I have had doubts too, about the shape of the point of the aspirating needle. The oocyte may enter from the side, and may do a violent turn as it enters. Entering a narrow needle would be worse than entering a broad needle. We have never seen any damage to the oocyte, especially to the zona pellucida. Is there any information on damage caused by a narrow needle?

Trounson: You may be right, but when I examine the size of the cumulus mass in the oocyte, 0.9 mm diameter does give them some room to move. The cumulus mass is soft and spongy, so it could take some movement without causing any pressure to the oocyte. We have a high fertilization rate, so we are satisfied with the situation. Perhaps we could make a reassessment about the size of the needle now that we have solved some other problems.

Does Ultrasound Influence the Time of Ovulation?

Conti: I would like to give one word of warning about the use of ultrasound to detect ovulation. Sometimes the pressure on the abdomen may be such as to distend or cause pressure in the ovulatory follicle, which may then burst or ovulate spontaneously. These follicles are those with a diameter greater than 2.4 cm. If follicles ''disappear'' after ultrasonic examination, my impression is that they may have been damaged during the examination.

Steptoe: It is possible to rupture a follicle when emptying the bladder before laparoscopy if too much pressure is applied. Nevertheless, I am a little surprised that this can be done during ultrasound with a moderately full bladder. Could you be sure that some follicles did not ovulate? The fact that you did not see a follicle rupture on the scan may not be sufficient evidence. Did you measure plasma progesterone to find out if ovulation had occurred?

Testart: It is usual to use sonography to estimate the number and size of the follicles, and also to be sure that the patient has not ovulated an hour or two before the laparoscopy is performed. We examined some patients by sonar 30 hours after HCG, but when they underwent surgery a few moments later, we found they had ovulated.

We therefore decided to find out what happened to follicles exposed to sonography. We discovered that if patients had no sonography at all, or had a single examination three days before the LH surge or before an injection of HCG, then none of them had ovulated by 36 hours after the ovulatory stimulus. In patients given HCG, we ensured that there was no endogenous rise of LH before the HCG was given.

Other groups of patients were exposed to sonography at various times up to three days before the LH surge began or before they received an injection of HCG. We observed five premature ovulations before 36 hours in 23 patients. A third group of patients were exposed to sonography after the LH surge began, i.e. between 0 and 34 hours after the LH surge, or after an injection of HCG. We observed eight premature ovulations out of 19 patients in this group. In other words, 42% of the patients displayed a premature ovulation before 36 hours. We verified that ovulation occurred by visualization of the ovaries during laparoscopy.

We could not equate premature ovulation with the number of sonographic examinations, and some patients showed premature ovulation with only a single examination. We have tried, using volunteers, to provoke premature ovulation using pressure, but we could not induce follicular rupture under these circumstances. We therefore believe that precocious ovulation is not due to the full bladder or the pressure exerted during sonography, but may arise through a direct effect of ultrasound on the wall of the follicle or because the patients drink water too quickly for filling the bladder, so resulting in an osmotic difference between the follicular fluid and the plasma. We have observed this phenomenon in patients examined during the natural cycle, but it seemed to be less serious in patients given clomiphene. Perhaps there is a slight difference in the timing of ovulation between these two groups, so that the phenomenon is less noticeable after Clomid treatment. We have the impression that ovulation takes place at 40 hours after Clomid and HCG, which is some 2 or 3 hours later than during the natural cycle. The median day of laparoscopy was the same in all three groups. The sound intensity was 1.5 megarads.

Edwards: Did you measure any stress hormones in your patients? I wonder about prolactin, or about the adrenal hormones being released in response to stress of the examination. Adrenal progesterone might be involved in stimulating ovulation in some species, and may be effective in man. I do not know if progesterone has any direct effects on follicles.

Cohen: We have the same impression that ultrasound can influence ovulation. We recommend that ultrasonic examination is not carried out three days before ovulation.

Edwards: Avoiding the use of sonography in the manner you describe is a further limit on the value of this technique in helping with the study of follicular growth. I distrust the use of the technique at ovulation anyway, which could exert effects on oocytes. The method seems to me to be of major value in identifying the sites of follicles in patients who may have only one accessible ovary.

If an interval of three days is required after sonography for ovulation to occur on time, is it possible that the follicle initially detected could regress and another could develop in its place, e.g. in the opposite ovary? And how is it possible to know when the sonography is done that the patient will not ovulate less than three days later?

Cohen: We have seen a follicle regress in one ovary, to be replaced by another in the opposite ovary within three days of ovulation. It does not occur very often. A follicle of say, 1.4 or 1.5 cm on one side can be superseded one day later by the growth of another on the opposite side. We have noticed premature ovulation in 4% of our cases. One of the patients would have had ultrasound within two days before the LH surge, and a percentage of them would have had ultrasound immediately prior to laparoscopy. We are using stimulated cycles, and we observe this rate of premature ovulation at 36 hours after the ovulatory stimulus.

Testart: I have read publications from various groups saying that there is a normal distribution of ovulation between 30 and 38 hours after the LH surge begins or after an injection of HCG. I am very surprised by this, because in all animal species we know that ovulation occurs within a very restricted period of time, and there is hardly any chance of a normal distribution since it occurs so quickly. In these papers, sonography was used to follow the ovulatory follicle, and this could have interfered considerably with the time of follicle rupture.

Trounson: I am sceptical about Testart's data. There is a considerable amount of variation in ovulation in different women and, in our data, there is actually an increase in the number ovulating between 34 and 37 hours. It is very important to analyse the data carefully, with large numbers of patients in properly randomized groups.

Were these patients completely randomized throughout this study?

Cohen: No, but we cannot avoid the observation that none of the patients without sonography did not ovulate before 36 hours, whereas those in other groups did. This is an observation, and your observations that some patients had ovulated within 36 hours may also have been due to the ultrasonic treatment.

Timing of Follicular Recruitment During Superovulation Treatments

Jones, H: I would like to know when follicular recruitment takes place during the human cycle. This is very important from the point of view of stimulating the ovary by clomiphene or HMG, in order to increase the harvest of follicles. Does anyone have any data on this?

Edwards: Some of the best data I know is the old information published some years ago by Gemzell & Johansson (1971). A single injection of HMG was given to amenorrhoeic patients who, presumably, had received no previous endogenous follicular stimulation. The follicle growing in response to his treatment could be induced to ovulate by HCG 8-10 days later. Some of the data presented at this conference may fit into this schedule because many groups appear to be carrying out a laparoscopy for oocyte recovery in "stimulated" patients around day 10, and this includes, of course, the period until just before the moment of ovulation. Perhaps such follicles had received an endogenous stimulation first.

Jones, H: I would still like to clarify how, during a normal cycle, we can induce the recruitment of oocytes over and above the normal one or two normally stimulated. When does this situation end? When can we no longer induce the extra follicles to grow? What is the latest time that one can expect to recruit additional follicles by some form of stimulatory treatment?

Trounson: It is not easy to answer these questions. Using HMG, we are undoubtedly rescuing some follicles which would usually undergo atresia. Follicles which respond to HMG will be of a certain size with an antrum and already well into their growth phase. It depends entirely on what happens in each particular patient, and whether she has follicles that can respond. Extensive work has been carried out in animals, without any standard method of treatment emerging for the ovulation of a precise number of follicles. And this is probably because the number of follicles that can reach the stage of responding to external stimuli are variable.

Jones, H: This appears to me to be the definition of recruitment, indicating which follicles are able to respond to the treatments we give. I would like to know the timing of this process; is there a day beyond which the growing follicles cannot be recruited into preovulatory growth?

Trounson: Follicles grow at different rates. A large follicle may carry on growing yet small follicles which grow more quickly may catch up in size by the time of ovulation. It is very difficult to sort out what may happen in a particular patient in her unique follicular situation when the stimulation is given. She may ovulate one large follicle very early in the cycle, yet still have small follicles apparently responding to stimulation in the growth phase.

Edwards: Studies in rabbits and other species have involved watching follicles grow and measuring their size with time. These studies revealed that large follicles can be overtaken, even close to ovulation, by smaller, rapidly-growing follicles (Smeaton & Robinson, 1971). The largest follicle in the ovary in the follicular phase is not necessarily the one that finally achieves ovulation. In other rabbits this did not happen, and the largest follicle went on to ovulation.

The situation in women will be equally complicated, and very difficult to prophesy. It is possible that some of these treatments arrest a large follicle and make it atretic, and too large a dose of hormones could interfere with development by internalizing LH receptors or by other means. It seems at the moment that it is a case of judging each patient separately: inject hormones and find out what happens.

Jones, G: From this I understand it is difficult to state a time which indicates when recruitment is possible, but I understand it is not impossible.

Edwards: In mice, it is possible to inject HCG or other hormones every day for four days, and a series of four ovulations take place in response to each treatment. In this species, therefore, it looks as if follicles are capable of being recruited for ovulation every 24 hours (Edwards & Fowler, 1961). I would be hesitant to say if such data from mice is relevant to the human ovary. Perhaps if HCG was given on, say day 10, and then another injection was given a day later, a fresh set of follicles may be stimulated to ovulate. Or it may be necessary to wait until the first batch have ovulated for the second injection of HCG to induce a second set. It is even possible that the use of two doses of HCG causes multiovulation *in vivo*. Perhaps similar rules apply to follicle stimulation too.

Jones, H: Some information has been published on the monkey. It suggests that oocytes are not recruited after day 5 of the menstrual cycle. Equally, it is impossible to recruit extra follicles if the hormone is given prior to menstruation. In other words, there is a very narrow window in the monkey where recruitment is possible.

Trounson: The timing of the HMG injection can be varied from woman to woman. If she has very long menstrual cycles, it can be started as late as day 10. She may then have a very nice response by day 20. In many women, ovulation may occur regularly but the cycle length may vary. We no longer trust the word of mouth of out patients, but insist on detailed records of the cycle lengths, where variation is considerable.

Conti: Some data has been recently published by McNatty, showing that in the human, secondary follicles are developing until day 4. At this time, they are about 3-4 mm in diameter, and after this stage they get smaller and atretic. This is why I believe it is essential to start treatment with clomiphene or other drugs before this stage is reached. There is no point in starting after day 4, when atresia has already begun.

Jones, H: We have taken this point seriously, and start our treatments at day 3. Yet we have heard of treatments beginning on day 5 and day 6, and other days at this meeting, which would imply that follicles were atretic when treatment was begun. But the treatment seems to work, so that one must believe that the situation is not as clear-cut as indicated.

Hamberger: It is important to distinguish between the patients treated with clomiphene in the past from those we are treating now. Previously, we treated patients with irregular cycles, some of them with very long and irregular follicular phases. On that basis, we decided to start on day 5 of the cycle. But some of our patients now have regular cycle lengths of 26 or 28 days, and by day 5 will already have had an endogenous stimulation of follicular growth. We begin our treatments on day 2 or 3, and because we have limited facilities for measuring oestradiol-17β and LH accurately, we believe that the chance of an endogenous LH peak is much less in such controlled cycles. If the treatment begins on day 5, or later, then a high proportion of cycles will have an endogenous LH surge and stimulate ovulation before HCG can be administered. We get excellent development in follicles with our corrected schedule.

Edwards: I would agree with that comment. Much of the data on which our ideas are based, e.g. the data by Gemzell & Johansson (1971), was collected from patients who were oligomenorrhoeic. Some of them had low levels of oestrogens, before and even after the treatment. In cyclic women, where their tonic levels of FSH and LH are being constantly secreted, we may be able to proceed much further in the cycle before follicles become atretic. Many follicles growing later in the cycle could be stimulated by a later treatment. The dynamics of follicle growth seem to ensure a steady supply of growing follicles at all times, irrespective of the stage of the menstrual cycle (Edwards, 1980). The response must depend on each follicle, and on each individual patient.

References

Edwards, R. G. 1980. *Conception in the Human Female*. Academic Press, London.

Edwards, R. G. & Fowler, R. E. 1961. Superovulation treatment of adult mice: their subsequent natural fertility and response to further treatments. *Journal of Endocrinology*, **21**, 147–157.

Gemzell, C. & Johansson, E. B. 1971. In: *Control of Human Fertility*, p. 15, Nobel Symposium. Eds. E. Diczfalusy and U. Borell. Almqvist & Niksell, Stockholm.

Le Maire, W. J. & Marsh, J. M. 1975. Interrelationships between prostaglandins, cyclic AMP and steroids in ovulation. *Journal of Reproduction and Fertility*, Supplement 22, 53–74.

Mastroianni, L. 1977. The tube. In: *Scientific Foundations of Obstetrics and Gynaecology*, p. 104. Eds. E. E. Philipp, J. Barnes & M. Newton. Heinemann Medical, London.

Smeaton, T. C. & Robertson, H. A. 1971. Studies on the growth and atresia of graafian follicles in the ovary of the sheep. *Journal of Reproduction and Fertility*, **25**, 243–252.

Wallach, E. E., Bronson, R., Hamada, Y., Wright, K. H. & Stevens, V. C. 1975. Effectiveness of prostaglandin $F_{2\alpha}$ in restoration of HMG–HCG induced ovulation in indomethacin-treated rhesus monkeys. *Prostaglandins*, **10**, 129–138.

Wood, C., Trounson, A., Leeton, J., MeKenzie-Talbot, J., Buttery, B., Webb, J., Wood, J. & Jessup, D. 1981. A clinical assessment of nine pregnancies obtained by in-vitro fertilization and embryo transfer. *Fertility and Sterility*, **35**, 502–508.

Laparoscopy of the Normal and Disordered Ovary

P. C. Steptoe and J. Webster

We wish to present a brief description of our current methods of laparoscopy for the purpose of oocyte recovery. These techniques are essential for programmes of in-vitro fertilization, and there are many points of procedure which must be carried out correctly if high rates of success are to be attained.

The techniques of operative procedures by laparoscopy were established in principle by Steptoe in 1967. These involved the use of unipolar high frequency diathermy instruments which have been replaced since 1977 by thermal coagulation generators, forceps and scissors, first introduced by Semm (1976). In a series of over 11,000 personally conducted laparoscopies, Steptoe has demonstrated the safety and versatility of thermal coagulation instruments as compared with both unipolar and bipolar electrical instrumentation.

Our work on recovery of human oocytes by laparoscopy began in 1969 (Edwards et al., 1969; Steptoe & Edwards, 1970). Techniques have inevitably been modified and improved with increasing experience. Following two years unavoidable interruption, our recent work began in Bourn Hall in October 1980 and observations are made on laparoscopies carried out during the past ten months.

The Patient

Almost 90% of patients accepted for treatment at Bourn Hall have occluded oviducts, or have had both of them removed because of tubal ectopic pregnancies or pelvic infection of marked severity. Many of them have been operated on more than once to attempt to restore tubal function. Multiple abdominal scars may be present with intraabdominal

Bourn Hall Clinic, Bourn, Cambridge, U.K.

and pelvic adhesions but these do not necessarily preclude treatment. Unfortunately, many patients have lost one ovary by operation and sometimes part of the remaining one also. The remaining 10% is made up of women with damaged but patent tubes, and of women with apparently healthy tubes with unexplained infertility of several years duration. A small number of patients were accepted for in-vitro fertilization because of oligospermia of the husbands, or cervical mucus hostility. Patients over the age of 40 were not usually accepted unless there was satisfactory evidence of ovulation occurring, and the couple were fully aware of the increased risk of abnormalities appertaining to any pregnancy at this age period.

Before any woman was admitted for treatment steps were taken to ascertain that she was ovulating regularly. Methods used included basal temperature charts, examination of cervical mucus, endometrial biopsies, progesterone and prolactin levels; follicle stimulating hormone and luteinizing hormone were also measured as necessary.

The husband should be potentially fertile. All semen samples were analysed in detail and cultured for infective organisms 4–6 weeks prior to admitting patients for in-vitro fertilization. The specimen had to be obtained by masturbation after thorough and repeated cleansing of the penis and hands to remove potentially infected smegma and other contaminants.

Observations on Laparoscopy

Preliminary Laparoscopy

Most of our patients needed a preliminary laparoscopy. Up to the 31 July 1981, 853 laparoscopies were performed of which 449 were carried out as assessment procedures. Of these assessments, 397 had laparoscopic operations, adhesolysis, tubal diathermy, placing of Bleier clips, hydrotubation, aspiration of cysts and ventrosuspension (Table 1). Even appendecectomy was performed on two occasions when this organ was found adherent to the right ovary. In 55 other cases it was necessary to proceed to immediate laparotomy or elective laparotomies because of severe adhesions involving bowel, appendages and uterus rendering the ovaries inaccessible, or for tubo-ovarian masses, and large distorted hydrosalpinges. Of these 55 cases, 18 have had successful oocyte recovery, 11 had failure of recovery and 26 are awaiting attempts at recovery.

Conventional laparoscopy was employed using CO_2 gas for the

Table 1
Laparoscopic operations (October 1980
to 31 July 1981)*

Adhesolysis-ovariolysis	368
Diathermy proximal tube	341
Bleier clips	6
Hydrotubations	21
Aspiration ovarian cysts	8
Ventrosuspension	5

*Many patients had more than one procedure performed.

pneumoperitoneum, high illumination by means of two light sources and a double guide, angled laparoscopes and one or two ancillary openings for operative procedures as necessary using two hands. The cervical canals and uterine cavities were explored, measured and assessed for future replacement of an embryo. The position of the uterus was noted. Uterine movement was controlled by an Eder–Cohen cannula locked into the uterus. Intra-abdominal gas pressures were constantly monitored. Thermal coagulating instruments were always used for probing, elevations, dissections, haemostasis, adhesolysis and cornual-isthmic diathermy (Steptoe et al., 1980). Short stumps of tubes and those which were found to be damaged or useless were occluded at the cornua, usually by diathermy at 140° for 30 seconds, or by the application of clips (Steptoe et al., 1980). Extensive adhesolysis was accompanied by pelvic aspirations of blood and in a few cases by instillation of hydrocortisone saline solution or Dextran 70 into the pelvis. During the last three months, no attempt was made to seal off the interstitial cornual portion of the tubes, because the amount of culture fluid used to introduce the embryo was reduced to a minute quantity.

Laparoscopy for Oocyte Recovery

Another 404 laparoscopies were carried out, 403 for oocyte recovery and one for replacing an embryo. We gave 10 mg valium orally for premedication. Anaesthesia was induced with thiopentone and flaxedil accompanied often by fentanyl or fentazin, and maintained with N_2O and O_2. Intubation was always carried out.

For oocyte recovery, laparoscopy was modified by avoidance of uterine manipulation and by the use of a gas phase of 5% CO_2, 5% O_2 and 90% N_2 for insufflation with continuous monitoring of intra-abdominal pressure. Most cases were performed with two ancillary instruments, one being the Palmer forceps which was found most reliable for holding and manipulating the ovary, and the second for the follicular aspiration needle. In some cases a third additional opening was found necessary and the thermal forceps were used as a probe or holder to move adhesions and bowel aside when they masked the ovary or ovaries.

Attempts were always made to identify the ovulatory follicle or follicles, and to manipulate the ovary so that the follicle or follicles to be aspirated presented upwards towards the anterior abdominal wall. Entry into the follicle was always made if possible in an avascular area away from the thinning operculum. Aspiration suction pumps were started at a force of 50 mmHg increased as necessary to 100 mmHg. The pneumoperitoneum was maintained by the gas mixture used for insufflation. Intra-abdominal pressure was never allowed to exceed 20 mmHg. When more than one ancillary forceps was used the risk of extraperitoneal emphysema was increased due to leakages, but only occurred in three cases causing temporary discomfort for between 3 and 5 days. No case of gas embolism occurred.

Gas Phase for Oocyte Recovery

A gas mixture containing 5% CO_2, 5% O_2 and 90% N_2 was used for oocyte recovery. If oocyte recovery was rapid and this was often achieved within two minutes of inserting the laparoscope, then exposure of oocyte or follicular fluid to the abdominal gas was minimal. When oocyte recovery takes much longer, i.e. 25–30 minutes, and involves several washings of the follicle, then exposure to the gases could influence the ovum environment. Follicles under such circumstances often leak and considerable bubbling of the aspirates with abdominal gas may occur. Gas also diffuses through the thin follicular wall. Acidity may be caused in these fluids if CO_2 is used for insufflation.

Another factor worthy of consideration in the use of the 5:5:90 gas mixture is the absence of peritoneal irritation which is usually observed when CO_2 is used. "Washing out" the abdomen with CO_2 has been abandoned during the last three months (Steptoe et al., 1980).

Puncturing Follicles and Aspirating Oocytes

Approaching the Follicle and Aspirating the Oocyte

The choice of site for inserting the needle through the abdominal wall is influenced by estimating the best line of approach to the difficult ovary. Transillumination of the abdominal wall is helpful in selecting an avascular area through which to insert the aspirating needle and avoid troublesome bleeding. Angled laparoscopes help in avoiding the clashing of instruments since the field of vision is wide and spacing can be planned. Adherent omentum does not often cause difficulty and can usually be traversed safely. Adherent bowel can cause serious problems but this does not always mean failure.

The ideal follicle appears to be one about 3 cm in diameter, thin walled, bluish pink in colour, presenting anteriorly with few easily identified vessels, and absent or few ecchymoses. It yields clear yellow fluid until almost empty, followed by blood-stained fluid, fragments of granulosa cells and viscous fluid. The less favourable follicles are deep blue or purple in colour with marked ecchymoses dotted around a central operculum. In these cases the aspirate is bloody and viscous from the start and does not flow easily. The follicle often needs washing out with heparin culture medium under increased power of suction.

Oocytes have been successfully recovered when only part of one ovary has been accessible and no follicle actually identified. The aspiration needle may probe deep into the ovary and "strike" clear or even bloody fluid of a hidden follicle.

Clomiphene therapy has been used for cases when ovulation has been irregular, with either shortened or lengthened cycles. It has also been used when access to the ovaries is poor or if less than one ovary is accessible, or in a later cycle after failure due to poor access when only one or less than two ovaries are accessible. Clomid is given in a dosage of 50 mg once daily from day 2 of the cycle for five days. An injection of 5,000 IU HCG has been given when urinary oestrogens have risen above 100 μg in 24-hour specimens in the absence of the onset of the LH surge. Such therapy may result in two or more follicles, which may be thin walled, often 4 cm in diameter in one or both ovaries. Two or more oocytes may be recovered, four being the maximum we have achieved. Occasionally the response to this therapy is poor with small follicles and no preovulatory oocytes. Sometimes a single cyst is found in the ovary, of 5–8 cm in diameter and anovulatory. Poor responses are treated by increasing the dose of Clomid to 150 mg daily or by the use of tamoxifen (Nolvadex) in doses of 20 mg daily for four days commencing on day 2, increasing to 40 mg if necessary.

Instrumentation for Follicular Aspiration

In the first series of cases the follicular aspiration was carried out with a single needle of 1.3 mm in diameter passed through a cannula (Purdy *et al.*, 1972). This often necessitated removal of the needle from the follicle, reinsertion and repeated aspirations as the follicle filled with blood. The oocyte would be trapped sometimes in a blood clot forming in the needle. Nevertheless oocyte recovery was very successful.

In the second series a double-channel needle was used, the aspiration channel was of 1.4 or 1.6 mm in diameter and the second channel 0.7 mm. The second channel was used to introduce heparin culture solution (2 IU ml^{-1}) into the follicle after the first emptying aspiration. In most cases the first aspirate consisted of clear pale yellow fluid containing a few granular cells. The second aspirate was blood stained containing viscous droplets and usually the oocyte. In some cases, the follicle did not yield the oocyte immediately and several washings with heparin saline were necessary. The fluid became increasingly blood-stained and so necessitated increasing the suction power. Nevertheless, even in these cases, the oocyte was frequently recovered after seven or eight aspirations. Manipulation of the needle increased the risk of leakage but allowed all parts of the follicle to be sucked out. Repeated aspirations were often accompanied by bubbling of the gas mixture into the collecting chambers.

Timing of Follicular Aspiration and Recovery of Oocytes

The highest rates of collection are achieved 32 hours after the injection of HCG or 22–26 hours after the onset of the rise of LH in urine. It is essential to time the onset of ovulation correctly. Should HCG be given after an endogenous surge of LH, ovulation may occur before aspiration begins. Diurnal rhythms in tonic LH release, sometimes reaching low surge levels over a few hours, can confuse the correct timing of the LH surge. If the ovary is accessible, and there are no other abdominal problems, oocytes can be collected during the natural cycle from 90% of patients, laparoscopy being completed within a few minutes (Table 2). Virtually none of our patients had ovulated when laparoscopy was performed and most of them had a large preovulatory follicle. Comparable results on patients given clomiphene are also given in Table 2.

Table 2

Aspiration of preovulatory oocytes from 214 patients in their natural cycle or given clomiphene*

Patients	Natural cycle	Clomiphene †
Total number	141	73
Adhesions obscuring both ovaries	7	7
Patients with follicles aspirated	134	66
Patients with one or more ovulatory oocytes	110 (82.1%)	54 (81.8%)
Remainder		
Very difficult access	9	3
Endometriosis	3 ⎫	1 ⎫
Ovulatory follicle?	1 ⎬ 14	1 ⎬ 6
Large hydrosalpinx	1 ⎭	⎭
Cysts		1
Failures due to method	10 (7.5%)	6 (9.1%)
Total number of follicles	140	129
Total number of oocytes	115 (82.1%)	103 (79.8%)
Mean number of oocytes per aspirated patient	0.86	1.90

* Compare data given in Edwards (1981).
† In our practice, patients with adhesions or other abdominal problems are given clomiphene. The clomiphene data includes those with a natural LH surge and those given HCG.

Preovulatory oocytes can be identified quickly. They are embedded in a viscous follicular fluid, to a diameter of ½ cm or more, and can be seen by eye. The viscosity of the cumulus mass serves as a guide to the stage of maturity of the oocyte. A few hours in culture in the presence of some follicular fluid helps to complete maturation, especially in those deliberately collected less than 26 hours after the LH rise which appear "unripe".

References

Edwards, R. G. 1981. Test-tube babies, 1981. *Nature*, **293**, 253–256.

Edwards, R. G., Bavister, B. D. & Steptoe, P. C. 1969. Early stages of fertilization *in vitro* of human oocytes matured *in vitro*. *Nature*, **221**, 632–635.

Purdy, J. M., Sekker, B., Edwards, R. G. & Steptoe, P. C. 1972. (Unpublished.)

Semm, K. L. 1976. *Pelviscopie und Hysteroscopie*, p. 214. Schattaver Verlag, Stuttgart.

Steptoe, P. C. 1967. *Laparoscopy in Gynaecology*. E. S. Livinstone, Edinburgh & London.

Steptoe, P. C. & Edwards, R. G. 1970. Laparoscopic recovery of preovulatory human oocytes after priming of ovaries with gonadotrophins. *Lancet*, **i**, 683–689.

Steptoe, P. C., Edwards, R. G. & Purdy, J. M. 1980. Clinical aspects of pregnancies established with cleaving embryos grown *in vitro*. *British Journal of Obstetrics and Gynaecology*, **87**, 757–768.

Changes in Hormonal Parameters Under Different Kinds of General Anaesthetics During Laparoscopic Oocyte Recovery

S. Szalay,[1] W. Feichtinger,[1] P. Kemeter,[1] A. Beck,[1] H. Janisch[1] and J. Neumark[2]

Introduction

Though there is a recent increase in the number of reports dealing with successful extracorporal fertilization, the overall success rate is still low (Edwards et al., 1980; Feichtinger et al., 1981; Lopata, 1980; Steptoe et al., 1980; Wood et al., 1981). The search for factors influencing success or failure is therefore most important. One factor influencing success rates could be the use of different types of general anaesthesia for the recovery of oocytes (Wood et al., 1981).

There are only a few investigations of hormone fluctuations during operations performed in general anaesthesia in relation to the menstrual cycle (Aono et al., 1972, 1976; Chalmers et al., 1969; Schneider & Bohnet, 1981; Sawers et al., 1977; Soules et al., 1980). There is an especial lack of information of the behaviour of hormones during anaesthesia at mid-cycle. The only report according such investigations was made in 1980 by Soules et al., but consisted only of two cases. The aim of this paper is to evaluate the changes in various hormones when general anaesthesia is performed for the laparoscopic recovery of oocytes at midcycle. Additionally, the influence of various anaesthetic drugs has been tested.

[1] Second Department of Gynecology and Obstetrics, University of Vienna, Austria.
[2] Department of Anesthesiology, University of Vienna, Austria.

Patients and Anaesthetics

A total number of 35 patients with an age between 22 and 41 years were included in this study. All the patients were undergoing laparoscopy for oocyte recovery during in-vitro fertilization. The methods being used and the results are reported elsewhere (Feichtinger *et al.*, 1981a, b). Only patients with a natural cycle, i.e. without stimulation by clomiphene citrate or gonadotropins, were evaluated. Five different kinds of general anaesthesia had been used (Table 1). These included:

(i) The induction of anaesthesia with thiopenthal and its continuation with halothane.

(ii) Induction with thiopenthal and continuation with a neuroleptic drug (Dehydrobenzperidol and Fentanyl).

(iii) Induction with etomidate and continuation with neuroleptic drug.

(iv) Induction with ketamine and continuation with neuroleptic drug.

(v) Induction with rohypnol and continuation with neuroleptic drugs.

All patients were intubated after relaxation with lysthenon and no premedication was applied. Blood samples were drawn 30 minutes before the beginning of anaesthesia, just before the beginning of anaesthesia, 10, 20, 30, 40, 50, 60 minutes after its onset, and also 120 minutes after anaesthesia, which was in all cases in the postoperative period. In some patients blood was also sampled after 240 minutes, after 720 minutes (6 hours) and after 1440 minutes (12 hours). The following hormones were evaluated in each sample: LH, FSH, PRL, progesterone, oestradiol-17β, cortisol and testosterone.

Table 1
Anaesthetics used for oocyte recovery in non-stimulated cycles

Induction	Continuation	Number
1. Thiopenthal	Halothane	10
2. Thiopenthal	Neuroleptic drugs	7
3. Etomidate	Neuroleptic drugs	7
4. Ketamine	Neuroleptic drugs	6
5. Rohypnol	Neuroleptic drugs	5
	Total	35

Radioimmunoassays

LH and FSH were estimated by the double antibody method described by Franchimont (1969) using kits of CIS.

Oestradiol-17β progesterone and testosterone were estimated according to the methods reported by Malvano *et al.* (1974) also with kits of CIS. The latter were performed without any chromatographic separation steps preceding the assay, therefore the specificity of the antisera used had to be sufficiently great to eliminate all major cross-reactions. This was found except with anti-testosterone. A 75% crossreaction with dihydrotestosterone was found in the testosterone assay and the results are therefore called "testosterone like activity".

Cortisol was estimated by a solid phase method (GammaCoat, Clinical Assays) without preceding extraction of the serum. The following crossreactions were determined: prednisolone 67%, 11-deoxycortisol 5.2%, prednisone 4.2%, cortisone 3.2%, deoxycorticosterone 0.3%, progesterone < 0.1%.

Prolactin was estimated by the method of Sinha *et al.* (1973) with kits of Serono.

The methodology and results of the hormone estimations mentioned above, except cortisol, have been published previously from our laboratory (Kemeter *et al.*, 1975, 1978).

For statistical evaluation, the BMDP 2 V-program of the University of California was used for computer processing. The Wilcoxon text was applied to evaluate significant increases or decreases relative to the prevalue. To evaluate differences between the various anaesthetic drugs, analyses of variance and covariances with repeated measures were performed. No Gaussian distribution of the values was observed, hence the non-parametric analysis of variance according to Kruskal and Wallis was carried out. The analyses of variance were calculated with the original values and also with the differences to the prevalues.

Hormonal Changes During and After Anaesthesia

The behaviour of the median LH values under different anaesthetic drugs is shown in Fig. 1. The elevated values reflect the end of the LH peak. During the operation, we observed no major changes. Instead of a further decrease, a slight but significant elevation was observed between 10 and 40 minutes after the onset of anaesthesia.

No striking changes could be seen in the values of FSH, progesterone, estradiol and testosterone (Figs. 2, 3, 4 and 5). Estradiol showed a slight decrease during and after the operation, reflecting the usual cyclic behaviour of this hormone. Testosterone showed a slight increase, which had most probably originated directly or indirectly from the stress-stimulated adrenals.

The evaluation of prolactin levels revealed distinct changes (Fig. 6). In all cases and under all types of anaesthesia a highly significant rise was evident. After two hours, there was a distinct decrease in the values, but they still remained elevated till the next day. Significant differences between the various anaesthetics could be observed at 30, 40 and 60 minutes after the onset of anaesthesia, due to a

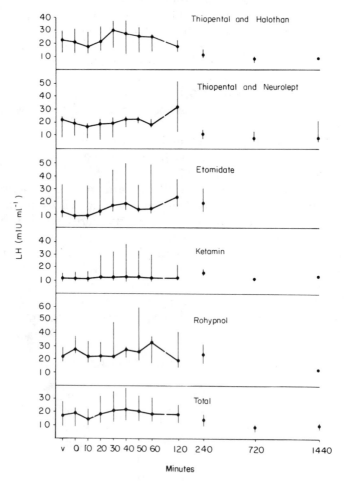

FIG. 1. LH levels in plasma after various anaesthetics.

diminished increase of prolactin under thiopental and halothane. Distinct changes were also observed when cortisol levels were evaluated (Fig. 7). There was a slight rise during the operation, but its maximal increase occurred postoperatively (120 minutes). This finding was obvious with all anaesthetics, and it was only reduced with the combination of thiopental and halothane. The difference between etomidate and rohypnol and the other anaesthetics was also statistically highly significant with respect to the period between 20 to 60 minutes after the onset of anaesthesia.

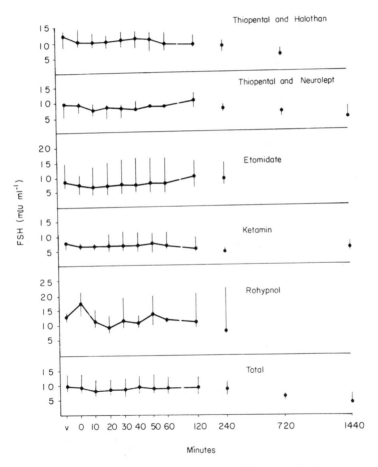

FIG. 2. FSH levels in plasma after various anaesthetics.

Discussion

There is but scanty information available on the nature of hormonal changes during anaesthesia as described in the introduction. First reports were made in 1969 by Charters *et al.* (1969) during studies on anterior pituitary function during surgical stress and covalescence. They investigated the behaviour of blood TSH, LH, FSH and growth

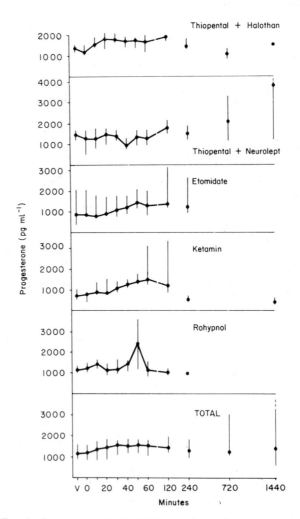

FIG. 3. Progesterone levels in plasma after various anaesthetics.

hormone during general anaesthesia in female patients, but failed to find any striking changes. Other investigators, e.g. Aono *et al.* (1972, 1976) confirmed these findings, but also found distinct differences in the response of LH in male and female patients. In all male patients, a rise in LH values was observed between 30 minutes and one hour after the beginning of general anaesthesia. Afterwards, the LH levels decreased slightly in men and women between 5–6 hours and 2 days after the onset of anaesthesia, though the decreases were not statistically significant, except in postmenopausal females. The LH levels then returned toward the baseline on the seventh postoperative day.

Soules *et al.* (1980) also measured the LH levels during different periods of the menstrual cycle under general anaesthesia, and reported

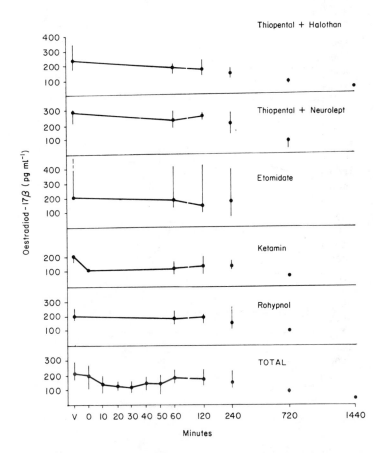

FIG. 4. Oestradiol-17β in plasma after various anaesthetics.

on LH levels at midcycle. Only few cases were analysed, giving the impression that the timing and magnitude of the LH peak at mid-cycle were not significantly altered by an operation or general anaesthesia. Our evidence confirms these findings. Apart from a significant brief increase after the onset of anaesthesia, no striking changes in LH were observed. The FSH values showed even less change, which also correlates well with reports in the literature.

During analyses of oestradiol-17β, Soules *et al.* (1980) found a slight

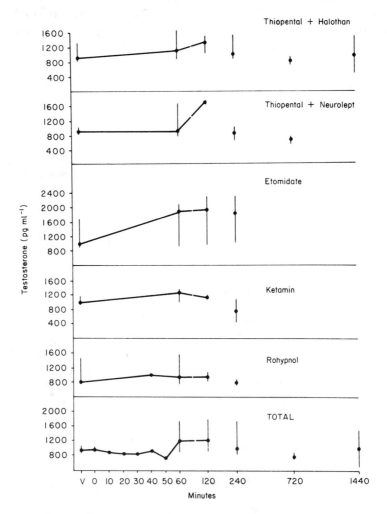

Fig. 5. Testosterone levels in plasma after various anaesthetics.

decrease in the postoperative period, which did not reach statistical significance. The same observation was made in our patients, but this decrease reflects the regular cyclic behaviour of this hormone after midcycle. Nor did progesterone show any significant changes during the observation period. In contrast, during their investigations of progesterone levels after general anaesthesia, Soules *et al.* reported a statistically significant decrease when compared with a control group

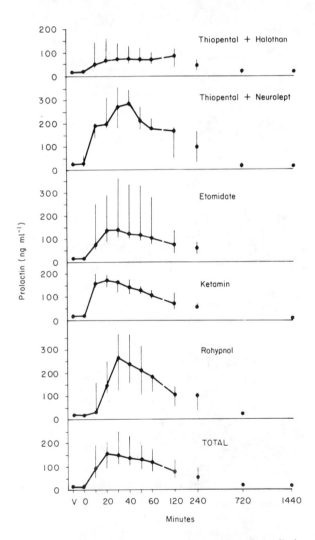

FIG. 6. Prolactin levels in plasma after various anaesthetics.

during the whole luteal phase. Perhaps this effect is explained by an inhibition of ovarian steroidogenesis through a direct toxic effect of the anaesthetic agents or by fluctuations in hormones such as prolactin which is able to inhibit gonadotrophin secretion if it is constantly raised (McNatty*et al.*, 1974; Noel *et al.*, 1972). This conclusion would fit well with our observation of an acute increase in prolactin following the induction of anaesthesia in all our patients.

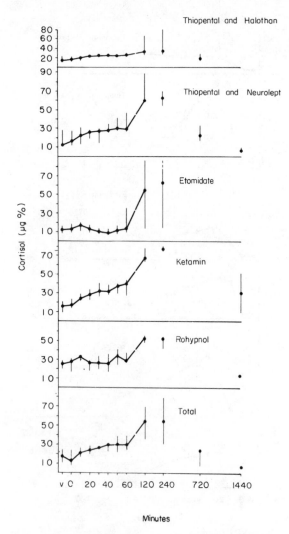

FIG. 7. Cortisol levels in plasma after various anaesthetics.

In contrast to Soules *et al.* we did not find a clear-cut luteal phase insufficiency in the vast majority of our patients after laparoscopy for oocyte recovery (Feichtinger *et al.*, 1981b and in press). But in most of their patients, the operation was carried out in different phases of the menstrual cycle, unlike our patients who were examined in the hormone-controlled preovulatory phase, making it difficult to compare both studies. It is well established that a striking elevation of serum prolactin is incompatible with a normal cyclic function, though it is still uncertain whether small or moderate increases can disturb the ovulatory period and/or corpus luteum function (Schneider & Bohnet, 1981).

The intraoperative and postoperative increase of cortisol which we found is a known reaction to operative stress (Sawers *et al.*, 1977). But this stress-dependent increase in cortisol might not influence the luteal phase. Kemeter *et al.* (1980) could not find lowered progesterone levels in the luteal phase of normal cyclic hirsute women even on the seventh day of a test involving 2 mg dexamethasone in comparison with such women without dexamethasone (Kemeter *et al.*, 1980).

We also compared the different anaesthetic drugs used for induction of general anaesthesia. A significant difference concerning their influence on cortisol was seen with respect to etomidate and rohypnol compared with the other drugs. There was a retarded increase in patients receiving etomidate and rohypnol (Fig. 7).

Differences were also evident regarding the two continuation anaesthetics. The use of halothane invoked minor increases in prolactin and cortisol compared with the neuroleptic drugs (DHP and Fentanyl) in the time period between 60 and 120 minutes. But further investigations are necessary to elucidate the possible advantage of halothane against neuroleptic drugs with respect to the luteal phase.

Summarizing our results, we can conclude that there is surprisingly little influence of anaesthetic agents on the genuine cyclic hormones, e.g. LH, FSH, oestradiol-17β and progesterone, hence it is justified to assume that no major disturbances of the ovulatory process and the corpus luteum function will occur. Increases in prolactin and cortisol over some hours may alter the cyclic hormones later in the cycle, but this will be the subject of further research. Even so, only slight changes can be expected because, as we mentioned above, the vast majority of our patients revealed normal luteal phases with respect to length and progesterone levels (Feichtinger *et al.*, 1981b and in press).

References

Aono, T., Kurachi, K., Mizutani, S., Hamanaka, Y., Upzumi, T., Nakasima, A., Koshiyama, K. & Matsumoto, K. 1972. Influence of major surgical stress on plasma levels of testosterone, luteinizing hormone, and follicle stimulating hormone in male patients. *Journal of Clinical Endocrinology and Metabolism*, **35**, 535.

Aono, T., Kurachi, K., Miyata, M., Nakasima, A., Koshiyama, K., Uozumi, T. & Matsumoto, K. 1976. Influence of surgical stress under general anesthesia on serum gonadotropin levels in male and female patients. *Journal of Clinical Endocrinology and Metabolism*, **42**, 144.

Charters, A. C., Odell, W. D. & Thompson, J. C. 1969. Anterior pituitary function during surgical stress and convalescence. Radioimmunoassay measurement of blood TSH, LH, FSH, and growth hormone. *Journal of Clinical Endocrinology and Metabolism*, **29**, 63.

Edwards, R. G., Steptoe, P. C. & Purdy, J. M. 1980. Establishing full term human pregnancies using cleaving embryos grown *in vitro*. *British Journal of Obstetrics and Gynaecology*, **87**, 737.

Feichtinger, W., Kemeter, P., Szalay, S., Beck, A. & Janisch, H. (in press). Could aspiration of the graafian follicle cause luteal phase deficiency? *Fertility and Sterility*, in press.

Feichtinger, W., Szalay, S., Kemeter, P., Beck, A. & Janisch, H. 1981a. Die Gewinnung reifer menschlicher Eizellen mittels Laparoskopie zum Zwecke der in vitro-Fertilisierung. *Geburtsh. u. Frauenheilk.*, **41**, 400.

Feichtinger W., Szalay, S., Kemeter, P., Beck, A. & Janisch, H. 1981b. In vitro-Fertilisierung menschlicher Eizellen sowie Embryotransfer. Erste Ergebnisse an der II. Univ. Frauenklinik, Wien. *Geburtsh. u. Frauenheilk.*, **41**, 482.

Franchimont, P. 1969. Le dosage radio-immunologique des gonadotrophines. *Ann. Endocrin.*, *Paris*, **29**, 403.

Kemeter, P., Salzer, H., Breitenecker, G. & Friedrich, F. 1975. Progesterone, oestradiol-17β and testosterone levels in the follicular fluid of tertiary follicles and graafian follicles of human ovaries. *Acta Endocrinologica*, **80**, 686.

Kemeter, P., Friedrich, F., Fulmek, R., Hermanns, U., Stöger, S., Polak, S. & Springer-Kremser, M. 1978. Das Prolaktin der Frau. *Wien. Klin. Wschr.*, **90**, 556.

Kemeter, P., Friedrich, F., Breitenecker, G. & Salzer, H. 1980. The recognition of ovarian androgen excess by dexamethasone-test in hirsutism. In: *Adrenal Androgens*, p. 289. Eds. A. R. Genazzani *et al.* Raven Press, New York.

Lopata, A. 1980. Successes and failures in human in-vitro fertilisation. *Nature*, **288**, 643.

Malvano, R. L., Troysi, C., Gandolfi, A., Attanasio, A. & Crosignani, P. C. 1974. In: *Recent Progress in Reproductive Endocrinology*, Serono Symposium No. 4, p. 229. Academic Press, New York.

McNatty, K. P., Sawers, R. S. & McNeilly, A. S. 1974. A possible role for prolactin in control of steroid secretion by the human graafian follicle. *Nature*, **250**, 653.

Noel, G. L., Suh, H. K., Stone, G. & Frantz, A. 1972. Human prolactin and growth hormone release during surgery and other conditions of stress. *Journal of Clinical Endocrinology and Metabolism*, **35**, 840.

Sawers, J. R., Raj, R. P., Hershman, J. M., Carlson, H. E. & McCallum, R. W. 1977. The effect of stressful diagnostic studies and surgery on anterior pituitary hormone release in man. *Acta Endocrinologica*, **86**, 25.

Schneider, H. P. G. & Bohnet, H. G. 1981. Die hyperprolaktinämische Ovarialinsuffizienz. *Gynäkologe*, **14**, 104.

Sinha, Y. N., Selby, F. W., Lewis, U. J. & Vanderloon, W. P. 1973. A homologous radioimmunoassay for human prolactin. *Journal of Clinical Endocrinology and Metabolism*, **36**, 509.

Soules, M. R., Sutton, G. P., Hammond, C. B. & Haney, A. F. 1980. Endocrine changes at operation under general anesthesia: reproductive hormone fluctuations in young women. *Fertility and Sterility*, **33**, 364.

Steptoe, P. C., Edwards, R. G. & Purdy, J. M. 1980. Clinical aspects of pregnancies established with cleaving embryos grown *in vitro*. *British Journal of Obstetrics and Gynaecology*, **87**, 757.

Wood, C., Trounson, A., Leeton, J., McKenzie Talbot, J., Buttery, B., Webb, J., Wood, J. & Jessup, D. 1981. A clinical assessment of nine pregnancies obtained by in-vitro fertilization and embryo transfer. *Fertility and Sterility*, **35**, 502.

Discussion on the Laparoscopic Recovery of Oocytes

The Gas Phase During Laparoscopy

Cohen: I would like to raise the question of the gas phase used during laparoscopy. I would like to know how many other groups are using the gas phase used by Steptoe and his colleagues.

Johnston: We are using the same mixture of 5% CO_2, 5% O_2 and 90% N_2 until about two months ago. When the Monash group came up with high rates of pregnancy using neat carbon dioxide, and other pregnancies were reported using the same mixture, we decided to change. We already had one embolus, and the woman lived, yet the embolus did happen. I felt that our team would be in a difficult medicolegal situation if we continued using that gas mixture. The change has not reduced our fertilization and cleavage rates.

Mettler: A case of embolism was reported in Germany, but this was not due to the gas mixture used by Steptoe and his colleagues. It was due to the use of nitrogen gas and no one in Germany is now using nitrogen alone.

Steptoe: This point must be discussed in relation to the emboli which arise with carbon dioxide. I think we cannot presume that because an embolus has occurred, it is the fault of the gas mixture being employed. It could be the fault of the operator, or an unexpected accident. Emboli occur if a needle carrying gas is put into a vessel, and it will occur just as rarely with any gas mixture. Carbon dioxide is soluble, so it is less likely to lead to a fatal result.

The problem, of course, is that the gas may enter the fluid being aspirated from the follicle. We have made some tentative observations on the pH of the fluid aspirated from follicles under CO_2 tension, our data being collected some years ago. This was carried out on patients who had been examined for purposes other than oocyte collection, but who happened to have preovulatory follicles.

Jones, H: One problem with aspiration concerns the entry of gases into the aspirating mixture, so influencing the pH of the medium in

119

which the oocyte lies. It is difficult, of course, to get pH results quickly enough, because the acidity of the fluid changes rapidly in air. We found the pH in the 7.4 range in follicular fluids, using carbon dioxide, following a delay of about a minute from the time they were obtained.

Steptoe: The problem is not really with the rapid aspiration. Problems arise when there is a difficult aspiration, and the laparoscopy may last for a period of time — 30 minutes or longer. This is when the situation becomes important.

Edwards: There are great difficulties in measuring the pH of follicular fluid freshly aspirated from the body. The moment it is removed and placed in air, the pH will begin to rise to very high levels as much as 7.8 or more. The correct buffering is approximately 5% CO_2, but the use of this would then modify the pH in the fluid being aspirated. The fact that Jones measured a pH of 7.4 some time after aspiration implies that it must have been much lower when it was collected. And a pH of 7.4, a few minutes after collecting fluid could be serious — it could imply a degree of acidity in the fluid when it was aspirated.

Trounson: Wood has measured the pH of fluid taken straight from the follicle and put through pH monitors. When using 100% CO_2 for the pneumoperitoneum, there is no change in the pH of follicular fluid for periods up to one hour, providing the follicle remains intact. This means that the intact follicle can buffer any CO_2 which diffuses through the follicle wall. However, ruptured follicles or fluid in the Pouch of Douglas will rapidly become acidic. Any oocytes exposed to these conditions will not be viable. Some of our patients with severe adhesions have been anaesthetized and under laparoscopy for an hour or more, yet the oocytes were collected, the embryo replanted, and they are now pregnant (Wood *et al.*, 1981). I doubt we are getting any acidosis in fluid to justify fearing any damage to the oocyte. I feel that there must be a justification of acidosis or an effect on the oocyte to use the 5 : 5 : 90 mixture.

Edwards: Some years ago in Oldham, we aspirated follicular fluid into growth medium, using CO_2, in order to observe the change in the indicator. We noted that it became very acid. In some of these cases we had bubbling of the fluid, and this presumably contained gas from the abdomen that was drawn into the fluid. In effect, the follicular fluid was being bubbled with the same gases from the abdomen which could be neat CO_2. I should imagine that the pH of any medium bubbled against 5% CO_2 will lower considerably in the presence of neat CO_2.

I think we must be extremely careful about any techniques which interfere with the oocyte in any way. I do not want to risk any damage whatsoever to it. We cannot tell when we begin the laparoscopy if the egg is going to be recovered quickly, or over a long period of time.

Trounson: If a gas is bubbled through 12 ml of follicular fluid, it takes 45 sec or thereabouts to get a major change in pH. It depends on the volume of the fluid, being gassed, and I feel that the use of high quantities of nitrogen must be justified. We seem to find no difference whether we use nitrogen or carbon dioxide but if you could demonstrate any damaging effect on the oocyte, then we would have to reconsider our position.

Edwards: We were worried about the pH shift when fluid from the follicle was added to our medium. Remember that the fluid may be bubbled for longer than 30–45 sec and the fluid may not be follicular fluid — it may be washing fluid.

Steptoe: With a suction pressure of 100 mm of mercury, there is always bubbling in my experience.

Edwards: I would like to know much more about the work carried out by Wood. Was it a beautiful clean aspirate? Were the bad aspirates thrown away and not measured? How was it taken to the machine to get such a rapid recording? Was there any artificial bubbling introduced?

Trounson: The needle pierced the follicle, and the fluid was taken directly to the pH meter at the side of the patient. We were doing this on patients from whom we were not collecting preovulatory oocytes for fertilization.

Edwards: This work should be done on those patients who have got a genuine preovulatory follicle in which the oocyte is being aspirated. The preovulatory follicle may have a much thinner wall than follicles being used for experimental purposes.

Trounson: We have had our patients under carbon dioxide for an hour, and we have obtained pregnancies. What more can we say?

Cohen: Well, we could say that you might have more pregnancies if you had used the gas mixture they employ. There is no guarantee that the pregnancy rate you obtain is optimal.

I think the question to be decided here is whether each group believes they are getting the best results by using their own particular gas. If there is a high rate of pregnancy with a specific gas, then perhaps the group should stay with it.

Jones, H: Is the only purpose of using special gas to control pH? What is the data to indicate that a pH shift of 0.2, for example, is undesirable for human embryos?

Edwards: We do not see any pH change in our culture fluids under the gas mixture of 5 : 5 : 90 we use. I do not know of any data on the human embryo using a pH as you describe and studying its effects on development. We prefer to avoid all the risks to the oocytes, we wish to leave everything as perfectly normal as we can. If we had many spare embryos, it would be possible to control studies with changes in pH, but I am not sure what changes would actually be measured, because the modifications in the pH of follicular fluid or flushing medium may take place for a brief time during aspiration.

Trounson: We regularly flush out follicles with a culture medium containing heparin and we do not notice any change in the pH.

Effect of the Gas Phase on Oocytes
During Difficult Laparoscopies

Edwards: I would like to relate the problems of the gas phase to the difficulties in aspirating follicles. If the oocyte is aspirated in a first aspirate, then there is no bubbling and everything is fine. But all too often we get it in the second pot, or even the later one. During that time, the aspirate is changing from follicular fluid to a washing solution, I do not know what the effect of carbon dioxide would be on that particular solution, which is a physiological saline containing heparin, diluted with plasma from the follicle. If there was a foolproof method of aspirating the oocyte first time, in follicular fluid, then we would probably abandon our gas mixture. So far, we have not been able to achieve this, and I do not know if any other group has been able to do so using methods such as ultrasound to guide the needle to the oocyte. Our washing solution has low levels of bicarbonate, and its pH may be changed much more readily by neat CO_2.

These pH effects could depend on the method of aspiration. If Leeton's method of aspiration is superior to ours, then oocytes might be collected from the follicle without exposure to CO_2. I still believe that I cannot place the oocyte in any jeopardy, or even take the chance of exposing it to any form of damage. From what I know of animal embryos, I would not jeopardize an oocyte at this stage when it is aspirated from the follicle. We are dealing with an oocyte in the final stages of meiosis, and must be wary about interfering with chromosomal segregation on the spindle. Some oocytes may be in metaphase of the first meiotic division, and others in metaphase-II, and any disturbance in the movement of chromosomes on the spindle, especially during meiosis-I, could lead to the disordered segregation of chromosomes. I would certainly not want to expose any oocyte under CO_2 for these reasons. We may be risking an increase in chromosomal disorders in the embryo. I hardly want to do the experiment — if someone else does it, I would be delighted to know that embryos are all diploid when exposed to the CO_2 after a difficult aspiration.

Trounson: We have had some abortions, but we cannot believe they are due to this gas phase. We are prepared to carry on using the gases we have employed already and to avoid exposing our patients to nitrogen.

Speirs: There is a very good blood supply to the ovulatory follicle, and this should take care of any carbon dioxide diffusing through the wall of the follicle. We found that thiopentane got into the follicular fluid within seconds, but even so I feel that any change in the pH before the follicle is punctured should not be a concern. But, when gas bubbles through the medium, then this may be a very different situation.

Steptoe: There are times when a very ripe follicle ruptures during laparoscopy, and we have to wash out what is virtually a crater on the surface of the ovary. Sometimes we can recover the egg from such a crater. Under these circumstances, the oocyte is exposed directly to the gas and this situation can occur with some frequency.

Leeton: I believe that this point about technique is important. We have not seen bubbling in our aspirates for over 12 months. We did not observe the bubbling or the bleeding that Steptoe described. I therefore believe that a lot of the problems may be associated with the method of aspiration.

Steptoe: We do not aspirate at 100 mm of mercury to begin with. If there is a large follicle, a snug fit with the needle, and there is no leakage of fluid, then the egg is collected within the first or second aspirate. That is all very nice. Under these circumstances, the gas has hardly had a chance to be in contact with the follicle or the aspirate. If the pressure has to be raised, for example if the fluid is viscous, then there is certainly bubbling, and also some leakage of the fluid from around the needle. The intra-abdominal pressure of the gas can also influence the amount of bubbling in the culture medium.

Edwards: Is Leeton saying that he recovered every oocyte without the need to use heparin? Does he collect all the oocytes now without having any bleeding from the follicle?

Leeton: We collect 100% of our eggs without any bubbling or bleeding.

Jones, G: We collect about 90% of our oocytes in the first aspirate, without the need to add any heparin solution.

Edwards: Our figure must be below that, and I would estimate about 70%. These oocytes are probably fine, but it is the remaining oocytes which worry me. It is the difficult cases where the chance of damage is highest, and we can never be sure before we start which cases will be difficult.

Trounson: I agree with Steptoe that those that are on the surface of the ovary, or can be collected from the Pouch of Douglas, will be exposed to high levels of carbon dioxide. The same situation would apply in an ovulated follicle, where the oocyte has to be aspirated from a cavity in the ovary.

Steptoe: In my opinion, as the intra-abdominal gas pressure is reached, and the aspirating needle is introduced through the cavity, then the high pressure within the abdomen will force gas into the aspirating chamber. The whole apparatus will thus be flushed with carbon dioxide, even before the aspirating needle has penetrated the follicle.

Trounson: It depends once again on the system being used. We use 5 ml tubes, so there is very little gas within them. After the aspiration is finished, they are disconnected, and a bung placed on them, so they are soon equilibriated with air.

Steptoe: It is a difficult decision to make about which gas phase to use. I have accepted the 5 : 5 : 90 because we have never yet had a gas embolism. By now, we have done over 12,000 laparoscopies, without such an event happening. In a medical-legal context, we might be in difficulties if an embolism did occur.

Jones, H: We would not use 5 : 5 : 90 in the United States. The medical-legal situation would be too complicated to justify its use.

Johnston: It was not only the single embolism which concerned me, because we continued using the high nitrogen gas for over two years after it occurred. There has been another case of embolism in private practice in Melbourne, using carbon dioxide. It was my belief that when teams using carbon dioxide obtained high rates of fertilization and cleavage, I could not expose the hospital to the risks of using high levels of nitrogen in our patients.

Steptoe: Some people have used air in laparoscopy. It was practised widely at one time.

Cohen: In France, Palmer has analysed several cases of embolism due to the use of air. There were many cases of embolism.

Lieberman: I have used nitrous oxide alone under local anaesthesia since 1972 for laparoscopy. So much depends on technique, e.g. on the how the needle is inserted, rather than the gas phase alone. Those cases of Palmer were probably carried out a long time ago, and under very different conditions to what are used today.

Lopata: We have moved to 100% carbon dioxide, as Johnston described. On the other hand, many of our aspirates are frothy, and we are using a single or a double needle. We have wondered whether there is a pH change in the aspirate.

Edwards: You could withdraw the aspirate into a pH indicator, e.g. that present in culture media. Any rapid change could then be noted visually. An immediate answer is vital, before any change can occur in the buffering of the fluid against the specific gas phase in the body.

Lopata: We have tried doing that, but we got a misleading colour change. The dominant yellow colour of the follicular fluid made it difficult to read any colour change in the indicator medium. The resulting orange colour did suggest acidity, but I was suspicious as to its meaning. I wish there was a rapid and accurate method of assessing pH of freshly aspirated fluid.

Jones, H: We attempted to avoid the bubbling problem by dispensing with wall suction. In this way, we avoided any suction on our needle until it was within the follicle. Suction is then discontinued before the needle is withdrawn. In this way, we hope to have a minimal amount of contact between the gas in the abdomen and any fluid in our aspirating device.

Edwards: I am very surprised that anyone can predict the outcome of a case, and a difficult case especially, to claim there will be no bleeding or gas from the abdomen entering the aspirating chamber. The follicle could be over-ripe, there could be adhesions, there could be many circumstances in which such a fine control of aspiration can be lost. It is one thing to have done a hundred cases, then decide not to use a gas phase of 5% CO_2, 5% O_2 and 90% N_2; it is another to predict each individual case.

I would like to know what would happen if neat CO_2 was used and the baby was born deformed. It is all right being wise after the event, but very difficult to know what to do before it begins. We have to do our best for every patient and the oocyte is a patient. It is a balance between accepting the surgical risks and accepting the best for the oocyte. Even when all the parameters appear to be right — a good rise in oestrogens, a good LH surge, a good knowledge of the ovary, we can still have difficulties in aspiration. I would not wish to risk getting a high incidence of trisomy or other anomalies by chancing an unknown factor against the wellbeing of the oocyte. I would be in a difficult a position as the surgeons obviously are now when considering the gas phase in the abdomen.

Rinsing Follicles During Oocyte Aspiration

Cohen: I would like to raise a general question, a second question, about the technique of aspirating follicles. Is the follicle washed out with a rinsing solution after the attempt at aspiration? I am specifically concerned with the situation when the oocyte is not aspirated during the first aspirate.

Steptoe: In our work, we aspirate a follicle and, as it empties, we observe the clear follicular fluid and perhaps the occasional flocculated mass within it. We then stop and wait, without removing the collecting chamber from the aspirating device. After an interval of 15–30 seconds, we then inject a small amount of solution containing heparin, and recommence aspiration. Very often at this point, we get a small bloodstained aspirate, and this sample may contain the oocyte. In many cases, the oocyte is not present in the original collection of clear fluid. The needle remains in position in the follicle throughout the procedure, and its double channel allows us to inject the heparin solution without removing the needle from the follicle. We may have to inject again if the oocyte has not been collected. When all is finished, we gently withdraw the needle from the follicle and end the case. We have used a single needle especially in our earlier work in Oldham, and the aspiration rates were quite good. We now prefer the double-channelled needle, using one channel to inject heparin.

Jones, H: At one time, it was suggested by one of the Melbourne groups that the addition of heparin to the washing medium precluded the chance of pregnancy. Are you concerned about the use of heparin?

Steptoe: No, not at all. I would imagine that in the vast majority of our successful pregnancies, the oocyte was exposed to at least some of this compound.

Trounson: Wood stated that heparin might not be helpful, when discussing our first 9 pregnancies.

Spiers: I have calculated the failure rate per follicle. It is then possible to determine the expected total failure rate when there are two follicles. In other words, the failure rate should be less with two or more follicles. Yet, when I look at the failure rate with two follicles, the observed failure rate is larger than one would expect. In other words, it is not only the difficulty with a particular follicle, there is also something wrong with the entire cycle or with the patient. We may be aspirating at the wrong time, e.g. the stimulus may be very viscous so we cannot unstick the egg from the wall of the follicle.

Should Diseased Oviducts be Occluded
During Preliminary Laparoscopy?

Cohen: I would now like to raise a further point. Steptoe described his methods for occluding the tubes when there was a risk of an ectopic pregnancy. I would like to open this to general discussion.

Leeton: We believe the risk of a tubal implantation following the replacement of an embryo is very unlikely, although it is a possibility. So far we have placed 300 embryos into patients with patent tubes, and there are none so far, so the risk is small. I would suspect that the risks of using sutures or tuboplasty are far greater than the risk of an ectopic pregnancy. I also believe that, if the tubes are patent, then the patient still has an inherent chance of pregnancy, which may be low, but is nevertheless now reduced to zero.

Steptoe: I would like to get one thing absolutely clear. We never seal off normal tubes; we would never contemplate it. Even if it was not a very good tube, we would not seal it off if it was patent. We only seal off those patients who are already sterile because of a distorted oviduct. There is no medical-legal situation for us, because we do not interfere with any patient who has the remotest chance of pregnancy. We deal with diseased tubes, not healthy tubes. With the great improvement in techniques, the risk of ectopic pregnancies is probably less now than it was 5 or 6 years ago. It is time perhaps that the method was abandoned, and I would be happy to do so, since this would enable us to treat the patient in the next cycle because there would be no tissue reaction. Of course, if other procedures such as adhesolysis had been performed, then we would have to wait longer anyway.

Leeton: Would you occlude tubes in a patient who has idiopathic infertility?

Steptoe: Of course not.

We often find in patients with a history of salpingectomies that the operation is incomplete. There is always a 2 cm stump there, and this is the kind of thing that we worry about. Many of our patients have had several years of pelvic inflammatory disease, and various operations. Some of these situations presenting to us are very difficult indeed. There have been claims that in animal studies, the tubes can be occluded and an embryo placed in the distal portion for implantation, and this is supposed to be a model for our work. I fully disagree, because patients who have had inflammatory disease over many years are in a very different situation. I think it would be criminal to put an embryo into such tubes in women.

Johnston: Have you ever noticed that the blockage placed in the oviduct has resulted over a period of time in an increase in the hydro-salpinx? In this case, the tube would be blocked at both ends, because in many of these patients there is also fimbrial agglutination. Have you had any problem with re-activating or increasing the incidence of pelvic inflammatory disease by blocking off the diseased oviduct?

Steptoe: The answer to the second question is no. But there may be an increase in the size of the hydrosalpinx. Sometimes a veiled transection occurs, and there is the risk of bleeding, and also the chance that tissues that were not adherent may become adherent after the treatment with diathermy. This is why we sometimes choose clips to occlude the oviduct.

Johnston: Have you ever lost an ovary as a result of the torsion on the oviduct?

Steptoe: No.

Trounson: In earlier work, Steptoe removed a disturbed oviduct. Is this still done?

Webster: If there are disorders in the tube at laparoscopy, we coagulate the isthmic portion in order to avoid the risk of an ectopic pregnancy.

Trounson: Is this necessary? We have not yet had a single ectopic implantation in all our pregnancies. I am aware that Steptoe & Edwards (1976) obtained an ectopic pregnancy early in their work, but this may not be significant. Coagulating the oviduct was a firm point in their method at one time, and is this still done today?

Leeton: I would also like to comment on this point. We feel strongly about occluding the oviducts in our patients, and we believe it may have strong medical and legal overtones. I accept that it could influence the implantation of the embryo following fertilization *in vitro* but there are three points which we must consider about the oviduct situation in these cases. First of all, there is the volume of medium replaced during replacement of the embryo. I believe Steptoe injected 0.4 ml of radio-opaque medium to test the flow of fluid in the uterus, but uses much less when embryo is replaced. The second factor is the site of replacement, and we like to replace our embryos 1 cm from the fundal region. Thirdly, the rate that fluid is injected will influence the results.

Steptoe: This is a question which I would like to see solved. We believe replacing an embryo to establish a pregnancy is a very responsible thing and made more difficult if there is a chance of an ectopic pregnancy, and especially if the patient is in her late thirties or early forties.

Many of the oviducts we observe are incapable of any function, and these worry us. We did show by X-ray examination and by radio-opaque dye that when media was expelled from a cannula placed near the fundus, small amounts of fluid entered the oviduct. This, combined with the observation of an ectopic pregnancy, has concerned us somewhat. We carry out our occlusion of the oviduct by coagulation and, of course, we have not been able to ensure that the oviduct is blocked because we cannot remove the uterus for examination! We are concerned about this point and would like to know what other groups think about this form of treatment. Certainly, if a tube has any possibility of functioning, we do not disturb it in any way.

The Value of Preliminary Laparoscopy

Cohen: We have abandoned the preliminary laparoscopy because it was extra work for nothing. We now prepare the patient as if we are going to collect the oocyte and, if there are adhesions, we divide them at the time. We may have lost the treatment, but we can then correct the damage and reintroduce the patient during the next cycle.

Steptoe: This is not easy if a patient has been staying in hospital 4 or 5 days before the laparoscopy for oocyte recovery is performed. Someone must pay the costs of such treatment. There may have been many hormone assays, and the patient may have been subjected to considerable expense both in time and money. This is a problem.

Mettler: I think it is perhaps preferable to introduce the patient for preliminary laparoscopy first so that we prepare the abdomen for oocyte collection and make the ovary accessible. The alternative, of course, is to take the chance and carry out the adhesolysis or whatever during the oocyte collection.

Steptoe: There are already too many "ifs" for the patient to face. If she gets an egg recovered, if it fertilizes, if the embryo cleaves. I would not like to add another "if", i.e. that the disturbance of adhesolysis is insignificant.

Edwards: A point to be borne in mind is that if we intend to replace an embryo, there is a better chance of establishing a pregnancy if the patient remains as quiet as possible. The last thing we want is adhesolysis or anything else during the cycle in which we are trying to establish a pregnancy. This is why we like to have all our patients coming to us with ovaries that are as accessible as possible. We do not want cauterization or drugs—think what may be released into the uterine cavity!

Cohen: If we see that oocyte recovery is not possible, we try to repair the damage and tell the patient the operation must be cancelled.

We cannot do more than this. She may stay in hospital, or go home, and we make sure that nothing extra is done at the time of laparoscopy for oocyte recovery. In effect, the eggs were collected in 85% of our patients undergoing laparoscopy. The remaining 15% unfortunately had the treatment for nothing, becuase we had to do some repair within the abdomen.

Webster: Many of our patients have come in with previous histories, e.g. they may have lost their oviducts through ectopic pregnancies, or pelvic infection. Many have had several operations, and we anticipate difficulties. We anticipate adhesions, or other problems.

Johnston: I would like to discuss the psychological problem of a patient waiting on a waiting list. We have a waiting list which will last for 1 or 2 years. If a preliminary laparoscopy is not carried out, she will not even know if she is a candidate for the programme; she will be waiting endlessly to see if she can even be admitted. The delay could even prevent her from making application for adoption. We therefore support the concept of a preliminary laparoscopy.

Webster: We have had to do laparotomies in some of our patients. In 12% of them we had to resort to laparotomy rather than laparoscopy in order to free the ovary.

Making Follicles Accessible Using Sonar or Surgery

Hamberger: We believe that follicles can be aspirated by ultrasound, and that there would be no major problem using a needle of 1.2 mm external diameter. It does not matter much if a bowel is penetrated by such a needle. Nothing serious happens in these cases, and we merely give an antibiotic prophylactically. In over 10 years of work with laparoscopy, we have not seen a single case of severe infection after having the bowel with an insufflatton needle.

Steptoe: I am not worried about the needle going through the bowel from the patient's point of view. I am concerned about the needle going through the bowel and then into the follicle.

Hamberger: I think it is very rare indeed that the bowel will be penetrated. I should estimate that the incidence is 1 in 1,000 or thereabouts. The patients are all prechecked with laparoscopy, and the aspiration by ultrasound should only be carried out on repeated cycles.

Johnston: We have recently tried avoiding laparoscopy and using sonar control to collect the oocyte and follicle. The ovary has been transferred to the anterior abdominal wall and we could hardly see any peritoneal cavity. We collected the cumulus cells from the follicle but, unfortunately, missed the oocyte. The operation was carried out under local anaesthesia.

Speirs: At laparotomy there was no hope that the patient could retain her ovary in any site that was accessible for oocyte recovery. Only after extensive sharp section could we reach the ovary itself at laparotomy. So we divided the ovarian ligament, swung the ovary into the anterior abdominal wall in the peritoneum, and returned it in place. We have done this so far with three patients, none have had any symptoms, and all have continued to ovulate. One of these patients was involved on two occasions in an attempt to collect her oocyte by sonar, and one embryo was replaced. I must stress that both ovaries were slung on to the anterior abdominal wall.

Johnston: This situation arose after problems with gaining access to the ovaries of a number of patients. About half of them developed post-operative lesions, and this prevented our finding the ovary during the subsequent laparoscopy. It was a desperate situation for the patients. I have always been impressed by the paucity of adhesions in the anterior fornix, in front of the round ligament. I thought this was the best side to place the ovary in order to collect oocytes at a later date. I divided the anastomotic vessel relative to the uterine artery, and mobilized the ovary so it literally hung on the infundibular pelvic ligament, and its vessels. After a hole is made in the broad ligament, the ovary can be placed in the anterior fornix, and tethered close to the internal iliac ring. Alternatively, the ovary can be sewn on to the anterior abdominal wall.

The ovaries have continued with their spontaneous ovulations, they do not appear to suffer diminution of blood supply, follicular development and ultrasound is normal, and they have a typical response to clomiphene. Those we have re-examined have given us access where it was impossible before.

Steptoe: We also sling the ovaries to this position in front of the broad ligament. Your approach seems to me to be perfectly logical. Do you take any further steps to prevent the formation of any new adhesions? We fear that the adhesions may reform after spending a long time in dissecting out the ovary.

Speirs: Making the ovary accessible was the reason we carried out the procedure. We usually instill 500 ml of Dextran 70.

Mettler: We have attempted in 25 cases to use ultrasound to locate the follicle. A reasonable percentage of eggs were recovered from the follicles and, on occasion, we had to pass through the bladder. There was no damage.

Steptoe: This approach may be possible in the normal patient, but I doubt it is in the type of patient with adhesions, etc., that we have to deal with. In those circumstances, the needle would almost certainly pass through the bowel or into a mesentery or somewhere else other than the ovary.

Anaesthetics and Stress

Johnston: With respect to the difference in the secretion of cortisol and prolactin after treatment with halothane, we may be witnessing a toxic effect. Halothane is a very toxic substance, and it may be poisoning the responses. Is Szalay worried about effects on oocytes?

Szalay: We usually use thiopentane and the neuroleptic drugs. The low levels of cortisol were ascribed to a reduction of stress in the patients.

Hamberger: I have understood from Szalay's lecture that most of the anaesthetic agents described were active at the level of the median eminence. We know, for example, that the LH surge is related to the actual levels of dopamine in this region and we know that decreases occur in levels of neurotransmitters after a major operation. Could there in addition be any local effects in the ovary?

Szalay: No, we do not ascribe any local effects to these anaesthetics.

References

Steptoe, P. C. & Edwards, R. G. 1976. Reimplantation of a human embryo with subsequent tubal pregnancy. *Lancet*, **i**, 880–882.

Wood, C., Trounson, A. O., Leeton, J., Talbot, J. Mc., Buttery, B., Webb, J., Wood, J. & Jessup, D. 1981. A clinical assessment of nine pregnancies obtained by in-vitro fertilization and embryo transfer. *Fertility and Sterility*, **35**, 502–508.

Part 3

FERTILIZATION AND PREIMPLANTATION GROWTH *IN VITRO*

Methods for Fertilization and Embryo Culture
in vitro

J. M. Purdy

The purpose of this paper is to give a brief description of some of the methods for in-vitro culture used in our laboratory. Careful quality control is essential to the success of in-vitro fertilization. I would like to include some of the difficulties in various stages of the procedure encountered over the years. I will also describe very briefly some of the different culture fluids used to support the pre-implantation embryos of mammals *in vitro*.

My intention is therefore modest, yet crucial for the success of the culture of human embryos *in vitro*. It is essential to maintain a careful and rigorous control over the methods used throughout each stage, the purchasing and testing of equipment, methods used in making and testing media, preparing spermatozoa, and achieving fertilization and embryo culture *in vitro*. Each laboratory will develop their own methods, depending on their own particular expertise. Some of the difficulties encountered during the past 15 years will be outlined. The methods described are offered as a guide to discussion; many more intriguing points of detail will undoubtedly come from other groups involved in similar studies.

Equipment and Containers

The equipment needed in a tissue-culture laboratory has been described extensively (Paul, 1970). We have found that great care is needed in the selection of glassware and washing it, the choice of plastic vessels, and the methods used for sterilizing media.

Bourn Hall, Cambridgeshire and Physiological Laboratory, Cambridge University, U.K.

Glassware and Washing

Most laboratories involved in tissue culture have steadily reduced the amount of necessary glassware. The time and effort spent in repeated rinsings can be dispensed with by the introduction of plastics, although some items of equipment still retain glass components, and the correct washing procedures must be adopted.

Pyrex glassware or its equivalent is used wherever possible. All used and new glassware is initially washed in detergent 7X (Hopkins & Williams), which has proved fully reliable and effective over many years. Each piece of glassware is then rinsed individually, using purified water, and numerous rinses (Paul, 1970).

Many laboratories use tap water for initial rinsing, moving to distilled water, and then to double distilled water. Tap water can introduce problems, especially in regions of hard water. Our earlier studies were carried out in Oldham, a soft water region. Rinsing could safely begin in tap water, to be completed in highly purified distilled water. Cambridge is a hard water region, and the adoption of similar methods resulted in deposits and stains on the glassware, presumably calcium salts, despite the most intense efforts to remove them. The formation of this deposit coincided with a period of low fertilization rates and retarded cleavage of embryos. We now completely avoid the use of tap water and use distilled water for diluting 7X and for the initial rinsing, and Analar water (British Drug Houses) for the final two rinses. There have been no difficulties with deposits or low rates of fertilization and cleavage since adopting these methods.

Tissue Culture Plastics

Various disposable plastics have been used during the course of our work. Their advantages are obvious, but we believe that care is needed in their use because they might exert deleterious effects on fertilization and embryonic growth. There are disadvantages with some plastics, and care must be taken to evaluate those requiring plasticizers during manufacture (Jaeger & Rubin, 1972; Lancet, 1975).

Falcon plastics have been most widely used in our work because spermatozoa and embryos survive excellently in them. The one disadvantage is that the surface can be scratched accidentally by a pipette or other glass instruments drawn lightly across them. Deeper-lying parts of the vessel are exposed, and substances might be released which are harmful to embryos growing in culture. We have tested the effects of scratching on the growth of mouse embryos *in vitro*. Scratches

Table 1
Growth of mouse embryos in culture dishes after the surface was scratched*

	A. Falcon	
Period of culture	24h	48h
2-cell	0, *1*	0, *1*
4-cell	3, *2*	3, *1*
8-cell	35 (67%), *32* (74%)	2, *1*
Morula	14, *8*	4, *6*
Blastocyst		46 (84%), *44* (83%)
	B. Another make	
Period of culture	24h	48h
2-cell	4, *2*	4, *2*
4-cell	29 (47%), *4*	11, *0*
8-cell	28 (45%), *61* (85%)	13, *4*
Morula	1, *5*	20, *17*
Blastocyst		14 (23%), *49* (68%)

*Embryos were collected on day 2, incubated overnight in medium 16 containing 4 mg l^{-1} bovine serum albumin, and divided into two groups next morning. In one group, the plastic remained intact; in the other, an X scratch was made with a glass needle. The embryos were scored 24 h and 40 h later; controls are italicized.

on Falcon plastic petri dishes did not harm mouse embryos growing in microdrops of medium, suspended in liquid paraffin (Table 1), but another make was unsatisfactory in this respect.

The design of plastic vessels is very important, simplifying the method of flaming the neck of a bottle or tube, minimizing the risk of introducing infection and increasing the ease of the procedure. Corning centrifuge tubes have proved to be of excellent design, and Falcon culture bottles permit the screw top lid to be handled easily as the bottle is opened and closed. We avoid push-fit tops, which are difficult to handle if sterility is to be maintained.

Sterilization by Membrane Filters

Almost all solutions are sterilized by filtration, using 0.22 μ Millipore filters almost entirely. They have given highly satisfactory and repeatable results, errors have been rare, and the ease and simplicity of the methods have been rewarding. Once an excessive amount of a wetting agent had been added to a batch of these filters during their manufacture. One or two filters from a new batch are used to filter distilled water, and a frothing on the surface of the filtered water indicates an excess of wetting agent.

Wetting agent-free filters are available and are preferable for tissue culture work. A minimal amount of frothing can sometimes be seen, but does not appear to be harmful. Contaminants such as this can perhaps be reduced by discarding the first few drops of the filtered samples.

Components of the Culture Solutions

Physiological Saline Solutions

Several media can be used to support cleaving human embryos *in vitro*. These include Earle's, Ham's F10, Hoppe and Pitts medium (1973), and several others. A protein source, albumin or serum, is also required. We have used serum for many years. Currently, we use Earle's solution, supplemented with pyruvate (Table 1) and serum (8% for fertilization and 15% for cleavage). These media are very simple, and have given excellent results.

The 10X concentrated media without bicarbonate is purchased (Flow Laboratories). These stock solutions can be maintained in refrigerators, and diluted when needed with a suitably pure water. For several years, pure "Analar" water has been purchased from British Drug Houses, because the double and treble distillation of local water gave inferior results. The media is freshly prepared at least once a week, and any remaining is discarded as fresh batches are prepared. The bicarbonate concentration is 0.21 gm % for culture media based on a gas phase including 5% CO_2 and 0.10 gm % for those used in air, e.g. for flushing follicles.

The osmotic pressure has consistently been between 282 and 286 mOsmol Kg^{-1}, close to the values found in follicular fluid. Each batch of medium is checked, using an osmometer to ensure that the correct reading has been obtained.

When culture media are to be used, the sterile serum is prepared and added. They are equilibrated against the gas mixture to be used in the incubator, usually 5% CO_2, 5% O_2 and 90% N_2, by bubbling gas from the cylinder through a wash bottle of sterile water with a sterilizing millipore filter at the terminal. They are then left to stand until the pH is attained, usually about 7.3. Care is needed in gassing media, because repeated hard gassing without humidification can lead to an increase in their osmotic pressure.

Some of the ionic constituents and energy sources in three media used by various groups are given in Table 2. The ratio of sodium : potassium varies in these media, e.g. it is low in Hoppe and Pitts medium. Energy sources also vary, the amount of pyruvate being

Table 2
Composition of the media used for fertilization and cleavage of human eggs in vitro
$(gm\ l^{-1})$

	Modified Earle's	Media for mouse eggs (Hoppe & Pitts, 1973)	Ham's F10* (Ham, 1963)
$CaCl_2 2H_2O$	0.2649	—	0.0441
KCl	0.400	0.356	0.285
$MgSO_4.7H_2O$	0.200	0.294	0.1527
NaCl	6.800	5.140	7.400
$NaH_2PO.2H_2O$	0.1583	—	—
Na_2HPO_4	—	—	0.156
KH_2PO_4	—	0.162	—
$NaHCO_3$	2.1	1.9	1.2
Ca lactate	—	0.527	—
Na pyruvate	0.011	0.025	0.110
Glucose	1.000	1.000	1.100
Na lactate (60% syrup)	—	$3.7\ ml\ l^{-1}$	—

*Also contains $CuSO_4$, $FeSO_4$, $ZnSO_4$, amino acids, etc.

much higher in Ham's F10. Fertilization and cleavage *in vitro* have been achieved in several media, including those in Table 2 and Tyrode's solution, and satisfactory results have been obtained with each of them. There appears to be no comparative data on their value at present.

Preparation of Serum

When a significant and maintained LH rise has been detected in urine, 20 ml of blood is taken for serum preparation. In order to avoid excessively fatty serum we prefer to venepuncture just before a meal is taken. We rely heavily on a visual check on the culture medium (it should remain absolutely clear) to exclude contamination or precipitation and very "milky", opaque serum obviously impedes this check.

There are several methods for preparing serum from samples of blood. The blood can be centrifuged immediately, and the plasma removed for clotting. Alternatively, blood can be allowed to clot, and as the clot contracts the serum is released and can be removed. We prefer the first method because clotting occurs in a cell-free plasma sample, and the preparations are clean with no evidence of lysis. Clotting must be complete before the sera are inactivated. This may not be necessary for successful embryonic development or to remove viruses, etc., but it is known that spermatozoa can bind immunoglobulins and fix complement. Reactions between human serum and spermatozoa are weak, nevertheless we routinely inactivate all sera at 56 °C for 30 minutes before use.

The sera are always handled as cleanly as possible using sterile procedures under a Laminair flow hood. Following heat inactivation they are millipored with a 0.22 μ sterilizing filter. Occasionally, the filtering is very difficult and a second filter is required to provide sufficient volume. A pre-filter is not routinely used, but may be helpful. All samples of serum, and of culture media, are stored at 4 °C.

Liquid Paraffin

Of all the components used in embryo culture, liquid paraffin perhaps presents some of the greatest difficulties. On several occasions, a particular batch of it has been suspected to interfere with fertilization or cleavage. It can be toxic to spermatozoa or embryos, exerting its effects quickly or, perhaps worse, gradually over a period of hours or days. All batches of paraffin must be tested before use in an in-vitro system, examining effects on the motility of human spermatozoa and/or the growth of mouse embryos *in vitro*. Only samples without any toxic effects should be used.

The preparation of the paraffin should be carried out carefully. Samples of liquid paraffin (British Drug Houses) are filtered through a coarse filter (Whatman) and are sterilized by autoclaving. Sterilization is a difficult step, because the admixture of steam will cause cloudiness in paraffin rendering it unusable. The tops of the bottles are screwed down tightly, ensuring that the lining and the bung are intact. The bottles are then autoclaved, reaching a temperature of 135 °C and 25 psi for 18 min. It is not clear how satisfactory sterility of the paraffin is achieved under these conditions. Nevertheless, this procedure works, and cultures have remained clean in our hands over many years. Once autoclaved, the paraffin appears to have an indefinite shelf life.

Before use, the sterile paraffin is equilibriated against culture media for several hours. This step is theoretically important to remove any toxic compound from the paraffin, and an approximate ratio of one part of culture medium to four parts of paraffin is used. The paraffin and medium are thoroughly mixed by gassing them together with the gas phase routinely used for embryo culture (5% CO_2, 5% O_2 and 90% N_2). The two layers, paraffin and culture medium, separate clearly in a few hours, and the underlying medium can be examined for pH and cleanliness. Fresh samples of equilibriated paraffin are prepared every 4–5 days.

The use of liquid paraffin to suspend small drops of culture medium is a considerable asset in culturing oocytes and embryos. But the difficulties in its use must be recognized and overcome. It will then help to maintain pH, osmotic pressure and cleanliness when media used against a gas phase containing 5% CO_2 have to be brought temporarily into air during the handling of gametes or embryos. It must be prepared and tested correctly, and also used under strict control during the culture of eggs and embryos, described later in this paper. Under these conditions, it permits the easy and rapid examination or manipulation of the cultures, and embryos can be grown if necessary through all stages of their preimplantation growth. Its advantages are so considerable that every care should be taken in preparing and using it correctly.

Assessing Materials and Media

All media and new materials are routinely tested by exposing them to human spermatozoa for some days. The sperm test is very simple. Spermatozoa are centrifuged twice, and suspended to a concentration of 10^5–10^6 ml^{-1}. The samples are prepared, and tested against any new material, or any freshly made medium containing a new component or a different batch of an existing component.

Samples of spermatozoa from most men remain highly motile for at least seven days at room temperature. If any component impairs the motility of spermatozoa, it is discarded and the original component is reintroduced into our system when possible. Sperm tests can give a rapid and simple assay of new materials and methods, carried out within the confines of our existing laboratory. A further quality control can be carried out, testing the suspect component against animal embryos. Mouse embryos are the easiest to obtain, and large numbers can be cultured in microdrops beneath paraffin; they are probably more sensitive to adverse materials and conditions than spermatozoa.

Samples of all newly-prepared media (without serum) are tested at 37 °C for several days to ensure that no growth occurs and that no deposits or other contaminants appear (i.e. that they remain sterile). Correct conditions must be established in any media being tested in this manner, e.g. equilibrating them with the correct gas phase. Fine white deposits will form in Earle's medium left ungassed and placed on the floor of an incubator (temperature $\pm$ 38 °C). The pH probably rises beyond the range of the phenol red indicator, causing calcium to precipitate. The buffering effect of gassing this medium or of adding serum presents the formation of a precipitate.

The Culture Rooms: Organization and Sterile Precautions

Every possible care should be taken in planning the relationships between culture rooms, the operating theatre, the sperm-preparation room and the washing and disposal areas. The reward will come when serious work begins, when a properly-designed layout will help the ease, efficiency and success of the culture methods, and facilitate collaboration between the scientific and medical teams. Obviously, the design adopted by each group of workers will be constrained by the available space and facilities. My comments are based on our experiences in Kershaw's Hospital, Oldham, where existing rooms were adapted, and here in Bourn Hall, where new but temporary accommodation could be designed before the work began.

When planning the design of the culture rooms, etc., we decided that sterile precautions must be used during oocyte recovery and fertilization and cleavage *in vitro* and during the replacement of the embryos. In Kershaw's Hospital, dishes containing oocytes and catheters carrying embryos had to be carried through an anaesthetic room intervening between the operating theatre and laboratory. The system was not ideal, but the work could be done efficiently.

In Bourn Hall, a new system was designed, although at present the accommodation is temporary. Twin culture rooms lie immediately adjacent to the operating theatre, so that one is used while the other is cleaned. A "stable-type" door separates each culture room from the theatre. During oocyte aspiration, the upper part of the door is open, and dishes are carried there from the surgeon to be transferred to the embryologist sitting close by. The aspirates can be examined within seconds, and a verbal report guides the surgeon in further aspiration. During embryo replacement into the mother, the door is fully opened, to permit easy access for the embryologist.

The sperm preparation room has been placed away from the culture rooms and a washing-up room is placed adjacent to it. The preparation of spermatozoa does not interfere with the techniques of oocyte aspiration, and the whole layout is convenient enough for surgeons and embryologists to carry out their procedures independently.

Full sterile precautions have been adopted in the culture rooms, operating theatre and sperm preparation room. The air conditioning has an absolute terminal filter and air turnover is 32 changes per hour, under positive pressure. Flow is outwards from the culture rooms. Walls and work tops are washable. The washable tops are all made with formica, and ultra-violet light is installed. Vinyl floors have been carefully laid and sealed with an appropriate edging to be washable.

Lighting is by Tungsten bulbs to avoid emission from fluorescent lighting. Laminated air flow cabinets are also used in each culture room and the sperm preparation room. Work can be carried out safely anywhere in these compact culture rooms without fear of infection, although the most exposed parts of the procedures are carried out in the laminated air flow cabinets.

Protective clothing is worn. Gowns, hats, masks, and special footwear or overshoes are essentially the same as those considered necessary in all operating theatres. Gloves are not worn, because they reduce dexterity, but hands are washed before beginning work. Indoor footwear is restricted to the theatre, culture room and sperm preparation room.

Preparations for Fertilization *in vitro*

Constant care is needed on the methods used to grow human embryos *in vitro*. A glance at a pathologist's report on some semen samples shows how pathogens and surface organisms are a constant threat to cleanliness. Some of these organisms may be resistant to antibiotics. An up-to-date report must be available on semen taken from each husband a few days before laparoscopy for oocyte recovery is due, and this must give a satisfactory indication of cleanliness. Nor are we sanguine about the cleanliness of samples coming from the operating theatre. The aspirating needle passes through the abdominal wall, and skin infections might persist after washing the abdomen.

So far, infections have been introduced through the semen only rarely, despite the fact that we routinely use only penicillin in our culture media. We have grown some embryos to blastocysts at five days of growth before replacing them in the mother, and most contaminants would have been revealed during this period.

Preparation of Spermatozoa

The neat semen sample is briefly examined microscopically for an approximate estimation of count and motility. Depending on these observations, an appropriate volume of semen is added using about 2 ml of Earle's solution containing 8% human serum from the wife. This is gently centrifuged for five minutes, the supernatant removed, and the procedure repeated a second time. After each centrifugation, care is taken to remove virtually all the suspending medium, hence the dilution of seminal plasma is considerable. Much of the non-cellular debris is also left in the supernate, at the low centrifugal force (150–200G) which is applied. This gentle centrifugation also removes some cellular deposits from spermatozoa, but increases the number of clumps in the final sediment.

Two centrifugations may not be necessary, but has proved highly successful in our hands. Excess washing can damage spermatozoa; in studies involving the fertilization of zona-free hamster oocytes, poorly-washed human spermatozoa were found to be ineffective in fertilization. The washing medium contained bovine serum albumin, and crude preparations were toxic to the gametes. A contaminant in the albumin, possibly lipoprotein, may have reacted with a polyamine, notably spermine, in seminal plasma. Oxidized spermine is known to be toxic to human spermatozoa (Pulkinnen *et al.*, 1977). We routinely use one medium for fertilization *in vitro*, i.e. Earle's solution with 8% of homologous serum, and avoid the use of albumin completely. Higher concentrations of serum are compatible with fertilization and cleavage.

There have been other recent reports of damage to spermatozoa caused by excess washing. Increasing the number of washes from 0 to 3 induced a progressive decondensation of DNA in up to 60% of human sperm heads. The damage increased proportionately with the number of washes (Blazak, 1981). We have been satisfied with our methods, and routinely achieve high rates of fertilization. If there is evidence of immunity to spermatozoa in the wife, an alternative source of serum is chosen; usually there are sufficient samples available for choice.

Some sperm samples contain massive amounts of cellular contamination. One method of removing many of these cells is to layer the washed sample of spermatozoa underneath a paraffin layer. After an hour or so, the cells have sedimented, while the spermatozoa are swimming over them. Clean samples of the spermatozoa can be obtained by gently pipetting off the supernate, and we have obtained fertilization *in vitro* with such semen samples.

Recovery of Oocytes

Many oocytes are aspirated in clear follicular fluid. They are transferred into a medium composed of a mixture of equal amounts of follicular fluid and fertilization medium (usually Earle's solution containing 8% of homologous serum) to complete maturation. Oocytes have been left in this medium for between 0 and 15 hours, depending on the "ripeness" of the oocyte and cumulus cells.

This interval in culture is sometimes important to permit the completion of oocyte maturation, which is presumably in its final stage when oocytes are aspirated, and to allow the full secretory properties of cumulus cells to appear. Changes can often be noticed in the secretory arrangement of cumulus cells after their incubation *in vitro* for a few hours. Culture *in vitro* for a few hours does not appear to damage the oocyte in any way, or to prevent normal embryonic growth. We established one pregnancy in Oldham from an oocyte which was cultured *in vitro* in this manner for 12 hours before insemination.

This routine must be changed if oocytes are aspirated after a follicle has been flushed several times by a flushing medium. In this case, the oocyte is suspended in flushing medium which usually contains heparin, and it might be found in media containing large or small amounts of blood. If possible, these oocytes are transferred to samples of their own follicular fluid before they are placed in culture. If follicular aspiration has not yielded clear fluid, the oocyte is rinsed in flushing medium containing heparin, and then in culture medium, to remove most of the blood and heparin. It is then transferred into droplets of culture medium beneath paraffin, to await insemination.

Fertilization *in vitro*

Fertilization is usually carried out in small drops of medium suspended under liquid paraffin. It can also be carried out in small culture tubes. The advantages of paraffin are obvious: the droplets can be examined rapidly to assess viability and number of spermatozoa, the condition of the oocyte, and the appearance of granulosa cells. Manipulations can be carried quickly with these microdrops, e.g. the oocyte can be transferred rapidly to a fresh droplet if numerous erythrocytes are present among the cumulus cells. Occasionally, the cells around the oocyte may remain very viscous, or tight, and these can be gently removed. The use of excessive light is rigorously avoided when examining oocytes under a stereomicroscope. Great care must be exercised in the use of microdrops beneath liquid paraffin, because the system can be easily insulted. It is highly satisfactory for maintaining the pH of high-bicarbonate media equilibriated against 5% CO_2. The liquid paraffin will hold the gas tension in the microdrop for a certain amount of time, but an equal period of time is needed for the paraffin to re-equilibriate when it is replaced in the incubator under its own specific gas phase.

Our paraffin cultures remain out of their own gas phase for a maximum of five minutes, and this only under exceptional circumstances. We prefer to replace them as soon as possible, to avoid the gradual decline in CO_2 tension. The penalty of maintaining paraffin cultures in air for a long time can be seen when the petri dish is replaced in the desiccator. The microdrops continue to lose CO_2 long after the gas phase has been replaced, the rising temperature drives it off more quickly and their pH rises steadily. If the petri dish has remained in air for 30 minutes, the pH of the microdrops continues to rise for about the same time in the incubator, so that the oocytes or embryos are exposed to highly alkaline conditions. We suspect that such changes in pH once the petri dish is replaced in its incubator are a major cuase of poor embryonic growth and perhaps low rates of fertilization (Edwards, 1973).

In our work, oocytes remain in the insemination droplet for between 4 and 24 hours after spermatozoa are added. We are still undecided about the optimum period. If the oocyte is seen to contain pronuclei, or if it has cleaved, then it is transferred into growth medium, usually modified Earle's solution containing 15% of homologous serum in a small plastic tube. We prefer to use Falcon plastics, and the small tubes can be quickly and easily gassed, sealed and placed in a dessicator, and no further changes of medium or conditions are needed. If there is no indication of fertilization, approximately 10,000 ml^{-1} spermatozoa are added to the oocyte in the plastic tube. We believe that this step gives a second chance of fertilization, which has apparently occurred in the plastic tube in some of our oocytes. Cleavage after such a delay in fertilization appears to be normal, or even more rapid, as if the embryo is "catching up" on a pre-existing timetable.

Culture of Embryos

Several methods have been tested for culturing embryos, including paraffin microdrops, plastic tubes, rotating cultures and feeder layers. We prefer paraffin drops or culture tubes at present, and are currently using tubes.

Cumulus cells remain adherent to many oocytes after fertilization *in vitro*. This situation differs from conditions *in vivo* where the enzymic and ciliary activity of the oviduct evidently ensure their complete removal. If the adherent cell mass is large and tight, it might affect embryonic growth, and we have seen a phenomenon resembling premature compaction in embryos surrounded by large numbers of cumulus cells. Two methods can be used for removing cumulus cells. The oocyte can be gently moved in-and-out of a fine pipette. Alternatively, the cells can be gently dissected from around the egg, using fine needles. Neither procedure is easy, and both risk damaging the egg.

We prefer to leave a few cumulus cells around the embryo pronucleate oocyte, as it is placed in the culture tube. They help to anchor it gently to the side of the plastic tube used for culture, and the embryo can then be examined easily under a stereomicroscope by simply rotating the tube so the embryo comes uppermost. Cleavage can be scored quickly, without altering the conditions of culture, and the embryo is exposed to minimal light. If the embryo is obscured by the cumulus cells, or when it is removed from the tube for re-placement into the mother, it must be dislodged from its position. This can be done carefully and gently with a fine, blunt-ended Pasteur pipette in a matter of moments. Most embryos can be scored *in situ*, without having to disturb them; the others are placed under paraffin in droplets. After 2 or 3 days in culture, all embryos are removed from the tube for replacement into the mother, and placed in the paraffin microdrop for a few moments until picked up into the replantation catheter.

Every care, including sterile technique, maintenance of temperature and humidity, minimum exposure to light or manipulation, is taken during embryo culture, and especially during the replacement of the embryo into the mother. With increasing experience, veterinary surgeons have found that cow embryos can tolerate wide variations in culture conditions, some embryos even being left open on a microscope stand at room temperature for several hours! We may also learn that human embryos are tougher than we imagine, but until then we will continue to exercise the care described above.

Conclusions

I have described briefly some of the methods adopted for the culture of human embryos. Many of them could perhaps be changed or modified or even abandoned. Complete media could be purchased, relying on the makers to establish the correct conditions. Different methods could be used for preparing spermatozoa and oocytes, or for culturing the embryos. Each method is legitimate if it produces the desired results. We hope that our methods are as simple as needed to be compatible with normal embryonic growth.

References

Blazak, W. F. 1981. Destabilization of human sperm nuclei induced by washing. *Biology of Reproduction*, **24**, suppl. 1.

Edwards, R. G. 1973. Studies on human conception. *American Journal of Obstetrics and Gynecology*, **117**, 587.

Ham, R. G. 1963. *Experimental Cell Research*, **39**, 515.

Hoppe, P. C. & Pitts, J. 1973. Fertilization *in vitro* and development of mouse ova. *Biology of Reproduction*, **8**, 420–426.

Jaeger, R. J. & Rubin, R. J. 1972. Migration of a phthalate ester plasticizer from polyvinyl chloride blood bags into stored human blood and its localization in human tissues. *New England Journal of Medicine*, **287**, 1114–1118.

Lancet. 1975. PVC, plasticisers and the paediatrician. *Editorial*, May 24.

Paul, J. 1970. *Cell and Tissue Culture*. E & S Livingstone, Edinburgh.

Pulkkinen, P., Sinervirta, R. & Jänne, J. 1977. Mechanism of action of oxidised polyamines on the metabolism of human spermatozoa. *Journal of Reproduction and Fertility*, **51**, 399–404.

Discussions on Methods of Culture

Gas Phase for Culturing Embryos

Testart: When embryos are placed in the desiccator at the start of incubation, there is a rapid build-up of gas and of pressure. Does this influence the growth of human embryos?

Purdy: When the desiccator is closed, we turn the tap to release any immediate build-up of pressure. This is repeated again after a minute or two, and then again, a few minutes after that. With gradually increasing intervals, the pressure inside the desiccator is maintained fairly steady, without getting too high.

Hamberger: We use similar methods, with desiccators for the growth of embryos. The pressure problem is avoided by having two glass tubes emerging from the desiccator, each with loosely-placed rubber plug. If there is a positive pressure, the plug is pushed away. The rubber plug is routinely moved for a short period after 2 and 10 minutes.

Trounson: I would like to raise a slightly controversial point with Jean Purdy and Bob Edwards. As far as I know from studies in the mouse, there is no distinct evidence that a lowered oxygen concentration is essential for embryonic development. Moreover, we have human pregnancies using 5% CO_2 in air, and I understand that Howard and Georgeanna Jones use this gas phase too. Moreover, I know that Carl Wood has measured the oxygen concentration in the tubes in the uterus, and concludes that it is close to 10% of oxygen, rather than 5%. Could we discuss this point, because using 5% CO_2 in air may be an easier system to work with.

Feichtinger: We are using a CO_2 incubator, using 5% CO_2 in combination with 5% oxygen by replacing the air with nitrogen. When the door of the incubator is opened, the oxygen concentration rises to between 10 and 15%, and after it is closed the tension then declines gently to 5% after ten minutes or so.

Edwards: We initially used a 5% O_2, 5% CO_2, and 90% N_2 gas mixture, because of the work described by Whitten (1971) some years

149

ago, which is rather old now. Both then and now, 5% CO_2 in air is the easiest system to work with, but we were impressed by Whitten's data. We must plead guilty to a great deal of inertia: if a system is working, we leave it severely alone. We often discover that a change can lead to an error, that it is very difficult to get back to where we were before making the change in the first place! Conditions are changed only when there is a very good reason to discard the old method.

Having said all this, I would like to stress that if other groups use 5% CO_2 in air and get high rates of pregnancies, then we will consider changing too.

Trounson: We do not have many pregnancies with 5% CO_2 in air. After obtaining the data from Carl Wood, we are now culturing embryos under 10% oxygen.

Fishel: We must bear another difference in mind between animal and the human studies. In man, we have to work with one or two embryos. In mice, there is always a great deal of statistical evidence based on large numbers of embryos. We can hardly use statistics when we have to grow a single embryo from one patient! We cannot change our methods, because of statistical evidence from animals that this or that method may give different results. We must stay close to our successful methods.

Edwards: I am interested to hear that the oxygen concentration in the oviduct is 10%. This contrasts with exhaled air, which is 5%, and is the reason why everyone tends to use the 5% system. Even at a 10% concentration in the oviduct, there is a great reduction from atmospheric oxygen, and the data from Wood indicates that some reduction is advantageous. Have two embryos from the same patient been cultured in different gas phases to find out if there were any differences in the cleavage rates?

Trounson: No, that particular experiment has not been done. The comparison has been between patients and, in all cases, rates of fertilization and embryonic growth appear to be very good. So the gas phase does not seem to be critical and we can find no statistical difference between gas phases, although more data is needed; it certainly seems to us that if there is any difference, large numbers will be required to demonstrate it.

Hillensjo: We have been using 5% O_2, 5% CO_2 and 90% N_2, and there are two ways of achieving this. One method is to use a premixed gas, but this is usually expensive to buy. The other is to mix the gases in the incubator, and to carefully monitor the level of CO_2 in it. With the latter method, we found a considerable variation, especially in the oxygen concentration. On occasions, it became clear that we had conditions virtually resembling anoxia in our incubator, even though there were no difficulties with CO_2 levels based on the pH of the media. The elaborate methods we had been using were not proving satisfactory, and we had to go back to the premixtures of gases and use a closed system.

Purdy: I would like to make the point that very little gas is used in flushing the desiccator. The expense is reduced to a minimum. Moreover, once the desiccator is flushed, it remains flushed with gas, and it need not be disturbed any more. The system is stable and simple and, in the end, not expensive.

Millipore Filtration

Feichtinger: I would like to query the use of a millipore filter for humidifying and gassing solutions. There is information that the addition of the millipore filter can reduce the humidity of the gas to 50%. Without the filter, there is 88–90% humidity. We use gas without filtering it.

Purdy: I had not seen that data but even 50% humidification would be sufficient to prevent a rapid elevation of osmotic pressure, which is what happens following repeated gassing with non-humidified gas phase.

Lopata: How much medium do you put through a millipore filter before it is rejected? Do you filter serum separately from medium?

Purdy: As far as I know, Millipore do not put any limit on the volume that can be put through a sterilizing filter. It depends on the nature of the solution being filtered. Filtering serum can block the filter very quickly after only a few ml. When filtering other solutions without serum, I routinely change a filter after about 500 ml, although I am not sure that this is necessary.

All sera are prepared and filtered separately, immediately after they have been inactivated. Media are prepared regularly, and are filtered and stored in the refrigerator.

Feichtinger: Why do you not avoid the use of filters for serum? If everything was maintained under sterile conditions, then there would be no need to filter. Millipore filters remove many components from serum.

Purdy: Once again, we have always used this system as a fail-safe method to ensure that the sera are clean, and it has been successful in the past. By the time the serum has been inactivated, it has been handled three or four times for spinning, removing of clots, inactivation, etc. We give it a final filtration to make sure it is still sterile.

Culture Media for Fertilization and Embryonic Growth *in vitro*

Feichtinger: I am interested in your comments about the use of Earle's medium. Could you let us know exactly what you do with it, because we have had very little success with it.

Purdy: We purchase the 10X concentrate, free of bicarbonate, and add pyruvate, bicarbonate and penicillin. We use 0.21 gm 100 ml^{-1} of bicarbonate in Earle's medium used for culturing embryos, although this is reduced to 0.1 gm 100 ml^{-1} in the heparinized flushing medium for follicles. The bicarbonate concentration differs slightly to that added to other media, e.g. F10 where it is 0.19 gm 100 ml^{-1}, which are buffered against 5% CO_2.

The levels of pyruvate are 0.0011 gm 100 ml^{-1}, and this is the concentration we have used for many years, whether adding pyruvate to Earle's, Tyrode's or any other solution being prepared at the time. The pyruvate concentration in our media is much lower—by a factor of ten—than in Ham's F10, and approximately one-third of the amount in Hoppe–Pitt's medium. I have always been worried about excess pyruvate in culture media, and so we keep it down to these levels which have appeared to be very successful. Although we have always added pyruvate, we are not aware of any work in which it has been removed from the culture media used to support human oocytes or embryos. Its addition to culture media for cleaving embryos is based largely on the work of Brinster (1972) in mice. To the best of my knowledge, pyruvate is not so essential for the growth of the rabbit embryo *in vitro*, although it is beneficial.

Edwards: The Earle's medium seems to be much more like serum in its composition of ions, especially in relation to the concentrations of sodium, potassium, chloride, magnesium, etc. In contrast, Hoppe–Pitt's medium seems to resemble a secretory fluid, because it has high levels of, for example, potassium. On the basis of these figures, I imagine that Hoppe–Pitt's medium is more similar to oviductal fluid than Earle's as we use it.

We then add 8% or 15% of serum to Earle's solution, which will repair some deficiencies in the composition of the medium and, of course, add antibodies, proteins, etc. Basically, the medium we use must be considered an undefined medium, because it is impossible to define the components of individual samples of serum. But our defence is that the system has worked, we have had wonderful embryos, very little polyspermy, and excellent growth even to hatched blastocysts. It has worked over the years, and so we have left the system alone.

Lopata: Could you describe the details of preparing serum?

Purdy: Yes, the way we take serum might be important. We spin the blood down immediately, remove the clear plasma, and let it clot separately. The clot can then be easily removed later. This blood is collected when the LH surge has begun, at least in most patients, although we do not believe that this is absolutely essential. We use good-quality disposable centrifuge tubes for spinning the blood and clotting the plasma, and after the clot is removed the serum is spun again to remove small particles. The serum is then decanted into a glass centrifuge tube and heat-inactivated at 56 °C for 30 minutes. Once again, we are not sure that inactivation is necessary, but we have done it for years and the system is successful, so we carry on doing it. Each serum is then millipored into a Falcon flask.

Jones, H: Do you test each sample of serum against spermatozoa, or use the mouse embryo test?

Purdy: No, we have had such excellent results with the medium we prepared, that we do not test each serum before use. Each sample of serum is actually inspected after filtration, and before it is added to the culture medium. We like to see a clear serum, without fatty contents or deposits.

Edwards: The thing that surprises me is that we can grow human embryos *in vitro* with far more success than the embryos of any other animal species. As far as I am aware, there is no other species, including mouse, where preovulatory oocytes can be collected from any female whatsoever, fertilized *in vitro*, grown to blastocysts, and replaced in the same female. I have often been told at meetings that our human embryos must grow more slowly *in vitro* than *in vivo* because mouse embryos do. But we can take the mouse data seriously only when an oocyte can be taken from any female, fertilized *in vitro* by sperm from any male, and grown to a blastocyst and then to a full-term pregnancy.

There are difficult problems with the embryos of most animal species. There are blocks in development at the 2-cell stage or elsewhere, in some species, e.g. hamster. Rabbit embryos grow well *in vitro*, but blastocyst formation is very different to mouse embryos. Even the media used for culturing mouse embryos, usually Hoppe–Pitt's or Brinster's media have an osmotic pressure of 280 mOsmol Kg^{-1}, which is different from that of mouse serum (approximately 310 mOsmol Kg^{-1}). I do not know the justification for this difference. Embryos of other species are even more refractile than mice and rabbit, indicating that the methods of care that Jean Purdy has outlined in her paper are perhaps responsible for the success we have had in culturing human embryos *in vitro*.

Mouse embryos are excellent models for human embryos in some respects, e.g. cleavage rates, formation of the cell mass and studies on implantation *in vivo*.

Use of Liquid Paraffin

Trounson: If an oil system is used for culturing embryos, all the steroids are drawn out of the culture media. It is not possible to use an oil and retain steroids in the microdrops. It was reported in a recent conference in Holland that steroids were removed within 30 seconds of the medium being exposed to paraffin.

Edwards: We have been curious about that, and feared that all the steroids would be removed by Millipore filtration or by the paraffin. Curiously though, when we have examined samples of media from beneath paraffin after fertilization *in vitro*, there have been large amounts of progesterone and other steroids in it. I really do not understand the variation in results here. Perhaps it depends on the type of paraffin in use.

Trounson: Do you bubble gas through the paraffin, or through the equilibrating medium and the paraffin together?

Purdy: Both together. I like the use of paraffin. It gives freedom of work in open air, rivalled by no other system. It is bacteriostatic, maintains the gas phase and prevents evaporation from the droplets while the necessary manipulations are carried out on the eggs. With careful handling, and provided the sperm tests are done and it is non-toxic, then I like its adaptability. We have had pregnancies from embryos grown under paraffin, hence I see no reason to abandon it.

Edwards: We use paraffin, but I am very suspicious of it. It see it misused so easily in many laboratories. It gives a false impression of safety. I have watched microdrops under paraffin held in open air for an hour or more, in the belief that the CO_2 tension would remain unchanged, trapped beneath the paraffin. Yet all the time the CO_2 has been slowly diffusing out, and the penalty is only seen when the culture is replaced in the incubator. The higher temperature drives off even more CO_2, and the microdrop goes alkaline over the succeeding hour or two. By now, the dish is tucked away in the incubator and no one examines it, yet this is the most critical time because it then takes a long time for the paraffin to be re-equilibriated against 5% CO_2, hence the pH of the microdrops can rise very high indeed. I feel such small tricks of the trade as this allowed us to grow embryos to the blastocyst in Oldham ten years ago, and to put human embryology *in vitro* far ahead of any other species.

Lopata: Do you put the drops of medium beneath the paraffin, or place the drops of medium into the dish first and then pour the paraffin over?

Purdy: It depends on whether it is Monday, Tuesday, Wednesday or Thursday. Simon Fishel is on on the early days, and puts the droplets in first; Bob Edwards and I put the paraffin in first and the droplets in second. We do not like to put the drops in first because the droplets spread more, and the cells surrounding the embryo are more adhesive to the plastic.

Fishel: I put the droplets in first, because they stay in one place, and I can place them exactly where I want them. I do agree that the cells can appear to stick more firmly to the plastic under these conditions. I do not like putting the drops in second because the plastic may be inadvertently scratched by the Pasteur pipette. As far as I can see, working with Falcon plastics is safe because light scratching does not appear to damage the growth of the embryos in the microdrops.

Plastic Tissue Culture Dishes

Purdy: We have made enquiries about the use of different plastics, and whether they have a protective surface coat which shields the culture droplets from the toxic compounds in the plastic. As far as I can see, various makers presumably use different qualities of polystyrene in their products, and this explains why there are differences between makes in the quality and properties of the plastic dishes used for culture.

Jones, H: Could you let us know when you transfer embryos from paraffin to tubes, and the reasons for doing so? Why do you use this system?

Purdy: Fertilization is always begun under paraffin, in order to remove many of the cumulus cells from around the oocyte. At some time later, the embryo is placed in culture tubes, and the exact timing depends on who gets their way, Bob Edwards or myself! We have transferred them at various intervals between 3 and 24 hours after insemination, and we could really see no difference in our results. Perhaps the difference may be subtle, and reflected in our pregnancy rates. We have not yet had time to analyse them. As far as we can see, embryos seem to grow well in both system, and I like paraffin.

The advantage of using a culture tube is that there is one component less (i.e. paraffin) and this may be important since we are all familiar with its toxic effects. In our system, the few remaining cumulus cells anchor the oocyte to the side of the culture tube, which can be gently rotated so the embryo can be examined fairly easily, but not so easily as in drops of medium held beneath paraffin. When it is time to replace the embryo into the mother, we take it from its tube, and place it into a drop of medium under paraffin, to be picked up in the transfer catheter.

We had pregnancies in Oldham from embryos grown in tubes and under paraffin. Perhaps it is not necessary to transfer from one to the other, and I think that paraffin is fully satisfactory provided it is handled carefully.

Trounson: I would like to warn about the use of plastics. Many of the plastics in general medical use are extremely toxic to mouse embryos, and each plastic should be tested for toxicity. Damage can be caused to the embryos, especially if they remain within the plstic for any length of time. PVC is totally toxic, liberating a dangerous gas, and such problems could cost years of work to people entering the field.

Jones, H: We have found that plastic varies from batch to batch. We routinely test plastics by the sperm survival test and other mouse embryo tests, and they are accepted when this is accomplished. However, there is variation from batch to batch, and we do not test each batch of new plastic samples, which gives us some concern.

Edwards: We always test each new batch of media, plastics, or anything else that is introduced into our system. This includes water, culture media, tubes for culture, paraffin, literally everything that is newly introduced.

References

Brinster, R. L. 1972. Developing zygote. In: *Reproductive Biology*, p. 748. Eds. H. Balin & S. Glasser. Excerpta Medica, Amsterdam.

Whitten, W. K. 1971. Nutrient requirement for the culture of preimplantation embryos *in vitro*. In: *Advances in the Biosciences*, **6**, 129–139. Ed. G. Raspé. Pergamon, London.

Discussions on fertilization and embryonic growth *in vitro* are given on pages 191 and 219 respectively.

Essentials of Fertilization

S. B. Fishel[1,2] and R. G. Edwards[2]

The fundamentals of fertilization in mammals are known in detail. However, the precise mechanism by which many of the finer processes occur, e.g. the stimuli initiating capacitation, still remain obscure. During the last few years, a considerable amount of information has been gained on the nature of the interactions between gametes, often by using studies on the sea urchin and other species. Extensive reviews have been published (Austin, 1965, 1975; Edwards, 1980).

Preliminaries to Fertilization

Spermatozoa gain their fertilizing ability in the lower regions of the male reproductive tract. After coitus they ascend the female reproductive tract rapidly, apparently as inert bodies with their own motility being important during the final stages of fertilization. Only small numbers reach the site of fertilization in the ampulla. In the female reproductive tract spermatozoa undergo a change known as capacitation.

The underlying mechanisms for capacitation, which can also be induced *in vitro* in a simple culture medium, are still unclear. It is generally accepted that subtle changes in the spermatozoal membrane are involved, e.g. the removal of surface coats deposited on the plasma membrane in the male tract. Using techniques such as freeze fracture, thin section and critical point drying, regional differences in the plasma membrane have been illustrated (Friend *et al.*, 1977; Phillips, 1977). Distinct morphological regions have been found, e.g. in the outer acrosomal membrane of guinea-pig and human spermatozoa, and these regions are probably involved in the initiation of capacitation.

The biochemistry of capacitation still remains to be elucidated.

[1]Beit Memorial Research Fellow.
[2]Physiological Laboratory, University of Cambridge, and Bourn Hall, Bourn, Cambridge, U.K.

Ultrastructural evidence exists suggesting the removal of surface coats which had restricted the permeability of the membrane and inhibited capacitation (Van Blerkom & Motta, 1979). Substances which inhibit capacitation may be present in the male reproductive tract and bind to the plasma membrane of the spermatozoa (Austin, 1975). Various compounds isolated from seminal plasma have been shown to prevent capacitation; such decapacitation factors include a glycoprotein of 37,000 MW (Olson & Hamilton, 1978), and a high molecular weight factor (Reddy et al., 1979; Van Der Ven et al., 1981). Various other substances with similar action have been postulated to be present in seminal plasma, e.g. sialoproteins and specific enzyme inhibitors (Bavister et al., 1978; Gwatkin, 1977). It has recently been suggested that the activity of a proteinase is required for capacitation and the subsequent acrosome reaction (Van Der Ven et al., 1981), and proteinase inhibitors in the cervical mucus may prevent capacitation. Although various enzymes such as glucuronidase and amylase have been used to induce capacitation the evidence of their involvement in capacitation remains unconvincing.

Many diverse substances have been shown to bind to the spermatozoal membrane, making it difficult to appreciate their function if any. These include LDH, cAMP, HCGβ, steroids, complement and immunoglobulins present in the normal serum of many animals including man (Beck et al., 1962). Albumin, however, is probably the most important protein involved in capacitation in vitro (Lui et al., 1977; Bavister, 1981), and it may act by sustaining sperm viability or be involved in the metabolism of cholesterol at the sperm membrane. Evidence exists to show that bovine serum albumin (BSA) reduces the cholestrol : lipid ratio in mouse spermatozoa, and BSA-mediated fluxes in spermatozoal membrane lipid may be essential for capacitation (Go & Wolf, 1981). Recently Hyne & Garbers (1981) have shown that biological fluids were required to capacitate guinea-pig spermatozoa at pH below 7.8, but were unnecessary at higher pH levels because spermatozoa capacitated spontaneously in very simple media (Table 1). This supports similar observations on the acrosome reaction in sea urchins (Dan, 1954). Catecholamines may be involved in capacitation since α- and β-adrenergic receptors have been demonstrated on spermatozoa (Cornett & Meizel, 1978) and they help to maintain spermatozoal viability at gamete ratios close to unity (Bavister, 1979).

The presence of cumulus cells is reported to assist human fertilization in vitro (Soupart & Morgenstern, 1973) possibly by providing a source of protein, steroids, ions or glycosidases (Gwatkin, 1977; Moore

Table 1

Capacitation and acrosome reaction of guinea-pig spermatozoa in response to pH and human plasma[a] (From Hyne & Garbers, 1981)

pH	Culture in Ca^{2+}-free medium (h)	Acrosome reacted (%)	Motility (%)
7.4	1.0	0	60
	1.5	0	60
	2.0	0	55
	3.0	<5	53
8.4	1.0	17	60
	1.5	30	62
	2.0	45	63
	3.0	40	60
7.4 + HBP[b]	3.0	4.3	—
7.4 + HPC[c]	3.0	24.3	—
7.4 + HPC[d]	3.0	1.7	—

[a] Spermatozoa were preincubated in Ca^{2+}-free medium without the addition of biological organic factors for up to 3 h, the percentage of acrosome-reacted and motile spermatozoa being scored 10 min after the addition of Ca^{2+}.
[b] 10% heat-treated human blood plasma (active molecular weight <1000).
[c] 20% human plasma concentrate (molecular weight 0–100,000).
[d] 20% human plasma concentrate (molecular weight <30,000).

& Bedford, 1978), but this is debatable. Oocytes can be fertilized in the absence of cumulus cells, although fertilization rates may be reduced. Cumulus and corona cells may help to restrict the number of spermatozoa reaching the oocyte and ensure correct orientation of spermatozoa to the zona pellucida. The zona pellucida could also have an important role by modifying spermatozoa and enabling them to bind to it, and attempts have been made to identify changes in receptors for lectins or the mobility of lectin-associated membrane particles.

The Acrosome Reaction

Capacitation leads to the acrosome reaction, a morphological change in the acrosomal cap of spermatozoa which is a prerequisite for fertilization in mammals. This process involves membrane fusion, which evidently releases enzymes which aid the penetration of spermatozoa between the cumulus cells, and their attachment and possibly movement through the zona pellucida. Morphological descriptions of membrane fusion in the acrosome region of spermatozoa have been extensively documented (Talbot & Franklin, 1976; Yanagamachi & Noda, 1970).

Initially, the anterior part of the acrosome cap begins to swell. Fusion then occurs between the outer acrosomal and plasma membrane resulting in vesiculation, subsequent shedding of the spermhead and release of the contents of the acrosome. The process may be analogous to other forms of membrane fusion, involving depolarization of the plasma and acrosomal membranes, movement of Ca^{2+} across the membrane, rising levels of cAMP and activation of intramembranal enzymes. Spermatozoa may resemble mast cells and resist depolarisation and the formation of calcium channels, until a ligand binds to the membrane during capacitation to depolarize it (Rink, 1977). Initial depolarization could be triggered by the binding of a protein or other molecule to the plasma membrane during capacitation, which might induce the opening of ion channels, activate antibody-complement like reactions or influence intramembranal lysolecithin. Lysophospholipids are involved in the guinea-pig spermatozoal acrosome reaction, but an external source of Ca^{2+} is necessary for the lipids to induce the process (Fleming & Yanagimachi, 1981) (Table 2).

Calcium is evidently involved in capacitation and the acrosome reaction, and magnesium appears to be inhibitory (Green, 1978a; Reyes et al., 1978; Rink, 1977; Talbot et al., 1976; Yanagimachi & Usui, 1974). Calmodulin, the calcium-dependent protein may also be involved in capacitation and vesiculation (Jones et al., 1980). An influx of Ca^{2+} may be mediated by α-adrenergic receptors, and the β-receptors may be involved in the mechanisms which raise the levels of cAMP (Meizel, 1978). Suggestions for the role of calcium ions in the acrosome reaction include neutralizing the negative charges on the outer acrosomal and plasma membranes, thus permitting the fusion of the two; their binding to phospholipids to change membrane permeability; the activation of phospholipases to generate lysophospholipids; and binding to the ATPase which is attached to the outer acrosomal membrane, so activating the acrosomal enzymes. Calcium ions may therefore have a direct effect on the plasma and outer acrosomal membranes, and a further effect modifying the acrosomal proteinases, e.g. activating proacrosin, although this specific function is in dispute (Green, 1978b, c).

A local change may occur initially in the acrosome spreading to the rest of the sperm surface. The tip of the acrosome might be the site where fusion begins (Friend et al., 1977; Green, 1978b). The essential difference between spermatozoa and sensory or secretory cells may

Table 2

The involvement of lysophospholipids and calcium in guinea-pig acrosome reaction[a] (From Fleming & Yanagimachi, 1981)

| | | | | Approximate percent of acrosome reacted spermatozoa | | | | | | |
| | | | | Lysophospholipid in control medium[b] | | | Lysophospholipid in Ca²⁺-free medium[b] | | | |
Time (h)	Control medium	Ca²⁺-free medium	Preincubation in Ca²⁺-free medium	LC	LE	LS	LC	LE	LS	LI
1	—	0	5	5–10	2	5	90	85	0–1	90
2	2	0	10	—	—	—	—	—	—	—
4	5	0	15	30	—	—	90	—	—	—
5	—	—	—	—	5	—	—	95	—	—
8	10	0	50	—	—	—	—	—	—	—
10	—	—	—	—	—	2	—	—	0–1	—
16–18	40	0	80	—	—	—	—	—	—	—

[a] Spermatozoa were continuously incubated with Ca^{2+}, i.e. control medium, with or without lipids; or in Ca^{2+}-free medium, with or without lipids. After preincubation in Ca^{2+}-free medium for various lengths of time, the percent of acrosome-reacted spermatozoa was assessed 10 min after the addition of Ca^{2+}.

[b] LC, lysophosphatidyl choline, 85 μg ml⁻¹; LE, lysophosphatidyl ethanolamine, 210 μg ml⁻¹; LS, lysophosphatidyl serine, 80 μg ml⁻¹; LI, lysophosphatidyl inositol, 140 μg ml⁻¹.

Table 3
Utilization of fructose and glucose by rat spermatozoa in utero *(From Leese* et al.*, 1981)*

	Approximate concentration of sugar (mM)			
	Normal male rat		Vasectomized male rat	
Time (h)	Fructose	Glucose	Fructose	Glucose
0	0.8	0.4	—	0.45
8	0.6	0.3	—	—
10	—	—	0.5	0.6
30	0.3	0.03	—	0.45
60	0.05	0	0.2	0.63

involve the method of opening calcium pores, achieved in the acrosome through the binding of a ligand rather than depolarization by potassium (Green, 1978c). More recently, a rise in the acrosomal pH by a net proton efflux, occurring by the induction of a proton channel in the outer acrosomal and plasma membrane has been suggested as initiating the acrosome reaction in hamster spermatozoa (Working & Meizel, 1981).

The events leading to the acrosome reaction and their timing remain to be explained. Ca^{2+}-dependant contractile microfilaments and microtubules may be involved in the fusion of the plasma and outer acrosomal sheath and post-equatorial segment after vesiculation (Peterson *et al.*, 1978; Stambaugh & Smith, 1978). Actin has also been found in human and animal spermheads associated with the acrosome and postacrosomal sheath (Clarke & Yanagimachi, 1978; Talbot & Kleve, 1978). There has been some disagreement over the energy sources required by spermatozoa during capacitation and the acrosome reaction. Fraser and Quinn (1981) have recently shown that glucose is necessary for the initiation of the acrosome reaction in mouse spermatozoa and the subsequent activated form of spermatozoal motility associated with it (Yanagimachi, 1970). Oxidative metabolism is not required, because glucose is utilized under strict anaerobic conditions. This is further supported by Leese *et al.* (1981) studying rat spermatozoa metabolism *in utero* (Table 3).

Binding of Spermatozoa to the Zona Pellucida

Spermatozoa pass through the cumulus cells, presumably assisted by hyaluronidase and esterases liberated from the acrosome, and oviductal fluid (Bradford *et al.*, 1976). They form a temporary initial attachment with the zona pellucida. The zona pellucida is rich in a network of mucopolysaccharides and glycoproteins and is dissociated by trypsin or related enzymes, mercaptoethanol and by low pH.

Specific molecules may be involved in the weak, temporary attachment. The spermatozoa eventually lay flat on the surface of the zona pellucida, forming a more adherent association prior to their migration through it (Austin, 1975). Specific chemical groups are involved in this attachment and antibodies may react with receptor sites raised against various macromolecules in the zona pellucida or the sperm membrane (Fig. 1) (Bedford, 1972; Dudkiewicz *et al.*, 1976; Hastings *et al.*, 1972; Sellens & Jenkinson, 1975).

Spermatozoal receptors are found throughout the structure of the zona pellucida. They can be extracted, and will bind to spermatozoa, so preventing fertilization (Fig. 1). Antibodies raised against the mouse

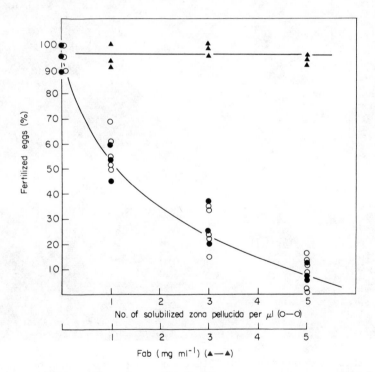

FIG. 1. Fertilizing ability of capacitated hamster spermatozoa, pretreated with different concentrations of heat-solubilized hamster zona pellucida (○) or with Fab antibodies against hamster ovary (▲) or both (●). Published with permission (Ahuja & Tzartos, 1981).

zona pellucida will also prevent fertilization. Nevertheless, the zona receptors do not appear to be antigenic, and the prevention of binding is due to steric hinderance, because the Fab fragments have no effect (Figs. 1 and 2). Three glycoproteins associated with the zona pellucida have been detected in the mouse oocyte, designated ZP1, ZP2 and ZP3; ZP3 has been identified as the probable sperm-binding receptor and this molecule is modified after fertilization (Bleil & Wassermna, 1980a, 1980b). Receptors on hamster and guinea-pig zona pellucida can be modified by trypsin or chymotrypsin, but not by glycosidases or lipases, and binding between spermatozoa and the zona pellucida appears to be independent of pH between 7.0 and 8.5, sensitive to calcium and inhibited by reducing agents. Furthermore, L-fucose seems to be involved in the molecule on the surface of the zona

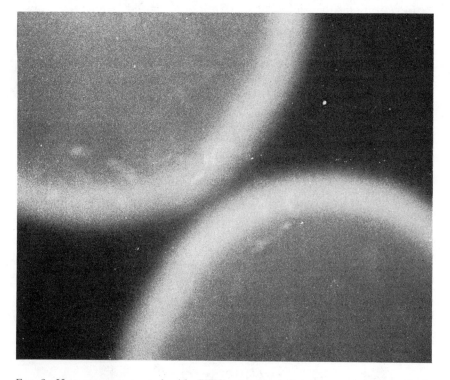

FIG. 2. Hamster eggs treated with FITC-conjugated Fab preparation of antibody against the zone pellucida, using a direct fluorescent antibody test. Only the zona pellucida is fluorescent. Control eggs exposed to FITC-conjugated preimmune Fab preparations were completely non-fluorescent. Published with permission (Ahuja & Tzartos, 1981).

pellucida to which spermatozoa bind (Ahuja, 1982b; Huang, 1981). In contrast with the receptors on the zona pellucida, those on the sperm surface are antigenic. Antigens on the surface of hamster spermatozoa appear to be necessary for spermatozoa to bind to the hamster zona pellucida. Binding is prevented by antisera against spermatozoa, and by Fab fragments prepared from immune sera (Tzartos, 1979).

The binding of spermatozoa to the zona pellucida is highly species specific. Only some closely related species will cross-fertilize, e.g. rabbit and hare. Human spermatozoa will attach to and penetrate the zona pellucida of the gibbon oocyte but not the baboon, rhesus or squirrel monkey.

Movement of Spermatozoa through the Zona Pellucida

The movement of spermatozoa through the zona pellucida may be assisted by enzymes associated with microfilaments and microtubules in the acrosome (Faltas *et al.*, 1975; Peterson *et al.*, 1978; Stambaugh & Smith, 1978). The microfilaments may even help draw the spermatozoa through the zona pellucida.

Acrosin is one of the ''zona lysins'' which is given most attention. It is closely bound to membranes and is localized in the perforatorium. Changes in acrosin in the acrosome during spermatogenesis in the male and during capacitation in the female have been analysed in detail in human spermatozoa (Tobias & Schumacher, 1976). Its formation by autocatalysis from its precurser molecule, proacrosin, is also well documented (Brown & Hartree, 1976; Meizel, 1978; Meizel & Mukerji, 1976). It is inhibited by the polyamine, spermine, which is present in seminal plasma, and must be removed by washing before in-vitro fertilization, because oxidized spermine has a detrimental effect on human spermatozoa (Pulkkeinen *et al.*, 1977). Other inhibitors of acrosin are found in oviductal fluid (Parrish & Polakoski, 1977). But the role of this enzyme in the movement of spermatozoa through the zona pellucida is in question, becuase the spermatozoa may pass through solely by their own motility (Bedford & Cross, 1978).

Three major classes of acrosomal glycoproteins probably exist, shown by the radioactive labelling of rabbit and guinea-pig spermatozoa during spermatogenesis (Kopecný & Fléchon, 1981). One class, such as hyaluronidase, is released prior to the acrosome reaction proper (Yanagimachi, 1977). Secondly, a group of glycoproteins form a firmer association with the outer acrosomal membrane, acrosome-reacted vesicles and the remnants of the acrosomal matrix. These acrosomal enzymes may be involved in the disaggregation of the acrosomal material during the acrosome reaction (Harrison *et al.*, 1982), leading to the diffusion of its contents through the vesiculated outer acrosomal membrane and to the loss of the acrosomal cap. Apparently, the majority of these glycoproteins remain on the surface of the zona pellucida.

The third class is a minor fraction (less than 20%) which remains associated with spermatozoa after their passage through the zona pellucida. Their nature is unknown: they are unlikely to include acrosin, but could encompass glycoproteins located in the equatorial segment since this remains intact after penetration.

No label was detected in the putative "penetration slit" in the zona pellucida suggesting that acrosomal glycoproteins such as acrosin are lost from spermatozoa after the acrosome reaction and before penetration. Movement through the zona pellucida may occur physically, because the motility of spermatozoa is highly exaggerated at this time and the perforatorium may provide a "cutting" edge (Gwatkin, 1977; Yanagimachi, 1970; Bedford & Cross, 1978). However, it is likely that a combination of biochemical and physical actions are utilized to assist spermatozoa in traversing the zona pellucida.

Fusion of the Gametes

Spermatozoa move through the zona pellucida and enter the perivitelline space in a few minutes. Capacitated spermatozoa do not live for long and soon become immotile. They form an initial contact with the plasma membrane of the oocyte, followed by a permanent merging or fusion.

The postacrosomal region is the segment of the spermatozoon involved in the gamete fusion (Austin, 1975). As in the Ascidian oocyte (De Santis *et al.*, 1980), restricted domains in the plasma membrane of the mammalian oocyte may be involved in fertilization. Microvilli on the surface of the oocyte may grasp the spermatozoon, to play an active role in drawing it into ooplasm (Yanagimachi, 1977; Wolf & Hamada, 1979).

The properties of the plasma membrane may be modified during sperm entry in the sea urchin and echinoderm, including changes in lipid and protein mobility (Conway & Metz, 1976; Schneider & Lennarz, 1976). Such modifications may make the membrane more viscous, restricting the mobility of its components after fertilization has occurred. Lysophospholipids may be involved in spermatozoon-egg fusion in mammals (Fleming & Yanagimachi, 1981), although Wolf *et al.* (1981) suggest that no large-scale reorganization of the mouse oocyte membrane occurs, in contrast to the sea urchin.

Specific receptors are obviously involved in fusion, but their chemical nature is obscure. Cholinergic receptors are present on the plasma membrane of mouse oocytes, and the membrane is depolarized by exposure to acetylcholine (Eusebi *et al.*, 1979). The membrane is also desensitized after fertilization, recovering its cholinergic activity in the 2-cell embryo. Acetylcholine receptors and the enzymes necessary for synthesizing this neurotransmitter are present in spermatozoa (Nelson, 1978).

Membrane sites rich in carbohydrates in the post-acrosomal region undergo aggregation during fusion, perhaps achieved by the action of microtubules (Clarke & Yanagimachi, 1978), but this modification may be related to the block to polyspermy rather than gamete fusion. Antibodies will interfere with fertilization, although there is some doubt about the nature of the reaction between antibodies and the plasma membranes; steric hinderance, rather than specific antibody–antigen reactions may prevent fertilization. Antibodies reacting with guinea-pig autoantigens probably located on the inner acrosomal membrane may bind with sperm receptors involved in fusion (Yanagimachi *et al.*, 1981), raising the possibility that similar antigens may also be involved in human fertilization.

Block to Polyspermy

Soon after fusion, a block to polyspermy is established. The most notable visible change is the exocytosis of the cortical granules, lying on the periphery of the egg, and this process is undoubtedly involved in blocking polyspermy. But two distinct blocks evidently exist, one occurring rapidly within a few minutes after fertilization, and the other involving the cortical granules, and occurring after several hours in mammalian eggs (Barros & Yanagimachi, 1972; Wolf, 1978; Yanagimachi, 1978). Polyspermy-blocking mechanisms can be expressed primarily at the egg membrane, as in the rabbit (Braden *et al.*, 1954; Yanagimachi, 1978), or at the egg investments — the zona reaction, e.g. sheep and pig. In some species a combination of both is apparently involved e.g. mouse and rat (Austin, 1975). However, some of the studies remain unconvincing (Dale & Monroy, 1981). The effective block to polyspermy in the ampulla is probably achieved partly by reorganization of the egg surface and partly by the relatively low successful collision rate because so few spermatozoa reach the site of fertilization.

The nature of the rapid block to polyspermy remains to be elucidated. There may be a propogated wave of depolarization, as in sea urchins, which induces the discharge of cortical granules (Gwatkin, 1977; Poste et al., 1975). The fast block does not appear to involve the cortical granules, which evidently require about 15 minutes to break down in vitro (Fraser et al., 1972; Fukuda & Chang, 1978; Sato, 1979). It has been suggested that a fast polyspermic block is electrically mediated (Jaffe, 1976) as the fertilizing spermatozoon induces a rapid overshooting depolarization across the egg plasma membrane, rendering the egg unreceptive to other spermatozoa. This hypothesis of a fast electrical block has been applied to other species (Cross & Elinson, 1980; Gould-Somero et al., 1979; Miyazaki & Hirai, 1979) but the experimental evidence is controversial (Dale & Monroy, 1981).

The exocytosis of cortical granules from the periphery of the oocyte may form a second, slower block to polyspermy by causing an extensive reorganization of the egg surface and the vitelline coat. The process has been extensively studied in the sea urchin where the vitelline coat and the plasma membrane are considered as forming a functional unit due to the "vitelline posts" that connect the two (Kidd, 1978; Chandler & Heuser, 1980). Due to the insertion of patches derived from the membrane of the cortical granules, an extensive alteration occurs in the organization of the egg surface, preventing the passage or binding of any additional spermatozoa.

Clearly, much more information on the block to polyspermy in mammalian eggs is required. Some factors suppressing fertilization have been identified, e.g. neuraminidase and lectins, but their effects may be exerted on the zona pellucida and not the depolarization of the cortical granules. Microtubules may be involved, because the exocytosis from the cortical granules is inhibited by procaine (Ahuja, 1982a) and the eggs become polyspermic.

Exocytosis from the cortical granules almost certainly modifies the plasma membrane and zona pellucida, and a trypsin-like enzyme released from the cortical granules may be responsible (Gwatkin, 1977; Wolf & Hamada, 1979). After exocytosis of the cortical granules, changes can be demonstrated in the egg membrane, which include modifications in the binding of concanavalin A, increased activity in membrane-bound enzymes, e.g. alkaline phosphatase and adenyl cyclase. Also the membrane of the mouse egg looses its sensitivity to acetylcholine after fertilization (Eusebi *et al.*, 1979).

The properties of the zona pellucida are also changed. Modifications include its sensitivity to digestion, and a deposit has been identified on its inner surface. The zona reaction varies in different species as mentioned earlier. It is reported to be strong in the sheep, pig and hamster, but weak in rabbits. On this evidence, it can be considered strong in the human, because few perivitelline spermatozoa have been identified after fertilization *in vitro* (Edwards, 1977). This observation further suggests a combined reaction between the zona pellucida and egg membrane.

If fertilization does not occur soon after ovulation the block to polyspermy is weakened. In some species, the cortical granules migrate centripetally, or they loose their ability to fuse with the egg membrane. In the hamster, the eggs become impenetrable as cortical granules display a spontaneous exocytosis by 24 hours after ovulation (Longo, 1974; Szollosi, 1975). The block to polyspermy may be temporary, becoming reversed with time even with fertilized eggs. This phenomenon has been called "refertilization" (Gulyas, 1974). Parthenogenesis may involve the exocytosis of the cortical granules, but it may be incomplete (Mintz & Gearhart, 1973), allowing fertilization to occur after the eggs have been activated. Once the fusion of egg and spermatozoon is completed, meiosis is resumed in the oocyte resulting in the expulsion of the second polar body, and development of the embryo is initiated.

Human Fertilization *in vitro*

Knowledge on the fundamentals of fertilization in mammals will assist clinical studies on the fertilization of human eggs *in vitro*. The conditions under which spermatozoa are prepared, and the presence of various clinical disorders in the patients, will influence the success of in-vitro fertilization, and we would like to conclude by presenting some of our initial findings on human fertilization.

Various techniques have been used for the preparation of spermatozoa and method of insemination. From observations on the timing of pronuclear development or the first cleavage division, it is clear that capacitation and the acrosome reaction must occur within a few hours in a simple culture medium with the addition of serum, and at a pH slightly above neutral. In our system, Earle's balanced salt solution plus 8% maternal serum is used (Purdy, 1982). The percentage of spermatozoa that are acrosome-reacted during storage at

23 °C has not been assessed, but it is likely to be quite low since spermatozoa remain motile for many days at this temperature. In our experience over more than ten years, the vast majority of eggs have two pronuclei, indicating that polyspermy is very rare (Edwards, 1980; Edwards et al., 1981). The high frequency of eggs with three pronuclei reported by other workers (Trounson et al., 1980, 1981) must have been due to factors such as the aspiration of immature oocytes, the use of high numbers of spermatozoa, deficient culture media, and the use of high levels of clomiphene.

Spermatozoa can be kept at room temperature for at least 48 hours and still successfully fertilize an oocyte, or up to seven days and fertilize zona-denuded hamster eggs (Fishel & Yodyingyuad, unpublished), although motility and activity obviously decline with time. The length of time the spermatozoa can be kept at room temperature, after preparation and before fertilization, is a function of the quality of the initial sample.

Serum albumin could be a major factor involved in capacitation, and substances released from the cumulus cells may also have a role (Soupart & Morgenstern, 1973). In most attempts at fertilization in vitro, there is abundant albumin and other proteins in serum, and numerous cumulus and corona cells surround the oocytes. It is not known if the acrosome reaction occurs before or during binding of the spermatozoa to the zona pellucida, but presumably the latter, because its premature loss would result in an early discharge of the acrosomal contents and, as in other species, this may be associated with a rapid loss of fertility (Gwatkin, 1977). Overall rates of fertilization exceed 75% of all oocytes, and reach over 85% when patients with certain clinical conditions are excluded. Difficulties arise with some semen samples, e.g. sperm agglutination, abnormal liquefaction, retarded activity, abnormal movement or progression, etc. (Tables 4 and 5).

One group with overt problems encompasses men with various types of sperm agglutination (Table 4). This primary difficulty is presumably caused by locally-secreted IgA (Edwards, 1976; Friberg & Tilley-Friberg, 1977). Many prefertilization and fertilization events in the guinea-pig and other animal species involve antigenic molecules on or in spermatozoa, and antibodies might also interfere with the function of receptor molecules, blocking sperm–egg interactions (Tung et al., 1980; Yanagimachi et al., 1981; Tzartos, 1979). In our studies, various types of agglutination of spermatozoa have been observed, from less severe duplets and triplets to the very severe and large clumps of spermatozoa. Maternal serum is used in the preparation of spermatozoa and might also contain IgG and/or IgM antibodies

Table 4

Success of fertilization in vitro in 182 patients classified according to sperm type. Data from natural cycle and clomiphene combined

Classification of spermatozoa	No. of patients	No. with 1 or more eggs fertilized (%)	Total no. of eggs	No. of eggs fertilized (%)
A. "Satisfactory" spermatozoa	95	87 (92%)	116	99 (85%)
B. Conditions compatible with high rates of fertilization				
Head clumping in small clusters, many immotile	6	6	11	11
Viscous seminal plasma[a]	5	4	7	6
C. Conditions slightly reducing rates of fertilization				
Some cells and debris	25	20	33	23
Many immotile spermatozoa, others sluggish and erratic	20	12	26	13[b]
D. Conditions seriously reducing rates of fertilization				
Massive clumping of spermatozoa	10	5	11	5
Severe oligospermia without other associated conditions[c]	2	1	3	2
Tail agglutination, many immotile in some patients	12[d]	5	12	5
Massive amounts of cells and debris	7	2	7	2

[a] One patient with severe oligospermia had one egg fertilized.
[b] Four of these unfertilized eggs in one patient. Three patients with oligospermia, two with eggs fertilized.
[c] Altogether eight of the patients in this table had oligospermia, and five had a fertilized egg (see Table 5).
[d] Two patients with severe oligospermia, one egg fertilized in one of them.

against spermatozoa or the zona pellucida. Fertilization *in vito* does sometimes occur with less severe forms of agglutination, indeed many females with immunity against spermatozoa are able to conceive naturally, but few of the men with seminal antibodies are ever fertile (Isojima *et al.*, 1974; Jones, 1976; Petrunia *et al.*, 1976). Treatment of immunity in men and women in the short term may be successful using corticosteroids (Shulman, 1976), but successful in-vitro fertilization may be preferable using medium containing heterologous serum. We have initiated a new method of collecting semen in cases where the wife has significant titres of sperm antibodies in serum and the husband has autoantibodies in the seminal plasma. Ejaculation is carried out into a pot containing medium with heterologous serum, and washing, centrifuging and resuspending an aliquot of this sample is performed within an hour. Storage of the spermatozoa in the same medium almost eliminates sperm agglutination and permits fertilization *in vitro*. Men with sperm agglutination might therefore be offered fertilization *in vitro* in an attempt to alleviate their infertility.

Cellular immunity could also arise against spermatozoa, e.g. in mice (Dorsman *et al.*, 1978) but evidence in the human is conflicting (Marcus *et al.*, 1978; Mathur *et al.*, 1980; Mettler *et al.*, 1980). In contrast to the literature on humoral immunity, little is known about cell-mediated immunity to spermatozoa; T lymphocytes may share a common antigen(s) with spermatozoa (Mathur *et al.*, 1980).

A further area where in-vitro fertilization is achieving success is in the treatment of oligospermia (Tables 4 and 5). Severe oligospermia is not a barrier to successful fertilization *in vitro* providing care is used in the preparation of spermatozoa and the activity of the motile spermatozoa is good. The total number of motile spermatozoa in the insemination drop is not critical, and we routinely use about 8×10^4 spermatozoa ml^{-1}. Good forward progress by the gametes is probably essential if fertilization is to occur. Two patients, whose husbands are oligospermic, have each recently delivered a healthy baby, and embryos have been obtained from several couples where the husband had oligospermia.

Another difficult condition is the presence of numerous cells or debris together with the spermatozoa. Some of these conditions seem to arise through inflammation in the male tract, or through the desquamation of spermatogenic cells. It is difficult to obtain clean samples, although the layering method under paraffin described earlier in this symposium by Purdy (1982) has greatly helped with a simple method to remove many of the cells. Fertilization rates are nevertheless low in this condition (Table 4). Massive clumping of spermatozoa

Table 5
Fertilization in vitro *in patients with idiopathic infertility or oligospermia*

I. Idiopathic infertility

Condition	No. of patients with one oocyte or more	No. of patients with one oocyte or more fertilized	Total no. of oocytes	Number of oocytes fertilized
Idiopathic	10	9 (90%)	15	12 (80%)
"Controls"[a]	95	87 (92%)	116	99 (85%)

II. Oligospermia

No. of spermatozoa $(10^6\,ml^{-1})$	Motility (% motile)	Total no. of patients with one oocyte or more	No. of patients with one or more oocytes fertilized	Total no. of oocytes	No. of oocytes fertilized
25–40	<20<20	3	2	3	2
10–<25	<20	7	6	9	7
5–<10	<20	6	4	6	4
V. few[b]		9	7	10	7
V. few[c]		6	2	6	2
Total		31	23 (74%)	34	22 (65%)
"Controls"[a]		95	87 (92%)	116	99 (85%)

[a] See Table 4; patients with "satisfactory" spermatozoa.
[b] Whole sample centrifuged to obtain sufficient spermatozoa; counts very low indeed, much less than 5×10^6, and many spermatozoa were immotile.
[c] Whole sample centrifuged and layered under paraffin to remove cells (Purdy, 1982).

also reduces rates of fertilization, although the cause is not clear.

Some "intermediate" conditions slightly depress rates of fertilization *in vitro*. The presence of a few cells and debris, or weak and sluggish motility are disadvantages which can be overcome in many patients (Table 4). Presumably, poor motility could result in the failure of spermatozoa to penetrate between the corona radiata, or to traverse the zona pellucida. Many more studies are needed to relate sperm motility with the causes of failure.

Some conditions do not seem to interfere significantly with fertilization *in vitro*. These include head clumps in small clusters, the presence of numerous immotile spermatozoa, the presence of viscous seminal plasma and idiopathic infertility in the couple (Tables 4 and 5). It is very encouraging that high success rates can be achieved even if only a few progressive, motile spermatozoa are available. We have not observed low rates of fertilization nor pronuclear anomalies in idiopathic patients, unlike the reports of Trounson *et al.* (1980). Introducing patients with the conditions described in Tables 4 and 5 brings considerable hope of alleviating these causes of infertility through fertilization *in vitro*. This is a major step forward since their combined number, plus those with tubal occlusion, form considerably more than one-half of all infertile couples (Edwards, 1980).

Acknowledgements

We wish to thank Miss Helen Izzard for help in the preparation of this manuscript.

References

Ahuja, K. 1982a. Inhibition *in vitro* of the block to polyspermy in the hamster eggs by tertiary amine local anaesthetics. *Journal of Reproduction and Fertility*, in press.

Ahuja, K. 1982b. Fertilization studies in the hamster: the role of cell-surface carbohydrates. *Experimental Cell Research*, in press.

Ahuja, K. & Tzartos, S. 1981. Investigation of sperm receptors in the hamster zona pellucida by using univalent (Fab) antibodies to hamster ovary. *Journal of Reproduction and Fertility*, 61, 257–264.

Aitken, R. J. & Richardson, D. W. 1981. Mechanisms of sperm-binding inhibition by anti-zona antisera. *Gamete Research*, 4, 41–47.

Austin, C. R. 1965. *Fertilization*. Prentice Hall, New Jersey.

Austin, C. R. 1975. Membrane fusion events in fertilization. *Journal of Reproduction and Fertility*, 44, 155–166.

Barros, C. & Yanagimachi, R. 1972. Polyspermy-preventing mechanisms in the golden hamster egg. *Journal of Experimental Zoology*, 180, 251–266.

Bavister, B. D. 1979. Fertilization of hamster eggs *in vitro* at sperm : egg ratios close to unity. *Journal of Experimental Zoology*, 210, 259–264.

Bavister, B. D. 1981. Bovine serum albumin is required for efficient capacitation of hamster spermatozoa *in vitro*. *Biology of Reproduction*, 24, Suppl. 1, 37A.

Bavister, B. D., Rogers, B. J. & Yanagimachi, R. 1978. The effects of cauda epididymal plasma on the motility and acrosome reaction of hamster and guinea-pig spermatozoa *in vitro*. *Biology of Reproduction*, 19, 358–363.

Beck, J. A., Edwards, R. G. & Young, M. R. 1962. Immune fluorescence and the isoantigenicity of mammalian spermatozoa. *Journal of Reproduction & Fertility*, 4, 103–110.

Bedford, J. M. 1972. An electron microscopic study of sperm penetration into the rabbit egg after natural mating. *American Journal of Anatomy*, 133, 213–254.

Bedford, J. M. & Cross, N. L. 1978. Normal penetration of rabbit spermatozoa through a trypsin- and acrosin-resistant zona pellucida. *Journal of Reproduction and Fertility*, 54, 385–392.

Bleil, J. D. & Wasserman, P. M. 1980a. Structure and function of the zona pellucida: identification and characterization of the proteins of the mouse oocyte's zona pellucida. *Developmental Biology*, 76, 185–202.

Bleil, J. D. & Wasserman, P. M. 1980b. Mammalian sperm-egg interaction:

identification of a glycoprotein in mouse egg zonae pellucidae possessing receptor activity for sperm. *Cell*, **20**, 873–882.

Braden, A. W. H., Austin, C. R. & David, H. A. 1954. The reaction of zona pellucida to sperm penetration. *Australian Journal of Biological Sciences*, **7**, 391–409.

Bradford, M. M., McRovie, R. A. & Williams, W. L. 1976. Involvement of esterases in sperm penetration of the corona radiata of the ovum. *Biology of Reproduction*, **15**, 102–106.

Brown, C. R. & Hartree, E. F. 1976. Comparison of neural proteinase activities in cock and ram spermatozoa and observations on proacrosin in cock spermatozoa. *Journal of Reproduction and Fertility*, **46**, 155–164.

Chandler, D. E. & Heuser, J. 1980. The vitelline layer of the sea urchin egg and its modification during fertilization. *Journal of Cell Biology*, **84**, 618–632.

Clarke, G. N. & Yanagimachi, R. 1978. Actin in mammalian sperm heads. *Journal of Experimental Zoology*, **205**, 125–132.

Conway, A. F. & Metz, C. B. 1976. Phospholipase activity of sea urchin sperm: its possible involvement in membrane fusion. *Journal of Experimental Zoology*, **198**, 39–48.

Cornett, L. E. & Meizel, S. 1978. Stimulation of in-vitro activation and the acrosome reaction of hamster spermatozoa by catecholamines. *Proceedings of the National Academy of Sciences*, **75**, 4954–4958.

Cross, N. L. & Elinson, R. P. 1980. A fast block to polyspermy in frogs mediated by changes in the membrane potential. *Development Biology*, **75**, 187–198.

Dale, B. & Monroy, A. 1981. How is polyspermy prevented? *Gamete Research*, **4**, 151–169.

Dan, J. C. 1954. Studies on the acrosome. III. Effects of calcium deficiency. *Biological Bulletin*, **107**, 335–349.

De Santis, R., Jamunno, G. & Rosati, F. 1980. A study of the chorion and of the follicle cells in relation to sperm-egg interaction in the Ascidian, *Ciona intestinalis*. *Developmental Biology*, **74**, 490–499.

Dorsman, B. G., Tumlooh-Oeri, A. G. & Roberts, T. K. 1978. Detection of cell-mediated immunity to spermatozoa in mice and man by the leucocyte adherence-inhibition test. *Journal of Reproduction and Fertility*, **53**, 277–283.

Dudkiewicz, A. B., Shivers, C. A. & Williams, W. L. 1976. Ultrastructure of the hamster zona pellucida treated with zona precipitating antibody. *Biology of Reproduction*, **14**, 175–185.

Edwards, R. G. 1976. Immunity and the control of human fertility. In: *Immunology of Human Reproduction*. Eds. J. S. Scott and W. R. Jones. Academic Press, London.

Edwards, R. G. 1977. Early human development: from the oocyte to implantation. In: *Scientific Foundations of Obstetrics and Gynaecology*, pp.175–252. Eds. E. E. Philipp, J. Barnes and M. Newton. Heinemann Medical, London.

Edwards, R. G. 1980. *Conception in the Human Female*. Academic Press, London.

Edwards, R. G., Purdy, J. M., Steptoe, P. C. & Walters, D. E. 1981. The growth of human preimplantation embryos *in vitro*. *American Journal of Obstetrics and Gynecology*, **141**, 408–416.

Eusebi, F., Mangia, F. & Alfei, L. 1979. Acetylcholine-elicited responses in primary and secondary mammalian oocytes disappear after fertilization. *Nature*, **277**, 651–652.

Faltas, S., Smith, M. & Stambaugh, R. 1975. The organised distribution of acrosomal proteinase within the acrosomes of rabbit spermatozoa. *Fertility and Sterility*, **26**, 1070–1074.

Fleming, A. D. & Yanagimachi, R. 1981. Effects of various lipids on the acrosome reaction and fertilizing capacity of guinea pig spermatozoa with special reference to the possible involvement of lysophospholipids in the acrosome reaction. *Gamete Research*, **4**, 253–273.

Fraser, L. R. & Quinn, P. J. 1981. A glycolytic product is obligatory for initiation of the sperm acrosome reaction and whiplash motility required for fertilization in the mouse. *Journal of Reproduction and Fertility*, **61**, 25–35.

Fraser, L. R., Dandekar, P. V. & Gordon, M. K. 1972. Loss of cortical granules in rabbit eggs exposed to spermatozoa *in vitro*. *Journal of Reproduction and Fertility*, **29**, 295–297.

Friberg, J. & Tilley-Friberg, I. 1977. Antibodies in human seminal fluid. In: *Human Semen and Fertility Regulation in Men*, pp.258–264. Ed. E. S. E. Hafez. C. B. Mosby, St. Louis.

Friend, D. S., Orci, L., Perrelet, A. & Yanacimachi, R. 1977. Membrane particle changes attending the acrosome reaction in guinea-pig spermatozoa. *Journal of Cell Biology*, **74**, 561–577.

Fukuda, Y. & Chang, M. C. 1978. The time of cortical granule breakdown and sperm penetration in mouse and hamster eggs inseminated *in vitro*. *Biology of Reproduction*, **19**, 261–266.

Go, K. J. & Wolf, D. P. 1981. BSA-mediated lipid fluxes in mouse spermatozoa: a molecular model for bovine serum albumin in mouse sperm capacitation. *Biology of Reproduction*, **24**, Suppl. 1, 37A.

Gould-Somero, M., Jaffe, L. A. & Holland, L. Z. 1979. Electrically-mediated fast polyspermy block in eggs of the marine worm, *Urechis cavpo*. *Journal of Cell Biology*, **82**, 426–440.

Green, D. P. L. 1978a. The induction of the acrosome reaction in guinea-pig sperm by the divalent metal cation ionophore A23187. *Journal of Cell Science*, **32**, 137–151.

Green, D. P. L. 1978b. The activation of proteolysis in the acrosome reaction of guinea-pig sperm. *Journal of Cell Science*, **32**, 153–164.

Green, D. P. L. 1978c. The mechanism of the acrosome reaction. In: *Development in Mammals*, Vol. 3, pp.65–81. Ed. M. H. Johnson. North-Holland, Amsterdam.

Gulyas, B. J. 1974. Electron microscopic observations on advanced stages of spontaneous polyspermy in rabbit zygotes. *Anatomical Record*, **179**, 285–296.

Gwatkin, R. B. L. 1977. *Fertilization Mechanisms in Man and Animals*. Plenum Press, New York.

Harrison, R. A. P., Fléchon, J.-E. & Brown, C. R. (1982). The location of acrosin and proacrosin in ram spermatozoa. *Journal of Reproduction and Fertility*, in press.

Hastings, R. A., Enders, A. C. & Schlafke, S. 1972. Permeability of the zona pellucida to protein tracers. *Biology of Reproduction*, **7**, 288–296.

Huang, J. 1981. On the nature of sperm-zona pellucida recognition in the guinea pig. *Biology of Reproduction*, **24**, Suppl. 1, 108A.

Hyne, R. V. & Garbers, D. L. 1981. Requirement of serum factors for capacitation and the acrosome reaction of guinea pig spermatozoa in buffered medium below pH 7.8. *Biology of Reproduction*, **24**, 257–266.

Isojima, S., Koyama, K. and Tsuchiya, K. 1974. The effect on fertility in women of circulating antibodies against human spermatozoa. *Journal of Reproduction and Fertility*, (Suppl) **21**, 125–150.

Jaffe, L. A. 1976. Fast block to polyspermy in sea urchin eggs is electrically mediated. *Nature*, **261**, 68–71.

Jones, H. P., Lenz, R. W., Palevitz, B. A. & Cormier, M. J. 1980. Calmodulin localization in mammalian spermatozoa. *Proceedings of the National Academy of Sciences*, **77**, 2772–2776.

Jones, W. R. 1976. Immunological aspects of infertility. In: *Immunology of Human Reproduction*, p.375. Eds. J. S. Scott and W. R. Jones. Academic Press, London.

Kidd, P. 1978. The jelly and vitelline coats of the sea urchin egg: new ultrastructure features. *Journal of Ultrastructural Research*, **64**, 204–215.

Kopecny, V. & Flechon, J.-E. 1981. Fate of acrosomal glycoproteins during the acrosomal reaction and fertilization: a light and electron microscope autoradiographic study. *Biology of Reproduction*, **24**, 201–216.

Leese, H. J., Astley, N. R. & Lambert, D. 1981. Glucose and fructose utilization by rat spermatozoa within the uterine lumen. *Journal of Reproduction and Fertility*, **61**, 435–437.

Longo, F. J. 1974. An ultrastructural analysis of spontaneous activation of hamster eggs aged *in vivo*. *Anatomical Record*, **179**, 27–56.

Lui, C. W., Cornett, L. E. & Miezel, S. 1977. Identification of the bovine follicular fluid protein involved in the in-vitro induction of the hamster sperm acrosome reaction. *Biology of Reproduction*, **17**, 34–41.

Marcus, Z. H., Freisheim, J. H., Houk, J. L., Herman, J. H. & Hess, E. V. 1978. In-vitro studies in reproductive immunology. I. Suppression of cell-mediated immune response by human spermatozoa and fractions isolated from human seminal plasma. *Clinical Immunology and Immunopathology*, **9**, 318.

Mathur, S., Goust, J.-M., Williamson, H. O. & Fundenberg, H. H. 1980. Antigenic cross-reactivity of sperm and T-lymphocytes. *Fertility and Sterility*, **34**, 469–476.

Meizel, S. 1978. The mammalian sperm acrosome reaction, a biochemical approach. In: *Development in Mammals*, Vol. 3, pp. 1–64. Ed. M. H. Johnson. North-Holland, Amsterdam.

Meizel, S. & Mukerji, S. K. 1976. Biochemical studies of proacrosin and acrosin from hamster cauda epididymal spermatozoa. *Biology of Reproduction*, **14**, 444–450.

Mettler, L., Schirwani, D. & Gradl, T. 1980. The occurrence of sperm antibodies in human reproduction. *American Journal of Obstetrics and Gynecology*, **136**, 106–116.

Mintz, B. & Gearhart, J. D. 1973. Subnormal zona pellucida changes in parthenogenetic mouse embryos. *Developmental Biology*, **31**, 178–184.

Miyazaki, S. & Hirai, S. 1979. Fast polyspermy block and activation potential. Correlated changes during oocyte maturation of a starfish. *Developmental Biology*, **70**, 327–340.

Moore, H. D. M. & Bedford, J. M. 1978. An in-vivo analysis of factors influencing the fertilization of hamster eggs. *Biology of Reproduction*, **19**, 879–885.

Nelson, L. 1978. Chemistry and neurochemistry of sperm motility control. *Federation Proceedings*, **37**, 2543–2547.

Olson, G. E. & Hamilton, D. W. 1978. Characterization of the surface glycoproteins of rat spermatozoa. *Biology of Reproduction*, **19**, 26–35.

Parrish, R. F. & Polakoski, K. L. 1979. Effect of polyamines on the activity of acrosin and the activation of proacrosin. *Biology of Reproduction*, **17**, 417–422.

Peterson, R., Russell, L., Bundman, D. & Freund, M. 1978. Presence of microfilaments and tubular structures in boar spermatozoa after chemically inducing the acrosome reaction. *Biology of Reproduction*, **19**, 459–466.

Petrunia, D. M., Taylor, P. J. & Watson, J. I. 1976. A comparison of methods of screening for sperm antibodies in the serum of women with otherwise unexplained infertility. *Fertility and Sterility*, **27**, 655–661.

Phillips, D. M. 1977. Surface of the equatorial segment of the mammalian acrosome. *Biology of Reproduction*, **16**, 128–137.

Poste, G., Papahadjopoulos, D. & Nicolson, G. L. 1975. Local anaesthetics affect transmembrane cytoskeletal controls of mobility and distribution of cell surface receptors. *Proceedings of the National Academy of Sciences*, **72**, 4430–4434.

Pulkkeinen, P., Sinervirta, R. & Janne, J. 1977. Mechanism of action of oxidized polyamines on the metabolism of human spermatozoa. *Journal of Reproduction and Fertility*, **51**, 399–404.

Purdy, J. M. 1982. Methods for fertilization and embryo culture *in vitro*. In: *Human Conception in vitro*. Eds. R. G. Edwards & J. M. Purdy. Academic Press, London (in press).

Reddy, J. M., Stark, R. A. & Zaneveld, L. J. D. 1979. A high molecular weight antifertility factor from human seminal plasma. *Journal of Reproduction and Fertility*, **57**, 437–446.

Reyes, A., Coicoechea, B. & Rosado, A. 1978. Calcium ion requirement for rabbit spermatozoal capacitation and enhancement of fertilizing ability by ionophore A23187 and cyclic adenosine $3':5'$-monophosphate. *Fertility and Sterility*, **29**, 451–455.

Rink, T. J. 1977. Membrane potential of guinea-pig spermatozoa. *Journal of Reproduction and Fertility*, **51**, 155–157.

Sato, K. 1979. Polyspermy-preventing mechanisms in mouse eggs fertilized *in vitro*. *Journal of Experimental Zoology*, **210**, 353–360.

Schneider, E. G. & Lennarz, W . J. 1976. Glycosyl transferases of eggs and embryos of *Arbacia punctata*. *Developmental Biology*, **53**, 10–20.

Sellens, M. H. & Jenkinson, E. J. 1975. Permeability of the mouse zona pellucida to immunoglobulin. *Journal of Reproduction and Fertility*, **42**, 153–158.

Shulman, S. 1976. Treatment of immune male infertility with methylprednisolone. *Lancet*, **2**, 1243.

Soupart, P. & Morgenstern, L. L. 1973. Human sperm capacitation and in-vitro fertilization. *Fertility and Sterility*, **24**, 462–478.

Stambaugh, R. & Smith, M. 1978. Tubulin and microtubule-like structures in mammalian acrosomes. *Journal of Experimental Zoology*, **203**, 134–141.

Szollosi, D. 1975. Mammalian eggs aging in the fallopian tubes. In: *Aging Gametes, their Biology and Pathology*, p. 98. Ed. R. J. Blandau. Karger, Basel.

Talbot, P. & Franklin, L. E. 1976. Morphology and kinetics of the hamster sperm acrosome reaction. *Journal of Experimental Zoology*, **198**, 163–169.

Talbot, P. & Kleve, M. G. 1978. Hamster sperm cross-react with antiactin (1). *Journal of Experimental Zoology*, **204**, 131–136.

Talbot, P., Summers, R. G., Hylander, B. L., Keogh, E. M. & Franklin, L. E. 1976. The role of calcium in the acrosome reaction: an analysis using ionophore A23187. *Journal of Experimental Zoology*, **198**, 383–391.

Tobias, P. S. & Schumacher, G. F. B. 1976. The extraction of acrosin from human spermatozoa. *Biology of Reproduction*, **15**, 187–194.

Trounson, A. O., Leeton, J. F., Wood, C., Webb, J. & Kovacs, G. 1980. The investigation of idiopathic infertility by in-vitro fertilization. *Fertility & Sterility*, **34**, 431–438.

Trounson, A. O., Wood, E. C., Leeton, J. F., Webb, J., Wood, J., Buttery, B., Mohr, L., McTalbot, J., Jessup, D. & Kovacs, G. 1981. A programme of successful in-vitro fertilization and embryo transfer in the controlled ovulatory cycle. In: *Third World Congress of Human Reproduction*, Berlin. Excerpta Medica, Amsterdam.

Tung, K. S. K., Okada, A. & Yanagimachi, R. 1980. Sperm autoantigens and fertilization. I. Effects of antisperm autoantibodies on rouleaux formation, viability and acrosome reaction of guinea pig spermatozoa. *Biology of Reproduction*, **23**, 877–886.

Tzartos, S. J. 1979. Inhibition of in-vitro fertilization of intact and denuded hamster eggs by univalent anti-sperm antibodies. *Journal of Reproduction and Fertility*, **55**, 447–455.

Van Blerkom, J. & Motta, P. 1979. *The Cellular Basis of Mammalian Reproduction*. Urban & Schwarzenberg, Baltimore.

Van Der Ven, H. H., Bhattacharyya, A. K., Kaminski, J., Binor, Z., Bauer, L. & Zaneveld, L. J. D. 1981. Inhibition of human sperm capacitation by proteinase inhibitors and a high molecular weight factor from human seminal plasma. *Biology of Reproduction*, **24**, Suppl 1, 38A.

Wolf, D. P. 1978. The block to sperm penetration in zona-free mouse eggs. *Developmental Biology*, **64**, 1–10.

Wolf, D. P. & Hamada, M. 1979. Sperm binding to the mouse egg plasmalemma. *Biology of Reproduction*, **21**, 205–211.

Wolf, D. E., Edidin, M. & Handyside, A. H. 1981. Changes in the organization of the mouse egg plasma membrane upon fertilization and first cleavage: indications from the lateral diffusion rates of fluorescent lipid analogs. *Developmental Biology*, **85**, 195–198.

Working, P. K. & Meizel, S. 1981. A role for acrosomal pH in the hamster sperm acrosome reaction. *Biology of Reproduction*, **24**, Suppl. I, 82A.

Yanagimachi, R. 1970. The movement of golden hamster spermatozoa before and after capacitation. *Journal of Reproduction and Fertility*, **23**, 193–196.

Yanagimachi, R. 1977. Specificity of sperm-egg interaction. In: *Immunobiology of Gametes*, p. 225. Eds. M. Edidin and M. H. Johnson. Cambridge University Press, Cambridge.

Yanagimachi, R. 1978. Sperm-egg association in mammals. *Current Topics in Developmental Biology*, **12**, 83–107.

Yanagimachi, R. & Noda, Y. L. 1970. Ultrastructural changes in the hamster sperm-head during fertilization. *Journal of Ultrastructural Research*, **31**, 465–485.

Yanagimachi, R., Okada, A. & Tung, K. S. K. 1981. Sperm autoantigens and fertilization. II. Effects of anti-guinea pig sperm autoantibodies on sperm-ovum interactions. *Biology of Reproduction*, **24**, 512–518.

Yanagimachi, R. & Usui, N. 1974. Calcium dependence of the acrosome reaction and activation of guinea-pig spermatozoa. *Experimental Cell Research*, **89**, 161–174.

Immunological and Other Problems with Human Spermatozoa

L. Mettler, V. Baukloh and H.-H. Riedel

Pathological conditions in the male reproductive tract, and in the seminal plasma, could impair the chances of achieving the fertilization of human eggs *in vitro*. Inflammatory conditions may lead to the presence of numerous leucocytes in the seminal plasma. Infections may impair the quality of samples of human spermatozoa. In man, as in many animals, immunological methods are known to influence the rate of fertilization (Mettler *et al.*, 1980, 1981; Edwards *et al.*, 1981). Compared with the magnitude of other causes of human infertility, the group with antibodies is rather small, but it is nevertheless significant.

We will first describe an experimental model in mice, in which antibodies against spermatozoa were demonstrated to interfere with fertilization. Next, we will consider the significance of antibodies, bacterial flora and various other pathological conditions which may impair human fertilization. Lastly, we will discuss briefly the value of the zona-free hamster egg as a model to test the fertilizing capacity of human spermatozoa.

Antibodies Against Spermatozoa and the Impairment of Fertilization in Mice

It is well recognized that mice immunized with mouse spermatozoa become infertile (Mettler *et al.*, 1980). The precise mechanisms involved are as yet unknown. The influence of antispermatozoal antibodies on fertility was established in an allogeneic mouse system by experiments investigating the interactions of antibodies with the

Department of Obstetrics and Gynaecology of the Christian Albrechts University, and Michaelis Midwifery School of Kiel, Hegewischstrasse 4, 2300 Kiel 1, Federal Republic of Germany.

following five levels of development:
  (a) Interactions with isolated gametes.
  (b) Interactions at fertilization.
  (c) Interactions on developing embryos prior to implantation.
  (d) Interactions during the implantation of the blastocyst.
  (e) Interactions during postimplantation development.

Inbred mice were used in the study. Epididymal spermatozoa, and spermatozoa of the deferent duct were obtained by gentle pressure on 2 cm of the deferent duct, and by tearing and squeezing the epididymis. These spermatozoa were used as antigens. Mouse spleen cells were obtained from male mice to serve as control antigens.

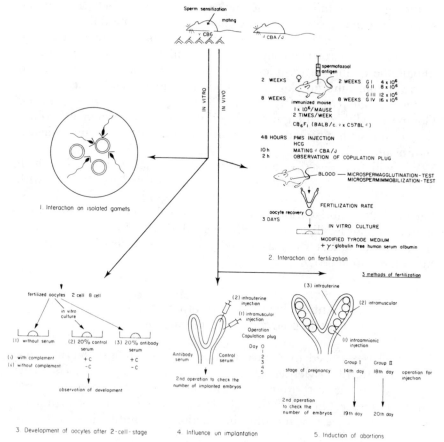

FIG. 1. Experimental system to investigate the influence of sperm antibodies on fertilization and early embryonic development.

Table 1
Influence of antisera against mouse spermatozoa on the rates of in-vitro fertilization of mouse oocytes

Treatment		Total no. of oocytes	No. of cleaving oocytes	Percent cleaving
Control	None	112	55	49.1
Control	Normal serum	51	21	41.2
Control	Sera prepared against erythrocytes	43	17	39.5
Treated	Antisera against spermatozoa	68	2	2.9
Treated	γ-globulin fraction of antisera against spermatozoa	80	1	1.3

High-titre antibodies against spermatozoa were produced by intraperitoneal injections of mice with spermatozoa. For controls, other mice were given similar intraperitoneal injections of spleen cells. Spermatozoal antibodies were assessed by microagglutination and microimmobilization tests using mouse spermatozoa, and by the use of immunofluorescence techniques (Friberg, 1974; Husted and Hjort, 1975; Mettler & Gradl, 1980).

A plan of the experiment is shown in Fig. 1. It was intended to test interactions between antispermatozoal antibodies and isolated gametes, and the effects of these antibodies on fertilization and implantation. We discovered that spermatozoal antibodies reduced the rates of fertilization *in vitro* in comparison with control antisera (Table 1). These antibodies also interfered with fertilization *in vivo*, or at least suppressed the early stages of growth after fertilization, as shown by the steady decline in the number of embryos reaching the 2-cell stage in various groups of immunized females, compared with controls (Fig. 2). The immunized females produced a reduced number of large blastocysts (Table 2).

We also analysed the interactions of these antibodies with developmental stages prior to implantation. Embryos were obtained at the 2-cell and 8-cell stages and were exposed *in vitro* to media containing 20% of antispermatozoal antibodies (see the experimental design in Fig. 1). There was no difference in cleavage, and in the morphology of embryos exposed to control sera and to antisera against spermatozoa. Nevertheless, after the incubation of embryos with antisera to spermatozoa from the 2-cell stage to blastocyst, a statistically significant reduction of hatching was observed in comparison with

Table 2
Size of blastocysts in control and immunized mice

Group of mice*	No. of large blastocysts	No. of small blastocysts (% in brackets)
Control	53	30 (36%)
Group 1	25	19 (43%)
Group 2	46	44 (49%)
Group 3	27	32 (54%)
Group 4	11	19 (63%)

*Groups of mice described in Fig. 1. Large blastocysts were >110 μ in diameter. Significantly more small blastocysts were found in the immunized groups (χ^2 = 13.5; p < 0.01).

controls. No such difference was seen when 8-cell embryos were treated in a similar manner, the proportion of embryos hatching being similar in all groups (Table 3).

Similar experiments were attempted *in vito* (see Fig. 1). High-titred antisera against spermatozoa were given via intrauterine or intramuscular injections to females during various stages of pregnancy. When these injections were given on day 0 and day 1 of pregnancy, there was no effect on implantation. Only in those groups given intramuscular injections on days 2, 3 and 4 after mating was a

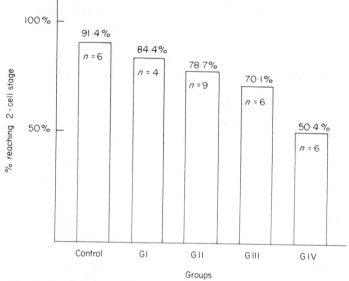

FIG. 2. The percentage of fertilized oocytes reaching the 2-cell stage. The various groups are described in Fig. 1. The percentage in group 4 was significantly lower than controls (p < 0.05).

Table 3
Influence of antisera against spermatozoa on the development of mouse embryos in vitro

Serum	Complement added	No. of embryos	No. reaching blastocyst	Percent hatching
1. Antisera added between 2-cell stage and blastocyst				
None	No	32	25	41
None	Yes	32	23	28
Control	No	31	22	39
Control	Yes	18	14	28
Antiserum	No	35	16	6
Antiserum	Yes	39	26	8
2. Antiserum added between 8-cell stage and blastocyst				
None	No	4	3	50
None	Yes	8	8	80
Control	No	6	6	67
Control	Yes	7	7	71
Antiserum	No	9	9	67
Antiserum	Yes	10	10	70

statistically significant decline noted in the rate of implantation in comparison with controls. Thus, the transformation of uterine tissues was impeded only by high titres of antispermatozoal sera.

The influence of sperm antibodies on postimplantation development was also tested. We attempted to induce abortions by means of these antibodies, injecting them into pregnant mice. No effect was observed in all three experimental groups as compared with controls.

Sperm Antibodies and Human Fertilization

These results indicate that the infertility effect of immunity to spermatozoa is primarily expressed as a block to fertilization. If men and women with such immunity are to be included in an in-vitro fertilization programme, it may then be advisable to use sera which have been typed for HLA, and found to be identical to the mother. These sera could be added to the growth media instead of the mother's serum, and also be used to wash the spermatozoa before fertilization. Moreover, in-vitro fertilization might reduce the exposure of spermatozoa to such antibodies and thereby improve rates of fertilization.

We have recently obtained results with hybridoma technique, to obtain monoclonal antibodies allowing the definition of relevant antigens on spermatozoa (Milstein & Kohler, 1977). When attached to a matrix, such antigens may be used to elute out specific antibodies from various serum samples before they are used for fertilization *in vitro*. At the present time, this approach has not been applied, but it promises to be of value in achieving fertilization *in vitro* using serum from patients with antibodies against spermatozoa.

Assessing Human Spermatozoa for in-vitro Fertilization

Ejaculates with certain criteria are a predominant prerequisite for successful in-vitro fertilization in man, and also in the human–hamster system. A careful investigation has been carried out on spermatozoa before the patients were introduced into an in-vitro programme. It is important to observe not only the concentration of spermatozoa in ejaculate, but also their motility and morphology, and to screen for certain round cellular elements and bacterial microorganisms. We routinely check all samples for anaerobic bacteria, mycoplasma and *Clamydia*. All of our sperm donors are investigated prior to in-vitro fertilization, and wherever possible a detailed bacteriological investigation is carried out. Using the human sperm : zona-free hamster egg system (Yanagimachi *et al.*, 1976), we have detected a correlation between the existence of pathological bacteria, e.g. *Staphylococci*, *E. coli*, etc., and the degeneration of hamster eggs *in vitro*.

The pathway between the site of fertilization, and the meeting point of egg and sperm, is obviously greatly shortened by in-vitro fertilization. But fertilization does not occur with literally any kind of spermatozoa. The criteria of sperm quality may not be as severe as is necessary for in-vivo fertilization, but they must nevertheless be identified. *In vivo*, a concentration of between 10 and 20 $\times$ 10^6 ml^{-1} spermatozoa does not lead to any significant reduction of fertilization if spermatozoal motility is good (McLeod and Gold, 1951; Smith *et al.*, 1977; Zuckermann *et al.*, 1977). The preparation of spermatozoa for in-vitro fertilization, e.g. by washing and centrifuging, leads automatically to a 10% reduction in the initial concentration. It is well known that for in-vitro fertilization of human and hamster eggs, a concentration of at least 50,000 to 100,000 of good motile and morphologically spermatozoa are needed. An initial concentration in the ejaculate of at least between 2 and 5 $\times$ 10^6 ml^{-1} motile spermatozoa is therefore necessary.

There are relatively few published accounts about the significance of sperm quality for in-vitro fertilization. Moreover, they are very contradictory. Between May, 1980, and Spring, 1981, we assembled a special collection of couples in order to assess the influence of andrological parameters on fertilization. Human in-vitro fertilization was assessed, and so too was the penetration of zona-free hamster eggs by human spermatozoa. Normal and pathological ejaculates were tested.

During these investigations, we performed 74 follicular punctures via pelviscopy, 46 in spontaneous cycles and 28 after previous stimulation by HMG and HCG or by clomiphene and HCG. Many oocytes were aspirated. In the four cases where cleavage was achieved, the husbands had normozoospermia. Only one of the husbands had a slight degree of oligospermia, having 31×10^6 ml^{-1} spermatozoa with normal morphology and motility.

In nine cases, the mature egg degenerated. We found a more or less pathological ejaculate in eight of the men. At present, we cannot discuss in detail the possible contribution of egg degeneration because both non-mature or over-mature eggs were aspirated in this group.

In 25 women, in-vitro fertilization was not achieved after the aspiration of one or more oocytes. In all these cases, the ejaculates of the husband showed a reduced sperm count and more or less pathological conditions according to our criteria (Table 4).

Table 4

Spermigrams of 25 husbands used for in-vitro fertilization where cleavage did not occur

Condition	Number
Oligozoospermia (10^7 sperm ml^{-1})	3
Oligoteratozoospermia ($<10^7$ sperm ml^{-1}, 30% normal morphology)	3
Oligoasthenozoospermia ($<10^7$ sperm ml^{-1}, $<30\%$ motility)	13
Asthenozoospermia ($<30\%$ motility)	1
Asthenoteratozoospermia ($<30\%$ motility, normal morphology)	4
Hyperzoospermia ($>1.8 \times 10^8$ ml^{-1})	1
Fructose deficiency ($<1200\ \mu g$)	1

These results demonstrate the need for a careful examination of the andrological parameters in men being introduced into programmes of in-vitro fertilization. Pathological conditions of virtually any type will impair success rates, and the couples should be cautioned accordingly.

The Zona-free Hamster Egg as a
Model for Assessing Human Spermatozoa

Different authors have described the wide variation in fertilization rates of zona-free hamster eggs by spermatozoa taken from fertile and infertile men. Yanagimachi *et al.* (1976) reported that about 56% of hamster eggs were fertilized using spermatozoa from normal, fertile men, compared with only 2–3% using spermatozoa from infertile men. In a group of men with a normal sperm count, we have established a fertilization rate of about 51%. With slightly pathological ejaculates, fertilization rates of 36% have been obtained, while pathological spermatozoa always result in a low fertilization rate of less than 10% (Table 5).

Table 5

Influence of sperm quality on the rates of penetration of human spermatozoa into zona-free hamster oocytes in vitro

Type of spermatozoa*	No. of samples	Percent penetration	Range (%)
Normal	19	53.9	38–80
Weakly pathological	37	34.2	21–64
Strongly pathological	35	9.5	0–32

*Weakly pathological: normal morphology > 50%, motile > 74%, numbers > 10^7 ml^{-1}. Strongly pathological: normal morphology < 50%, motile < 40%, numbers < 10^7 ml^{-1}. The difference between penetration rates in the normal and pathological samples were significant ($p \leq 0.01$).

The statistically significant increase in fertilization rates of hamster eggs with normal spermatozoa illustrates the relationship between successful fertilization and sperm concentration, motility and morphology. According to our investigations, we believe that the in-vitro fertilization of human eggs requires similarly high sperm qualities as in the hamster egg system. Perhaps we should only consider couples for an in-vitro fertilization programme if the andrological parameters of the husbands are normal or slightly pathological. Before a couple can be introduced into such a programme, two or three andrological investigations are necessary, including an extensive bacteriological analysis.

In attempts to identify some of the causes of low rates of fertility under "Pathological" conditions, we have tried to investigate some of the problems with sperm capacitation and penetration into hamster eggs. We have added ascorbic acid, fluid from the Pouch of Douglas, and kallikrein to the pathological ejaculates prior to incubation with oocytes. The addition of L-ascorbic acid and body fluids to the pathological samples of spermatozoa resulted in an increased motility of at least 15%, and also in penetration rates of 15% greater. This positive effect could be due to an increased sperm motility, or to a better capacitation process, although more investigations are obviously needed. Similar attempts to improve human in-vitro fertilization have not yet been made.

Summary

Sperm antibodies influence gametes during and after fertilization and impair embryonic development prior to implantation in mice. The immunobiological consequences of sperm immunity may perhaps be avoided by the use of in-vitro fertilization. Certain other criteria must be fulfilled in the human spermiogram to obtain fertilization *in vivo* or *in vitro*. A better fertilization rate may be obtained *in vitro* than *in vivo* with minimal sperm concentrations of between 10^6 and 5×10^6 ml^{-1}, more than 30% motility and more than 30% normal morphology, provided the ejaculates are free of bacteria. These criteria could also be applied to cases of oligospermia and to cases where antibodies exist.

Meeting these conditions could help many infertile couples. Follicular puncture via laparoscopy, even in cases of many adhesions due to previous operations, does not prevent the aspiration of many oocytes (Mettler *et al.*, 1981). At present, our cleavage rates are still poor, and embryo replacement has only been tried in three cases, each of them unsuccessful. Nevertheless, we hope to greatly improve fertilization rates and replacement procedures for our patients as described by others (Steptoe *et al.*, 1980; Lopata *et al.*, 1980; Trounson *et al.*, 1980), and to extend our work to helping couples with pathological problems involving spermatozoa.

References

Edwards, R. G., Mettler, L., Talwar, P., Goldberg, E., Wegman, T. & Bratanov, K. 1981. Will immunology ever help in the control of human fertility? *Round table, III World Congress of Human Reproduction*, Berlin. Excerpta Medica, Amsterdam.

Friberg, J. 1974. Immunological studies on sperm agglutinating sera from women. *Acta. Obstet. Gynec. Scand.*, Suppl. **36**, 31.

Husted, S. & Hjort, T. 1975. Microtechnique for simultaneous determination of immobilizing and cytotoxic sperm antibodies. *Clinical and Experimental Immunology*, **22**, 256–264.

Lopata, A., Johnston, I. W. H., Hoult, I. J. & Speirs, A. I. 1980. Pregnancy following implantation of an embryo obtained by in-vitro fertilisation of a preovulatory egg. *Fertility and Sterility*, **33**, 117.

McLeod, J. & Gold, R. Z. 1951. The male factor in fertility and sterility. II. Spermatozoon counts in 1000 cases of known fertility and in 1000 cases of infertile marriage. *Journal of Urology*, **66**, 436.

Mettler, L., Seki, M., Baukloh, V. & Semm, K. 1980. Different factors influencing mice in-vitro fertilization. *Infertility*, **3**, 217–229.

Mettler, L. & Gradl, T. 1980. The occurrence of sperm antibodies in human reproduction. *American Journal of Obstetrics and Gynecology*, **136**, 106–116.

Mettler, L., Seki, M., Baukloh, V. & Semm, K. 1981. Erste Ergebnisse zur extrakorporalen Befruchtung am Menschen. *Geburtshilfe und Frauenheilkunde*, **41**, 62.

Milstein, C. & Köhler, G. 1977. Cell fusion and the derivation of cell lines producing specific antibodies. In: *Antibodies in Human Diagnosis and Therapy*. Eds. E. Haber and R. M. Krause. Raven Press, New York.

Smith, K. D., Rodriguez-Rigau, L. J. & Steinberger, E. 1977. Relation between indices of semen analysis and pregnancy rate in infertile couples. *Fertility and Sterility*, **28**, 1314–1319.

Steptoe, P. C., Edwards, R. G. & Purdy, J. M. 1980. Clinical aspects of pregnancies established with cleaving embryos grown in vitro. *British Journal of Obstetrics and Gynaecology*, **87**, 757–768.

Trounson, A. O., Leeton, J., Wood, J. F., Webb, J. & Kovacs, G. 1980. The investigation of idiopathic infertility by in-vitro fertilization. *Fertility and Sterility*, **34**, 431–438.

Yanagimachi, R., Yanagimachi, H. & Roger, B. J. 1976. The use of zona-free animal ova as a test-system for the assessment of the fertilizing capacity of human spermatozoa. *Biology of Reproduction*, **15**, 471–476.

Zuckermann, Z., Rodriguez-Rigau, L. J., Smith, K. D., & Steinberger, E. 1977. Frequency distribution of sperm counts in fertile and infertile males. *Fertility and Sterility*, **28**, 1310–1313.

Discussion on the Fertilization of
Human Oocytes *in vivo* and *in vitro*

Capacitation, the Acrosome Reaction, and Gamete Fusion

Jones, H: Does the spermatozoa at the vitelline membrane have to be acrosome-reacted or not? This may not be of importance in the normal situation, but could be in the oligospermic situation, where the number of spermatozoa are limited. If there was a choice, would it be preferable to have a maximum number of acrosome-reacted spermatozoa from an oligospermic patient?

Fishel: There may be species variations in mammals in the timing of the reaction. An acrosome reaction at the vitelline membrane has recently been demonstrated in the guinea-pig, and it is required for the binding of the sperm to the egg. There have been suggestions that the acrosome reaction is necessary in other species before binding occurs between the sperm and the zona pellucida. But, whatever happens, the acrosome reaction must occur either at, or during binding, prior to penetration of the zona pellucida. This must, presumably, occur with oligospermic patients too, although there is no such detailed data on the human. In every species that we know of, it appears that the reaction must take place before ordinary binding occurs. Perhaps the best answer about numbers of acrosome-reacted spermatozoa is that, if the eggs are fertilized, then spermatozoa from oligospermic men must, presumably, have undergone the acrosome reaction beforehand.

Jones, H: Is there information on the lowest number of motile spermatozoa that can be used for fertilization *in vitro*?

Mettler: In studies on the penetration of hamster eggs by human spermatozoa, we did not feel able to go below 200,000 ml^{-1}. Below this, rates of penetration decline.

Fishel: We can go to half that amount, and perhaps much lower. In some cases, if the spermatozoa are highly progressive and motile, the addition of 200,000 ml^{-1} to an insemination droplet appears to reduce the chances of fertilization by causing a premature removal of cumulus

191

and corona cells from the oocyte. We have obtained fertilization with numbers as low as 50–100,000 ml^{-1}, and even lower.

Jones, H: This returns debate to the situation regarding the acrosome reaction and fertilization *in vitro*. Is there any idea of the number of acrosome-reactive spermatozoa there must be in those numbers just quoted? It is pertinent to the oligospermic situation where, I assume, as many acrosome-reacting spermatozoa would be needed as possible.

Fishel: There is some data in the hamster, where it was shown that 10% of acrosome-reactive spermatozoa in any particular sample are sufficient to achieve fertilization *in vitro* (Fleming & Yanagimachi, 1981).

Jones, H: But if the number of spermatozoa with an acrosome reaction could be manipulated, should there be 25% or 50% of them in oligospermic patients in order to achieve fertilization *in vitro*? The longer they are washed, the more will have had an acrosome reaction.

Edwards: I am not sure how the number of spermatozoa with an acrosome reaction could be manipulated in the human situation. I know of no evidence to indicate the number of acrosome-reacted spermatozoa in relation to the conditions of washing and the components of the culture media. It would depend on the medium being used, its pH, etc. Capacitation may take place *in vitro*, but the acrosome reaction, that is the "true" acrosome reaction, might occur only near the oocyte. Other acrosome reactions may be "false" (Meizel, 1978). Perhaps lysophospholipids or catecholamines would help if added to the culture media.

Trounson: There is one further point we must consider here. If spermatozoa are left *in vitro* for some time, e.g. for two days, many of them will be acrosome-reacted. Is it a good thing to leave eggs in contact with acrosome-reactive spermatozoa like this? Will they have any deleterious effects on the egg?

Edwards: I do not know the answer to that point but many acrosome-reacted spermatozoa soon die. We spin the spermatozoa down twice, and suspend them at room temperature. We do not put them in the incubator during the preincubation phase, so there may be a difference due to temperature. There is also a second point to be considered. We obtain the spermatozoa before the oocytes are recovered, wash them, and leave them standing at room temperature *in vitro* for at least two hours and usually more before fertilization occurs. In this way, we hope that capacitation is happening while the oocyte is maturing, so that both will be coincident when insemination takes place. The number of acrosome-reacted spermatozoa may be different under these conditions to other conditions. I believe that motile spermatozoa will have an intact acrosome, at least most of them. When the eggs are added, spermatozoa in the vicinity of the egg might undergo an acrosome reaction very quickly.

Lopata: There are several reports that microfilaments are involved in fertilization. Are these present in the sperm, the oocyte, or the zona pellucida?

Fishel: The microfilaments are present on the surface of the sperm. They are not present in the zona pellucida. I was not referring to the grasping of the egg by the microvilli on the plasma membrane of the oocyte.

Edwards: There are some beautiful pictures in mammalian species showing how microfilaments and microtubules are associated with the acrosomal membrane (Peterson *et al.*, 1978; Stambaugh & Smith, 1978). Actin and tubulin have been found in sperm heads, in association with the acrosome (Talbot & Kleve, 1978). Microfilaments and microtubules could be involved in the acrosome reaction, sperm movement through the zona pellucida and gamete fusion.

Testart: There were claims for the presence of antifertilisin in mammalian oocytes (Thibault & Dauzier, 1960). During the early days of fertilization *in vitro*, Thibault suggested that it was necessary to wash the egg many times to remove this substance before fertilization occurred.

Fishel: I have no direct evidence, and there must be doubts that it exists. We get high rates of fertilization without washing the eggs.

Testart: Yes, but we are now told that it is preferable to leave the eggs maturing *in vitro* for five hours after collection before insemination. During this time, the antifertilisin could be removed from the eggs, and this could result in your higher rates of fertilization.

Fishel: You may be right. We may lose such compounds from eggs which are not fully mature when they are collected and inseminated. But I strongly doubt that washing removes any antifertilization factor from a ripe egg. The oocytes are simply left in culture with the intention of completing maturation, and some eggs can be fertilized immediately they are withdrawn if they are ripe already.

Abnormal Spermatozoa, Oligospermia and Fertilization *in vitro*

Trounson: There has been some discussion about the possibility of abnormal spermatozoa fertilizing human eggs *in vitro*. What sort of abnormalities have been involved in various studies, and what effects do they have on fertilization rates *in vitro*?

Fishel: This is an interesting point. We see various forms of abnormality in samples of spermatozoa, including some with many cytoplasmic droplets, others with erratic movement, some with bent tails. In most cases, they do not seem to affect our fertilization rates. In one recent case, a particular man had 80% of spermatozoa which appeared to consist solely of a sperm head and perhaps a mid-piece, but no tail. Nevertheless, the two oocytes available from his wife were fertilized and they were replaced as cleaving embryos a few days later. I know of no other similar case in the literature. We would normally expect a lower rate of fertilization in such cases. Presumably, the few remaining sperm with tails were able to achieve fertilization.

We can break down our failure in fertilization into two groups. One group, which we call unexplained, and the "problematical" group, where extraneous factors are preventing fertilization, as opposed to our techniques. Our fertilization rate is 90% approximately of all oocytes if we exclude cases of severe agglutination, non-ovulatory oocytes that were inseminated, abnormal liquefaction of the semen, etc. There is very little difference between the natural cycle and clomid stimulation.

Lopata: We had an unusual case arising from an oligospermic man. All his spermatozoa were immotile, and he was treated with corticosteroids. Motility then rose to 10%, and samples of his sperm were frozen. When thawed for fertilization *in vitro*, we were able to fertilize the two oocytes available. This is a remarkable example of a man initially with immotile spermatozoa being able to fertilize an egg ultimately.

Fishel: It is important to make sure that spermatozoa are scored after washing. Sometimes, there is an increase in motility after washing, so care must be taken about scoring them as zero motility until this test is performed. Some of our cases have had a very weak sperm motility but, after washing, and letting them stand for a few hours, many spermatozoa showed an improved activity.

Jones, G: What were the actual number of motile spermatozoa used for fertilization in Lopata's case?

Johnston: 500,000 ml^{-1} were used for fertilization *in vitro*. The reason for freezing these spermatozoa was the presence of high levels of immobilizing antibody. The man was treated with extremely high levels of cortisol for a few months, and the spermatozoa were then held in frozen storage for 2–3 months before fertilization *in vitro*. This was necessary because the man could not accept further treatment with cortisol.

Steptoe: Many gynaecologists face problems with oligospermia and weak sperm motility in their patients. We often get figures sent to us describing very low counts of sperm numbers and motility, e.g. 400,000 ml^{-1} with a motility of 20% or less. What would you offer us here? Is there a good chance of achieving fertilization *in vitro*?

Fishel: We have fertilized eggs *in vitro* using samples in which only 10% of the spermatozoa are active. In a sense, we also have the opposite situation concerning oligospermia, where most of the few spermatozoa are active. Many patients have been referred as oligospermic, sometimes severely so. Yet, for the purposes of fertilization *in vitro*, they had adequate numbers of spermatozoa, and only in very severe cases, in virtually azoospermic men or those with other problems, are we concerned about the possibility of obtaining fertilization.

Care is required about what we mean about oligospermia. In some patients who are known clinically to be oligospermic, various conditions of stress or duress may lead them to produce an oligospermic sample. In cases of severe oligospermia, more than one-third have had at least one egg fertilized and an embryo replaced and one such patient has given birth to a healthy girl. In cases of idiopathic infertility, we have fertilized 90% of the eggs, and replaced the embryos in most of the patients.

Mettler: There is still a difficult problem in relating the number of spermatozoa in the ejaculate to fertilization *in vitro*. What are the minimum number required, and how about their motility?

Fishel: We have achieved fertilization *in vitro* with astonishingly low numbers of spermatozoa. Fertilization can be achieved in most of these men, but success really depends on factors other than number. We like to see good, active spermatozoa, and a good forward, progressive movement. Under these conditions, a total of 10^6 spermatozoa is quite sufficient to make an attempt at fertilization *in vitro*.

Antibodies Against Spermatozoa

Johnston: We cannot use hamsters in Australia because they are not indigenous and we cannot import them! We have looked at 45 cases of men with oligospermia and other problems. As far as we can see, the fertilization and cleavage rates *in vitro* in these cases were exactly the same as in patients with tubal occlusion. The eggs were taken from the wife in the usual way, so the comparison was made in a strictly human system. Our results thus differ from those given by Mettler, and it will be interesting to see how the two systems evolve. I must stress that these included all kinds of patients, including those with antibodies.

Edwards: What are the immunoglobulin classes found in human seminal plasma that react with human spermatozoa? Can anything be done about it when the information is available?

Mettler: We keep a close watch on antibodies in the semen, because some men may produce local IgA, which is a strongly agglutinating antibody and might interfere with fertilization. We have screened some ejaculates using sperm agglutination for the presence of immuno-globulins, and have found IgA. It is possible that the presence of IgA does interfere with fertilization, but a lot of data are needed before a satisfactory answer can be given to this question. In the woman, we have found IgG and IgM, and local IgA in cervical secretions.

Trounson: A group of immunologists in Australia have suggested that the ejaculate should be collected directly into culture medium, to reduce the titre of antibodies. Is there any validity to this idea, or in the use of ejaculates collected in this way?

Mettler: It is a very good idea. It should be tested, although I know of no evidence on it.

Edwards: I would suggest that the important thing is to dilute the seminal plasma as quickly as possible, and in as specific a way as possible. Perhaps adding large amounts of serum to the culture medium would be beneficial, so that the seminal plasma and spermatozoa come into contact immediately with immunoglobulins in the serum. In this way, the serum immunoglobulins might coat the spermatozoa, perhaps even binding to the same sites that the agglutinating IgA would compete for. Another method is to add a monovalent antibody to the culture fluid, which will bind specifically to the binding sites, but will not cause sperm agglutination. The monovalent antibody may not prevent fertilization. There is also some possibility of using F_{ab} fragments of immune IgA in the culture medium to prevent the binding of a specific IgA.

Bacteriology of Semen and Fertilization *in vitro*

Hillensjo: Is it necessary to carry out bacterial analyses as a routine on all the semen samples collected for fertilization *in vitro*?

Mettler: Our experience is not extensive, and our fertilization and cleavage rates are lower than other groups, so they may give preferen-tial answers. Nevertheless, we often have great difficulty in obtaining fertilization and cleavage in the presence of bacteria in the semen. It seems as if the normal systems are disrupted in some way, and the infection prevents normal growth. Approximately 20% of the sperm samples are contaminated.

Edwards: The bacteriology of semen should be taken very seriously in our opinion. Many of the samples are infected with either pathogens or surface contaminants. Could other groups give some idea of their method to prevent contamination, including the use of antibiotics? We use only penicillin routinely. Our men are tested frequently, including an examination just before they come for treatment, but we are still very much aware of the problem.

Trounson: All our men are screened as they first come into the programme, and, more importantly, during the cycle of treatment. On day 7 or 8 of the cycle, we take a swab from the cervix of the wife, and a semen sample from the husband. We receive the microbiological information back in about two days, and if we find any excessive infection, then the patient is not treated during that month. He is given the antibiotics and in-vitro fertilization is performed when the infection is controlled. If there is a viral infection, we have at times reluctantly gone ahead, and we have not noticed any deleterious effects. We use streptomycin and penicillin in our culture media, at the normal levels that many other people have described. One of the most severe infections we had was from Brewer's Yeast, and I do not know where that came from.

Lieberman: When you take swabs from the vagina, do you mean the vagina, or the cervix?

Trounson: We use a random high vaginal swab.

Storing Spermatozoa *in vitro* or in the Deep Freeze

Feichtinger: There was a great deal of discussion in earlier times about the interval needed for spermatozoa to undergo capacitation *in vitro*. Excessive duration of incubation was even believed to reduce their fertilizing capacity. What is the current situation?

Trounson: There is one piece of information here. Quinn *et al.* (1982) have recently been looking at human spermatozoa incubated overnight. The sperm have been incubated for a period of 12–18 hours, and were still able to fertilize hamster eggs.

Edwards: We have been able to fertilize human eggs 48 hours after aspiration, using spermatozoa that were 48 hours old. But, once again, it is important to define the situation. The spermatozoa had been left at room temperature after washing, and were maintained under the correct gas phase. The critical conditions must be defined, e.g. the addition of albumin, serum, or anything else to the culture media.

Fishel: On one occasion, we have inseminated a human oocyte with spermatozoa that were aged 24 hours since collection, and an embryo was transferred and a pregnancy has resulted. This shows that spermatozoa can be kept in the fertilizing state for this length of time under the conditions of our clinic.

Feichtinger: What is the shortest period spermatozoa can be preincubated for fertilization *in vitro*?

Trounson: We use spermatozoa almost immediately they are collected. We spin them down, and leave them to migrate up the tube from the sediment for about 20 minutes. We achieve very high rates of fertilization. Our electron-microscopic studies, indicate that fertilization occurs very rapidly under these conditions. But let me stress that we do incubate the oocyte for six hours before the spermatozoa are added.

Fishel: In recent work, we have found that spermatozoa can be left in dishes in culture medium, under correct gas conditions, at room temperature, for up to 14 days. Many remain motile, and they retain their fertilizing capacity as judged by their ability to fertilize hamster eggs *in vitro*. This approach may be useful in oligospermic cases, if two or three samples are produced within that interval.

Trounson: Using spermatozoa which has been frozen, with similar characteristics as that used for A.I., we have exactly the same fertilization as with non-frozen semen. There is probably a reasonable case to do a proportion of inseminations with frozen semen, particularly where the husband has to travel quite long distances. There is a psychological advantage in having the couple together, but there are many reasons why it is often difficult for the husband to always be there. We centrifuge the sperm sample, but let spermatozoa swim into the medium from the pellet for between 20 and 45 minutes. We are testing five different culture media at present.

With frozen spermatozoa in approximately 18 cases, our fertilization rate as determined by pronuclei is similar to that with unfrozen sperm. The criteria of semen quality for freezing and artificial insemination are an excess of 6×10^6 ml^{-1} spermatozoa and motility in excess of 60%. If freezing immobilizes more than 50% of the motile spermatozoa, then we reject the sample.

The Husband as a Patient

Edwards: We have practised collecting the sperm sample before laparoscopy, so that we know we have the spermatozoa before the oocytes are collected. We have been loathe to ask the surgeon to proceed until we know there are sufficient active spermatozoa for fertilization. Sometimes, the semen sample may be very delayed, and has not arrived by the time the laparoscopy is due. This is a difficult situation because we do not wish to expose the wife to laparoscopy if the sperm sample should not arrive at all. We wish to help the husband as much as possible, and consider him just as much a patient as the wife. In fact, we generally find that virtually all of the husbands eventually produce a sperm sample, so the problem is probably not severe. Would others comment on the methods of collection of the sperm sample? We must be very sympathetic to the husband in this situation.

Trounson: I agree that this problem is slight. We ask husbands for a sperm sample when they first come to the clinic, so that we have some idea what to expect eventually when they enter the programme. They come to the hospital to produce a sample, rather than bringing it from home, and at that time we find out if any problem exists about masturbation, and encourage them to practice. If they have already produced one or two samples in the hospital before in-vitro fertilization was attempted, and this is the usual case, then we do not have any problems. A few men are unable to masturbate by themselves. Our anaesthetist can usually arrange a reasonably light anaesthesis and the wife is soon awake if they prefer to participate together. Psychiatrists, in fact, believe that we should try to encourage this as a form of behaviour.

Johnston: In the investigation of infertility in Melbourne, we are more and more asking men to produce their sperm samples at the laboratory. For various reasons, we get a much better idea of what the motility is, and we are sure that the sample we have is, in fact from the husband, and not from one of his friends. In the process, the men are therefore trained, to work under less-than-ideal conditions for sperm production. We have changed recently from asking the husband to produce his sample before laparoscopy to producing it afterwards, and my impression is that they find it easier. Beforehand, they were worried about their wife's laparoscopy an hour or two hence, and if they are having trouble, then time runs out on them. When they know the egg is there and they have upwards of 3–4 hours to produce a sample, the pressure on them seems to be less.

Trounson: We do not ask husbands to produce a sample if there is no egg. That is one slight advantage to some husbands. Another advantage arises for husbands who cannot produce a sample under such a stressful situation. Five or six hours later, his wife has usually recovered and can assist.

References

Fleming, A. D. & Yanagimachi, R. 1981. Fertilizable lifetime of acrosome-reacted guinea-pig spermatozoa. *Biology of Reproduction*, **24**, Suppl. 1, p. 108A.

Meizel, S. 1978. The mammalian sperma acrosome reaction, a biochemical approach. In: *Development in Mammals*, vol. 3, pp. 1–64. Ed. M. H. Johnson. North-Holland, Amsterdam.

Peterson, R., Russel, L., Bundman, D. & Freund, M. 1978. Presence of micro-filaments and tubular structures in boar spermatozoa after chemically inducing the acrosome reaction. *Biology of Reproduction*, **19**, 459–466.

Quinn, P., Barros, C. & Whittingham, D. G. 1982. Preservation of hamster oocytes to assay fertilizing capacity of human spermatozoa. *Journal of Reproduction and Fertility* (in press).

Stambaugh, R. & Smith, M. 1978. Tubular and microtubule-like structures in mammalian acrosomes. *Journal of Experimental Zoology*, **203**, 134–141.

Talbot, P. & Kleve, M. G. 1978. Hamster sperm cross react with antiactin (1). *Journal of Experimental Zoology*, **198**, 163–169.

Thibault, C. & Dauzier, L. 1960. "Fertilisines" et fécondation *in vitro* de l'oeuf de Lapine. *Comptes Rendus Hebdomadaires des Seances de l'Academie des Sciences*, **250**, 1358–1359.

A discussion on methods of culture for fertilization *in vitro* is given on page 149.

Factors Influencing the Success of Fertilization and Embryonic Growth *in vitro*

A. O. Trounson

Introduction

When assessing in-vitro fertilization and the factors which influence the successful outcome of embryo transfer we are dealing with multifactorial systems which interact in varying degree and direction depending on the procedures set at any one time. During optimization of the treatment, factors identified as important at one point in time may no longer be critical after procedures have changed. There are many examples of this in the past and there will be many more in the future. However, there are a number of basic components which are themselves critical to the success of in-vitro fertilization. An appreciation of their significance will ensure that groups introducing these methods will at least have the potential to initiate a successful programme.

Oocyte Maturation and Follicular Oestrogen Secretion

One way to ensure that the ovulating follicle and oocyte is completely mature is to monitor the ovulatory cycle for the preovulatory LH surge. The potential of this procedure was recognized and used by Edwards *et al.* (1980). Under these circumstances the ovulatory follicles generate sufficient oestrogen to induce LH release and furthermore those follicles are then capable of binding and responding to endogenous LH release which initiates the final phase of oocyte maturation.

The difficulties of this system reside in the resources required and the

Department of Obstetrics and Gynaecology, Monash University and Queen Victoria Medical Centre, Melbourne, Australia.

precision of detecting LH release (Trounson *et al.*, 1981b). One way of overcoming these problems is to use HCG to initiate the final phase of oocyte maturation, instead of relying on detection of the LH surge. However, if this is done, the function of the growing follicles must be assessed, as premature exposure of the follicles to HCG will lead to the production of abnormal oocytes and embryos (Trounson, 1982).

Follicle function may be assessed by examination of plasma or urinary oestrogen levels and this has been reviewed by Trounson (1982). Rising oestrogens in the natural cycle or rising oestrogens in combination with one or two ultrasound reviews of follicle size and number in the stimulated cycle, will identify the time of HCG injection. The criteria for HCG injection used in our own studies has been described by Trounson *et al.* (1981a).

Ultrasound cannot be used as the sole criterion for HCG injection in the stimulated cycle because of the poor relationship between follicle size and the onset of the LH surge (Trounson, 1982). An analysis of follicle size, as determined by ultrasound, and oestrogen levels has shown that oestrogen levels increase at a variable follicle size (1.5 to 2.5 cm diameter), so that injection of HCG at some arbitrary follicular diameter (e.g. 1.8 cm) will be inappropriate in many cases. As a consequence, non-viable oocytes and embryos will be obtained and pregnancy rates after embryo transfer will be low (Trounson, 1982).

Oocyte Maturation and Delayed Insemination

Follicular oocytes obtained at laparoscopy may not have completed maturation, despite the appearance of cumulus and changes in the nuclear chromatin. In studies on the maturation of sheep oocytes (Moor & Warnes, 1978; Trounson *et al.*, 1981a), delayed insemination resulted in a dramatic improvement of the proportion of normally fertilized oocytes, blastocysts and live young. In our experiments with human oocyte, we obtained a marked increase in the proportion of fertilized oocytes and apparently normal embryos by incubating oocytes in culture media for 5 to 6 hours after collection and before insemination (Trounson *et al.*, 1982). The consequences of insemination of oocytes immediately after recovery at laparoscopy were:

(a) Reduced fertilization, due probably to failure of complete maturation of the zona pellucida. In most of the oocytes, spermatozoa were unable to fully penetrate the zona, a situation similar to that when immature oocytes are inseminated at the germinal vesicle stage.

(b) Increased incidence of polyspermy, due to incomplete maturation of cortical granules (Sathananthan & Trounson, 1982). Immediately after oocyte recovery, cortical granules may still be forming and migrating to the surface of the vitelline membrane. Supernumery spermatozoa can enter the oocyte before the oocyte is capable of discharging sufficient cortical granules to enable the zona reaction to occur.

(c) Delayed fertilization of up to 12 hours leading to delayed cleavage, fragmentation and retarded embryo development.

All the pregnancies obtained by our group have resulted from oocytes preincubated for 4 to 8 hours before insemination, and includes at least one case of an ovulated oocyte recovered from the Pouch of Douglas.

Culture Media and Quality Control Procedures

All culture media and materials in contact with oocytes and embryos must be non-toxic and suitable for tissue culture. In our laboratory, we go to great lengths to check this. We do not accept culture media which does not support the growth of more than 90% of mouse embryos from the 2-cell stage to hatched blastocysts. A similar criterion is used to check all new introductions of culture tubes, dishes, transfer catheters and glassware. In this way we have isolated toxic components and suboptimal procedures.

At the present time we are testing a variety of culture media including Hams F10, modified Whittens medium (Hoppe & Pitts, 1973), Earle's medium and Whittinghams T6. There are no apparent differences in fertilization or embryo cleavage rates in these media and we are evaluating the resulting pregnancy rates in a 12-month randomized trial.

The nutritional requirements of human oocytes and embryos have not been established and present studies are complicated by the addition of human serum to culture media. In a comparative study of hatched human, mouse and cattle blastocysts (Mohr & Trounson, 1982) we concluded that at the levels of the light and electron microscope, human embryos grown *in vitro* can show the normal developmental changes expected of other species fertilized and grown *in vivo*. Any culture system used for human in-vitro fertilization should be capable of supporting development *in vitro* to the hatched blastocyst stage. If this cannot be done the system should be examined and re-optimized. The procedures presently used for embryo culture in our laboratory are described in detail by Trounson & Wood (1981) and Trounson *et al.* (1982).

Fertilization and Cleavage

Semen is obtained from the husband after collection of oocytes from the wife, and spermatozoa are prepared by the normal methods of centrifugation and resuspension (Trounson *et al.*, 1980, 1982). We inseminate the oocyte in 1 ml of culture medium in Falcon 5 ml culture tubes with 20,000 to 50,000 spermatozoa. These numbers have been titred by the number of spermatozoa bound to the zona pellucida of oocytes examined by interference-light microscopy.

Oocytes are examined about 16 hours after insemination for pronuclei. The criteria for normal fertilization is cleavage of pronuclear oocytes. Furthermore, cleavage should be within the intervals expected for that stage (Trounson *et al.*, 1982). The first cleavage should occur between 22 and 30 hours after insemination and thereafter at 10- to 12-hour intervals.

Regular cleavage and even division is an important element of normal embryo development. Fragmentation and uneven cleavage is indicative of abnormal development or sub-optimal culture conditions. All our pregnancies have arisen from embryos with normal cleavage states (Trounson *et al.*, 1982), although some have had small cytoplasmic fragments in association with equal sized blastomeres. The presence of small anucleate particles or fragments in viable sheep embryos has been described by Killeen & Moore (1971).

Temperature, Humidity and Gas Phase

Although it may be ideal to maintain oocytes and embryos at culture temperature (37 to 37.5 °C), this is usually impracticable. We are not concerned by short periods of handling oocytes and embryos at 21 to 25 °C, as this appears to have no effect on their cleavage rates. We have also reduced temperatures to 4 °C for a few embryos to evaluate their sensitivity to cooling, a situation known to be deleterious to pig embryos and early cleavage stage cattle embryos (Trounson *et al.*, 1976). Human embryos continued development *in vitro* after cooling to 4 °C. However, this is not a recommended procedure for fertilization *in vitro*.

If oil is not used for embryo culture, the maintenance of 100% humidity is necessary to maintain the correct osmolarity of culture media. Some incubators are unable to achieve this and humid chambers are recommended to ensure evaporation of culture media does not occur. We do not use oil in our work with human oocytes or embryos and large volumes of media are used when the embryos are handled outside the humid chamber.

When using bicarbonate-based culture media, a 5% CO_2 gas phase must be maintained to control pH. The use of 5% O_2 is debatable as pregnancies have been obtained using 5%, 10% and 20% O_2. The oxygen tension in the human oviduct is closer to the equivalent of 10% O_2 than 5% O_2 (C. Wood, unpublished data).

References

Edwards, R. G., Steptoe, P. C. & Purdy, J. M. 1980. Establishing full-term human pregnancies using cleaving embryos grown *in vitro*. *British Journal of Obstetrics and Gynaecology*, **87**, 737–756.

Hoppe, P. C. & Pitts, S. 1973. Fertilization *in vitro* and development of mouse ova. *Biology of Reproduction*, **8**, 420–426.

Killen, I. D. & Moore, N. W. 1971. The morphological appearance and development of sheep ova fertilized by surgical insemination. *Journal of Reproduction and Fertility*, **24**, 63–70.

Mohr, L. R. & Trounson, A. O. 1982. *Journal of Reproduction and Fertility* (in press).

Moor, R. M. & Warnes, G. M. 1978. In: *Control of Ovulation*, pp. 159–176. Eds. D. B. Crighton, G. R. Foxcroft, N. B. Haynes & G. E. Lamming. Butterworths, London.

Sathananthan, A. H. & Trounson, A. O. 1982. Ultrastructural observations on cortical granules in human follicular oocytes cultured *in vitro*. *Gamete Research* **5**, 191–198.

Trounson, A. O., Willadsen, S. M., Rowson, L. E. A. & Newcomb, R. 1976. The storage of cow eggs at room temperature and at low temperatures. *Journal of Reproduction and Fertility*, **46**, 173–178.

Trounson, A. O., Leeton, J. F., Wood, C., Webb, J. & Kovacs, G. 1980. The investigation of idiopathic infertility by in-vitro fertilization. *Fertility and Sterility*, **34**, 431–438.

Trounson, A. O., Leeton, J. F. & Wood, C. 1981a. In-vitro fertilization and embryo transfer in the human. In: *Proceedings of the Van de Graaf Symposium*, Nijmegen. Excerpta Medica, Amsterdam.

Trounson, A. & Wood, C. 1981. Extracorporeal fertilization and embryo transfer. *Clinics in Obstetrics and Gynaecology*, **8**, 681–713.

Trounson, A. O., Leeton, J. F., Wood, C., Webb, J. & Wood, J. 1981b. Pregnancies in humans by fertilization *in vitro* and embryo transfer in the controlled ovulatory cycle. *Science*, **212**, 681–682.

Trounson, A. 1982. In-vitro fertilization. In: *The Endocrinology of Pregnancy and Parturition*. Eds. L. Marini & V. James. Academic Press, New York.

Trounson, A. O., Mohr, L. R., Wood, C. & Leeton, J. F. 1982. Effect of delayed insemination on in-vitro fertilization, culture and transfer of human embryos. *Journal of Reproduction and Fertility*, **64**, 285–294.

Factors Influencing the Growth of Human Preimplantation Embryos *in vitro*

A. Lopata

I wish to describe some of the factors which influence the cleavage of human embryos grown in culture. When we began our work, we initially used the natural cycle, monitoring the excretion of urinary LH. A distinct diurnal rhythm occurred in the timing of the LH discharge in our patients, very few beginning their LH surge between 2100 hours and 0300 hours. After this, there was a rapid increase in numbers, similar to the data described by Edwards *et al.* (1980). We have now turned to cycles stimulated by clomiphene and HCG, using 5,000 IU of HCG to induce preovulatory maturation.

Use of Ham's F10 in Embryo Culture

We have used various culture media, although Ham's F10 has been most widely employed. We have tested it as originally composed, with additional calcium lactate, and sometimes with raised levels of potassium by the addition of potassium bicarbonate up to 5 or 10 mM, while reducing the amount of sodium bicarbonate to 20 mM. The pH is 7.35, and this medium is used for fertilization and cleavage *in vitro* (Lopata, 1980; Lopata *et al.*, 1978, 1980a and b).

When we began working with this modified Ham's F10 medium, our first problem was to decide on its suitability. We decided to measure the development of embryos of the 8-cell stage to blastocysts, and the intermediate stages, using 5 mM potassium. Our overall success rate was 42%, covering all stages from the 8-cell to the blastocyst. We obtained a higher yield of blastocysts (52%) when the potassium concentration was increased to 10 mM. However, the lower level of potassium was evidently sufficient to sustain the growth of the embryos.

Department of Obstetrics and Gynaecology, Royal Women's Hospital, Melbourne.

We then carried out a more complex analysis, using a programme devised by Dr. A. Speirs, which enabled us to isolate various aspects of the culture conditions. In this programme, the work was extended to include all stages from the fertilized egg to the blastocyst. Overall, 30% of fertilized eggs developed into blastocysts, as compared with 50% if calculations were made from the 8-cell stage. We made the necessary corrections for those embryos which were replaced in the uterus, or were fixed and prepared for analytical study.

Steroids and Prostaglandins in the Culture Medium

We have analysed levels of various steroids and prostaglandins in the culture media. The analyses included both the insemination medium, and the growth medium for the embryos. There is likely to be a "cocktail" of these compounds in the insemination medium; some steroids must come from follicular fluid, for even after "washing" the oocyte, large amounts of hormones must be present in the fluid between the egg and its adjacent cells. Likewise, prostaglandins may be introduced from follicular fluid and from seminal plasma, despite the considerable dilution of semen during the washing of spermatozoa (Lopata, 1980).

The composition of steroids in the embryo culture medium depends on whether the corona cells are left adjacent to the eggs, or are removed before the embryo is placed into the medium. These cells release both oestradiol-17β and progesterone into the medium, which will obviously modify its content over a period of time. If the embryos are cultured under paraffin oil, then a similar situation may not apply if the oil removes these steroids from the aqueous medium.

Timing of Cleavage *in vitro* and the Size of Preovulatory Follicles

We have examined the duration of time needed for an embryo to reach the 8-cell stage and beyond, and related this to the origin of the egg from follicles of different sizes. There appears to be no significant difference in the cleavage rates of embryos, irrespective of the follicular diameter from which the oocyte was taken. Oocytes from larger follicles reach the 8-cell stage at about 68 hours, and those from smaller follicles at 72 hours, but the difference is not significant.

What are the chances of an oocyte developing to the 8-cell stage, and into a later pregnancy? We have studied the follicle sizes which will yield an oocyte capable of developing to the 8-cell stage. A clear relationship emerged: the larger the follicle, the greater chance of obtaining an 8-cell embryo. Likewise, the chance of establishing a pregnancy after replacement of an embryo is related to follicular size. The pregnancies we have obtained have arisen from follicles which were between 2.0 cm and 2.6 cm in diameter (Lopata *et al.*, 1980a).

We were disappointed initially with the use of clomiphene, because more than 60% of the follicles were in the group with a lower chance of producing an 8-cell embryo. Between 20 and 25% of the follicles were in the "good performance" group. After an analysis of 500 follicles, we decided to change the timing of the injection of HCG. It had been based on a sonar assessment of follicle growth from the 1.7 cm diameter to 2.0 cm (Lopata, 1980; Lopata *et al.*, 1978). Giving HCG at a size of 1.7 cm locked us into a situation where too many follicles were of small size. The largest follicle must now be 2.0 cm before HCG is given.

Overall, the rate of oocyte recovery does not differ from follicles of different diameters, except in the case of the very small follicles. Apart from this, there is no difference between follicles of moderate or large size, recovery rates being 60% in the medium-size and 70% in the larger sized follicles. Likewise, fertilization rates are similar using oocytes from follicles of these sizes, apart from the two extremes, i.e. very small or very large. Once again, the smallest follicles averaged out at a slightly lower level, although it is not significant. Similar results were obtained on cleavage rates, with perhaps a slight advantage to larger follicles.

These conclusions stand, even though we have tried to analyse the data in different ways. Arbitrarily classifying follicles into groups greater or less than 2 cm in diameter during the spontaneous cycle, or during the stimulated cycle, produced no significant differences in fertilization or cleavage, even though the pregnancies resulted from larger follicles.

Replacement of Embryos in Relation to Cleavage Rates

We have replaced embryos at all stages from the 2-cell stage to the 8-cell stage. We have also analysed the time after insemination when the embryos were replaced. Most embryos were replaced in the 8–10 cell stage, and those resulting in pregnancy were transferred between 70 and 76 hours after insemination. We now have several pregnancies following the replacement of 4-cell embryos, and another after the replacement of a 7-cell embryo.

The rate of cleavage in our cultures appears to be slightly slower than that described by Trounson (1982). Most of the embryos were produced from oocytes which were inseminated immediately after recovery. Recently, the oocytes have been incubated for 4–6 hours before spermatozoa are added. Embryos resulting from such preincubated oocytes appear to cleave more rapidly than those inseminated immediately.

We have a practical question to solve now that we have decided to replace embryos in the 4-cell stage. Should they be replaced when they reach the 4-cell stage, or should we wait until later? Is it possible to wait for a brief time after it is first seen as a 4-cell embryo, and improve the rates of implantation? At the present time, we have not decided on the optimal time for replacement.

Morphology of Cleavage

We have examined embryos histologically at various stages after fertilization *in vitro*. One 8-celled embryo that we have examined looks remarkably similar to that described by Pereda & Croxatto (1978), which was recovered from the oviduct 77 hours after the beginning of the LH surge. They described metachromasia in some of the blastomeres and we have observed a similar phenomenon in this embryo which we stained with toluidine blue. Some of the blastomeres were darker than the others, perhaps indicating that some form of differentiation had occurred in these early cleavage stages (Pereda & Croxatto, 1978). Alternatively, the difference in metachromasia may be due to differing intervals between the previous cleavage and the moment of observation. A similar difference in cytoplasmic density can be seen when embryos are examined under the electron microscope.

Similar observations have been made on baboon embryos recovered from the reproductive tract, and the denser cells may be tro-phectoderm. The situation appears to be different in the embryo of the rhesus monkey, where trophectoderm and the inner cell mass appear to stain similarly, although there may be differences within the cells of the inner cell mass. In the human embryo, we could observe no differences between the trophectoderm and the inner cell mass in the degree of metachromasia.

We have examined some blastocysts grown *in vitro*. Several interesting features have been seen. In one embryo, endoderm was seen migrating out from the inner cell mass. In some blastocysts, lighter cells, with vacuoles, were sequestered between the zona and trophectoderm, and we refer to these as "discarded" cells. This blastocyst developed from an embryo that appeared to be damaged early in growth, and we had not imagined it would develop so far. This observation raises a question about embryo replacement. Should we avoid replacing a "bad looking" embryo into the mother, for fear that it may not grow normally? This embryo developed normally to the blastocyst after a poor morphological appearance during cleavage, hence we now believe that such embryos should be replaced because some may implant and grow to full term. Human embryos are apparently quite effective at discarding damaged cells, and the remaining normal blastomeres had the potential to go on, as shown first in animal embryos by Tarkowski & Wroblewska (1967).

References

Edwards, R. G., Steptoe, P. C. & Purdy, J. M. 1980. Establishing full-term pregnancies using cleaving embryos grown *in vitro*. *British Journal of Obstetrics and Gynaecology*, **87**, 737.

Lopata, A. 1980. Successes and failures in human in-vitro fertilization. *Nature*, **288**, 643.

Lopata, A., Brown, J. B., Leeton, J. F., Talbot, J. Mc. & Wood, C. 1978. In-vitro fertilization of preovulatory oocytes and embryo transfer in infertile patients treated with clomiphene and human chorionic gonadotrophin. *Fertility and Sterility*, **30**, 27–35.

Lopata, A., Johnston, I. W. H., Hoult, I. J. & Speirs, A. I. 1980a. Pregnancy following intrauterine implantation of an embryo obtained by in-vitro fertilization of a preovulatory egg. *Fertility and Sterility*, **33**, 117.

Lopata, A., Sathananthan, A. H., McBain, J., Johnston, I. W. H., & Speirs, A. I. 1980b. The ultrastructure of the preovulatory human egg fertilized *in vitro*. *Fertility and Sterility*, **33**, 12–20.

Pereda, J. & Croxatto, H. B. 1978. Ultrastructure of a 7-cell human embryo. *Biology of Reproduction*, **18**, 481–489.

Tarkowski, A. & Wroblewska, J. 1967. Development of blastomeres of mouse eggs isolated at the 4-cell and 8-cell stage. *Journal of Embryology and Experimental Morphology*, **18**, 155–180.

Trounson, A. O. 1982. Factors influencing the success of fertilization and embryonic growth *in vitro*. In: *Human Conception in Vitro*. Eds. R. G. Edwards & J. M. Purdy. Academic Press, London (this volume, pp. 201–205).

Microcinematographic Recordings as a Tool for Monitoring the Development of the Human Embryo in Culture

B. G. Erikson, L. Hamberger, T. Hillensjö, P. O. Janson,
C. O. Löfman, Lars Nilsson, Lennart Nilsson, Anita Sjögren and
M. Wikland

The early development of human ova, fertilized and cultured *in vitro* prior to implantation, is infuenced by numerous factors which may cause physiological disturbances of the early cleavage stages. Such disturbances may be revealed by transmission electron microscopy or chromosome analyses, but such methods cannot be used when embryo transfers are to be made. Attempts to visualize the early embryonic development by continuous cinematographic recording have, hitherto, been hampered by the fact that exposure of the cells to visible light may, in itself, induce cellular damage. For such reasons a new technique was developed utilizing light of extremely low intensity during short periods coupled to time-lapse exposure equipment, thus making possible microphotographic-documentation.

Patients and Oocyte Recovery

The cell material to date is limited to 24 oocytes obtained from 18 women. Most of the cycles (n = 15) were stimulated with a combined treatment of clomiphene and HCG according to the schedule illustrated in Fig. 1. The time chosen for HCG injection was based exclusively on repeated ultrasonic examinations for reasons recently clarified by Kerin *et al.* (1981). Three natural cycles were monitored with repeated ultrasonic examinations combined with serum determinations of LH.

Department of Obstetrics & Gynecology and Department of Physiology, University of Göteborg, The Karolinska Institute and the Swedish Television, Stockholm, Sweden.

213

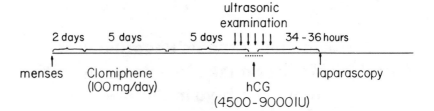

FIG. 1. Time schedule of hormonal treatment and ultrasound examinations during cycles intended for aspiration of oocytes at laparoscopy.

Table 1
Composition of different media used for collection and culture of human oocytes and embryos*

	Tyrode medium
NaCl	120.00 mmol l^{-1}
KCl	5.27 mmol l^{-1}
NaH_2PO_4, H_2O	1.13 mmol l^{-1}
$NaHCO_3$	11.90 mmol l^{-1}
D-glucose	5.55 mmol l^{-1}
$CaCl_2$, $2H_2O$	1.97 mmol l^{-1}
$MgCl_2$, $6H_2O$	0.80 mmol l^{-1}
BSA	0.05 mmol l^{-1}
Na-pyruvate	1.00 mmol l^{-1}
Streptomycin-sulphate	5.00 mg l^{-1}
Phenol red	12.00 mg l^{-1}
Benzyl-penicillin-G	10,000 IU l^{-1}
	Collection medium
Tyrode medium	1,000 IU l^{-1}
+ heparin	Culture medium
Tyrode medium	2.5 mmol l^{-1}
+ $NaHCO_3$	Cleavage medium
Ham's F10 (Gibco Bio-Cult)	
Patient serum	15%
Na-pyruvate	0.6 mmol l^{-1}
Benzyl-penicillin-G	10,000 IU l^{-1}

*The medium was sterilized (Millipore filter) and adjusted to 285 mOsmol Kg^{-1} (280–290) and pH 7.4. The medium was bubbled with a 90% N_2, 5% O_2, 5% CO_2 gas mixture for 30 min before use. (Media compositions adopted from Dr. Glenn Lauritsen, Copenhagen, Denmark.)

Follicular oocytes were aspirated at laparoscopy using a stainless steel needle (inner diameter 1.0 mm) connected by teflon tubing to a small glass bottle which in turn was connected to a vacuum pump. The negative pressure at aspiration varied between 90–110 mmHg and the aspiration time did not exceed 1 min. Carbon dioxide was used to induce the pneumoperitoneum necessary for the laparoscopy. The small bottle containing the oocyte in follicular fluid plus 2 ml of collection medium (composition see Table 1) was kept in darkness at a constant temperature (36.8–37.1 °C) during transportation to the laboratory (2–3 min). Generally within 2–8 min, the oocytes were identified using a Zeiss stereomicroscope in a temperature controlled room (36–37 °C) and were transferred to 0.5 ml culture medium (composition given in Table 1) under paraffin oil (Kebo Ltd., Sweden 7161).

Culture and Photography of Embryos

The incubations were carried out at 36.8–37.1 °C in an atmosphere of 5% O_2, 5% CO_2, 90% N_2. After 3–4 h incubation, the oocytes were transferred to 0.5 ml medium of the same composition containing approximately 3×10^5 spermatozoa (washed, diluted and preincubated for 1–3 h). After 20–24 h the oocytes were transferred to cleavage medium (see Table 1), and their subsequent development was followed continuously by cinematographic recording.

A Zeiss photomicroscope with Nomarski interference optics was equipped with a small tissue culture chamber surrounding the objectives and stage. An electronically induced conductivity camera (Siemens–Heimann with an EIC Vidicon tube ZQ) having a maximal sensitivity around 500 nm (range 400–820 nm) was connected to a time-lapse unit (Wild Ltd., Switzerland) and a television screen. The specimens were kept in complete darkness and the intervals between each exposure (0.5 sec) varied between 30 and 120 sec. The exposures were also transmitted to a second monitor outside the temperature controlled room and recorded on videotape (Fig. 2).

Observations on the Embryos

The first cell division occurred between 18 and 50 h (mean 30 h) after the aspiration and the interval between all successive divisions varied between 15 and 25 h (mean 17 h). The first division was generally seen as a slowly occurring elongation of the cell without changing the shape of the zona pellucida. A few hours prior to the division the pronuclei could generally be visualized (Fig. 3), whereas a clear indentation appeared indicating the exact position of the cleavage. The cleavage was, in itself, a rapid process requiring not more than 5–15 min. Fertilized ova were followed from the 1-cell to the 16-cell stage and detailed observations of cellular morphology and the kinetics of cell division were made. Both normal and apparently abnormal cell divisions have been observed. The abnormal cell divisions were those with persisting variability in cellular size.

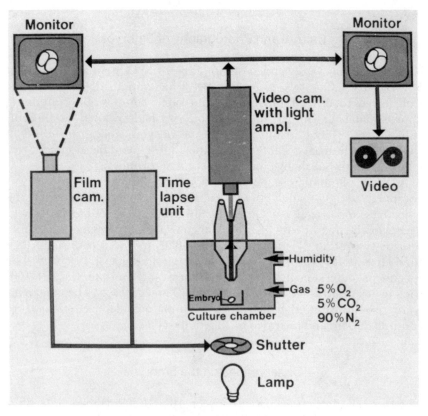

FIG. 2. Schematic illustration of the microcinematographic equipment used for time-lapse filming of developing human embryos in culture.

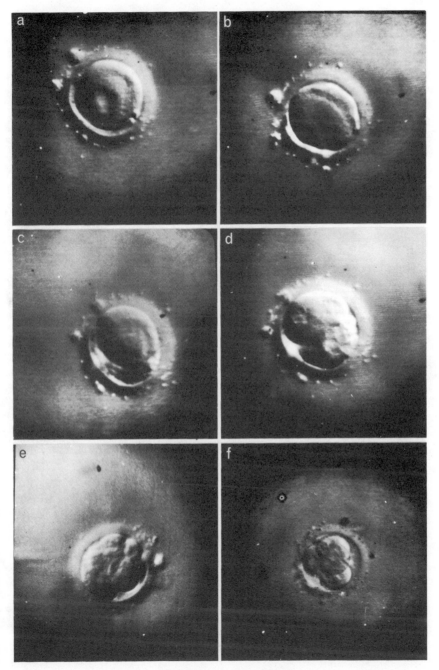

FIG. 3. Development of a fertilized human oocyte from the 1- to the 4-cell stage.

Comments

The development of fertilized ova in culture may, theoretically, be influenced in an abnormal direction by a number of known and unknown factors. It is this possibility that has created some uncertainty regarding the replacement of human embryos. Pertubations at these early stages of development might cause spontaneous abortions during the first trimester or allow persistence of pregnancies with chromosomal aberrations. Workers in this field cannot be totally convinced, so far, that such risks are negligible following the in-vitro fertilization procedure. The present technique may prove to be a useful tool in the arsenal of techniques available for evaluation of the quality of cultured embryos before implantation is attempted. At present, the equipment utilized may seem both expensive and complicated but it is our belief that a simpler arrangement of equipment could serve the same purpose.

In conclusion, we cannot exclude yet the possibility that even light of extremely low intensity may cause damage to the developing embryo. Experiments with fertilized rat oocytes aimed at investigating this possibility have therefore been set in progress in our laboratory.

Reference

Kerin, J. F., Edmonds, D. K., Warnes, G. M., Cox, L. W., Seamark, R. F., Matthews, C. D., Young, G. B. & Baird, D. T. 1981. Morphological and functional relations of Graafian follicle growth to ovulation in women using ultrasonic, laparoscopic and biochemical measurements. *British Journal of Obstetrics and Gynaecology*, **88**, 81–90.

Discussion on the Growth of Human Embryos
in vitro

The Timing of Embryonic Growth *in vitro*

Edwards: It is clear that several groups are now obtaining good rates of cleavage *in vitro*. Our earlier data has been published over several years, and the rate of cleavage here at Bourn Hall approximates to it. Are there any data of the effect of different media or other conditions on the rate of embryonic growth *in vitro*?

Lopata: We have not observed any differences due to different media. On occasion, embryos have slowed down, and this is when we have raised the level of potassium to 15 mM. The rates of growth appear to be improving considerably now that we are preincubating oocytes for up to six hours *in vitro* before fertilization.

Edwards: Our estimates of cleavage were as follows: the first 2-cell were found at 26 hours after insemination, 4-cell after 38 hours, and so on. The examinations of the embryos were often made only once a day, so the variation in the data must be considerable. How does this compare with the cleavage rates found by other groups? Our mean cleavage times were as follows: 2-cell, 34 hours; 4-cell, 50 hours; and 8-cell, 64 hours (Edwards, 1973; Edwards *et al.*, 1981).

Trounson: We have been examining some eggs from the pronuclear stages onwards. Syngamy occurs at 24 hours, and the first cleavage begins at about this time or shortly afterwards. The first 4-cell embryos are seen at about 36 hours. These figures seem to be slightly different from Edward's data published in 1977 (Edwards, 1977), and our pregnancies evidently arise from the left hand side of that distribution, i.e. the more rapidly-dividing embryos.

Lopata: We also found that our embryos cleaved faster than Edwards's data published in 1977.

Edwards: Our data goes back to about 1970, when many eggs were inseminated immediately they were collected and others were incubated for only a short period beforehand. It really is a mixture of data, from the very early stages of our work, and an interval should be inserted for the period of oocyte maturation to be completed *in vitro*. This would reduce cleavage time by 2–3 hours.

Purdy: We have discovered that oocytes can be matured *in vitro* for a long period of time, and fertilization and cleavage still occur normally. Some oocytes have matured overnight *in vitro*, usually in a medium containing follicular fluid, and they developed to the 8-cell stage or later after fertilization. One patient has become pregnant after replacing such an embryo, and has now delivered a normal baby.

It is interesting to note that the second pregnancy we obtained in Oldham was from an oocyte incubated for seven hours before spermatozoa were added. We had become concerned about the time needed for the migration of cortical granules to the surface of the oocyte, and so delayed insemination for this reason.

Trounson: The cleavage of embryos in culture is very successful. The cleavage rates are very high, in excess of 85%. It is very unusual for embryos not to cleave, even with delayed fertilization.

Edwards: Our data are similar and I believe that the problems of fertilization and cleavage have been largely solved, even as long ago as 1970. The human embryo can obviously tolerate a wide variety of culture media, as witnessed by the different types of media described at this meeting.

Jones, H: I would like to ask about the success of the cultures, especially since Edwards feels that the problems are basically solved. We should perhaps keep an open mind, because any difficulties may be reflected in the pregnancy rate.

Trounson: Our results include all the idiopathic and tubal cases, and success rates are improving all the time. The important thing is that methods of fertilization and cleavage differ a little between the various clinics but they are working well. The total number of pregnancies is really not so important any longer, because we now need statistical analyses to discover the problems of replacing embryos.

Edwards: I agree with those remarks. I still feel that the conditions of fertilization and cleavage are solved. The growth of embryos through cleavage does not give us concern; perhaps some problems might arise by the blastocyst stage, because the zona pellucida might "trap" the embryo, and we have not examined enough blastocysts in detail. By now, the replacement of embryos into the mother is the part of the work which is giving us the most difficulty. A similar situation existed in the cow with low pregnancy rates after embryo transfer, until there was a sudden improvement.

In most cases, the problems of establishing a pregnancy are clearly not connected with cleavage *in vitro*. Some of the replacements into patients have been very difficult, but must be included in our data for purposes of comparison. Neater transfers with our new catheters may improve the rates of pregnancy.

Another essential line of enquiry concerns the study of foetal growth. We must be on our guard about trisomy because we are handling oocytes and embryos when the chromosomes are segregating. Following the use of ultrasonics, if the pH in the media goes wrong, or if men produce many abnormal spermatozoa, we may then initiate trisomic or triploid embryos. But these are different problems than cleavage *in vitro*, and we have clearly passed the initial stages of the work and can now obtain many embryos for replacement.

Testart: We do not fertilize as many oocytes as other groups, but the patterns of cleavage are excellent. We believe our medium to be good. Moreover, we also obtain a relatively high proportion of pregnancies — more than 20% — when the embryos are replaced. Our series is presently small, but using our culture media, we observe a more constant interval between each cleavage stage than described by other workers.

Plachot: We use the same medium, but our results are not so good as those of Testart.

Size of Follicles and Cleavage of Embryos

Edwards: The size of the follicles may influence cleavage rates, because the milieu of the oocyte within its fluid might vary. Feichtinger pointed out that there were variations in the sizes of human oocytes, and differences in their ability to cleave. Many years ago, Chang (1955) showed that oocytes had to mature for some time after an injection of HCG, otherwise embryonic growth was abnormal.

Feichtinger: Smaller oocytes show a high incidence of pathological anomalies. There were two or three examples where the egg contained three or more pronuclei, and other eggs in this group failed to cleave.

Trounson: I believe that the different-sized oocytes in culture probably indicate a problem with follicular maturation and the aspiration of immature follicles. The egg grows during the final stages of antral formation, and if it is taken too soon after the injection of HCG, or early in its growth phase, then it is immature. The incidence of polyspermy will be expected to be greater under these circumstances. Small follicles would be expected to produce fewer pregnancies under such conditions, although we have established one from a follicle with a volume of 2.5 ml. We do not know if the surgeon aspirated all the follicular fluid, or whether some was left inside the follicle itself. In general, we get more pregnancies from larger follicles, provided they have not become too large, a fact which was very noticeable in the earlier stages of our work.

Cohen: It is very difficult to estimate the diameter of a follicle with any accuracy. It can be done either by measuring the fluid, or by ultrasound.

Our studies on the sonography of follicles have revealed many variations of between 1 and 3 mm in their mean size. Renault, in France, prefers a mean diameter of 2.8 cm for a preovulatory follicle, whereas some American publications have indicated that 2.0–2.1 cm is the correct size. Sonography may not therefore be a good method of measurement. Nor do I believe that follicular diameter observed during laparoscopy is a good parameter either. Many of the follicles obtained after stimulation lie deep in the ovary, and they cannot be seen so clearly as those developing during the natural cycle. The only method of measuring a follicle is to assess the volume of follicular fluid.

Lopata: We measure follicle size in two ways. Initially, we carry out an ultrasonic scan, when the follicle is measured in three dimensions. We then measure the volume of follicular fluid, after its complete aspiration. There is a good correlation between the two estimates.

Fishel: Has Lopata attempted to correlate the size of a follicle with the difficulty of its aspiration? If there is any problem in aspiration, can the fertilization or cleavage rates be impaired because of attendant problems?

Lopata: Speirs found no significant difference in fertilization and cleavage rate between eggs that were obtained from follicles between 1.5 and 2.0 cm in diameter, and those from follicles greater than 2.0 cm in diameter. Also, if the follicle has to be irrigated, the oocytes fertilize equally well if they are obtained in the first flush or during later irrigations of the follicle.

Rapid and Delayed Cleavage *in vitro*

Fishel: A phenomenon which we call ''catching up'' seems to occur in our cultures. If an egg is inseminated after a long delay, or if fertilization is delayed after a normal insemination, then cleavage occurs slightly more quickly. The embryo appears to catch up on normal growth. Have other groups seen a similar phenomenon, or found an intrinsic rate of growth which is followed irrespective of external factors such as the time of insemination?

Trounson: We have noticed that those eggs which have pronuclei much later than expected, e.g. after a delay of 24 hours, cleave at a much slower rate. They never catch up. It is important to be precise about the formation of the pronuclei. In our experience, those that have delayed a long time certainly cannot catch up.

Edwards: Fishel is describing some embryos which were not fertilized at the first insemination and were reinseminated 24 hours later. They seemed to cleave more rapidly and catch up on their delayed time sequence. The exact interval between the 2-cell and 4-cell stage of one of these embryos was timed, and seemed to occur very quickly.

Fishel: Perhaps some fragmentation occurred after delayed fertilization, but it was not obvious. The embryos were watched very closely, and the second cleavage of both blastomeres in a 2-cell embryo were recorded, and so too was its later division into an 8-cell embryo. Cleavage seemed to be normal. We have seen more than one embryo doing this.

Edwards: This embryo was replaced in its mother. We would be delighted to know if delayed fertilization of an oocyte, followed by a more rapid cleavage, can give rise to pregnancy.

At least one of our pregnancies has arisen from an embryo that was cleaving more slowly than expected. In one of our patients in Bourn Hall, who has now delivered, the embryo was 8-cell when we expected it to be 16-cell.

Fishel: The human embryo is surprising in comparison with those of other animal species. There does not seem to be a narrow implantation window as in species such as the mouse. The human embryo and uterus are perhaps much more flexible in this sense.

Lopata: We have also observed some unusual phenomena. In two instances, the patient was discharged when the embryo was still 2-cell at 48 hours after insemination. Then, the next afternoon, the embryo was found to be 8-cell, and the patient returned for replacement. This has happened with two embryos.

Edwards: Particular blocks exist in the development of animal embryos at specific stages of growth, and the 2-cell block is very well known in some species. Occasional human embryos will stop growing *in vitro*, but there does not seem to be anything resembling a regular block at the 2-cell stage. If the culture media are right, the embryos simply carry on dividing. I was surprised at some of the figures given by Lopata, showing embryos becoming arrested in cleavage, for our experience indicates that most of them will develop into morulae and blastocysts *in vitro*. The number arrested in cleavage, and so not replaced in the mother, is very few indeed.

Lopata: The success rate for the growth of an embryo from one stage to the next is about 90% at all stages of growth. Occasionally, it stops at about 86%. The stage of growth with the highest frequency of arrest is the morula, and our rate for the transition into a blastocyst drops to about 70%.

Testart: Our medium was effective with animal embryos when used alone. In the early days, we decided not to add serum for human embryos too. Under these circumstances, the systematic block was seen at the 4-cell stage. With serum, this stage is passed easily, hence it seems essential to add serum to ensure satisfactory cleavage.

Edwards: We have been very satisfied with the Earle's medium containing serum that we routinely employ. It gives us excellent cleavage, and we have often considered using it to sustain the growth of embryos of other species. Are there any data on the value of human serum to sustain embryos of other species, e.g. cow embryos?

Trounson: We have used human serum to culture both mouse and cow embryos, and they grow very nicely. It is especially interesting how mouse embryos grow well in human serum, but badly in mouse serum. In fact, the human serum we now have in quantity is regularly used for the culture and freezing of cow embryos.

Fishel: We also find that human serum is very beneficial to mouse embryos *in vitro*. The embryos seem to like it, and grow well in it. It does not seem to overcome the 2-cell block which can arise in this species, but it serves remarkably well after these stages of growth.

It is important to evaluate the components of a culture medium by carefully assessing the capacity of embryos to respond to them. Ions and macromolecules are most important. As mouse embryos develop into blastocysts, they become increasingly dependant on serum macromolecules in the medium for the synthesis of optimal levels of RNA (Fig. 1). Likewise, components of low molecular weight, e.g. Ca^{2+} and Mg^{2+} are essential for optimal metabolism, and RNA synthesis is impaired if these components are restricted (Fig. 2).

The Need to Examine Pronuclear Stages

Jones, H: Is it essential to examine eggs for the presence of pronuclei after insemination, in order to ensure that they have been fertilized? We examined our eggs during their cleavage, so we do not have data on the fertilization rate as such. What is the advantage of knowing that they are fertilized before cleavage?

Edwards: We are not greatly concerned if a 1-cell egg cannot be

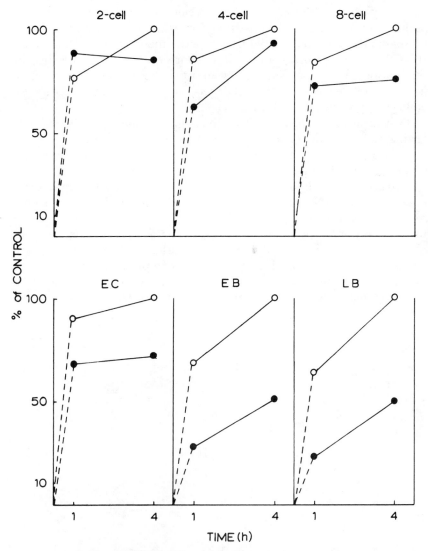

FIG. 1. Differential effects of media containing serum (○) or bovine serum albumin (●) on RNA synthesis in mouse embryos growing *in vitro*. The stimulatory effect of serum is pronounced after compaction (EC) and in early and late blastocysts (EB, LB) (Fishel & Surani, 1978).

seen sufficiently clearly to score its pronuclei. Some persistent cumulus cells may obscure the egg, and we prefer to leave them alone. It is perhaps an advantage to know that fertilization has occurred, in the sense that the addition of any further spermatozoa can then be avoided. If in doubt, we usually add a little more on the day following inseminations. If two pronuclei are seen, the embryo is obviously well on its way and cleavage can be predicted, and we expect to replace the embryo in virtually every patient.

Trounson: I would encourage those groups having difficulty with fertilization or cleavage to look for pronuclei. At least, they will again be assured that fertilization has been achieved, and their problem is in embryonic development.

Testart: I believe that it is not necessary to disturb the egg in order to see pronuclei. Nor do we look for polar bodies, because polar body history is not a reliable guide. Initially, we got no fertilization because the preparation of spermatozoa was poor; in those conditions, we never obscured true cleavage. The human egg perhaps cleaves correctly only when it is fertilized, and cleavage histories can probably be taken as an indication of successful fertilization. We examine undivided or fragmented eggs by serial sections, to check if fertilization has occurred.

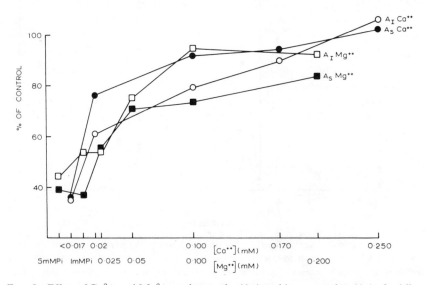

FIG. 2. Effect of Ca^{2+} and Mg^{2+} on the uptake (A_S) and incorporation (A_I) of uridine into mouse blastocysts *in vitro*. Control embryos were grown in optimal culture medium. The limiting levels were 0.250 mM Ca^{2+}, and 0.200 nM Mg^{2+}, levels substantially lower than present in standard culture media (Fishel, 1980).

Risks of Triploidy Arising Through Polyspermy *in vitro*

Edwards: One of the questions to be solved about fertilization *in vitro* is the possibility of polyspermy, leading to triploidy in the embryo, or to even more extreme forms of chromosomal imbalance. Polyspermy is associated with a delayed fertilization *in vivo* in several animal species, and may not arise *in vitro* with the same frequency if penetration occurs within an hour or two after insemination.

Fishel: Could Trounson give some indications of polyspermy in his cultures? It was fairly high at one time; has it changed during recent work, and are there any differences in the rate of polyspermy between the natural and induced cycles? Data from fertilization *in vivo* in animals would indicate that there may be such a difference.

Trounson: When inseminating at zero hours, i.e. when the oocytes were freshly collected, we had a high rate of polyspermy at about 19%. All the eggs which do not cleave or are not replaced because of abnormalities, are examined by our electronmicroscopist, Henry Sathananthan. Since we moved away from immediate inseminations, the rate has become very low indeed, perhaps even as low as 1%. Nevertheless, we do occasionally see eggs with three pronuclei, and we have carried out chromosome studies on five such eggs which divided. In three of them, there were far too many chromosomes, indicating that the embryos were not diploid, and probably all three pronuclei had fused at syngamy. The other two embryos were diploid.

We gave up using the natural cycle some years ago, so we do not have a great deal of data on the comparison with induced cycles. Nevertheless, my impression is that there is very little difference between the natural and stimulated cycle.

Edwards: We have been impressed over many years by the astonishing rareness of eggs with three pronuclei in our cultures. Indeed, they are so rare that there is no necessity to look for them; if there is a slight cumulus cloud over the fertilized egg, we are now fully prepared to accept that there are two pronuclei.

The egg is put at risk each time we manipulate it to count the pronuclei, whether we remove the surrounding cumulus cells mechanically or enzymically. Almost always, we have found two pronuclei in fertilized eggs, even from the earliest stages of our work in Oldham (Edwards *et al.*, 1981). We may get so few polyspermic eggs because the oocytes are collected fairly late in maturation, close to ovulation. Another reason may be because we routinely add serum, and the concentration of the culture medium could make a difference to the rate of polyspermy.

Trounson: Parallel studies using serum, or bovine serum albumin, in different culture media have not made any difference as far as we can see. Polyspermy does not seem to be a problem with the medium, but essentially one of oocyte maturation. Sections of eggs obtained immediately after laparoscopy have shown that the cortical granules are still moving towards the surface of the oocyte (Sathananthan & Trounson, 1982). After six hours in culture, this migration appears to be completed. Insemination of eggs before the maturation of cortical granules is completed can lead to polyspermy.

The low incidence of triploidy may not be important anyway in our work. Triploidy at birth is rare indeed. We would obviously like to avoid the situation, but it is probably not essential to look for multiple pronuclei. At one time, I thought that pronuclear examination was very important, but I have changed my mind since. However, I would advise groups with low rates of fertilization and cleavage that it would be well worthwhile checking they are not obtaining polyspermy.

Chromosomal Analyses on Preimplantation Embryos for Trisomy and Triploidy

Mettler: We have applied for research grants, although the referees have stressed that we must examine cleaving embryos for their chromosomal complement. This was a prerequisite to our obtaining the grant. We know from studies on mice that triploidy is not an important component of early embryonic growth *in vitro*. Could Trounson comment on whether chromosomal studies should be done on human embryos, and would they be difficult?

Trounson: The studies would probably be difficult to do. Part of the problem would depend on the source of material. All our patients expect their eggs to be replaced, or frozen and replaced during the later cycle. We do not take the ownership of oocytes away from the patients, so their wishes are paramount. We ask them to sign a document giving us permission to freeze the embryos, and a further document to re-place them. This is essentially a protection system for ourselves, recommended by our Ethical Committee. If some patients did not object to our having the spare embryos, then it would be a good idea to use them for chromosomal analyses. But we believe there are few such patients in our clinic.

Edwards: We know that trisomic and triploid fetuses arise during fertilization *in vivo*, so obviously some will arise during fertilization *in vitro*. They could arise through various causes. It is possible that the incidence of polyspermy *in vitro* is less than it is *in vivo*, because we avoid delayed fertilization, whereas the situation could obviously arise *in vivo* if intercourse was delayed for some time after ovulation. Delayed fertilization of human eggs, as in animals' eggs, is probably an essential component of polyspermy.

If it can be avoided by good culture technique, there may actually be a reduced rate of triploidy *in vitro* as compared with fertilization *in vivo*. Obviously, the incidence would also depend on all the other causes of triploidy, which include delayed fertilization, fertilization by a diploid spermatozoon, and failure of the first or second polar body to form. If the incidence of some of these anomalies in our cultures was lower than in the oviduct, then it would be an advantage of fertilization *in vitro*. If all the data were placed together, and triploidy was found to occur more rarely, then it would be a great bonus to have clear evidence of one anomaly at a lower incidence in our work than during conception *in vivo*.

Trounson described some eggs with three pronuclei which developed as diploid embryos. This is intriguing, because in certain animals, one pronucleus can be excluded from syngamy. There appears to be a corrective factor excluding the extra pronucleus.

Trounson: I agree. We decided that one of the pronuclei had been extruded at syngamy or later. Extrusion almost certainly occurred at syngamy.

Lopata: Another mechanism has been described whereby the mouse egg protects itself from polyspermy. Accessory spermatozoa can be extruded from the egg, and this obviously is a most fascinating mechanism.

Edwards: Deciding the incidence of trisomy and monosomy will be much more difficult because excellent chromosomal spreads will be needed. At present, there appears to be no detailed evidence, and this is a deficiency that should be remedied even though it is going to prove difficult with the few mitoses available in cleaving embryos. Perhaps the best thing is to grow embryos to as late a stage as possible, to the blastocyst or later, and so increase the number of cells. This may provide more evidence on karyotypes.

We examined more than 30 embryos by squashed preparations in the early 1970s, and many had no mitoses whatsoever. Altogether, a total of 15 embryos had chromosome spreads that could be counted with some accuracy, but only to exclude triploidy (Edwards, 1977). We could not exclude trisomy, although all of the embryos seemed to have an approximately diploid number of chromosomes. There were always two or more chromosomes overlying each other, or some other defect in the flattening process which made exact scoring impossible. Mouse embryos have been examined karyotypically at the first cleavage division, but syngamy may nevertheless be an unreliable guide if a pronucleus or a group of chromosomes can evade the spindle and segregate abnormally into later blastomeres.

The risks of trisomy can be assessed by amniocentesis. In effect, our patients will be in a similar situation to those couples, one of whom carries a translocation, and where a trisomic-like state may thus arise in the embryo. Nevertheless, many of our patients are now declining amniocentesis, especially those in their late thirties.

Fragmentation of Blastomeres

Jones, H: Some embryos do not appear to cleave normally. Could Trounson clarify the circumstances under which fragmentation of blastopheres is most likely to take place?

Trounson: Fragmentation takes place under two types of conditions. First, it arises if an oocyte is taken from a follicle in which the granulosa cells are slightly atretic, and the cumulus cells are abnormal. This condition is a fairly frequent cause of fragmentation. The second cause is a shock, e.g. pH, osmolarity or temperature, and fragmentation may then occur immediately in one or two minutes. There is also a possibility that oocytes which are immature when fertilized begin normal cleavage, but then fragment at the 2- or 4-cell stage. This may be due to suboptimal culture conditions, but it can also arise if the oocyte is not handled correctly.

Fishel: It would be very helpful to distinguish between cytoplasmic fragments and fragmentation of the embryo. Sundström et al. (1981) have shown that cytoplasmic fragments can arise in cleaving human embryos, but do not appear to be compatible with normal growth. Cytoplasmic fragments have occasionally been seen in our embryos and, on occasions, the embryos were not replaced into the mother for that reason. Nevertheless, the embryos carried on to form into perfectly normal healthy blastocysts a few days later. Do other groups replace embryos with fragmented blastomeres?

Trounson: These types of fragments are commonly seen in sheep and cows (Killen & Moore, 1971). I have a healthy respect for the amount of fragmentation that can take place, especially small non-nucleated fragments. The presence of fragments is not incompatible with normal development in sheep and cattle, although they are rarely seen in the mouse. It is difficult to see them in the pig, because the embryo compacts so early, but in species where the embryos compact later, and the human is one of these, a small bleb can be isolated during division or compaction, and such fragments do not have a role in cleavage thereafter. But it is essential to distinguish between fragmentation, regular cleavage, and regular cleavage with a few fragments. We have obtained pregnancies from the last group.

Testart: The most important problem we have with cleavage is the presence of polynucleate blastomeres. This could be a problem of polyspermy or other factors. The 1-cell egg might have many undivided nuclei, and sometimes embryos in the 2- or 4-cell stage might have more than one nucleus per cell. This occurs more frequently in patients given clomiphene.

Trounson: This was also reported recently in Berlin (Wramsby & Liedholm, 1981). It is an indication of degenerating embryos, due to nuclear division occurring without cytoplasmic division. It does not happen very frequently in our early human embryos and, indeed, the incidence is still declining. It was not uncommon in our early studies on blastocysts. At the present time, our Ethical Committee would prefer us to deal only with early cleavage stages, and not to experiment with later stages.

Parthenogenesis, Andrenogenesis and Gynogenesis *in vitro*

Edwards: We seldom see any sign of parthenogenesis in our oocytes. Hardly any of them display any signs of pronuclei or any other indications of artificial stimulation, even when cultured for up to three days without fertilization taking place. An astonishingly high number of them remain in metaphase-II with the first polar body. Whenever a nucleus is seen, I suspect that it is a germinal vesicle, and the egg is immature. The situation in the human egg develops from that in several laboratory animals; the hamster egg is remarkable in showing parthenogenetic activation if it is unfertilized.

Trounson: I agree that parthenogenesis is very rare in human eggs, but a different point would concern me. A whole range of circumstances can induce parthenogenetic development in mice and hamsters, including a deficiency of calcium, the presence of chelating agents, high temperature, etc. If a mistake occurs in the preparation of culture media, e.g. if calcium is omitted, or if glassware is incorrectly washed, then it may be easy to induce parthenogenesis. The condition would undoubtedly be lethal, and would equally cause a great deal of interest.

Quality control procedures may be very important in ensuring parthenogenetic activation does not occur. This is one reason why we check all our media with mouse embryos and do not accept media which will not sustain the growth of 90% of embryos from the 2-cell stage to hatched blastocysts. This test is carried out in the same incubator in which human embryos are grown. On one occasion, an incubator overheated to 45 °C and the cultures of mouse embryos identified the deficiency. Quality control is essential if we hope to obtain high standards of fertilization and growth.

Jones, H: Parthenogenesis is often associated with the fragmentation of an embryo. Is it possible to distinguish between the two?

Edwards: In our work, parthenogenesis is the activation of an egg without fertilization. Gynogenesis is a variant, occurring when an oocyte is fertilized by a spermatozoon which has been genetically inactivated by ultraviolet light or some other cause. The parthenogenetic activation of an egg can lead to fragmentation of the oocyte, involving disruption of the chromosomes on the spindle, fragmentation of pronuclei, and fragmentation of cells and their constituent nuclei during cleavage. But parthenogenesis can be very highly ordered, especially in experimental studies in animals, and the embryos are capable of development well past implantation.

We do not know if parthenogenetic or gynogenetic human embryos can also develop through stages of growth up to and beyond implantation. In a sense, the counterpart of gynogenesis is androgenesis, where only paternal chromosomes are present in the embryo, and we know that androgenetic human embryos can progress to implantation and beyond *in vivo* (Kajii & Ohama, 1977). Androgenesis could have arisen in the embryos with three pronuclei which ultimately gave rise to diploid embryos as described by Trounson. Some anomalies of syngamy observed in our work, in which one pronucleus seemed large, could lead to androgenetic or gynogenetic embryos.

Fishel: Evidence of the growth of parthenogenetic embryos has been given by several workers, including Kaufman *et al.* (1977). They studied the growth of parthenogenetic mouse embryos to the 20-somite stage of growth. Some degree of parthenogenetic activation may occur in human systems, and in other animal embryos maintained *in vitro*. Was the parthenogenetic embryo described by Trounson due to spontaneous or experimentally-induced parthenogenesis?

Trounson: We were trying to mature sheep eggs in culture tubes or in the rabbit oviduct, and one control group was maintained without spermatozoa. Spontaneous cleavage occurred in this control group.

Jones, H: In human embryos if the X chromosomes are retained, then the result is a cystic teratoma. If the embryo is androgenetic, it results in a hydatidiform mole (Kajii & Ohama, 1977; Vassilakos *et al.*, 1977).

Edwards: Trounson described five eggs with three pronuclei, of which three developed as triploid embryos. The other two were diploid, indicating that one pronucleus was excluded from syngamy. If the single female pronucleus is extruded, the embryos would have been androgenetic diploids. Was the chromosomal constitution of the two embryos identified? Did they have, for example, two Y chromosomes indicating they were androgenetic in origin?

Trounson: Some studies were made on the chromosomes of these two embryos. I believe one Y chromosome was found in one of the embryos, and the other embryo appeared to have X chromosomes. We are hoping to develop a better technique for karyotyping which will allow us to identify the chromosomes more easily.

References

Chang, M. C. 1955. The maturation of rabbit oocytes in culture and their maturation, activation, fertilization and subsequent development in the Fallopian tubes. *Journal of Experimental Zoology*, **128**, 379–405.

Edwards, R. G. 1973. Studies on human conception. *American Journal of Obstetrics and Gynecology*, **117**, 587.

Edwards, R. G. 1977. Early human development from the oocyte to implantation. In: *Scientific Foundations of Obstetrics and Gynaecology*, pp. 175–252. Ed. E. E. Phillipp, J. Barnes & M. Newton. Heinemann Medical, London.

Edwards, R. G., Purdy, J. M., Steptoe, P. C. & Walters, D. E. 1981. The growth of human preimplantation embryos *in vitro*. *American Journal of Obstetrics and Gynecology*, **141**, 408–416.

Fishel, S. B. 1980. The role of divalent cations in the metabolic response of mouse embryos to serum. *Journal of Embryology and Experimental Morphology*, **58**, 217–229.

Fishel, S. B. & Surani, M. A. H. 1978. Changes in responsiveness of preimplantation mouse embryos to serum. *Journal of Embryology and Experimental Morphology*, **45**, 295–301.

Kajii, T. & Ohama, K. 1977. Androgenetic origin of hydatidiform mole. *Nature*, **268**, 633–634.

Kaufman, M. H., Barton, S. C. & Surani, M. A. H. 1977. Normal post-implantation development of mouse parthenogenetic embryos to the forelimb bud stage. *Nature*, **265, 53–55**.

Killen, I. D. & Moore, N. W. 1971. The morphological appearance and development of sheep ova fertilised by surgical insemination. *Journal of Reproduction and Fertility*, **24**, 63.

Sathananthan, A. H. & Trounson, A. 1982. Ultrastructural observations on cortical granules in human follicular oocytes cultured *in vitro*. *Gamete Research* **5**, 191–198.

Sundström, P., Nilsson, O. & Liedholm, P. 1981. *Acta Obstet. Gynec. Scand.*, **60**, 109.

Vassilakos, P., Riotton, G. & Kajii, T. 1977. Hydatidiform mole: two entities. *American Journal of Obstetrics and Gynecology*, **127**, 167–170.

Wramsby, H. & Liedholm, P. 1981. Multinucleated blastomeres in early cleavage stages of in-vitro inseminated human oocytes. In: *Third World Congress of Human Reproduction*, Berlin. Excerpta Medica, Amsterdam.

Part 4

THE LUTEAL PHASE UTERUS AND REPLACEMENT OF EMBRYOS

Animal Studies on Embryo Transfer and Storage

J. Testart[1] and J.-P. Renard[2]

Introduction

The considerable differences between embryo transfer in animal and human species (Table 1) result from the nature of the objective being sought: embryo transfer in animals is used in experimental studies on reproduction or in genetic improvement (e.g. farm animals) whereas in humans it is only used for treatment of sterility. Thus animal embryos are usually collected from a donor female in order to be transferred to a recipient female (either immediately or after storage). The success rate of this technique is about 40–70% in all species studied.

Embryo transfer following in-vitro fertilization has been carried out in only a few species: rabbit (Chang, 1955), mouse (Whittingham, 1968; Hoppe & Pitts, 1973), rat (Toyoda & Chang, 1974) and bovine (Brackett et al., 1981), and several hundred births have resulted from this process. There has apparently been no attempt to transfer animal embryos in the same conditions as human embryos, namely in-vitro fertilization and culture followed by uterine implantation in the female from whom the oocyte was collected. Thus, the term ''embryo replacement'' proposed by the Bourn Hall group accurately indicates the specific method used in humans.

This paper deals only with the principal results in storage and transfer of animal embryos. It however seems important to emphasize the usefulness of animal experiments for human research, particularly as regards the preparation of gametes, in-vitro fertilization and culture (Fishel & Edwards, 1982). Moreover, a certain number of original methods used in animal studies deserve to be mentioned. For example,

[1] INSERM, U. 187, Physiologie et Psychologie de la Reproduction Humaine Maternité, Hôpital Antoine Béclère, 157, Rue de la Porte de Trivaux, 92141 Clamart, France.
[2] INRA, Station Centrale de Physiologie Animale, Centre National de Recherches Zootechniques, 78350 Jouy-en-Josas, France.

237

Table 1
Some differences between human embryo replacement and animal embryo
transfer

	Embryo transfer (in animals)	Embryo replacement (in human)
Recruitment	Excellent fertility — Male and females	Infertility
Object	Experimental Studies on reproduction Genetic Improvement	Treatment of infertility Occluded or absent tubes Oligoasthenospermy Idiopathic infertility
Hormonal treatment	Superovulation PMSG or FSH + HCG or $PGF_{2\alpha}$	Spontaneous cycle LH surge onset detection or Stimulated cycle HMG or Clomiphene + HCG
Egg collection	Follicular or tubal oocytes Sacrified females or Uterine cleaved eggs Surgical or non-surgical flushing	Follicular oocytes Laparoscopy
Fertilization	Mainly *in vivo* or *in vitro* (rat, mouse, rabbit, cow)	*in vitro*
Egg transfer	Homotransfer Surgical or non-surgical techniques in estrous synchronized recipient	Autotransfer Non-surgical (cervical)

xenogenous fertilization has been proposed as an alternative to in-vitro fertilization: hamster or squirrel monkey oocytes have been fertilized *in vivo* in the oviducts of rabbit with a success rate of 60 and 36%, respectively (de Mayo *et al.*, 1980). It has also been shown the rabbit oviduct allows in-vivo culture for some days of eggs from foreign species: cattle (Lawson *et al.*, 1972b), sheep (Lawson *et al.*, 1972a), pig (Polge *et al.*, 1972) and horse (Allen *et al.*, 1976). Finally, other techniques used in animal experiments might be useful in improving the human embryo replacement. For example, sexing or chromosomal analysis of the embryo appear to be possible (Gardner & Edwards, 1968; Hare *et al.*, 1978). It has also been shown that embryo duplication can be carried out relatively easily by using micro-manipulation in early stages of development: monozygotic twins can be obtained from 2- to 8-cell embryos of sheep (Willadsen, 1980) or cattle (Willadsen & Polge, 1981). These techniques of chromosomal analysis and embryo duplication, taken together, might be useful in determining the quality of the human embryo prior to uterine replacement.

Egg Preservation

The first successful studies on the preservation of mammalian embryos by Chang (1947) reported the development of 2-cell rabbit embryos transferred following in-vitro storage at 10 °C. A few years later, it was clearly established that the exposure of rabbit eggs to very low temperatures (-79 and -196 °C) was not incompatible with further development: some of these eggs divided after freezing in the presence of 15% glycerol (Smith, 1952). Several authors have reviewed the main experiments that have been conducted to determine the effects of low temperatures on the viability of laboratory (Whittingham, 1977a) or farm animals (Maurer, 1976; Polge & Willadsen, 1978). Until now, the embryos of six mammalian species including mouse, rabbit, rat, bovine, sheep and goat had been successfully preserved and stored at -196 °C before producing viable offspring when transferred to appropriate foster mothers (Whittingham et al., 1972; Bank & Maurer, 1974; Whittingham, 1975; Wilmut, 1973; Willadsen et al., 1976; Bilton & Moore, 1976).

The reactions of oocytes and embryos to the shock produced by low temperatures are typical of mammalian cells in general (Leibo, 1977). The main modifications that occur may be summarized as follows:

(a) Lowering the temperature of a cell brings about a modification in the hydraulic conductivity of its membrane, which induces water elimination. The survival of cells depends on the kinetics of water loss (Mazur, 1970) determined by several factors including the size of the cell and the cooling rate.

(b) At suprazero temperatures, the cell begins to shrink and is subjected to modifications (known as cold shock) (Lovelock, 1955) as a result of the increasing concentration of electrolytes.

(c) At low temperatures, ice nucleation occurs and ice forms progressively as temperature drops.

(d) Survival depends not only on the cooling rate but also on the minimum subzero temperature to which the cells are cooled; an excess of intracellular ice is lethal but excessive shrinkage makes the cells vulnerable to the large amount of extracellular ice and solutes.

(e) Cryoprotective agents such as glycerol or dimethylsulfoxide (DMSO) are an effective measure against slow cooling injury. They allow the cell to be less dehydrated when frozen, and under these conditions rapid thawing prevents recrystallization.

The main features of the technique used to freeze mammalian eggs are based on these principles and follow the original method proposed for mouse embryos by Whittingham *et al.* (1972). After collection, embryos are incubated in the presence of cryoprotectant (1.0 to 1.5 M glycerol or DMSO) in phosphate-buffered saline. Ice is induced in the suspending medium at $-7\,°C$ and slow cooling (0.2 to $0.8\,°C$ min^{-1}) is performed to $-80\,°C$ before direct immersion of the embryo in liquid nitrogen. After storage, slow thawing (4 to $25\,°C$ min^{-1}) precedes gradual dilution of the cryoprotectant at suprazero temperatures. However, several combinations of cooling and warming rates may be equally effective for the survival of embryos which can tolerate rapid rates of thawing and dilution (Whittingham *et al.*, 1979).

Survival Assays Following Egg Preservation

The optimal test of survival after egg storage is the production of viable offspring following transfer to foster mothers. Indications of the optimum survival rates obtained to date in six different species are given in Table 2. Survival rates of frozen-thawed embryos are variable, depending on the species under study and the nature of the experiment. The best results obtained in specific conditions of freezing, which depend on the developmental stage of the embryo (cf. infra), are shown in Table 2.

Table 2
Overall survival rates in several species following freezing-thawing and embryo transfer

| | | Survival rates | | |
| | | No. liveborn offspring | | |
Species	Embryo stage at freezing	No. frozen embryos	Percent	References
Mouse	8-cell	38/85	44.8	Whittingham *et al.*, 1977
Rat	8-cell	3/33	9.0	Whittingham, 1975
Rabbit	Morula	48/86	55.8	Renard *et al.* (unpublished data)
Bovine	Blastocyst	8/12	66.6	Willadsen *et al.*, 1978
Sheep	Blastocyst	17/26	65.3	Willadsen *et al.*, 1976
Goat	Blastocyst	3/25	12.0	Bilton & Moore, 1976

Apart from the conditions of the freezing itself, several factors affect the survival rate of frozen-thawed and transferred embryos. For example, the breed or strain of the recipient female have been shown to play a role in mouse and rabbit (Miyamoto *et al.*, 1977; Maurer & Haseman, 1976).

In-vitro culture has often been used to verify the survival of frozen-thawed embryos. In several species such as the mouse or the sheep the number of mitotic divisions observed after 20 to 24 hours of in-vitro culture was generally lower in surviving frozen-thawed embryos than in non-frozen embryos (Whittingham, 1977a; Willadsen *et al.*, 1976). In spite of this developmental delay, transferring mouse embryos led to the same survival rate for blastocysts cultured from 8-cell frozen embryos as for non-cultured frozen blastocysts (Whittingham *et al.*, 1977). Thus in-vitro culture conditions appear to be more suitable than the uterine milieu for restoring the viability of the frozen mouse embryo. In the rabbit, it has been shown that temporary postponement of development by the storage of 2-cell embryos at 10 °C for 24 hours did not impair nucleic acid and protein synthesis after warming (Anderson & Foot, 1975), but the viability of cultured rabbit embryos was low following transfer to recipient females (Binkerd & Anderson, 1979). Furthermore, the in-vitro culture of frozen-thawed bovine embryos for 24 hours reduced their viability but in-vitro development through one or two divisions provided a good indication of the success of the freezing-thawing techniques (Renard *et al.*, 1981).

Optimum Stages of Development for Egg Preservation

The viability of stored oocytes increases with advancing stages of maturation at the time of storate, e.g. in rats (Kasai *et al.*, 1979). Since fertilization rarely occurs using non-frozen oocytes collected before the metaphase-I stage of maturation (Thibault, 1977), it appears necessary to freeze the oocytes only when this stage has been reached. Approximately one half of mature rat oocytes collected from the oviducts could be fertilized *in vitro* after freezing, but 62% of them showed anomalies (Niwa *et al.*, 1979). The proportion of mature oocytes which survive freezing differs from species to species: hamster oocytes collected from oviducts 15 to 16 h following HCG administration apparently survived freezing with no great difficulty whereas mouse oocytes showed a poor survival rate when frozen in the same conditions (Tsunoda *et al.*, 1976). Comparison of the results obtained in two separate studies indicates that the survival rate following transfer of mouse embryos fertilized *in vitro* was higher when freezing was performed after fertilization than when it was performed before (Nagakata & Toyoda, 1980; Whittingham, 1977b). Freezing 2-cell embryos reduced their potential viability to about 65% of that of non-frozen embryos (10% vs 15% survival), whereas freezing the oocytes led to a viability of only 37% of that of non-frozen oocytes (12% vs 32% survival).

The choice of the stage of embryonic development for freezing is generally contingent upon the propitious time for egg collection and transfer (cf. infra: egg transfer). It also depends on the vulnerability of embryos to cooling and freezing, which varies according to their developmental stage. As yet, only mouse embryos have been successfully frozen at various stages from the 1-cell to the blastocyst stages (Whittingham *et al.*, 1972; Whittingham, 1974). Mouse embryos are generally frozen at the 8-cell stage; this facilitates estimates of their survival after thawing when cultured *in vitro* before transfer at the blastocyst stage.

The survival rate of 8- to 16-cell bovine embryos was low after cooling to below 10 °C (Wilmut *et al.*, 1975) but increased for the late morula or early blastocyst stages (Trounson *et al.*, 1976). This increase in embryo survival was apparently associated with the disappearance of the numerous vesicular inclusions between the 8-cell stage and the blastocyst stage. Fortunately, the blastocyst stage in cattle is one during which embryos can easily be collected and transferred by simple cervical techniques (cf. infra: transfer methods). Bovine-hatched blastocysts at later stages of development did not survive *in vivo* after freezing (Tervit *et al.*, 1981). This stage is characterized by an increase in the total amount of lipid content (Ménezo *et al.*, 1982); lipid inclusions, either within cytoplasmic vesicles or else bound to proteins in cell membrane, are known to be non-conducive to embryo preservation at low temperatures (Edidin & Petit, 1977). Embryonic cells of pig embryos contain large amounts of lipids and globular inclusions, and these embryos do not develop after cooling to below 15 °C (Norberg, 1976; Wilmut, 1972).

Duration of Storage

Mouse oocytes and pronuclear eggs tolerate only a few hours of storage at 0 to 5 °C (Lin, 1968; Sherman & Lin, 1959). When stored at 10 °C, 8-cell mouse embryos survive only two days (Farrant, 1980), whereas rabbit and sheep embryos have been successfully preserved for 14 and

9 days respectively (Hafez, 1965; Trounson *et al.*, 1976). The proportion of bovine embryos that developed *in vivo* was roughly the same when storage had lasted 24 h at 2 °C as when it had lasted 6 months at -196 °C (Renard *et al.*, 1981). Thus only the storage of embryos at temperatures maintained by liquid nitrogen constitutes a practical method of long-term preservation. At this temperature, only photophysical reactions, such as ionizing radiations, can occur. The genetic damage from such radiations has been estimated to be the equivalent of 200 years' background radiation when embryos are stored for two years at -196 °C (Whittingham *et al.*, 1977).

Embryo banks have been created over the past several years for certain strains of mice. Because of their economic interest, banks of frozen bovine embryos are now being developed (Whittingham *et al.*, 1977; Seidel, 1981). The advantages and risks of freezing human embryos have been discussed (Edwards & Steptoe, 1977). Some attempts have been made to freeze human oocytes or embryos (Edwards & Steptoe, 1977; Whittingham, 1977c; Trounson *et al.*, 1981). As in animal species, success in this field depends not only on the methodological procedures employed but also on the stage of development reached by the embryo before freezing. Ultrastructural studies of human early embryo (Lopata *et al.*, 1980) could be helpful in determining the optimal stage for freezing, taking into account the presence of lipid inclusions.

Egg Transfer

An historical survey of embryo transfer was recently completed by Betteridge (1981). The story begins 90 years ago in Cambridge where Heape (1891) performed the first embryo transfer from donor to recipient rabbit does. Between 1933 and 1951, a certain number of embryo transfers were successfully performed in rodents: rat (Nicholas, 1933); mouse (Fekete & Little, 1942) and in farm animals: sheep (Warwick *et al.*, 1934); bovine (Umbaugh, 1949); goat (Warwick & Berry, 1949); pig (Kvasnickii, 1951). There has been spectacular development of embryo transfer in cattle over the past ten years, since commercial applications of the method for increasing the reproductible rate of valuable cows became obvious. The various techniques involved (superovulation, egg collection, storage and transfer) are increasingly simple and efficient. According to Seidel (1981), approximately 17,000 bovine pregnancies were induced by superovulation and embryo transfer in North America in 1979, the cost of each being about $1,500.

Relatively little research has been done on egg transfer or replacement in non-human primates. Only a few successes have been reported in the baboon (Kraemer *et al.*, 1976) and the macaque (Marston *et al.*, 1977; Kreitman & Hodgen, 1980). Thus, information concerning egg transfer in mammals is mainly derived from results in cattle, mouse and rabbit. Three main variables in embryo transfer could affect the success rate of pregnancy, namely:

(a) The embryo's stage of development (i.e. the age of the embryo).

(b) The time interval between ovulation in the recipient and the transfer (i.e. the "age of the uterus").

(c) The method used for transferring the embryo.

Other factors, such as the respective ages of donor and recipient females, or the hormonal environment following superovulation induction, are not dealt with in the present study. The possible effects of seasonal influence must be mentioned, since it appeared that the transfer of frozen bovine embryos (Bilton, 1980) resulted in a higher rate of pregnancies during spring time (58%) than during autumn or winter (35%). Research in this field usually makes no reference to a possible influence of the time of day at which the transfer is performed.

Time of Egg Transfer: Post-ovulatory Day and Embryo Stage

In all species studied, transfers are most successful when the egg is placed in the portion of the genital tract (either the uterus or the tubes) at a time corresponding to its developmental stage. Since egg transfer has been used in humans, at least until now, essentially as a treatment for tubal sterility, the egg must be placed either in the uterus or in the lower portion of the tube.

Extrapolating from animal studies, the human embryo must not be transferred until the third day following fertilization, when it reaches the 8-cell stage. However, earlier transfers have proved to be successful in man and it should be recalled that fertilization can occur within the human uterus (Estes & Heitmeyer, 1934). Although there are cases of rabbit oocytes being fertilized within the uterus (Chang, 1955), this possibility has not been confirmed in other species: none of 392 hamster oocytes transferred into the uterus of inseminated females were fertilized (Hunter, 1968), and similar attempts have failed in the macaque (Kreitman; Marston, personal communications) and in man (Frydman and Testart, unpublished data). By contrast, five pregnancies followed low tubal transfer of 31 macaque oocytes

(Kreitman & Hodgen, 1980). This success rate (16%) was greater than the one reported hitherto in cases of in-vitro fertilization and embryo replacement in humans. The primate uterus, unlike that of other species is apparently able to receive very young eggs, since Marston (personal communication) obtained two pregnancies following uterine autotransfer of three tubal pronucleate eggs.

Conversely, embryo transfer too late after ovulation is not compatible with implantation. In sheep, pregnancy can regularly result from the uterine transfer of 12- to 13-day embryos at 12 days after ovulation occurs in the recipient female, whereas one day later, pregnancy does not occur (Moor & Rowson, 1964). Ruminants differ from most other species in that the length of the oestrous cycle (21 days in cows) is shorter than the time between ovulation and implantation (35 days in cows), and a luteotrophic signal must be emitted from the free blastocyst before the time of implantation. It would seem that in man as in many other mammals, the embryo can be transferred until a time quite close to the time of implantation.

A special phenomenon occurs when the embryo is placed inside the uterus through the cervical canal rather than by surgical intervention. In this case, the physiological response of the uterus is related to the day of the recipient's cycle, which can affect the result of the transfer as has been shown in cattle. Non-surgical embryo transfer in cows at least 6 days after oestrus is considerably more successful than transfer earlier in the cycle (Lawson et al., 1975). Bovine embryos must be transferred into the uterus through the cervical canal at least two days after the normal time the embryo enters the uterus from the fallopian tube (cf. infra: transfer methods).

For each mammalian species, a specific developmental stage of the embryo guarantees the maximal success of embryo transfer. The analysis of 2,286 non-surgical embryo transfers in cows revealed a better rate of pregnancy when blastocysts (65%) rather than morulae (44%) were transferred into synchronized recipients (Wright, 1981). According to the same study, the rate of pregnancy depended on the embryo stage rather than on the cycle day of the recipient. A 36-hour interval between the respective dates of oestrus of donor and recipient cows had no effect on the result.

Contrary to animal species, the human embryo has always been transferred into the uterus of the patient from which the oocyte was collected. Thus, apart from cases of embryo storage, the problem of synchronizing the cycles of the donor and recipient females does not exist in humans. However, a delay has been observed between the stage reached by embryos cultured *in vitro* when compared with those growing *in vivo*, e.g. rabbit (Maurer *et al.*, 1970), mouse (Bowman & McLaren, 1970). Although in-vitro culture of rabbit embryos did not result in ultrastructural or biochemical degradation (Van Blerkom *et al.*, 1973, 1974), the success of transfers of cultured embryos decreases as the duration of in-vitro culture increases.

We have already described how the luteal stage of the recipient must be timed in order to coincide with the developmental stage of the transferred rabbit embryo, rather than with its chronological age, and the pregnancy rate was maximal when rabbit eggs cultured from 26 to 96 h *post coitum* (*p.c.*) were transferred to a recipient doe at 48 h *p.c.* (Binkerd & Anderson, 1979). This demonstrates that the maternal environment at 48 h *p.c.* corresponds to the maturational stage of embryos that have been cultured for 3 days. Because of the poor information about the in-vivo stage of dated early embryos, it is not known whether the same effect of in-vitro culture occurs with human embryos. If it does, it would be advantageous to store human embryos until transferring them at a propitious moment.

There are other negative effects of in-vitro culture which have no relation to delayed development. When bovine embryos were transferred following in-vitro culture for 24 h (Renard *et al.*, 1980) the pregnancy rate was identical to that obtained with non-cultured embryos, but after in-vitro culture embryonic mortality often occurred at the time of implantation (between 35 and 60 days). The exceptionally late implantation in the cow makes it possible to distinguish between preimplantation and postimplantation survival of transferred embryos. In most species, including man, there is no clinical evidence of pregnancy before implantation. This prevents estimates of embryo survival during the period immediately following embryo transfer. It is possible that many transferred human embryos continue their development *in utero* until the time of implantation, despite the fact that pregnancy rate is low.

An important problem is the establishment of criteria for the quality of human embryos before their replacement in the uterus following in-vitro fertilization and culture. This should lower the risk of anomalies in newborn babies and also help to avoid the psychic stress of patients whose badly-wanted pregnancies result in abortion. The subjective evaluation of embryo quality on the basis of appearance is the only criterion used at present, but it has proved to be valid at least to some extent in cattle. The success rates were 64, 45 and 33% when the transferred bovine embryos were evaluated grade 1, 2 and 3, respectively (Wright, 1981).

Methods for Transferring Embryos *in utero*

The first successful embryo transfers were performed by surgical intervention using laparotomy of anaesthetized recipient females. Over the past 30 years, there have been numerous attempts to avoid surgery by placing the embryo in the uterus through the cervical canal. The first births using this method were obtained by Beatty in 1951; he proposed the term "inovulation" for this technique which resulted in a success rate of 10% in mouse. This rate was later improved and has reached 50% in mouse (Marsk & Larsen, 1974), about 30% in rat (Vickery *et al.*, 1969) and between 47 and 59% in rabbit (Dauzier, 1962; Hafez, 1962). However, the cervical method of embryo transfer had a low success rate (2 to 4%) in goat (Otsuki & Soma, 1964) and in pig (Polge & Day, 1968). The first calf was obtained by Mutter *et al.*, 1965, following non-surgical transfer. Numerous investigations in cattle have led to recent improvements with results nearly as positive as those obtained using surgical intervention (30–60% vs. 50–70% pregnancies using non-surgical and surgical techniques, respectively.

It is worth mentioning that various other techniques have been explored in order to avoid both true surgery and the cervical canal method. The possibility of putting the human arm into the vagina or into the rectum of a cow did nothing but stimulate the imagination of certain investigators. . . . The transrectum introduction of a transfer needle into the uterine lumen has been tried without success (Avery *et al.*, 1962). Two techniques have been proposed for introducing the embryos inside the uterus through the vaginal cul-de-sac (Sugie, 1965; Testart & Leglise, 1971), resulting in success rates of about 30% (Sugie *et al.*, 1972; Testart *et al.*, 1975). The transvaginal route also met with some success in the mare, whereas the cervical route did not (Oguri & Tsutsumi, 1972, 1974). Avery *et al.* (1962) also tried to induce pregnancy in the cow by transferring the eggs directly to the abdominal cavity, in hopes that they would be captured by the fimbria. However, particles or eggs placed into the abdomen reached the uterus only in very low and highly hazardous proportions (Dauzier, 1962; Croxatto *et al.*, 1973).

Six years ago, Rowson's group in Cambridge (Lawson *et al.*, 1975) established that the success rate of cervical embryo transfer was greatly improved when the transfer was performed later in the cycle (6 to 9 rather than 3 to 5 days following oestrus). This result laid the foundations for the extensive use of embryo transfer in cattle. Two negative consequences of early transfers via the cervix might be avoided by later transfers: uterine infection, and expulsion of embryos.

Uterine Infection After Transfer

The first success obtained by cervical embryo transfer in cattle (Mutter *et al.*, 1965) occurred when daily injections of antibiotics were made *in utero* between oestrus and the date of transfer. Rowson and Moor (1966) assigned an antiseptic function to the CO_2 they insufflated into the uterus, and uterine sensitivity to bacterial contamination at the beginning of the luteal phase has been demonstrated (Dzuik *et al.*, 1958). Blood serum was injected *in utero* at 3- to 7-days following oestrus in inseminated cows, and the pregnancy rate dropped only when the injected serum was free of antibiotics. We showed in the rabbit that vulval or vaginal stimulations at the time of embryo transfer did not affect the rate of implantation of 4-day transferred blastocysts (Testart, 1969). However, crossing the cervical canal by the catheter used for transfer brought about a severe drop in the implantation rate (45% vs 77%, Table 3). This drop was the result of uterine contamination rather than of egg expulsion toward the vagina because some eggs were recovered in the vagina when transferred at day 2 but expulsion did not occur following transfer at day 3 or 4.

Table 3
Effect of vaginal (speculum) or cervical (catheter through the cervical canal) stimulations on the result of rabbit embryo transfer at 4 days (From the data of Testart, 1969)

Stimulations		Number of does			Non-infected does		
Vagina Cervix		Total	Uterine infection	Number not pregnant	Number of transferred blastocysts	Implantations (%)	Embryo survival at day 11 (%)
Control		18	0	0	211	77.7	85.9
+	0	16	1	1	164	76.2	87.2
0	+	11	5[3]*	4[1]	64	45.3[4]	96.5
+	+	28	7	8[2]	169	44.9[5]	85.5

*Differences with control group: [1,2]$p < 0.05$; [3]$p < 0.01$; [4,5]$p < 0.001$.

Expulsion of Embryos After Transfer

Radioactive spheres placed inside the cow uterus during the luteal phase were recovered *in situ* 4 h after having been deposited across the uterine wall, whereas they were expelled in the vagina within 1.5 h when transferred through the cervix (Bennet & Rowson, 1961). In addition, rabbit eggs introduced through the cervical canal in the cow uterus were expelled 2 h later (Testart & Leglise, 1970). This phenomenon might have an influence on the entire genital tract, since the alien tubal egg reached the mare uterus earlier when the cervical canal was stimulated (Oguri & Tsutsumi, 1972). However gold radioactive microspheres were significantly retained within the cow uterus when transferred at 7- to 8-days rather than at 4- to 5-days following oestrous. Furthermore, the myometrial activity of the cow uterus decreases sharply as of the 4th day following oestrus, attaining a very low level at days 6–7 (Brand, 1976). Uterine contractions in the ewe have been shown to be rarely (35%) in direction of the cervix during oestrus, contrary to what can be observed two days later (70%) (Croker & Shelton, 1973).

Only a few attempts have been made to understand the physiological mechanism of the contractile uterine response to cervical stimulus. Uterine contractions can be induced by injections of oxytocin, but oxytocin was not detected in blood following cervical stimulation (Rowson et al., 1972). Uterine or cervical dilatation in lactating cows can produce the milk ejection reflex although the fact that oxytocin was not detected in blood might reflect a false estimation of oxytocin levels in plasma (Testart and Martinet, unpublished observations). Nor could prostaglandins ($PGF_{2\alpha}$) be detected in ovarian blood following cervical stimulation in the cow (Manns et al., 1975).

Although the release of these substances could not be demonstrated in these conditions, some attempts have been made to prevent egg expulsion from the uterus by using various drugs. Adrenalin was ineffective in cows (Harper et al., 1961), even when combined with atrophin in subcutaneous administration (Rowson et al., 1964). Uterine instillation of procaine or papaverin produced only weak or no effects. Local anaesthesia of the cervix produced no effects in the goat, whereas success was reported when a specific parasympathetic antagonist was used (Otsuki & Soma, 1964). Finally, uterine instillation of CO_2 at the time of transfer in the cow limited egg expulsion from the uterus (Testart & Leglise, 1970; Hafez & Sugie, 1963; Rowson & Moor, 1966). Studies in this direction have not been undertaken in primates, which is a serious omission in our knowledge.

Conclusions

In conclusion, it is worth noting that the pregnancy rate following human embryo replacement, as reported in this book, was similar for some groups of investigators, despite the fact that different types of cannulae were used for the introduction of the embryo into the uterine cavity through the cervical canal. Between 15 and 20% pregnancies were obtained by some groups after embryo replacement at 2- or 3- days following fertilization *in vitro*.

It is possible that human in-vitro fertilized eggs are frequently non-viable and this might explain the low success rate; however, this poor result is reminiscent of the similar situation in cattle when the cervical transfer of early embryos was first attempted ten years ago. It is important to recall that improvements were obtained by modifying either the method used (transvaginal or surgical techniques) or the day of embryo transfer. It is not yet known whether prolonged in-vitro culture of human embryos might increase the pregnancy rate following uterine replacement of morula or blastocyst 4 to 6 days after fer-tilization. Conversely, neither is it known how the pregnancy rate would be modified if 4- to 8-cell human embryos were replaced *in utero* using the non-cervical route.

These questions must be resolved in order to improve the efficiency of human embryo replacement. Freezing the embryo might allow either the storage of supplementary embryos obtained when hormonal stimulation is used, or the postponement of embryo replacement until a later, non-treated cycle. The developmental stage allowing for the optimum survival of frozen-thawed human embryos remains to be determined. It must also correspond to a favourable period for embryo culture and a propitious day for embryo replacement.

References

Allen, W. R., Stewart, F., Trounson, A. O., Tischner, M., Kosiniak, K. & Bielanski, W. 1976. Viability of horse embryos after storage and long-distance transport in the rabbit. *Journal of Reproduction and Fertility*, **47**, 387–390.

Anderson, G. B. & Foote, R. H. 1975. Effects of low temperature upon subsequent nucleic acid and protein synthesis of rabbit embryos. *Experimental Cell Research*, **90**, 73–78.

Avery, T. L., Fahning, M. L., Pursel, V. G. & Graham, E. F. 1962. Investigations associated with the transplantation of bovine ova. IV. Transplantation of ova. *Journal of Reproduction and Fertility*, **3**, 229–238.

Bank, H. & Maurer, R. R. 1974. Survival of frozen rabbit embryos. *Experimental Cell Research*, **89**, 188–196.

Beatty, R. A. 1951. Transplantation of mouse eggs. *Nature*, **168**, 995.

Bennett, J. P. & Rowson, L. E. A. 1961. The use of radioactive artificial eggs in studies of egg transfer and transport in the female reproductive tract. *Proceedings of the 4th Congress of Animal Reproduction*, **2**, 360.

Betteridge, K. J. 1981. An historical look at embryo transfer. *Journal of Reproduction and Fertility*, **62**, 1-13.

Bilton, R. J. 1980. Preservation of embryos of the large domestic species. *Proceedings of the 9th International Congress of Animal Reproduction, Madrid*, 245-253.

Bilton, R. J. & Moore, N. W. 1976. In-vitro culture, storage and transfer of goat embryos. *Australian Journal of Biological Sciences*, **29**, 125-129.

Binkerd, P. E. & Anderson, G. B. 1979. Transfer of cultured rabbit embryos. *Gamete Research*, **2**, 65-73.

Bowman, P. & McLaren, A. 1970. Cleavage rate of mouse embryos *in vivo* and *in vitro*. *Journal of Embryology and Experimental Morphology*, **24**, 203-207.

Brackett, B. G., Bousquet, D., Boice, M. L., Donawick, W. J. & Evans, J. F. 1981. Pregnancy following cow in-vitro fertilization. *Biology of Reproduction*, **24**, 109 (Abstract).

Brand, A. 1976. Non-surgical embryo transfer in cattle. In: *Egg Transfer in Cattle*, pp. 41-56. Ed. L. E. A. Rowson. E.E.C., Luxembourg.

Chang, M. C. 1947. Normal development of fertilized rabbit ova stored at low temperature for several days. *Nature*, **159**, 602-603.

Chang, M. C. 1955. In: *La Fonction Tubaire et ses Troubles*, pp. 40-52. Masson et Cie, Paris.

Chang, M. C. 1959. Fertilization of rabbit ova in vitro. *Nature*, **184**, 466-467.

Croker, K. P. & Shelton, J. N. 1973. Influence of stage of cycle, progestogen treatment and dose of oestrogen on uterine motility in the ewe. *Journal of Reproduction and Fertility*, **32**, 521-524.

Croxatto, H. B., Vogel, C. & Vasquez, J. 1973. Transport of microspheres in the genital tract of the female rabbit. *Journal of Reproduction and Fertility*, **33**, 337-341.

Dauzier, L. 1962. Nouvelles données sur la transplantation des oeufs chez la lapine, par voie vaginale ou intrapéritonéale. *Ann. Biol. anim. Bioch. Biophys.*, **2**, 17-24.

De Mayo, F. J., Mizoguchi, H. & Dukelow, W. R. 1980. Fertilization of squirrel-monkey and hamster ova in the rabbit oviduct (xenogenous fertilization). *Science*, **208**, 1468-1469.

Dziuk, P. J., Donker, J. D., Nichols, J. R. & Petersen, W. E. 1958. Problems associated with the transfer of ova between cattle. *University of Minnesota Agricultural Experimental Station Technical Bulletin*, **222**, 75.

Edidin, M. & Petit, V. A. 1977. The effect of temperature on the lateral diffusion of plasma membranes proteins. In: *The Freezing of Mammalian Embryos*. Ciba Foundation Symposium, **52**, pp. 155-164. Elsevier, Excerpta Medica, North-Holland, Amsterdam.

Edwards, R. G. & Steptoe, P. C. 1977. The relevance of the frozen storage of human embryos. In: *The Freezing of Mammalian Embryos*. Ciba Foundation Symposium, **52**, pp. 235-250. Elsevier Excerpta Medica, North-Holland, Amsterdam.

Estes, W. L. & Heitmeyer, P. L. 1934. Pregnancy following ovarian implantation. *American Journal of Surgery*, **24**, 563-580.

Farrant, J. 1980. General observations on cell preservation. In: *Low Temperature Preservation in Medicine and Biology*, pp. 1-18. Eds. M. J. Ashwood-Smith and J. Farrant. Pitman Medical, Tunbridge Wells.

Fekete, E. & Little, C. G. 1942. Observations on the mammary tumor incidence of mice born from transferred ova. *Cancer Research*, **2**, 525-530.

Fishel, S. & Edwards, R. G. 1982. Essentials of fertilization. In: *Human Conception in vitro*. Eds. R. G. Edwards & J. M. Purdy. Academic Press, London (this volume, pp. 157-179).

252 J. TESTART AND J.-P. RENARD

Gardner, B. L. & Edwards, R. G. 1968. Control of the sex ratio at full term in the rabbit by transferred sexed blastocysts. *Nature*, **218**, 346–348.

Hafez, E. S. E. 1962. Effect of progestational stage of the endometrium on implantation, fetal survival and fetal size in the rabbit. *Journal of Experimental Zoology*, **151**, 217–226.

Hafez, E. S. E. 1965. Storage media for rabbit ova. *Journal of Applied Physiology*, **20**, 731–736.

Hafez, E. S. E. & Sugie, T. 1963. Reciprocal transfer of cattle and rabbit embryos. *Journal of Animal Science*, **22**, 31–35.

Hare, W. C. D., Singh, E. L., Betteridge, K. J., Eaglesome, M. D., Randall, G. C. B. & Mitchell, D. 1978. Embryo sexing with particular reference to cattle. In: *Control of Reproduction in the Cow*, pp. 441–449. Eds. J. M. Streenan & M. Nijhoff. La Haye.

Harper, M. J. K., Bennett, J. P. & Rowson, L. E. A. 1961. Movement of the ovum in the reproductive tract. A possible explanation for the failure of non-surgical ovum transfer in the cow. *Nature*, **190**, 789.

Heape, W. 1891. Preliminary note on the transplantation and growth of mammalian ova within a uterine foster-mother. *Proceedings of the Royal Society*, **48**, 457–458.

Hoppe, P. C. & Pitts, S. 1973. Fertilization *in vitro* and development of mouse ova. *Biology of Reproduction*, **8**, 420–426.

Hunter, R. H. F. 1968. Attempted fertilization of hamster eggs following transplantation into the uterus. *Journal of Experimental Zoology*, **168**, 511–515.

Kardymowicz, O., du Mesnil du Buisson, F., Wintenberger-Torres, S. & Zapletal, S. 1976. The long-distance transport of fertilized sheep ova stopped *in vitro* at a temperature above 0 °C. *Proceedings of the 8th Congress of Animal Reproduction*, **3**, 254–257.

Kasai, M., Iritani, A. & Chang, M. C. 1979. Fertilization of rat ovarian oocytes after freezing and thawing. *Biology of Reproduction*, **21**, 839–844.

Kraemer, D. C., Moore, G. T. & Kramen, M. A. 1976. Baboon infant produced by embryo transfer. *Science*, **192**, 1246–1247.

Kreitman, O. & Hodgen, G. D. 1980. Low tubal ovum transfer: an alternative to in-vitro fertilization. *Fertility and Sterility*, **34**, 375–378.

Kvasnickii, A. V. 1951. Interbred ova transplantation. *Animal Breeding Abstracts*, **19**, 224.

Lawson, R. A. S., Adams, C. E. & Rowson, L. E. A. 1972a. The development of sheep eggs in the rabbit oviduct and their viability after re-transfer to ewes. *Journal of Reproduction and Fertility*, **29**, 105–116.

Lawson, R. A. S., Rowson, L. E. A. & Adams, C. E. 1972b. The development of cow eggs in the rabbit oviduct and their viability after re-transfer to heifers. *Journal of Reproduction and Fertility*, **28**, 313–315.

Lawson, R. A. S., Rowson, L. E. A., Moor, R. M. & Tervit, H. R. 1975. Experiments on egg transfer in the cow and ewe: dependance of conception rate on the transfer procedure and stage of the oestrous cycle. *Journal of Reproduction and Fertility*, **45**, 101–107.

Leibo, S. D. 1977. Fundamental cryobiology of mouse ova and embryos. In: *The Freezing of Mammalian Embryos*. Ciba Foundation Symposium, **52**, pp. 69–91. Elsevier, North-Holland, Amsterdam.

Lin, T. P. 1968. Survival of pronuclear mouse eggs kept at different temperatures. *Journal of Experimental Zoology*, **168**, 501–510.

Lopata, A., Sathananthan, A. H., McBain, J., Johnston, H. & Speirs, A. L. 1980.

The ultrastructure of the preovulatory human egg fertilized *in vitro. Fertility and Sterility*, **33**, 12–20.

Lovelock, J. E. 1955. The haemolysis of human red blood cells by freezing and thawing. *Biochimica et Biophysica. Acta*, **10**, 414–416.

Manns, J. G., Newcomb, R. & Rowson, L. E. A. 1975. Effect of cervical stimulation on $PGF_{2\alpha}$ release into ovarian vein blood of heifers. *Veterinary Record*, **96**, 384–385.

Marsk, L. & Larsson, K. S. 1974. A simple method for non-surgical blastocyst transfer in mice. *Journal of Reproduction and Fertility*, **37**, 393–398.

Marston, J. H., Penn, R. & Sivelle, P. C. 1977. Successful autotransfer of tubal eggs in the Rhesus monkey. *Journal of Reproduction and Fertility*, **49**, 175–176.

Maurer, R. R. 1976. Storage of mammalian oocytes and embryos: a review. *Canadian Journal of Animal Science*, **56**, 131–145.

Maurer, R. R. & Haseman, J. K. 1976. Freezing morula stage rabbit embryos. *Biology of Reproduction*, **14**, 256–263.

Maurer, R. R., Onuma, H. & Foote, R. H. 1970. Viability of cultured and transferred rabbit embryo. *Journal of Reproduction and Fertility*, **21**, 417–422.

Mazur, P. 1970. Cryobiology: the freezing of biological systems. *Science*, **168**, 939–949.

Menezo, Y., Renard, J. P., Pageaux, J. F. & Delobel, B. 1982. Kinetic study of fatty acid composition of D7 to D14 embryos. *Biology of Reproduction* (in press).

Miyamoto, H., Katsuura, G. & Ishibashi, T. 1977. Strain differences in survival of frozen thawed mouse embryos. *Japanese Journal of Zootechnical Science*, **48**, 634–640.

Moor, R. M. & Rowson, L. E. A. 1964. Influence of the embryo and uterus on luteal function in the sheep. *Nature*, **201**, 522–523.

Mutter, L. R., Graden, A. P. & Olds, D. 1965. Successful non-surgical bovine embryo transfer. *A.I. Digest*, **12**, 3.

Nakagata, N. & Toyoda, Y. 1980. Normal young after transfer of frozen-thawed 2-cell mouse embryos obtained by fertilization *in vitro. Japanese Journal of Zootechnical Science*, **51**, 740–744.

Nicholas, J. S. 1933. Development of transplanted rat eggs. *Proceedings of the Society for Experimental Biology and Medicine*, **30**, 1111–1113.

Niwa, K., Kasai, M. & Iritani, A. 1979. Fertilization *in vitro* of rat eggs after freezing and thawing. *Japanese Journal of Zootechnical Science*, **50**, 747–752.

Norberg, H. S. 1976. Ultrastructural aspects of the preattached pig embryo: cleavage and early blastocyst stages. *Z. Anat. Entwickl. Gesch.*, **143**, 95–114.

Oguri, N. & Tsutsumi, Y. 1972. Non-surgical recovery of equine eggs and an attempt at non-surgical egg transfer in horses. *Journal of Reproduction and Fertility*, **31**, 187.

Oguri, N. & Tsutsumi, Y. 1974. Non-surgical egg transfer in mares. *Journal of Reproduction and Fertility*, **41**, 313–320.

Otsuki, K. & Soma, T. 1964. Transfer of fertilized ova through the cervix in goats. *Bull. Nat. Inst. Anim. Ind.*, **6**, 27–32.

Polge, C. E. & Day, B. N. 1968. Pregnancy following non-surgical egg transfer in pigs. *Veterinary Record*, **82**, 712.

Polge, C. E. & Willadsen, S. M. 1978. Freezing eggs and embryos of farm animals. *Cryobiology*, **15**, 370–373.

Polge, C. E., Adams, C. E. & Baker, R. D. 1972. Development and survival of pig embryo in the rabbit oviduct. *Proceedings of the 7th Congress of Animal Reproduction*, 513–517.

Renard, J. P., Heyman, Y. & Ozil, J. P. 1980. Importance of gestation losses after non-surgical transfer of cultured and non-cultured bovine blastocysts. *Veterinary Record*, **107**, 152–153.

Renard, J. P., Ozil, J. P. & Heyman, Y. 1981. Cervical transfer of deep-frozen cattle embryos. *Theriogenology*, **15**, 311–320.

Rowson, L. E. A. & Moor, R. M. 1966. Non-surgical transfer of cow eggs. *Journal of Reproduction and Fertility*, **11**, 311–312.

Rowson, L. E. A., Bennett, J. P. & Harper, M. J. K. 1964. The problem of non-surgical egg transfer to the cow uterus. *Veterinary Record*, **76**, 21–23.

Rowson, L. E. A., McNeilly, A. S. & O'Brien, C. A. 1972. The effect of vaginal and cervical stimulation on oxytocin release during the luteal phase of the cow's oestrous cycle. *Journal of Reproduction and Fertility*, **30**, 287.

Seidel, G. E. 1981. Superovulation and embryo transfer in cattle. *Science*, **211**, 351–358.

Sherman, J. K. & Lin, T. P. 1959. Temperature shock and cold storage of unfertilized mouse eggs. *Fertility and Sterility*, **10**, 384–396.

Smith, A. U. 1952. Behaviour of fertilized rabbit eggs exposed to glycerol and to low temperatures. *Nature*, **170**, 374–375.

Sugie, T. 1965. Successful transfer of a fertilized bovine egg by non-surgical technique. *Journal of Reproduction and Fertility*, **10**, 187–202.

Sugie, T., Soma, T., Fukumitzu, S. & Otsuki, K. 1972. Studies on the ovum transfer in cattle, with special reference to transplantation of fertilized ova by means of non-surgical techniques. *Bull. Nat. Inst. Anim. Ind.*, **25**, 27–33.

Tervit, H. R., Rowson, L. E. A. & McDonald, M. F. 1974. Application of the egg transfer technique in cattle and sheep. *Proceedings of the New Zealand Society of Animal Production*, **34**, 56–60.

Tervit, H. R., Elsden, R. P. & Farrand, G. M. 1981. Deep freezing 7 to 8 and 10 to 11-day-old cattle embryos. *Theriogenology*, **15**, 114.

Testart, J. 1969. Comparaison de différentes techniques de transplantation, des blastocystes chez la lapine. *Ann. Biol. anim. Bioch. Biophy.*, **9**, 351–360.

Testart, J. & Leglise, P. C. 1970. Recherche d'une technique de transplantation des oeufs chez la vache. *Ann. Biol. anim. Bioch. Biophys.*, **10**, 147–153.

Testart, J. & Leglise, P. C. 1971. Transplantation d'oeufs divisés, chez la vache, par voie transvaginale. *C.R. Acad. Sc., Paris*, **272**, 2591–2592.

Testart, J., Godard-Siour, C. & du Mesnil du Buisson, F. 1975. Transvaginal transplantation of an extra egg to obtain twinning in cattle. *Theriogenology*, **4**, 163–168.

Thibault, C. 1977. Are follicular maturation and oocyte maturation independent processes? *Journal of Reproduction and Fertility*, **51**, 1–15.

Toyoda, Y. & Chang, M. C. 1974. Fertilization of rat eggs *in vitro* by epididymal spermatozoa and the development of eggs following transfer. *Journal of Reproduction and Fertility*, **36**, 9–22.

Trounson, A. O., Willadsen, S. M., Rowson, L. E. A. & Newcomb, R. 1976. The storage of cow eggs at room temperature and at low temperatures. *Journal of Reproduction and Fertility*, **46**, 173–178.

Trounson, A. O., Mohr, L. R., Pugh, P. A., Leeton, J. F. & Wood, E. C. 1981. The deep-freezing of human embryos. In: *World Congress of Human Reproduction*, Berlin (in press).

Tsunoda, Y., Parkening, T. F. & Chang, M. C. 1976. In-vitro fertilization of mouse and hamster eggs after freezing and thawing. *Experientia*, **32**, 223–224.

Umbaugh, R. E. 1949. Superovulation and ovum transfer in cattle. *American Journal of Veterinary Research*, **10**, 295–305.

Van Blerkom, J. & Manes, C. 1974. Development of preimplantation rabbit embryo in vivo and in vitro. II. A comparison of qualitative aspects of protein synthesis. Developmental Biology, 40, 40–51.

Van Blerkom, J., Manes, C. & Daniel, J. C. 1973. Development of preimplantation rabbit embryo in vivo and in vitro. I. An ultrastructural comparison. Developmental Biology, 35, 262–282.

Vickery, B. H., Erickson, G. I. & Bennett, J. P. 1969. Non-surgical transfer of eggs through the cervix in rats. Endocrinology, 85, 1202–1203.

Warwick, B. L. & Berry, R. D. 1949. Inter-generic and intra-specific embryo transfers. Journal of Heredity, 40, 297–303.

Warwick, B. L., Berry, R. D. & Horlacher, W. R. 1934. Results of mating rams to Angora female goats. Proc. 27th ann. Meet. Am. Soc. anim. Prod., 225–227.

Whittingham, D. G. 1968. Fertilization of mouse eggs in vitro. Nature, 220, 592–593.

Whittingham, D. G. 1974. The viability of frozen-thawed mouse blastocysts. Journal of Reproduction and Fertility, 37, 159–162.

Whittingham, D. G., 1975. Survival of rat embryos after freezing and thawing. Journal of Reproduction and Fertility, 43, 575–578.

Whittingham, D. G. 1977a. Some factors affecting embryo storage in laboratory animals. In: The Freezing of Mammalian Embryos Ciba Foundation Symposium, 52, pp. 93–108. Elsevier, North-Holland, Amsterdam.

Whittingham, D. G. 1977b. Fertilization in vitro and development to term of unfertilized mouse oocytes previously stored at −196 °C. Journal of Reproduction and Fertility, 49, 89–94.

Whittingham, D. G. 1977c. In "The Freezing of Mammalian Embryos". Ciba Foundation Symposium, 52, p. 243. Elsevier Excerpta Medica, North-Holland, Amsterdam.

Whittingham, D. G., Leibo, S. P. & Mazur, P. 1972. Survival of mouse embryos frozen to −196 °C and −269 °C. Science, 178, 411–414.

Whittingham, D. G., Lyon, M. F. & Glenister, P. H. 1977. Re-establishment of breeding stocks of mutants and inbred strains of mice from embryos stored at −196 °C for prolonged periods. Genetical Research, Cambridge, 30, 287–299.

Whittingham, D. G., Wood, M., Farrant, J., Lee, M. & Hasley, J. A. 1979. Survival of frozen mouse embryos after rapid thawing from −196 °C. Journal of Reproduction and Fertility, 56, 11–21.

Willadsen, S. M. 1980. The viability of early cleavage stages containing half the normal number of blastomeres in the sheep. Journal of Reproduction and Fertility, 59, 357–362.

Willadsen, S. M. & Polge, C. 1981. Attempts to produce monozygotic quadruplets in cattle by blastomere separation. Veterinary Record, 108, 211–213.

Willadsen, S. M., Polge, C., Rowson, L. E. A. & Moor, R. M. 1976. Deep freezing of sheep embryos. Journal of Reproduction and Fertility, 46, 151–154.

Willadsen, S. M., Polge, C. & Rowson, L. E. A. 1978. The viability of deep-frozen cow embryos. Journal of Reproduction and Fertility, 52, 391–393.

Wilmut, I. 1972. The low temperature preservation of mammalian embryos. Journal of Reproduction and Fertility, 31, 513–514.

Wilmut, I. 1973. The successful low temperature preservation of mouse and cow embryos. Journal of Reproduction and Fertility, 33, 352–353.

Wilmut, I., Polge, C. & Rowson, L. E. A. 1975. The effect on cow embryos of cooling to 20, 0 and −196 °C. Journal of Reproduction and Fertility, 45, 409–411.

Wright, J. M. 1981. Non-surgical embryo transfer in cattle. Embryo-recipient interactions. Theriogenology, 15, 43.

The Human Uterus in the Luteal Phase and Early Pregnancy

R. G. Edwards[1] and S. B. Fishel[1,2]

Studies on the uterus and the implanting embryo are too numerous to review in detail. Extensive reference works are available (Dallenbach-Hellweg, 1975; Wynn, 1977; Edwards, 1980). We will describe some properties of the uterus and early conceptus which could influence the success of work on replacing human embryos for the cure of infertility. Especial reference will be made to the primate uterus, and to the luteal phase of the cycle.

The uterus is stimulated primarily by oestrogens during the follicular phase, and by oestrogens and progesterone during the luteal phase. Responses to these hormones dictate its typical cyclic changes in histology, glandular structure, secretion and myometrial activity. Some essential aspects of uterine physiology are poorly understood, e.g. the importance of its changing secretions, and the attachment of embryos to the epithelium during implantation. More knowledge is urgently needed for studies on the replacement of human embryos; the low rate of implantation is the major stumbling block to the attainment of high rates of pregnancy, since fertilization and cleavage *in vitro* have been achieved with very high rates of success.

Physiological and Biochemical Changes in Uterine Tissues During the Reproductive Cycle

Cell division during the proliferative phase leads to an increase in thickness of the endometrium under the influence of oestrogens, and the typical development of the uterine glands. Towards mid-cycle, the stroma becomes increasingly vascular, the arteries spiralized, and the

---

[1] Physiological Laboratory, Cambridge University, and Bourn Hall, Cambridge.
[2] Beit Memorial Research Fellow.

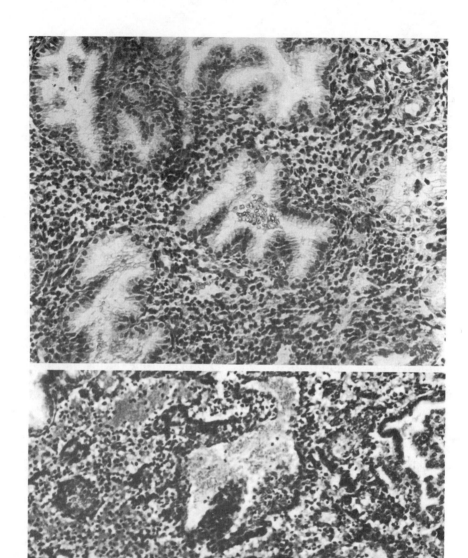

uterine glands developed. There is a further thickening of the endometrium during the luteal phase, with vascularization and oedema of
the stroma, and an accumulation of secretions in the now highly-
convoluted uterine glands (Fig. 1). The glandular secretions are rich in
carbohydrates, and glycogen is secreted into the lumen. The glands
enlarge further during pregnancy. At menstruation, the coiled arteries
of the basal layer constrict as their spiralling becomes intense, and the
superficial zone of the endometrium is blanched for hours at a time.
Glandular activity decreases, interstitial fluid is lost, and leucocytes
invade the tissues (Fig. 1). The histological changes in the uterus
provide the basis for menstrual dating, and the interpretation of the
action of the various exogenous steroids, natural or artificial, used for
contraception and other purposes (Noyes *et al.*, 1950).

Physiological changes during the menstrual cycle include alterations
in the permeability of blood vessels and tissues, the release of

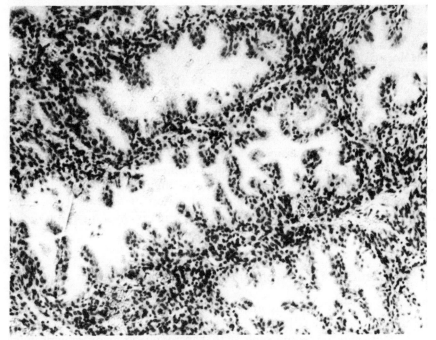

FIG. 1. Histology of the human uterus (Edwards, 1980). (a) Late secretory phase, with
the endometrium at maximum thickness, branching glands and extensive secretion,
and the nuclei at the base of cells of the glandular epithelium. (b) Menstruation. The
glands are tortuous, and the tissue is infiltrated by erythrocytes and polymorphs.
(c) Pregnancy. The glands are hypertrophied, with saw-toothed convolutions, low
epithelium and thin interglandular septae.

histamines and changing rates of blood flow. Cell division is involved in the proliferative renewal of the uterine tissue after menstruation, and in the luteal phase. Specific peaks of RNA synthesis have been identified, e.g. one during oestrus and another on day 4 of the luteal phase of the rat (Blahna & Yochim, 1975; O'Grady et al., 1975). The second period of RNA synthesis may result in the production of proteins specifically concerned with implantation.

The changing levels of oestrogen and progesterone control enzymic pathways involved in protein synthesis and carbohydrate metabolism. Levels of glycogen increase in the human uterus during the luteal phase. Enzymatic activity in the uterus is modified. Alkaline phosphatase activity changes during the early luteal phase in the human uterus, and during the preimplantation phase of various mammals, implying it may have a role in decidualization or in membrane transport (Connell, 1972). Acid phosphatase activity increases towards menstruation, and changes occur in levels of β-glucuronidase, leucine aminopeptidase and other enzymes including collagenase, indicating there may be a remodelling of collagen in uterine tissues.

Many other modifications occur in uterine physiology during the menstrual cycle. Cytoplasmic lipids vary in the epithelial cells of the oviduct and uterus, accumulating in the cow uterus as the corpus luteum is being formed (Wordinger et al., 1977). Lipid metabolism is modified in rats and other species. Levels of iron, potassium and trace elements such as copper and zinc are highest in the proliferative stages, and other elements fluctuate throughout the cycle (Hagenfeldt et al., 1977). Levels of $PGF_{2\alpha}$ rise in the second half of the luteal phase in women, perhaps, under the combined action of oestradiol-17β and progesterone, whereas PGE_2 appears to remain constant throughout the cycle (Downie et al., 1974; Singh et al., 1975).

The Activity of the Myometrium During the Reproductive Cycle

The activity of the myometrium is also modified during the reproductive cycle. Its response to neurotransmitters, steroid hormones, and to trauma such as that introduced during replantation of an embryo could obviously influence the success rate following fertilization in vitro. Its electrical and muscular activity have been measured using intrauterine balloons, catheters, transducers, external tachometers, hysterograms, cultures in vitro, etc. (Edwards, 1980). Many observations are contradictory, especially those derived from studies *in vitro*. Several reviews on myometrial activity are available (Kao, 1977; Wood, 1972). Daily variations have been reported in the myometrial activity of the human uterus, activity being lowest at night and high during the day (Akerlund *et al.*, 1976; Lindström *et al.*, 1981).

Both α- and β-catecholaminergic receptors are present in the uterus. Its α receptors are more sensitive to adrenalin, and are usually excitatory, and so invoke contractions. The β-receptors are inhibitory, relaxing the uterus. Low levels of progesterone reduce the threshold of α-receptors, and increase contractility, whereas high levels reduce the threshold of β-receptors and inhibit uterine contractions. β-mimetics such as isoxsuprine, ritodrine, and terbutaline are inhibitory, and terbutaline and fenoterol may act on β_2-receptors and so avoid effects on the β_1-receptors of the heart (Edwards, 1980). Such β_2-mimetics may alleviate the pain of severe primary dysmenorrhoea (Akerlund *et al.*, 1976), although side effects may include tremor.

Compounds such as reserpine and $PGF_{2\alpha}$ inhibit the release of catecholamines, and augment uterine contractions. PGE_2 inhibits contractions and β_2-mimetics prevent the uterine action of $PGF_{2\alpha}$. Antiprostaglandins such as flufenamic acid or ibuprofen prevent the high myometrial activity during dysmenorrhoea (Halbert *et al.*, 1976; Schwartz *et al.*, 1974; Wiqvist *et al.*, 1975).

The parasympathetic system is served from elements in the spinal cord, and fibres project to plexuses in the ovary, uterus and vagina. The major neurotransmitter is acetylcholine, and its synthesis and activation are promoted by oestrogens. Oestrogens also sensitize the myometrium and depress cholinesterase activity, to result in an accumulation of the neurotransmitter. Inhibitors of acetylcholine synthesis inhibit uterine contractility.

Receptors for oxytocin in the uterus appear to have an increased affinity for the hormone in uteri dominated by oestrogens. The number of endometrial and myometrial receptors rises in sheep with the approach of oestrus (Roberts *et al.*, 1976). Oxytocin stimulates the release of $PGF_{2\alpha}$ from the endometrium, and this may coincide with the action of oestrogens in stimulating the synthesis of prostaglandins, perhaps by increasing levels of prostaglandin synthetase.

Muscle activity may be local or propagated down the uterus (Kao, 1977; Wood, 1972). One pacemaker may initiate bursts of discharges at intervals of several seconds, while another controls the numbers of spikes in each burst. Bursts initiate the frequency of contractions, and the number of spikes determines their intensity. Local activity is of high frequency and low active pressure, with irregular contraction cycles. Propagating activity is sensitive to oxytocin, and has a low frequency and high active pressure, with regular contractions during the cycle and quadratic increments of pressure from fundus to cervix. Calcium is involved in myometrial contractions, and calcium antagonists such as Nifedipine relax the myometrium, and may help in reducing the pain of dysmenorrhoea (Ulmsten et al., 1978).

Steroid hormones influence myometrial activity. Contractions vary in amplitude and frequency during the different phases of the cycle, and bursts of action potentials and muscle contractions are frequent when oestrogen levels are high during pro-oestrus and oestrus in animals. Progesterone impairs conductivity and reduces contractions, and evidently dampens uterine contractions during late pregnancy (Kao, 1977; Wood, 1972; Edwards, 1980). Rapid increases in uterine pressure occur at menstruation, perhaps due to an increased mechanical activity as the oestrogen is withdrawn.

Uterine contractility in women is influenced by external factors. Pain or fear probably act through the release of adrenalin. Sexual arousal arising from visual stimuli, excitation and orgasm or the insertion of IUDs, increase uterine contractility. Stress may raise the secretion of prolactin. The frequency and amplitude of spontaneous contractions of the rat uterus are raised by prolactin and specific receptors may be present in the membranes of the human myometrium (Bigazzi & Nordi, 1981). There is no information on the effect of intrauterine catheters on changes in uterine contractility.

Steroid Receptors

The regulation of target tissues by steroid hormones involves the binding of the steroid to its receptor, translocation of the hormone-receptor complex to the nucleus, perhaps to a particular acceptor site, and the modulation of gene expression (Baulieu et al., 1972; Gorski, 1973; O'Malley & Means, 1973). Oestrogen receptors have proved easier to study than progesterone receptors, which are labile and have a rapid dissociation rate.

The content of oestrogen receptors in the uterus fluctuates during the menstrual cycle, being maximal during the proliferative phase (Bayard et al., 1978; Martel et al., 1980; Pollow et al., 1976; Tseng & Gurpide, 1975), or during pro-oestrus in rodents. Oestrogens induce the de-novo synthesis of their own receptors. Progesterone appears to have a variable action, increasing the content of oestrogen receptors in the rat endometrium, but not in the myometrium, and it inhibits the action of oestrogens in stimulating the synthesis of their own receptors

(Martel & Psychoyos, 1980). The response of epithelial cells to oestrogens is reduced in the luteal phase, whereas the response of stromal cells is enhanced (Finn, 1977; King et al., 1979). Similar mechanisms could occur in all species in which implantation is regulated by a precise sequence of oestrogen and progesterone.

The number of oestrogen receptors in the human uterus, rhesus monkey and the baboon decrease during the preimplantation period as levels of progesterone increase (Elsner et al., 1977; Martel & Psychoyos, 1980). Progesterone may reduce the number of oestrogen receptors, as indicated in studies on postmenopausal women (King et al., 1979).

The content of progesterone receptors in the primate uterus maximizes during the proliferatory phase, under the influence of oestrogens. Progesterone is ineffective in a uterus that has not been primed with oestrogens, because of a lack of receptors. In the human endometrium, the number of cytosol progesterone receptors reached their nadir during the early secretory phase, when concentrations of nuclear receptors are high (Bayard et al., 1978; Pollow et al., 1976). During the implantation phase in all species studied, the levels of progesterone receptors become undetectable in the cytoplasm, with measurable amounts present in the nucleus. The hormonal regulation of progesterone receptors may be more uniform in various species, in contrast to oestrogen receptors.

The number of oestrogen and progesterone receptors are high in uteri with well-differentiated tumours, variable in cystic hyperplasia, and low in a hyperplastic proliferative endometrium. Artificial steroids compete for steroid receptors, and can induce long-term transcription. Antioestrogens such as MER-25 and clomiphene bind to oestrogen receptors, causing them to be retained in the nucleus for a long period (Ruh & Baudendistel, 1977). Tamoxifen also binds to oestrogen receptors, causing them to move sluggishly into and out of nuclear acceptor sites (Koseki et al., 1977). These drugs are being used to stimulate the pituitary gland and induce superovulation in patients treated by fertilization in vitro; they will presumably also exert their action on the reproductive tract.

Uterine Prostaglandins

The roles of prostaglandins in uterine physiology and the implantation of the embryo are not clear. The role of prostaglandin E in myometrial activity is obscure; there are various reports implying that it increases or decreases uterine activity, but it is believed to increase myometrial contractions during the preovulatory period (Toppozada *et al.*, 1977; Vijayakumar & Walters, 1981). The ratio of PGE : PGF is approximately unity in the proliferatory phase, but levels of $PGF_{2\alpha}$ rise in both the endometrium and myometrium during the secretory phase (Downie *et al.*, 1974; Maathuis & Kelly, 1978; Vijayakumar & Walters, 1981). Uterine $PGF_{2\alpha}$ rises in the late secretory phase, but this is not reflected in plasma levels (Singh *et al.*, 1975). There is no evidence to suggest that $PGF_{2\alpha}$ is luteolytic in women, although its production during endometriosis has been suggested to have a role in infertility, acting via luteolysis (Moon *et al.*, 1981).

The changing ratios of myometrial prostaglandins correlate with alterations in the ratio of oestrogen and progesterone during the menstrual cycle. The higher levels of oestradiol-17β in uterine venous plasma are related to increasing amounts of PGF in the progesterone-primed myometrium. Oestradiol-17β might stimulate the synthesis or inhibit the catabolism of the prostaglandins (Vijayakumar & Walters, 1981). The greater concentration of myometrial PGF in the late secretory phase also appears to be correlated with a decline in peripheral plasma progesterone. A progesterone-primed endometrium evidently induces the preferential synthesis of PGF under stimulation by oestrogens.

Prostaglandins may exert other roles in the uterus besides their action on the myometrium. They may be associated with the formation of decidual cells, because uterine sensitivity for decidualization corresponds with the maximum ability of the endometrium to respond to PGE_2. Prostaglandins of the E and/or I series increase the vascular permeability of the endometrium (Kennedy, 1980), and trauma could induce the release of prostaglandins associated with a reduction in progesterone (Helvacioglu *et al.*, 1981).

Prostaglandins may also be involved in implantation. Unfortunately, reports on their roles are contradictory, since the prostaglandins or their antagonists may exert stimulatory or inhibitory effects on implantation in mammals. In association with histamine, prostaglandins might modify the permeability of uterine capillaries at the site of implantation, and thus have a role in the early stages of nidation (Edwards, 1980). They may also have a role in the escape of the blastocyst from its zona pellucida (Baskar *et al.*, 1981).

Endocrinology of Implantation

Most knowledge on the endocrinology of implantation has been gained from animal species. Exposure to oestrogens appears to be essential for full uterine growth before ovulation, and progesterone is apparently essential for implantation in virtually all species. This steroid may be bound preferentially at the sites of implantation of the embryos (Sartor, 1980; Ward et al., 1978), a conclusion questioned in recent studies on receptor content (Martel & Psychoyos, 1980). In some species, the embryo itself may contribute towards the steroidal milieu of the uterus, although this is unlikely before implantation in women (Edwards, 1980). Various steroid conversions occur in the reproductive tract, and metabolites of oestrogen, progesterone and the androgens have been identified.

Striking examples of the hormonal milieu needed for implantation are shown during delayed implantation in animal species. Blastocysts can lie dormant in the uterus, sometimes for months, awaiting the correct balance of steroid hormones for implantation to occur. The role of the central nervous system and pituitary gland in delayed implantation await clarification, but the simple manipulation of the oestrogen : progesterone ratio is a powerful tool in regulating it. Excision of the ovaries soon after mating, as cleaving embryos are traversing the oviduct, will normally destroy the chances of implantation in some species, e.g. the rat and mouse. The continued administration of progesterone will sustain the embryos in the oviduct and uterus, and the blastocysts will remain quiescent in the uterine cavity for many days or weeks (Fig. 2). An injection of oestrogen will then induce implantation (Finn, 1977; Fishel, 1979; Martel & Psychoyos, 1980). Likewise, heavy lactation or seasonal effects induce delayed implantation, presumably by interfering with the central control of ovarian steroidogenesis.

Similar situations do not seem to arise in primates. Unfortunately, the number of studies on steroidal regulation of uterine activity during the luteal phase in primates is meagre. In mammals not exhibiting delayed implantation, implantation may occur in the presence of progesterone alone. The gradual rise in plasma oestradiol-17β during the luteal phase in women (Fig. 3) and in species such as marmosets (Hearn, 1980) does not occur in baboons, rhesus monkeys, or the stump-tailed macaque (Goncharov et al., 1976; Koyama et al., 1977; Hotchkiss et al., 1971; Wilks, 1977). The increased rate of secretion of progesterone after ovulation induces and maintains the secretory phase of the uterus. These changes are inhibited or impaired in women with

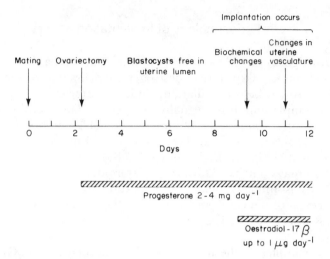

FIG. 2. Model for the experimental delay and induction of implantation in rats. The interval between ovariectomy and treatment with oestrogen can be varied (Edwards, 1980).

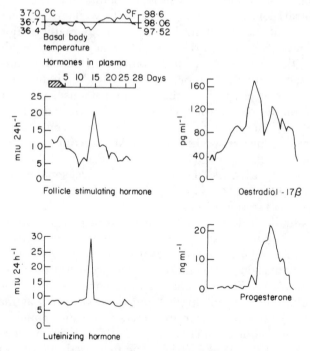

FIG. 3. Plasma levels of FSH, LH, oestradiol-17β and progesterone during the human menstrual cycle (Edwards, 1980).

a short luteal phase; implantation may occur, as shown by transitory increases in HCG, but the pregnancy terminates within a few days (Seppälä *et al.*, 1978). The progesterone deficiency can sometimes be corrected by administering large amounts of this steroid (Jones, 1976).

The levels of steroids in plasma vary during the luteal phase and early pregnancy in women. The placenta becomes active in steroidogenesis during early gestation (Fig. 4), oestriol and oestradiol-17β being its major oestrogenic secretions, while the gradual increase in the production of progesterone by the placenta relieves the corpus luteum of this function after about six weeks.

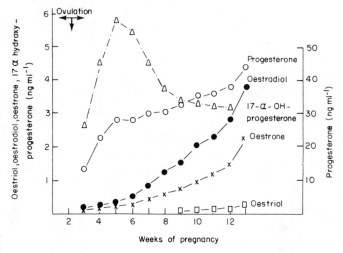

FIG. 4. Levels of various steroids in plasma during early human pregnancy. The arrow indicates the presumed time of ovulation (Tulchinsky & Hobel, 1973).

The hormone most widely recognized as typical of human pregnancy is chorionic gonadotrophin (HCG), presumably produced by the implanting embryo. It is widely accepted as a luteotrophin, rescuing the corpus luteum, which otherwise falters at around day 7 of the luteal phase (Ross, 1979). There is increasing evidence that a similar type of hormone is important in many species including rodents and other primates, and glycoproteins are synthesized and released from blastocysts of laboratory and domestic animals (Figs. 5 and 6) (Fishel, 1981; Fishel & Surani, 1980c).

HCG is synthesized in syncytiotrophoblast and perhaps in cytotrophoblast form remarkably early in pregnancy, perhaps soon after implantation by 6–7 days after fertilization (Fig. 7). Amounts increase very rapidly, individual trophoblast cells in the human embryo having

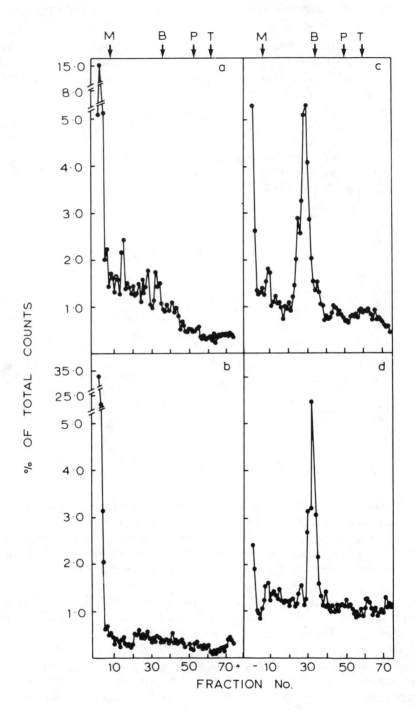

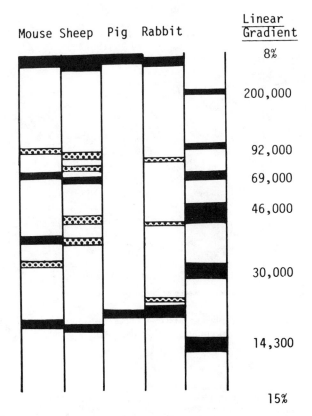

Mouse Sheep Pig Rabbit

Linear
Gradient

8%

200,000

92,000

69,000

46,000

30,000

14,300

15%

FIG. 6. Representative profiles of glycoproteins released from blastocysts of four animal species *in vitro*, and detected on polyacrylamide-gel autoradiograms. The dark and stippled areas represent high and low concentrations of glycoproteins respectively. Two groups of MW proteins with molecular weights of approximately 20,000 and >200,000 are conserved in each species. No comparable data exists for human embryos; HCG has a molecular weight of 39,000 (Fishel, 1981).

FIG. 5. Types of glycoproteins synthesized (a) and released (c) from mouse blastocysts *in vitro*. Comparable results in (b) and (d) show the effects of suppressing glycoprotein synthesis with tunicamycin. Overall synthesis is depressed in the embryo, but the production and release of the major glycoprotein continues. Marker proteins and their molecular weights: M, myosin (220,000); B, bovine serum albumin (66,500); P, peroxidase (40,000); T, trypsin (23,000) (Fishel & Surani, 1980).

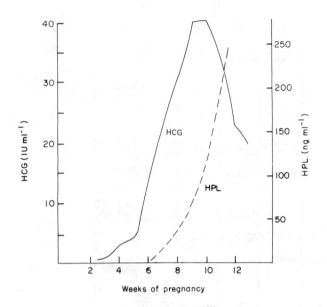

FIG. 7. Levels of HCG and placental lactogen (HPL) in plasma during early human pregnancy (Edwards, 1980).

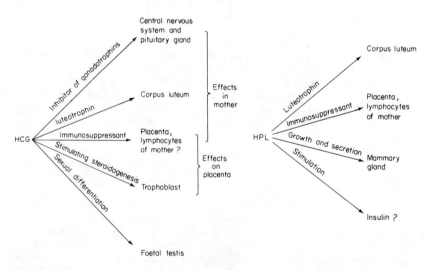

FIG. 8. Roles postulated for HCG (left) and placental lactogen (HPL) (right) during human pregnancy (Edwards, 1980).

been estimated to secrete 1.4×10^{-2} IU day^{-1} at 10 days of gestation, declining to 7.9×10^{-4} IU daily at 16 days (Ross, 1979). HCG is credited with various roles in pregnancy, depressing the release of LH from the pituitary gland, acting as a luteotrophin, abrogating the mother's immune response against the fetus, etc. (Fig. 8).

Prolactin is also a hormone of the late luteal phase and early pregnancy (Fig. 7). It is known to be synthesized by human decidual cells, whether an embryo is present or not (Maslar & Riddick, 1979). The classic role of prolactin is on mammary tissue (Fig. 8). It is not clear if this hormone has a role in maintaining the luteal phase of the human uterus, or assisting in implantation. It is known to arrest corpora lutea and stimulate progesterone secretion in rats (Smith *et al.*, 1975), and it is probably involved in maintaining the seasonal delay of implantation in some animal species (Tyndale-Biscoe, 1979). It is well known as a stress hormone, and so could influence success rates if there is trauma during the replacement of human embryos. High levels of prolactin in the luteal phase have been given as an explanation for infertility in some normoovulatory women (Ranta *et al.*, 1979). Prolactin might also help in abrogating the mother's immune response against her fetus.

The human follicle and corpus luteum also produces relaxin. Its levels in the peritoneal fluid of women are very high between days 5 and 10 post ovulation (Thomas, 1981), and prolactin appears to act as an antagonist to it (Bigazzi & Nardi, 1981). Relaxin is detectable in serum during early pregnancy, soon after implantation, although no role has yet been identified for it at nidation (Quac-Liarello *et al.*, 1979).

The Uterine Milieu During Implantation of the Embryo

The changing levels of steroid hormones in the luteal phase are believed to modify the secretions of the uterus, and so regulate the activity of the blastocyst during implantation.

The growth of blastocysts in species with delayed implantation appears to be regulated by the changing properties of the uterine milieu. Alternatively, contact inhibition may regulate the activity of blastocysts, suspending their growth during certain stages of the reproductive cycle or under specific physiological conditions (Fishel, 1980a). Steroids seem to influence embryos by modifying the uterine milieu, rather than acting directly upon them. Some specific uterine proteins are believed to be associated with implantation. Uteroglobulin, stimulated initially by the action of oestradiol-17β and then by large amounts of progesterone, is present in certain species, including rabbits (Beato, 1977; Beier, 1974). It appears in secretions on day 2, and declines by day 9, and it may transport steroids such as progesterone, inhibit trypsin-like proteases, and exert direct effects on the embryo. A similar protein has been found in other tissues, including the oviduct and lungs. Other specific proteins include a proteolytic β-glycoprotein in rabbits, and small amounts of several proteins and glycoproteins as implantation begins in rats and mice, their profile depending on the ratio of oestrogen and progesterone (Fig. 9) (Surani, 1977; Fishel, 1979; Edwards, 1980).

There is evidently a significant decline in the protein content of the uterine lumen during the secretory phase in women, without any qualitative changes during other stages of the menstrual cycle (Maathuis & Aitken, 1978; Aitken, 1979). The plasma proteins do not appear to alter greatly in amount in the uterus during the menstrual cycle in women, and evidently migrate to the lumen, crossing the epithelium relatively easily. Larger molecules, including γ-globulins are excluded in some species by the uterine epithelium (Beier, 1974; Surani, 1977).

There are also some indications of the presence of specific proteins in the lumen of the human uterus. The profile is dominated by the plasma proteins, although there are occasional reports of the presence of compounds such as uteroglobin, which may exert specific effects on embryo or uterus (Edwards, 1980). Pieces of human endometrium incubated *in vitro* with specific precursors secrete glycoproteins for several hours, and the addition of oestrogen and progesterone stimulates the activity of the endometrium (Shapiro & Forbes, 1978). Specific proteins have been found in the pre-albumin or post-transferrin fractions, and two characteristic proteins have been found, one appearing before ovulation, and another soon afterwards (Wolf & Mastroianni, 1975). Lactoferrin has also been found in uterine secretions, and it might bind and remove iron.

Proteins in the uterine lumen might have diverse roles. Enzymes could digest the zona pellucida from around implanting embryos, because in mice, rats, and other species the zona is removed either by lytic factors in the uterus, or by the activity of the embryo itself, which "hatches". Some human embryos have hatched from the zona pellucida *in vitro* but there is no knowledge of the situation *in vivo* (Edwards & Surani, 1977). Specific proteins may modify the surface of the trophoblast and uterine epithelium, to enhance apposition and adhesion of the embryo to the uterine epithelium; enzymes such as sialidase and glycosidase are known to act on cell surfaces. Other proteins might be mitogenic; mouse embryos becoming increasingly sensitive to serum mitogens and other compounds at the 8-cell stage (Fishel & Surani, 1978; Surani, 1977). Transport systems differentiate successively in the blastocyst (Powers & Tupper, 1977), and might be influenced by uterine proteins.

Changes have been found in the non-protein composition of uterine secretions. Potassium levels remain unchanged throughout the cycle,

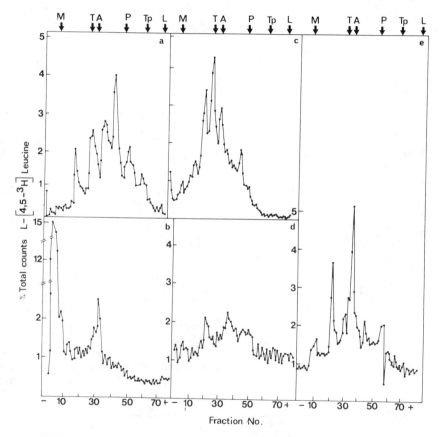

FIG. 9. Radiolabelled proteins in the uterine fluid of the mouse at (a) pro-oestrus, and (b)–(e) days 1–4 of pregnancy, respectively. Notice the fluctuations in the types of proteins released into the lumen. Amounts are small on day 3 (d), the day before implantation, in contrast with the two major peaks appearing on the day of implantation. Marker proteins and their molecular weights: M, myosin (220,000); T, transferrin (82,000); A, bovine serum albumin (66,500); P, peroxidase (40,000); Tp, trypsin (23,300); L, lysozyme (14,300) (Fishel, 1979).

but its concentration rises during the luteal phase as the volume of fluid declines (Clemetson *et al.*, 1973). Levels of calcium and magnesium may vary, as in animals, and changes in calcium levels could influence the metabolism of blastocysts (Fig. 10) (Fishel, 1980b, 1981). Fructose and glucose are detected during the luteal phase of the human uterus (Douglas *et al.*, 1970). Heparin-like activity has been identified in human uterine fluid, increasing in amounts during the cycle and decreasing during menstruation.

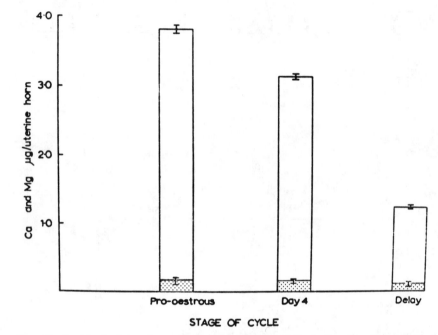

FIG. 10. Levels of calcium (open bars) and magnesium (stippled) in the uterine fluid of mice during early pregnancy. Notice the considerable changes in levels of calcium, especially during delayed implantation (Fishel, 1981).

Implantation of the Embryo

In man, implantation occurs around days 6–7, and is interstitial (Hertig & Rock, 1945). The haemochorial placenta develops later. Three main stages are usually described for this type of implantation; pre-attachment or apposition, attachment and invasion (Smith & Wilson, 1974); Enders, 1975). During apposition the epithelia lining the opposing surface of the endometrium move closer together and come into close contact with the blastocyst. This process probably occurs as a result of the pinocytosis of uterine fluid by pinopods. The opposing epithelial microvilli, and the microvilli of the epithelium and trophoblast cells interdigitate, microvilli becoming more numerous over the polar trophoblast at this stage.

During the attachment stage, the apposing trophoblast and epithelium flatten, contact becomes intimate and the microvilli disappear. These changes are concomitant with increased uterine vascular permeability, in which histamine, prostaglandins and cAMP may each exert a role (Edwards, 1980).

Contact between the trophoblast and endometrial stroma signifies the invasive stage. In man, the trophoblast overlying the embryonic disc differentiates into the syncytiotrophoblast which proliferates and penetrates between the epithelial cells, disrupting them from the basement membrane and possibly phagocytosing them. The secretion of proteolytic enzymes by the trophoblast may aid this process (Owers & Blandau, 1971).

The embryo is always orientated at implantation, the trophoblast over the embryonic disc invading the endometrium, normally on the posterior wall near the mid-line. By this stage the embryos have shed their zona pellucida by "hatching" or it has been dissolved by uterine enzymes. This stage is referred to as stage 4 (O'Rahilly, 1973). Many biochemical and ultrastructural changes occur in the embryo and uterine tissues reflecting their preparation for implantation, and possibly for communications between the two tissues (Edwards, 1980; Fishel, 1981). The trophoblast is a highly specialized tissue; in mice, trophoblastic vesicles devoid of an embryonic disc can implant in the uterus and apparently induce normal changes in the decidua (Gardner, 1971).

The cytotrophoblast overlying the inner cell mass is composed of large polyhedral cells whereas the syncytiotrophoblast has large nuclei near the cytotrophoblast and small nuclei in the invasive region. The syncytiotrophoblast surrounds small capillaries of the stratum compactum which probably represents the incipient formation of trophoblastic lacunae. Extensive microvilli, glycogen and filaments are seen in the mural trophoblast, and the chromatin is characteristically more diffuse (Fig. 11). Generally, there is an increase in ribosomes and granular endoplasmic reticulum and a reduction in the number of dense bodies. The abembryonal trophoblast accumulates glycogen and multivesicular bodies. The syncytiotrophoblast contains smaller mitochondria, unusually dense cytoplasm and the chromatin is more condensed (R. G. Kleinfeld, personal communication; Edwards, 1980).

Embryos at implantation have large amounts of glycoproteins of high molecular weight on the outer surface, and these may be involved during adhesion (Pinsker & Mintz, 1973; Schlafke & Enders, 1975; Fishel, 1981). Many changes occur in energy metabolism, the synthesis of macromolecules and properties of the cell surface. More studies are needed, especially in man, to elucidate the mechanisms in the uterus and embryos that are involved in implantation. By day 9, the uterine stroma is undergoing decidualization, and the endometrial stromal cells are beginning to hypertrophy.

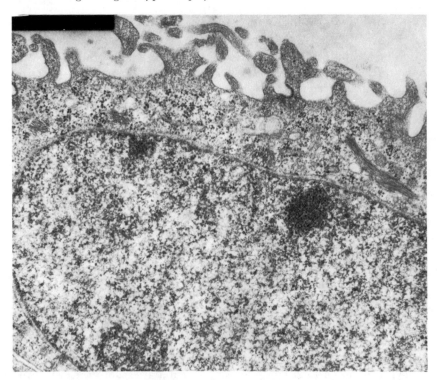

FIG. 11. Cell of the mural trophoblast of a human embryo grown *in vitro* for nine days. Extensive microvilli, filaments and glycogen are seen in the cytoplasm. The chromatin is typically diffuse (Edwards, unpublished).

Decidualization in the Uterus

The uterine stroma, with its eleven or more cell types (Glasser & McCormack, 1980) is a dynamic tissue, containing static and transient cell populations within an extracellular matrix. During implantation, the stroma differentiates into decidual tissue after priming by oestrogen and progesterone and, in some species, probably as the result of embryo-epithelial interactions. The nature of these interactions, and the induction of decidualization remain major mysteries in the physiology of implantation (Edwards, 1980; Glasser & Clark, 1975; Sartor, 1980).

There is much conjecture about the origin and function of decidual cells, too plentiful to describe here. Several recent reviews are available (Edwards, 1980; Glasser & McCormack, 1980). Human decidual cells possess large Golgi complexes, a well-developed granular endoplasmic reticulum and are secretory. Gap junctions exist between these cells, cellular extensions project deeply into the cytoplasm of adjacent cells and extracellular matrices persist between contiguous cells (Fig. 12). Lymphocytes migrate into the uterine tissues during decidualization, to form close associations with decidual cells (Figs. 13 and 14). The association of small decidual cells with lymphoblasts was found in the vicinity of precapillary arterioles and capillaries (Tekelioglu-Uysal *et al.*, 1975). No specific role has yet been assigned to the function of lymphocytes in the deciduotrophoblastic region.

Decidualization occurs only in the sensitized endometrium during a limited time period (Finn, 1977). Such changes occur around day 25 of the menstrual cycle in the non-pregnant and pregnant human uterus. Decidualization depends on relatively high rates of progesterone: oestrogen in rats and mice, but the precise hormonal regulation of the luteal phase endometrium in women is unclear.

Embryo-epithelial interactions probably play a major role in the normal induction of decidualization. But in certain species, non-specific effects will induce decidualization, e.g. scratching the uterine horn, the electrical stimulation of the myometrium, instillation of histamine, oil droplets, carbon dioxide, prostaglandins, etc. The passage of a catheter during the placement of a human embryo might act in a similar manner in women.

The precise endocrine control of decidualization may become unnecessary when decidualization is induced by trauma (Finn, 1977). Trauma might bypass or injure the epithelium, and act on the stroma directly. The epithelium has an obligatory role in inducing decidualization in several species (Lejeune *et al.*, 1981), and disruption of the epithelial-stromal topography prevents the decidual cell reaction. Regardless of the stimulus, embryo or non-specific, the epithelium might therefore act as a transducer to stroma during decidualization.

In rodents, decidualization is restricted to the site of implantation, but longitudinal propagation can be induced artificially (Lejeune and

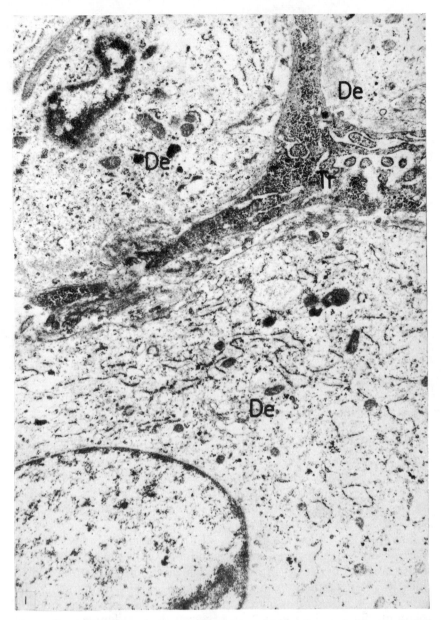

FIG. 12. Human deciduotrophic complex. An extension of a trophoblastic cell (Tr) sandwiched between three large decidual cells (De). The cytoplasm of the decidual cell is pale, with short profiles of tubuli of granular endoplasmic reticulum and small mitochondria. The trophoblast cell is darker, with filaments, large ovoid mitochondria, glycogen aggregates and lipid droplets (× 24,000) (Tekelioglu-Uysal *et al.*, 1975).

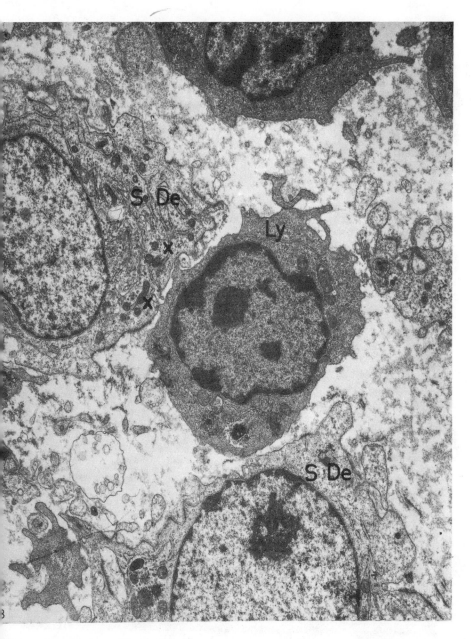

FIG. 13. Association between small decidual cells (S De) and a lymphoblastic cell (Ly) in the human uterus. Notice the close relationship (X) between the two cells (× 8,000) (Tekelioglu-Uysal *et al.*, 1975).

Leroy, 1980). In the human uterus, a longitudinal wave of decidual-ization occurs naturally, and decidual-like changes (predecidual changes) occur in the stroma during the luteal phase, even in the absence of an embryo. The human blastocyst implants interstitially, completely embedded in the stroma, and the epithelium is almost undisturbed. Extensive decidualization occurs in the stroma before the embryo enters it.

Decidualization in women differs from that in the rhesus monkey and baboon. Only a superficial attachment to the endometrium occurs in the rhesus monkey, the epithelium forming a characteristic epithelial plaque, while in baboon there is no epithelial plaque. Neither species exhibits the extensive stromal hypertrophy typical of man, and the small decidual swellings are not comparable to the human (Ramsey *et al.*, 1976).

Successful implantation in non-primates involves precise synchrony between sensitization of the endometrium and the arrival of the blastocyst in the uterus. This may not be the case with the rhesus monkey (Marston *et al.*, 1977). The human situation is not clear,

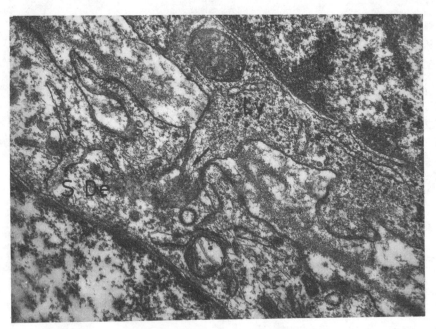

FIG. 14. Close association between a small decidual cell (S De) and a lymphoblast (Ly). A projection from the lymphoblast into the decidual cell is arrowed (× 24,000) (Tekelioglu-Uysal *et al.*, 1975).

although the elevated levels of oestradiol-17β during the luteal phase differ from the situation in rhesus monkey and baboons. Why should this difference occur? The signal to decidualization in some species may be embryonic (Fishel, 1981; Logeat *et al.*, 1980), whereas in man it may initially be maternal, with embryonic enforcement later.

The nature of the regulation of decidualization, its sensitivity, and the necessity for embryo-uterine synchrony during the luteal phase in women needs to be clarified. Embryo replacement at an unfavourable stage of the luteal phase may result in a severe asynchrony between the embryo and uterus inducing decidualization too early. The stress of replacement could also upset the normal endocrine regulation of implantation and studies are urgently needed on, for example, the secretion of prolactin during this process.

Human Fertility and the Luteal Phase

Many concepts on uterine physiology remain to be applied to studies on embryo replacements in women. These include the use of β-mimetics or inhibitors of prostaglandin synthesis to modify the activity of the endometrium, the administration of progesterone, the use of tranquillizers, antioxytoxics, and inhibitors of prolactin. The better design of catheters, or replacement at different stages of the menstrual cycle, have resulted in sharp improvements in success rates. Studies in rabbits have shown that the endometrium, myometrium and embryo must be coincident for embryo transfer to be highly successful (Adams, 1980).

We do not know if the uterine installation of hormones, carbon dioxide, drugs or other compounds might assist in implantation by exerting local effects on the uterus. The highly secretory and vascular endometrium could easily be damaged during reimplantation of embryos, causing damage or trauma, releasing histamines, prostaglandins, vasodilators and other compounds adversely influencing the endometrium.

What success rates are possible after the replacement of human embryos? Implantation occurs in 50–90% of females after embryo transfer in animals; are similar success rates possible in man? The groundwork is laid because embryos are replaced in 80% of patients. Unfortunately, implantation occurs in less than one-quarter.

Some evidence implies that this low rate of implantation is all that can be expected. Epidemiological studies show the proportion of women conceiving during any particular menstrual cycle is 28% when coitus occurs six times, rising to 45% if it occurs twelve times in the cycle (Tietze & Potter, 1962), approximately 30% after the discontinuation of contraception (Tietze et al., 1950) and lower in other studies (Short, 1976). Approximately one-half of oligomenorrhoeic women given clomiphene conceive after three cycles of treatment, a ratio similar to that occurring in the general population (Gorlitsky et al., 1978). There is a 30% chance of conception after the first cycle of treatment with AID, increasing by approximately 20% in one or two successive cycles (Chong & Taymor, 1975).

Such low rates of natural fertility could arise through a failure of fertilization in many women. Spermatozoa may not be present in the ampulla when ovulation occurs, which is presumably one reason why the frequency of intercourse influences human fertility. Hidden problems in sperm or ovum transport could also exist in many women as suspected in some of those with idiopathic infertility, and some men may have undiagnosed oligospermia.

The high rate of embryonic mortality in the first trimester, and especially in the first month of pregnancy, could also reduce human fertility. Tissues resembling blastocysts, and casts of decidual tissue which may be the remains of an early implantation site have been identified in women, and the well described "blighted ovum" dies soon after implantation (Hertig, 1975). Some implanted embryos may be represented only by a brief rise in plasma or urinary $HCG\beta$ towards the expected time of menstruation (Batzer et al., 1981), a fate which might afflict almost half of all conceptuses. Some of these embryonic disasters could arise through delayed fertilization in vivo. Infrequent intercourse could result in spermatozoa arriving at the site of fertilization long after ovulation had occurred, so that polyspermy, the fertilization of over-ripe oocytes, and asynchrony between embryo and the mother's luteal phase could each lead to disordered or delayed implantation and embryonic mortality.

Unique disadvantages could equally arise with conception in vitro, e.g. damage to the uterus caused by the use of catheters for replacement. Such disadvantages could be offset: two embryos can be replaced to raise the chances of one implanting, the mother can be rested and treated during the delicate period of implantation, and luteal deficiency can be rapidly recognized and corrected. Even today, approximately 20–25% of replaced embryos will implant, already very close to the "natural" rate; it will be fascinating to see if there is an improvement over the coming years.

References

Adams, C. E. 1980. Retention and development of eggs transferred to the uterus at various times after ovulation in the rabbit. *Journal of Reproduction and Fertility*, **60**, 309–315.

Aitken, R. J. 1979. The hormonal control of implantation. In: *Maternal Recognition of Pregnancy*, pp. 53–83. Ciba Foundation Symposium, no. 64.

Akerlund, M., Andersson, K. E. & Ingermarsson, I. 1976. Effects of terbutaline on myometrial activity, uterine blood flow, and lower abdominal pain in women with primary dysmenorrhoea. *British Journal of Obstetrics and Gynaecology*, **83**, 673–678.

Basker, J. F., Torchiana, D. F., Biggers, J. D., Corey, E. J., Andersen, N. H. & Subramanian, N. 1981. Inhibition of hatching of mouse blastocysts *in vitro* by various prostaglandin antagonists. *Journal of Reproduction and Fertility*, **63**, 359–363.

Batzer, F. R., Schlaff, S., Goldfarb, A. F. & Corson, S. L. 1981. Serial β-subunit of human chorionic gonadotropin doubling time as a prognosticator of pregnancy outcome in an infertile population. *Fertility and Sterility*, **35**, 307–312.

Baulieu, E. E., Atger, M., Best-Belpomme, M., Corvol, P., Courvalin, J. C., Mester, J., Milgrom, E., Robel, P., Rochefort, H. & Catalogne, D. 1975. Steroid hormone receptors. *Vitamins and Hormones*, **33**, 649–731.

Bayard, F., Damilano, J., Robel, P. & Baulieu, E. E. 1978. Cytoplasmic and nuclear oestradiol and progesterone receptors in human endometrium. *Journal of Clinical Endocrinology and Metabolism*, **46**, 635–648.

Beato, M. 1977. Hormonal control of uteroglobin synthesis. In: *Development in Mammals*, vol. 1, p. 361. Ed. M. H. Johnson. North-Holland, Amsterdam.

Beier, H. M. 1974. Oviducal and uterine fluids. *Journal of Reproduction and Fertility*, **37**, 221–238.

Bigazzi, M. & Nordi, E. 1981. Prolactin and relaxin : antagonism on the spontaneous motility of the uterus. *Journal of Clinical Endocrinology and Metabolism*, **53**, 665–667.

Blahna, D. G. & Yochim, J. M. 1975. Protein and RNA synthesis in endometrium of the rat uterus during early progestation. *Biology of Reproduction*, **13**, 527–534.

Chong, A. P. & Taymor, M. L. 1975. Sixteen years' experience with therapeutic donor insemination. *Fertility and Sterility*, **26**, 791–795.

Clemetson, C. A. B., Kim, J. K., de Jesus, T. P. S., Mallikarjuneswara, V. R. & Wilds, J. H. 1973. Human uterine fluid potassium and the menstrual cycle. *Journal of Obstetrics and Gynaecology of the British Commonwealth*, **80**, 553–561.

Connell, E. B. 1972. Endometrial histochemistry. In: *Reproductive Biology*. Eds. H. Balin & S. Glasser. Excerpta Medica, Amsterdam.

Dallenbach-Hellweg, G. 1975. *Histopathology of the Endometrium*. Springer, Berlin.

Downie, J., Poysner, N. L. & Wunderlich, M. 1974. Levels of prostaglandins in human endometrium during the normal menstrual cycle. *Journal of Physiology*, **236**, 465–472.

Douglas, C. P., Garrow, J. S. & Pugh, E. W. 1970. Investigation into the sugar content of endometrial secretion. *Journal of Obstetrics and Gynaecology of the British Commonwealth*, **77**, 891–894.

Edwards, R. G. 1980. *Conception in the Human Female*. Academic Press, London.

Edwards, R. G. & Surani, M. A. H. 1977. The primate blastocyst and its environment. *Uppsala Journal of Medicine*, **522**, 39–50.

Elsner, C. W., Illingworth, D. V., de Groot, K., Flickinger, G. & Mikhail, G. 1977. Cytosol and nuclear oestrogen receptor in the genital tract of the rhesus monkey. *Journal of Steroid Biochemistry*, **8**, 151–155.

Enders, A. C. 1975. The implantation chamber, blastocyst and blastocyst imprint of the rat: a scanning electron microscope study. *Anatomical Record*, **182**, 137–150.

Finn, C. A. 1977. Implantation reaction. In: *Biology of the Uterus*, pp. 245–308. Ed. R. M. Wynn. Plenum Press, New York.

Fishel, S. B. 1979. Analysis of mouse uterine proteins at pro-oestrus, during early pregnancy and after administration of exogenous steroids. *Journal of Reproduction and Fertility*, **55**, 91–100.

Fishel, S. B. 1980a. *Regulation of blastocyst metabolism and implantation in the mouse*. Ph.D. thesis, University of Cambridge.

Fishel, S. B. 1980b. The role of divalent cations in the metabolic response of mouse embryos to serum. *Journal of Embryology and Experimental Morphology*, **58**, 217–229.

Fishel, S. B. 1981. The blastocyst and its environment. In: *Human Reproduction*. Eds. K. Semm & L. Mettler. Third World Congress of Human Reproduction, Berlin. Excerpta Medica (in press).

Fishel, S. B. & Surani, M. A. H. 1978. Changes in responsiveness of preimplantation mouse embryos to serum. *Journal of Embryology and Experimental Morphology*, **45**, 295–301.

Fishel, S. B. & Surani, M. A. H. 1980. Evidence for the synthesis and release of a glycoprotein by mouse blastocysts. *Journal of Reproduction and Fertility*, **59**, 181–185.

Gardner, R. L. 1971. Manipulations on the blastocyst. *Advances in the Biosciences*, **6**, 279–296.

Glasser, S. R. & Clark, J. H. 1975. A determinant role for progesterone in the development of uterine sensitivity to decidualization and ovoimplantation. In: *Developmental Biology of Reproduction*, pp. 311–345. Eds. C. Markett and J. Papaconstantinou. Academic Press, New York.

Glasser, S. R. & McCormack, S. A. 1980. Role of stromal cell function diversity in altering endometrial cell responses. *Progress in Reproductive Biology*, **7**, 102–144. Karger, Basel.

Goncharov, N., Aso, T., Cekan, Z., Pachalia, N. & Dicsfalusy, E. 1976. Hormonal changes during the menstrual cycle of the baboon (*Papio hamadryus*). *Acta Endocrinologica*, **82**, 379–412.

Gorlitski, G. A., Kase, N. G. & Speroff, L. 1978. Ovulation and pregnancy rates with clomiphene citrate. *Obstetrics and Gynecology*, **51**, 265–269.

Gorski, J. 1973. Estrogen binding and control of gene expression in the uterus. In: *Handbook of Physiology*, vol. **7**, pp. 525–536. Eds. R. O. Greep and E. B. Astwood. Waverley Press, Baltimore.

Hagenfeldt, K., Landgren, B.-M., Plantin, L.-O. & Diczfalusy, C. 1977. Trace elements in the human endometrium and decidua. *Acta Endocrinologica*, **85**, 406–414.

Halbert, D. R., Demers, L. M. & Jones, D. 1976. Dysmenorrhoea and prostaglandins. *Obstetrical and Gynecological Survey*, **31**, 77–81.

Hearn, J. P. 1980. Endocrinology and timing of implantation in the marmoset monkey, *Callithrix jaachus*. *Progress in Reproductive Biology*, **7**, 262–269.

Helvacioglu, A., Auletta, F. & Scommegna, A. 1981. Antifertility effect of azastene mediated by prostaglandin. *American Journal of Obstetrics and Gynecology*, **141**, 138–144.

Hertig, A. T. 1975. Implantation of the human ovum: the histogenesis of some aspects of spontaneous abortion. In: *Progress in Infertility*, p. 411. Eds. S. J. Behrman & R. W. Kistner. Little, Brown & Co., Boston.

Hertig, A. T. & Rock, J. 1945. Two human ova of the pre-villous stage having a developmental age of about seven and nine days respectively. *Contributions to Embryology*, **31**, 65–84.

Hotchkiss, J., Atkinson, L. E. & Knobil, E. 1971. Time course of serum estrogen and luteinising hormone concentrations during the menstrual cycle of the rhesus monkey. *Endocrinology*, **89**, 177–193.

Hsueh, A. J. W., Peck, E. J. & Clark, J. H. 1976. Control of uterine estrogen receptor levels by progesterone. *Endocrinology*, **98**, 438–444.

Illingworth, D. V., Wood, C. P., Flickinger, G. L. & Mikhail, G. 1975. Progesterone receptor of the human myometrium. *Journal of Clinical Endocrinology and Metabolism*, **40**, 1001–1008.

Jones, G. S. 1976. The luteal phase defect. *Fertility and Sterility*, **27**, 351–356.

Kao, C. Y. 1977. Electrophysiological properties of uterine smooth muscle. In: *Biology of the Uterus*, p. 423. Ed. R. M. Wynn. Plenum Press, New York.

Kennedy, T. G. 1980. Prostaglandins and the endometrial vascular permeability changes preceding blastocyst implantation and decidualisation. *Progress in Reproductive Biology*, **7**, 234–243.

King, R. J. B., Whitehead, M. I., Campbell, S. & Minardi. 1979. Effect of estrogen and progestin treatments on endometria from postmenopausal women. *Cancer Research*, **39**, 1094–1101.

Koseki, Y., Zava, D. T., Chamness, G. C. & McGuire, W. L. 1977. Estrogen receptor translocation and replenishment by the antiestrogen tamoxifen. *Endocrinology*, **101**, 1104–1110.

Koyama, T., Delapena, A. & Hagino, N. 1977. Plasma estrogen, progestin and LH during normal menstrual cycle in baboon — role of LH. *American Journal of Obstetrics and Gynecology*, **127**, 67–72.

Lejeune, B. & Leroy, F. 1980. Role of the uterine epithelium in inducing the decidual cell reaction. *Progress in Reproductive Biology*, **7**, 92–101. Karger, Basel.

Lejeune, B., Van Hoeck, J. & Leroy, F. 1981. Transmitter role of the luminal uterine epithelium in the induction of decidualization in rats. *Journal of Reproduction and Fertility*, **61**, 235–240.

Logeat, F., Sartor, P., Vu-Hai, M. T. & Milgrom, E. 1980. Local effect of the blastocyst on estrogen and progesterone receptors in the rat endometrium. *Science*, **207**, 1083–1085.

Lundström, V., Eneroth, P., Granström, E. & Swahn, K.-L. 1981. In: *Human Reproduction*. Eds. K. Somm & L. Mettler. Third World Congress of Human Reproduction, Berlin. Excerpta Medica, Amsterdam (in press).

Maathuis, J. B. & Aitken, R. J. 1975. Cyclic variation in concentrations of protein and hexose in human uterine flushings collected by an improved technique. *Journal of Reproduction and Fertility*, **52**, 289–295.

Maathuis, J. B. & Kelly, R. W. 1978. Concentrations of prostaglandin $F_{2\alpha}$ and E_2 in the endometrium throughout the human menstrual cycle, after administration of clomiphene or an oestrogen-progestogen pill and in early pregnancy. *Journal of Endocrinology*, **77**, 361–371.

Makler, A. & Eisenfeld, A. J. 1974. In-vitro binding of ^{3}H-oestradiol to macromolecules from the human endometrium. *Journal of Clinical Endocrinology and Metabolism*, **38**, 628–633.

Marston, J. H., Penn, R. & Sivelle, P. C. 1977. Successful autotransfer of tubal eggs in the rhesus monkey, *Macaca mulatta*. *Journal of Reproduction and Fertility*, **49**, 175–176.

Martel, D. & Psychoyos, A. 1980. Behaviour of uterine steroid receptors at implantation. *Progress in Reproductive Biology*, **7**, 216–233. Karger, Basel.

Martel, D., Malet, C., Olmedo, C., Monier, M. N., Dubouch, P. & Psychoyos, A. 1980. Oestrogen receptor in the baboon endometrium: cystolic receptor, detection, characterization and variation of its concentration during the menstrual cycle. *Journal of Endocrinology*, **84**, 261–272.

Maslar, I. A. & Riddick, D. H. 1979. Prolactin production by human endometrium during the normal menstrual cycle. *American Journal of Obstetrics and Gynecology*, **135**, 751–754.

Moon, Y. S., Leung, P. C. S., Yuen, B. H. & Gomel, V. 1981. Prostaglandin F in human endometriotic tissue. *American Journal of Obstetrics and Gynecology*, **141**, 344–345.

Noyes, R. W., Hertig, A. T. & Rock, J. 1950. Dating the endometrial biopsy. *Fertility and Sterility*, **1**, 3–25.

O'Grady, J. E., Moffatt, G. E., McMinn, L., Vass, M. A., O'Hara & Heald, P. J. 1975. Uterine chromatin template activity during the early stages of pregnancy in the rat. *Biochimica et Biophysica Acta*, **407**, 125–132.

O'Malley, B. W. & Means, A. R. 1973. *Receptors for Reproductive Hormones*. Plenum Press, New York.

O'Rahilly, R. 1973. *Developmental Stages in Human Embryos*, Part A. Carnegie Institute, Washington.

Owers, N. O. & Blandau, R. J. 1971. Proteolytic activity of the rat and guinea-pig blastocyst *in vitro*. In: *Biology of the Blastocyst*, p. 207. Ed. R. J. Blandau. University of Chicago Press, Chicago.

Pinsker, M. C. & Mintz, B. 1973. Change in cell-surface glycoproteins of mouse embryos before implantation. *Proceedings of the National Academy of Science*, **70**, 1645–1648.

Pollow, K., Boquoi, E., Schmidt-Gollwitzer, M. & Pollow, B. 1976. The nuclear estradiol and progesterone receptors of human endometrium and endometrial carcinoma. *Journal of Molecular Medicine*, **1**, 325–342.

Powers, R. D. & Tupper, J. T. 1977. Developmental changes in membrane transport and permeability in the early mouse embryo. *Developmental Biology*, **56**, 306–315.

Psychoyos, A. 1973. Hormonal control of ova implantation. *Vitamins and Hormones*, **31**, 201–256.

Quag-Liarello, J., Steinets, B. G. & Weiss, G. 1979. Relaxin secretion in early pregnancy. *Obstetrics and Gynecology*, **53**, 62–63.

Ramsey, E. M., Houston, M. L. & Harris, J. W. S. 1976. Interactions of the trophoblast and maternal tissues in three closely related primate species. *American Journal of Obstetrics and Gynecology*, **124**, 647–652.

Ranta, T., Lehtovirta, P., Stenman, V. H. & Seppala, M. 1979. Serum prolactin and progesterone concentrations in ovulatory infertility. *Endocrinological Investigation*, **2**, 71.

Roberts, J. S., McCracken, J. A., Gavagan, J. E. & Soloff, M. S. 1976. Oxytocin-stimulated release of $PFG_{2\alpha}$ from ovine endometrium *in vitro*: correlation with estrous cycle and oxytocin-receptor binding. *Endocrinology*, **99**, 1107–1114.

Ross, G. T. 1979. Human chorionic gonadotropin and maternal recognition of pregnancy. In: *Maternal Recognition of Pregnancy*, pp. 191–208. Ciba Foundation Symposium, no. 64.

Ruh, T. S. & Baudendistel, L. J. 1977. Different nuclear-binding sites for antiestrogen and estrogen receptor complexes. *Endocrinology*, **100**, 420–426.

Sartor, P. 1980. Cell proliferation and decidual morphogenesis. *Progress in Reproductive Biology*, **7**, 115–124. Karger, Basel.

Schlafke, S. & Enders, A. C. 1975. Cellular basis of interactions between trophoblast and uterus at implantation. *Biology of Reproduction*, **12**, 41–65.

Schwartz, A., Zor, U., Lindner, H. R. & Naor, S. 1974. Primary dysmenorrhoea: alleviation by an inhibitor of prostaglandin synthesis and action. *Obstetrics and Gynaecology*, **44**, 709–712.

Seppälä, M., Lehtovirta, P. & Rutanen, E.-M. 1978. Detection of chorionic gonado-trophin-like activity in infertile cycles with a short luteal phase. *Acta Endocrinologica*, **88**, 164–168.

Shapiro, S. S. & Forbes, H. H. 1978. Alterations in human endometrial protein synthesis during the menstrual cycle and in progesterone-stimulated organ culture. *Fertility and Sterility*, **30**, 175–180.

Short, R. V. 1976. The evolution of human reproduction. *Proceedings of the Royal Society, B*, **195**, 3–24.

Singh, E. J., Baccarini, I. M. & Zuspan, F. P. 1975. Levels of prostaglandins $F_{2\alpha}$ and E_2 in human endometrium during the menstrual cycle. *American Journal of Obstetrics and Gynecology*, **126**, 652–656.

Smith, A. F. & Wilson, I. B. 1974. Cell interaction at the maternal-embryonic interface during implantation in the mouse. *Cell and Tissue Research*, **152**, 525–542.

Smith, M. S., Freeman, M. E. & Neill, J. D. 1975. The control of progesterone secretion during the estrous cycle and early pseudopregnancy in the rat: prolactin, gonadotropin and steroid levels associated with rescue of the corpus luteum of pseudopregnancy. *Endocrinology*, **96**, 219–226.

Surani, M. A. H. 1977. Cellular and molecular approaches to blastocyst uterine interactions at implantation. In: *Development in Mammals*, vol. 1, p. 245. Ed. M. H. Johnson. North-Holland, Amsterdam.

Tekelioglu-Uysal, M., Edwards, R. G. & Kisnichi, H. A. 1975. Ultrastructural relationships between decidua, trophoblast and lymphocytes at the beginning of human pregnancy. *Journal of Reproduction and Fertility*, **42**, 431–438.

Thomas, K. 1981. Relaxin structure, function and evolution. KROC Foundation Conference. *Annals of the New York Academy of Science*.

Tietze, C., Guttmacher, A. F. & Rubin, S. 1950. Time required for conception in 1727 planned pregnancies. *Fertility and Sterility*, **1**, 338–346.

Tietze, C. & Potter, R. G. 1962. Statistical evaluation of the rhythm method. *American Journal of Obstetrics and Gynecology*, **84**, 692–698.

Tseng, L. & Gurpide, E. 1975. Effects of progestins on oestradiol receptor levels in the human endometrium. *Journal of Clinical Endocrinology and Metabolism*, **41**, 402–404.

Topposada, M., Khowessah, M., Shaala, S., Osman, M. & Rahman, H. A. 1977. Aberrant uterine responses to prostaglandin E_2 as a possible etiological factor in functional infertility. *Fertility and Sterility*, **28**, 434–439.

Tulchinsky, D. & Hobel, C. J. 1973. Plasma human chorionic gonadotropin, estrone, estradiol, estriol, progesterone and 17α-hydroxyprogesterone in human pregnancy. III. Early human pregnancy. *American Journal of Obstetrics and Gynecology*, **117**, 884–893.

Tyndale-Biscoe, C. H. 1979. Hormonal control of embryonic diapause and reactivation in the tammar wallaby. In: *Maternal Recognition of Pregnancy*, pp. 173–190. Ciba Foundation Symposium, no. 64.

Ulstem, U., Andersson, K. E. & Forman, A. 1978. Relaxing effects of Nifedipine on the nonpregnant human uterus *in vitro* and *in vitro*. *Obstetrics and Gynecology*, **52**, 436–441.

Vijayakumar, R. & Walter, W. A. W. 1981. Myometrial prostaglandins during the human menstrual cycle. *American Journal of Obstetrics and Gynecology*, **141**, 313–317.

Ward, W. F., Frost, A. G. & Ward, M. O. 1978. Estrogen binding by embryonic and interembryonic segments of the rat uterus prior to implantation. *Biology of Reproduction*, **18**, 598–601.

Wiqvist, N., Martin, J. N., Bygdeman, M. & Green, K. 1975. Prostaglandin analogues and interotonic potency: a comparative study of seven compounds. *Prostaglandins*, **9**, 255–269.

Wilks, J. W. 1977. Endocrine characterization of the menstrual cycle of the stump-tailed monkey (*Macaca arctoides*). *Biology of Reproduction*, **16**, 474–478.

Wolf, D. P. & Mastroianni, L. 1975. Protein composition of human uterine fluid. *Fertility and Sterility*, **26**, 240–247.

Wood, C. 1972. Myometrial and tubal physiology. In: *Human Reproductive Physiology*, p. 324. Ed. R. P. Shearman. Blackwell, Oxford.

Wordinger, R. J., Dickey, J. F. & Ellicott, A. E. 1977. Histochemical evaluation of the lipid droplet content of bovine oviductal and endometrial epithelial cells. *Journal of Reproduction and Fertility*, **49**, 113–114.

Wynn, R. M. (Editor) 1977. *Biology of the Uterus*. Plenum Press, New York and London.

Discussion on Embryo Transfer in Animals and its Relevance to Man

Cervical Versus Fundal Replacements

Edwards: The work on cattle may point to a parallel for work on human embryos. It was the work of Testart, and of Rowson and his colleagues in Cambridge which showed that cervical transfers were more successful if done at 8 or 9 days, than at three days. This was a major advance in the application of embryo transfer in cattle, because success rates had been very low before this. Why does this difference arise? Perhaps all of us here are in the situation now of wondering whether to transfer on day 1, 2, 3 or 4, or whether to go to surgical transfers via the fundus. Could Testart analyse for us some of the factors that changed in cattle when the timing of cervical transfers was altered?

Testart: Many people have tried to detect physiological changes in the cattle uterus during these early days of the luteal phase. They have analysed the results of embryo transfer with and without catheters. Two sequelae of cervical transfers appear to be responsible for the difference in success rates. The first is the stimulation of the cervix during transfer, which could induce contractions in the uterus. The second is the inflammatory or infectious responses of the uterus. In sheep, for example, contractions in the uterus three days after ovulation are mainly from the oviduct towards the cervix, and after this time they change direction. A small stimulation to the uterus may therefore influence this type of contraction, and if it is increased the egg may be expelled into the vagina after transfer.

Edwards: Cervical transfers in mice were frowned upon for a long time. Up to about 1972, cervical transfers in almost any species were regarded as anathema. Coincident with the cattle work, two Swedish workers began to transfer mouse embryos via the cervix, and they obtained 50% of pregnancies (Marsk & Larsson, 1974). This compares with a figure of approximately 70% in this species after surgical transfer. What had been thought difficult or impossible suddenly started to work, giving acceptable rates of implantation. There is no obvious reason why the system suddenly improved, but it does not appear to become as popular as it has in cattle, and most people still use surgical transfers.

In many respects, the mouse embryo is a good model for man. The form of implantation is very similar, the cervical canal is straight, although double, the formation of the blastocyst is similar, although the inner cell mass is on the opposite pole of the embryo during implantation.

Jones, G: I believe that the mouse is a better model than the horse and other farm animals for the human being. The method of implantation and the formation of the embryo is very different in the horse.

Trounson: It depends entirely on which aspect of reproduction is being considered. Transfer via the cervix in the mouse is very difficult if you want to develop models for comparing with the human.

Edwards: I always found it remarkably easy to pass the cervix in mice, using a fine blunted needle. The two cervices had to be penetrated separately, but it was possible to do it without difficulty.

Trounson: I understand the method is much more difficult if transfers are made at day 3 or 4 in mice. The cervix closes right down at these stages of the luteal phase.

Leeton: We have now tried using the transfundal method in women. In three cases I could find the cavity without any difficulty during laparoscopy. But we have no pregnancies. It is very simply done by inserting a needle through the uterine wall into the cavity, then inserting a catheter through it. We have checked this procedure with patients not in the in-vitro fertilization programme, and there was virtually no bleeding in the washings. We have also looked through the hysteroscope and found little blood inside the uterine cavity. There was bleeding from the serosal end as the needle was removed, but there was very little into the uterine cavity itself.

Steptoe: I am bothered about bleeding into the abdomen. It can be controlled. Which method do you use? A small amount of current will stop the bleeding immediately.

Leeton: The bleeding stops within a few minutes. We do not have to take any steps to control it.

Mettler: Are there any difficulties in locating the endometrial cavity?

Leeton: The necessity is to control the utero-vaginal relationships, by manipulation. The needle must be kept at right angles to the fundus, and vaginal control through the fingers allows the uterus to be held stiffly, so that it can be penetrated by the needle. Under these conditions, a slight give in pressure can be felt as the uterine cavity is entered. I find it easier to do it by this method than by actually holding directly on to the cervix.

Steptoe: We carried out about six transfundal transfers in Oldham, and before that I carried out a number of tests on how it could be done and the results of the technique. We put a holding forceps on to one of the round ligaments, penetrated the fundus, and then passed a catheter into the lumen. We passed blue dye into the lumen and radio-opaque substances, to see that the fluids were entering the lumen of the uterine cavity. The method is extraordinarily easy if the mid-point of the fundus is chosen. The characteristic resistance of the uterus is succeeded by a slight give as the endometrial cavity is entered, and then it is possible to move about 1 cm into the uterine cavity without further resistance.

My concern is that a rather large Tuohy needle is required to pass into the uterus, and this worried me in relation to the amount of bleeding there may be in the endometrial cavity. This has been my only criticism of the method. The stilette in the Tuohy needle enables this procedure to be carried out with minimum interference to tissue. Of course, the Tuohy needle is slightly curved at the end, and this does create slight difficulties in passing the catheter. None of the cases we did resulted in pregnancy but, of course, some of these were done in the early days when we were using HMG and HCG and getting short luteal phases.

Infections and the Replacement of Embryos

Testart: There is also the possibility that infection might influence success rates. Even a subclinical dose could be important because at this time the uterus is very sensitive to bacteria and other con-taminants. But, having said all this, no one yet knows why it is not easy to transfer an embryo on day 3 in cattle.

Jones, H: Veterinarians at our Agricultural Research Station in Virginia have indicated that infection is the key to the difference. They believe that an early transfer is apt to fail because the infection destroys the embryo, whereas later the endometrium is more resistant.

Testart: I doubt this is the answer. We know that we can transfer on day 3 by surgery, and the results are very good.

Jones, H: But surgical transfers are cleaner than cervical transfers. This could still be the explanation, that the endometrium is damaged by the infection, and cannot catch up later to sustain the embryo. At day 9, the damage is less. The veterinarians use antibiotics in the medium to protect the embryo and the endometrium against infection.

Trounson: Numerous studies have been reported, but many are conflicting. Some groups have found no advantage in adding antibiotics, and no effect associated with microbiology of the transfer catheter in cattle (Trounson *et al.*, 1978). In effect, the cow is a bad model for human and the horse may be preferable. In that species, non-surgical transfers are simpler, and the cervix is easier to pass. The cow cervix is very convoluted, and a rigid instrument must be used to pass through it. A soft catheter must have a metal stilette down the centre, whereas the horse cervix is a much simpler, and straighter. Horse embryos can be transferred much easier, hence I suggest that the uterus and the cervix of the horse may be preferable as models rather than cattle.

Fishel: Infections could be very important in their influence on reimplanting human embryos in another respect. Contaminants may be present in human semen, and these could persist in low amounts in the culture fluid. We must be very careful about the introduction of contaminants via this route, which could influence the rate of implantation.

Jones, H: We have been persuaded by the work in animals to give our patients tetracyclines 24 hours before reimplantation. This should be long enough for them provided they are given in a sufficiently high dose. The dose is given orally, and continued until 24 hours after transfer. We do not have the slightest idea if it is effective or otherwise.

Conti: We have data to show that if suppositories are given for five days in succession, there is no effect on the flora of the cervical mucus inside the cervical canal. The bacteria in the vagina are removed, but not those in the cervical canal. In my opinion, the tetracycline should be taken orally.

Jones, G: This was also our experience a number of years ago. The organism that concerned us most was ureaplasma, which is sensitive to tetracycline and why we selected that particular drug.

Cohen: We have to be careful with the addition of antibiotics to spermatozoa. We know that furadin is very toxic to spermatozoa. Tetracyclines are not toxic.

Steptoe: We have carried out a large number of studies on women who were presenting for in-vitro fertilization. Only very rarely have we found what may be regarded as pathogens in cervical mucus. Frequently, *Staphylococcus faecalis*, *S. alba*, and other organisms were present. They do no harm in the women, and are not so easy to eliminate. But carrying them up into the uterus through the cervical mucus during reimplantation of the embryos could well be a different matter.

Pharmacological Inhibition of Uterine Contractions

Feichtinger: Frölich (1974) has measured contractions in the non-pregnant human uterus, using catheters similar to those used for replacing embryos. Small, frequent contractions occur in the follicular phase, but they have a greater amplitude in the luteal phase.

Hamberger: We have been studying uterine and cervical activity, both *in vivo* and *in vitro*. When there is an increased activity, there appears to be a concomitant release of prostaglandins, either from the endometrium or the myometrium. We accordingly believe that the less manipulation, the better. We also believe that if the replacements are done transabdominally, there will be a release of prostaglandins lasting for several hours. The activity of the uterus is raised for many hours before it returns to basal levels. We have considered using prostaglandin synthetase inhibitors, but we suspect they might interfere negatively with the implantation process. Likewise, the use of β_2-mimetics to dampen uterine contractions could interfere with the activity of the corpus luteum: the catecholamines and prostaglandins are very much involved in regulating the function of the early corpus luteum.

Feichtinger: We have tried giving patients Ritodrine infusions. This resulted in short luteal phases in two out of three patients. We have also tried to glue the cervix together, using fibrin. It was not introduced as far as the internal os, and we felt that it was not being detrimental. The sample was a human frozen fibrin, and we had to double the injection system to add the clotting factors. The block remained at the external os for about 24 hours.

Trounson: We have tested mefanomic acid, to eliminate contractions. It had no effect on the success of the replantations. We have also tested prostaglandin inhibitors and also β_2-mimetics, but without effect. We have even suspected that they may be reducing the chance of implantation in some patients.

Effects on Implantation of Stage of Embryonic Growth and Time of Day

Edwards: In our work, embryos have been transferred at all stages between the 4-cell and the blastocyst. All replacements are carried out during the evening at 5 p.m. or 9 p.m. The days after fertilization have varied from day 2 to day 5, to cover these embryonic stages. We wished to know if changes in, for example, uterine contractility and levels of progesterone during the early luteal phase would influence implantation of the embryos. Even though we now have more than 40 pregnancies, we still feel in no position to evaluate the different methods with any reliability. There are too many variables, including the day of transfer, the position of the patient, the amount of medium injected (in our case between 0.015 and 0.04 ml). I believe that an occasional pregnancy using a particular technique or catheter is good information, but it does not prove that the method is reliable or even satisfactory.

Steptoe: We ask our patients to stay in one position for as long as possible. It is very difficult, of course, when they are in the knee–chest position. This is one reason why we do our replacements in the evening, so the patient can go to sleep immediately after the replacement is completed. We also keep our patients in for four days, to make sure that the implantation process is well advanced before they leave the clinic.

Trounson: We keep our patients in hospital for 24 hours. I know that some groups send their patients home immediately after replacement, and they have had some success. We have found no difference in the time of day when replacements are carried out, in contrast to the Bourn Hall team.

Jones, H: Most of the teams here transfer the embryos at any convenient time, during the normal working day or whenever they can. Only the Bourn Hall team replaces embryos during the evening.

Feichtinger: Does the presence of corona cells around the embryo make any difference to the success rate of implantation? It is possible that they might interfere with the implantation process.

Edwards: We will continue to replace embryos in the evening, perhaps a little earlier as winter comes on and darkness comes earlier. There is evidence of a diurnal rhythm in uterine activity, contractions being less at night (Akerlund *et al.*, 1976; Lundstrom *et al.*, 1981), and evening transfers suit our work programme.

Corona cells do not seem to influence implantation if there are not too many of them. Some patients have established pregnancies after the replacement of an embryo with some corona cells around it, and we prefer to leave them rather than take measures to remove them that could damage the embryo.

Testart: It seems to me that all groups appear to be getting about the same rate of success with replacement—between 15 and 20%.

Perhaps the catheter, or whatever, does not make any difference. We may have to think similarly to animal studies, where the post-ovulatory day is important.

References

Akerlund, M., Andersson, K.-E. & Ingermarsson, I. 1976. Effects of terbutaline on myometrial activity, uterine blood flow and lower abdominal pain in women with primary dysmenorrhea. *British Journal of Obstetrics and Gynaecology*, **83**, 673–678.

Fröhlich, H. 1974. Steuermechanismen der Motilität des nichtgraviden Uterus *in situ*. *Wein Klin. Wschr.*, **86**, Supplement 24.

Lundström, V., Eneroth, P., Granström, E. & Swahn, K.-L. 1981. Third World Congress of Human Reproduction, Berlin (in press).

Marsk, L. & Larsson, K. S. 1974. A simple method for non-surgical blastocyst transfer in mice. *Journal of Reproduction and Fertility*, **25**, 451–454.

Trounson, A. O., Rowson, L. E. A. & Willadsen, S. M. 1978. Non-surgical transfer of bovine embryos. *Veterinary Record*, **102**, 74–75.

A discussion on the replacement of human embryos is given on page 315.

Luteal Phase Evaluation
in in-vitro Fertilization

G. S. Jones, J. Garcia and A. Acosta

Theoretically, for successful implantation of a fertilized oocyte, both the luteal phase and the endometrial response to hormonal stimulation must be normal. Secondarily, the development of the blastocyst must be in phase with the endometrial development. More specifically, the endometrium must not be in advance of the trophoblastic development. The question to be answered is, does in-vitro fertilization disrupt luteal function, either by (1) the stress of anaesthesia theoretically due to the ensuing hyperprolactinemia, or (2) by mechanical removal of the granulosa cells during aspiration? If so, is supplementation of the luteal phase necessary or helpful? To answer these questions, we initiated a study prior to beginning our in-vitro fertilization programme.

Mechanical Removal of Granulosa Cells
During Oocyte Aspiration in the Natural Cycle

Thirty-two patients who were to be admitted to the programme were monitored during 45 cycles prior to an aspiration attempt. Forty-two cycles were studied during an egg retrieval in a natural cycle. The retrieval cycles were divided into four categories according to the estimated amount of follicular granulosa cell disruption, as judged by the numbers of follicle washes and the estimated vigour of the washing.

Further groups of patients were evaluated according to the presence of progesterone supplementation. Group one consisted of eight cycles in which a mature oocyte was recovered, but no fertilization or cleavage occurred. No progesterone supplementation was given in these eight cycles. Group two consisted of eight cycles, again in which a

Department of Obstetrics and Gynecology, Eastern Virginia Medical School, Norfolk, Virginia.

mature oocyte was obtained, an embryo was replaced, and progesterone supplementation was given. Group three consisted of nine cycles in which no oocyte was retrieved, and during which multiple aspirations were done with vigour. Group four consisted of nine cycles in which ovulation had occurred and a recent corpus luteum with stoma was seen. The corpora lutea were aspirated unsuccessfully and probably most vigorously.

All of these cycles were natural cycles monitored with an LH serum radioimmunoassay to determine the initiation of the LH surge. An attempt was made to time the aspiration to 27 hours after the onset of the LH surge was detected. As these cycles represent the initiation of the program, it is understandable that some aspirations were not always properly timed and the monitoring was occasionally misinterpreted. More details can be obtained by consulting the previous publications (Garcia *et al.*, 1982a, b). Fifteen of the unaspirated cycles were also evaluated by endometrial biopsy and diagnosed as normal according to the biologic response of the endometrium by Dr. J. Donald Woodruff, Department of Obstetrics and Gynecology, Johns Hopkins Hospital, Baltimore, Maryland.

The total length of the secretory phase of the menstrual cycle was determined by counting the day of ovulation as day one, and calculating the interval to the first day of the menstrual period. The day of ovulation is counted as beginning 10 hours from the estimated LH peak (Pauerstein *et al.*, 1978).

During oocyte retrieval attempts, the patient was hospitalized. Medications consisted of Demerol 50 mg, Vistaril 50 mg, and Robinul 0.2 mg, on call to the operating room. Subsequently, this type of premedication has been discontinued in in-vitro fertilization patients. P-tubocurarine 5 mg IM; Fentanyl 1–2 cc IV, according to the patient's weight; sodium pentothal 250–300 mg IV; succinylcholine and L.T.A. topical to the trachea, and endotracheal intubation followed by N_2O_2 2–5 : 2 ratio were used as anaesthesia. Neat oxygen was given by mask during the recovery from anaesthesia until the patient was alert and reoriented. Laparoscopy was performed using carbon dioxide for peritoneal insufflation. Serum assays for LH, progesterone and estradiol-17β were done by radioimmunoassay, the details having been published elsewhere (Abraham *et al.*, 1971; Garcia *et al.*, 1982a, b; Midgley, 1967; Pauerstein *et al.*, 1978).

The unpaired Student's t-test was used to analyse the difference between progesterone and oestradiol levels on specific cycle days. In order to test the difference between the progesterone values and the oestradiol values in the groups throughout the entire cycle, an analysis of variance with co-variance was used. The day of the cycle and the square of the day of the cycle were used as co-variates in the analysis in order to eliminate the effect of position in the cycle on the overall progesterone or oestradiol values. The number of viable granulosa cells was estimated by actual counts in 19 aspirates.

Hormone Levels in Various Groups of Patients

Figure 1 illustrates the radioimmunoassay LH values during the cycles studied. In this assay, the value of 60 mIU ml^{-1} was used to mark the beginning of LH surge, and values were taken every four hours during the peri-ovulatory and post-ovulatory 24-hour period. The length of the cycles cannot be inferred from the day of the last value, as many cycles were not studied during the last few days. This is true for all of the figures given. Ovulation was assumed, arbitrarily, to have occurred 10 hours after the peak LH value.

The second figure (Fig. 2) shows the serum progesterone values obtained during the 45 monitored cycles without follicle aspiration.

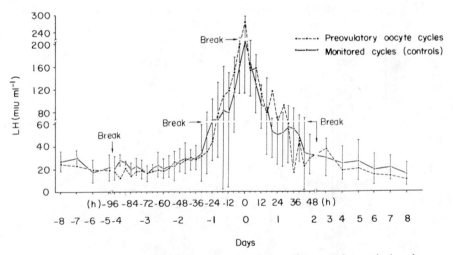

FIG. 1. Serum LH values by radioimmunoassay, daily and every 4 hours during the periovulatory phase of the cycle, in 45 cycles from 32 women with normal menstrual interval ovulation and, in 15 patients, normal endometrial biopsy reports. These cycles were studied prior to a cycle for attempted egg retrieval for in-vitro fertilization. Onset of LH surge is estimated at 60 mIU ml^{-1} in this assay. These values are compared with those found in 16 cycles in which follicle aspiration was accomplished and a pre-ovulatory oocyte obtained. No statistical difference is seen.

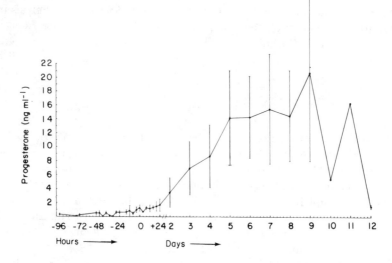

FIG. 2. Progesterone serum values by radioimmunoassay during 45 monitored cycles in 32 women prior to follicular aspiration for in-vitro fertilization. All women had normal menstrual histories and 15 of the abnormal cycles were associated with an histologically normal endometrial pattern. No evaluation can be made of cycle length from this figure.

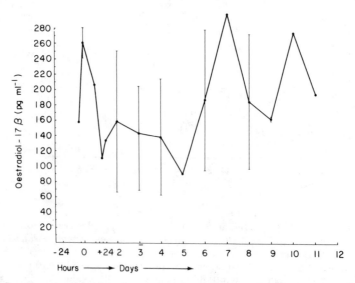

FIG. 3. Serum oestradiol values in a series of control, normal patients without follicle aspiration. Blood assays are every other day rather than every day as in Figs. 1 and 2.

It is of interest that there is an initial rise in progesterone simultaneous with the rise in LH and a sharp decline in the curve after day 9, which contrasts to the steady, gradual increase in the progesterone to peak values from day 0 to day 5. This is not unlike the curve found in previous studies of normal cycles (Aksel & Jones, 1974). Figure 3 represents the radioimmunoassay values for serum oestradiol-17β found in pre-aspiration cycles. Note that the frequency of these values is less than the frequency in the progesterone samples, being every other day. The preovulatory oestradiol surge in this assay is somewhat lower than in other assays reported, being between 250–280 pg ml^{-1}, rather than the usual 300–400 pg ml^{-1}.

Figure 4 shows the serum progesterone values in eight cycles in which a mature oocyte was obtained, but cleavage failed. No replacement occurred and no progesterone supplementation was given. The dotted line represents the aspiration cycle, and the solid line the pre-aspiration monitoring cycles. There was a small but statistically significant decrease in the aspiration cycles.

Figure 5 represents the serum oestradiol values in this same group of eight cycles, with mature oocytes and failed fertilization. Again, there

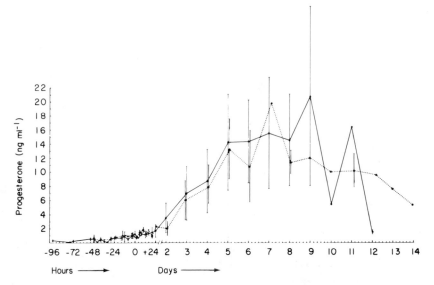

FIG. 4. Serum progesterone values in the normal control patients (——) plotted against serum progesterone values in 8 cycles in which a mature oocyte was obtained, but cleavage failed (······). No replacement occurred and no progesterone supplementation was given. There was a small but statistically significant decrease in the aspiration cycles.

is also a small statistical decrease between the oestradiol values of the aspirated and unaspirated cycles.

Figure 6 represents the serum progesterone values in eight cycles in which follicle aspirations secured a mature oocyte and embryo replacement occurred. These cycles were supplemented with progesterone therapy, 25 mg progesterone suppositories, b.d., or 12.5 mg of progesterone IM daily, beginning on the day after embryo placement. It can be seen that the cycles were significantly lengthened. There was no statistically significant different in the serum progesterone values.

Figure 7 represents the serum oestradiol values in the same cycle as Figure 6. Again, the dotted line represents the aspiration cycles, the solid line the control, monitored cycles. Again, no difference was seen in the statistical evaluation of the oestradiol values.

Figure 8 shows the serum progesterone values in nine cycles in which no oocyte was retrieved. These nine patients had multiple aspirations which were vigorously performed, in an effort to obtain an oocyte. There is a statistically significant decrease in the amount of progesterone in the aspirated cycles from those of the control unaspirated cycles. Again, no inference can be made as to the length of the cycle.

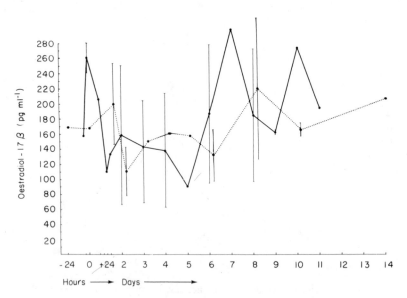

FIG. 5. Serum oestradiol values in the same group of 8 cycles with mature oocytes and failed fertilization (———) represents the values in the controlled cycles while (········) represents values in the aspiration cycles. Again there is a small statistical decrease between the oestradiol values of the aspirated and unaspirated cycles.

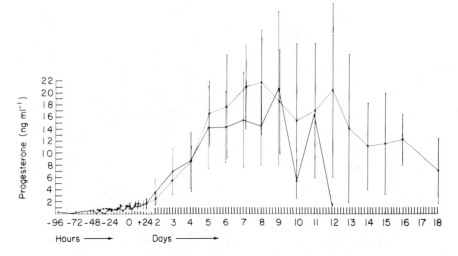

FIG. 6. Serum progesterone values again in the normal, control patients (———) plotted against 8 cycles in which egg retrieval was accomplished, a mature oocyte recovered, and the embryo replaced (······). In these patients progesterone vaginal suppositories 50 mg daily, or 12.5 mg in oil daily was given I.M. the day after egg replacement. As can be seen, there is no decrease in progesterone values during the retrieval cycles, and the substitution therapy produces a slight increment.

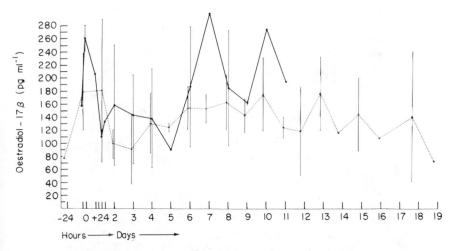

FIG. 7. The same 8 cycles as described in Fig. 4, showing the serum oestradiol values from aspiration cycles (······), plotted against the control (———). In this group, unlike the unsubstituted group (Fig. 3) there is no demonstrable statistical decrease in the levels of oestradiol, in spite of the fact that there was no oestradiol therapy. The progesterone is assumed to have acted as an oestradiol substrate.

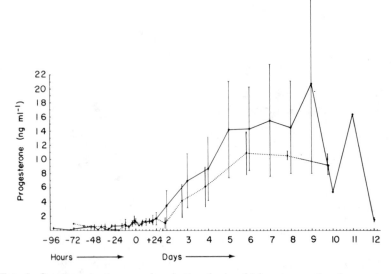

FIG. 8. Serum progesterone values in 9 cycles in which oocyte retrieval was attempted, and no oocyte retrieved. Therefore, multiple, vigorous aspirations were performed (·····). These are once more plotted against the normal control, unaspirated cycles (——). There is a statistically significant decrease in the amount of progesterone in the aspirated cycles compared to the unaspirated control cycles.

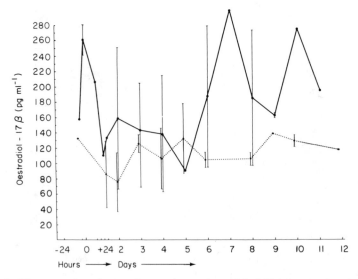

FIG. 9. The same 9 cycles as shown above, in which follicle aspiration for oocyte retrieval was attempted and no oocyte retrieved. Oestradiol values are shown as the above (·····). Control cycles are shown by (——). There is a statistically lower oestradiol in the aspiration cycles.

Figure 9 represents the oestradiol values in the same nine cycles in which no oocyte was retrieved. As with progesterone, the oestradiol values showed a decrease compared to the control non-aspirated cycles.

Figure 10 shows the serum radioimmunoassay progesterone values from nine cycles during which a recent corpus luteum was seen at laparoscopy. Nevertheless, these corpora were aspirated vigorously, although unsuccessfully in an effort to obtain a mature oocyte. The values show a decreased progesterone in the aspiration cycles compared to the control cycles, which is similar to but slightly greater than seen in the unsuccessful aspiration cycles (Fig. 8).

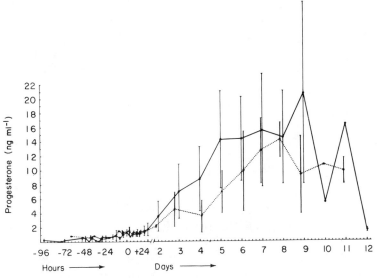

FIG. 10. Nine cycles in which a recent corpus luteum was found at laparoscopy, and aspiration was attempted unsuccessfully. These follicles were apparently most vigorously aspirated (·····). Values are plotted against the control, unaspirated cycles (——). The values were statistically lower in the aspiration cycles. The duration of the cycle cannot be interpreted by the charts.

Figure 11 shows the serum oestradiol values plotted by the broken line in the same nine cycles showing recent ovulation with corpus luteum aspiration. Again, there is a decreased serum oestradiol compared to those in the control cycles.

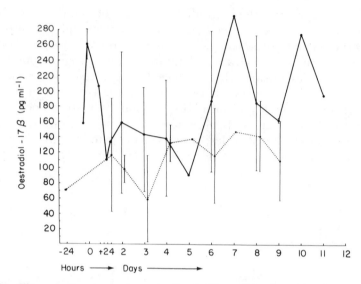

FIG. 11. The same 9 cycles as shown in Fig. 8. Oestradiol values following aspiration of a recently ovulated corpus luteum (······), plotted against the unaspirated, control cycles (———). The aspiration cycles show a statistically decreased amount of oestradiol compared to the control, unaspirated cycles.

Does the Mechanical Aspiration of Granulosa Cells Impair the Luteal Phase?

The results of a statistical analysis of the total surgical procedures for oocyte aspiration in the natural cycle during in-vitro fertilization leads to the conclusion that there is a decrease of luteal steroidogenic function following aspiration and that this is probably associated with the mechanical aspiration of granulosa cells. The most severe disruption of function in both progesterone and oestrogen steroidogenesis seems to occur in those cycles in which the most vigorous and repetitive aspirations of follicles were carried out. As the anaesthesia technique in all patients was the same, this seems to preclude an anaesthetic stress phenomenon. The psychogenic stress as far as can be evaluated should have been the same in all groups of patients. No prolactin assays were made on these patients, as reports by Steptoe *et al.* (1980) and Soules *et al.* (1980) indicate that prolactin values in the serum may be elevated.

The disruption of oestradiol steroidogenesis which was also statistically demonstrated in the cycles following follicular aspiration

(Figs. 9 and 11) is assumed to be due to the decrease of progesterone, the steroid substrate for oestradiol. This assumption perhaps is strengthened by the finding that the values for oestradiol-17β are within normal limits in those cycles in which progesterone supplementation occurred (Fig. 7).

In this series, the average figure of viable granulosa cells per aspiration was 3×10^6. The number of active granulosa cells in the mature human follicle has been estimated to be approximately 50 million (Hodgen, personal communication). Thus, the number of granulosa cells removed at aspiration, particularly when multiple procedures are done, is theoretically of some concern. In the subhuman primate, progesterone insufficiency has been shown by Hodgen (personal communication) to occur in the early part of the post-ovulatory phase following follicle aspiration. The individual pattern of corpus luteum disruption in our patients, however, did not follow the same curve.

We think that the re-documentation of the increased serum progesterone paralleling the LH rise may be of significance and as suggested by Wramsby et al. (1980) may serve as a marker for oocyte maturation. This is a point which needs to be checked by all groups interested in in-vitro fertilization.

Although luteal function can be shown to be impaired after follicle aspiration in relation to controlled cycles in the same individuals, these mathematical computations may not be of biological significance. It is important at this time to state that this study relates only to overall statistics. The relation of individual case findings to these statistics is required in order to understand the biological significance of the statistical findings. This possibility is emphasized by the fact that cycles having the most vigorous and multiple aspirations (Figs. 8, 9, 10 and 11), and showing the most marked alteration in steroidogenesis, showed no associated shortening of the secretory phase. The mean duration of the luteal phase in the unaspirated cycles was 12.3 days with variations between 12 and 16 days. In the most vigorously aspirated cycles, the mean duration was 13.6 days with variations between 13 and 15 days for the aspiration failure cycles, and 13.7 days with extremes of 11 to 16 days in the luteum aspirated cycles.

In the cycles supplemented with progesterone, there was a statistically significant prolongation of the luteal phase, the mean being 19.6 days which is highly significant. Again, this needs to be evaluated in respect to individual patients, as some continued to show a normal 14-day span in spite of supplementation, while others were greatly prolonged, one being 26 days, almost 2 weeks past the expected time of the period. This was of particular interest as in the study of supplemented cycles both in infertility patients with either normal corpus luteum function, or inadequate corpus luteum function, no such prolongation was seen. The longest delay was 4 days in an inadequate luteal phase cycle (Aksel & Jones, 1974). In our experience of many years with supplementing the luteal phase using this dosage of progesterone, such pseudo-pregnancy reactions have never occurred. However, in none of the cycles reported here was it possible with serum available, to document any significant changes in the levels of HCGβ. We have nevertheless queried if this could possibly represent a failure of the embryo, matured *in vitro*, to develop a trophoblastic hormone function. If this were the case, such a fundamental defect would probably be associated with other defects incompatible with continued embryo development.

Does the Aspiration of Granulosa Cells Cause Luteal Phase Defects in Cycles Stimulated by HMG and HCG?

During the last six months, as reported in this conference, we have been using ovulation induction with human menopausal gonadotrophin (Perganol) followed by HCG and attempted oocyte aspiration at 36½ hours after the HCG injection. A low-dosage regime has been employed beginning on day 3 of the cycle, and modified according to the clinical parameters and the serum oestradiol findings, but in the main using 2 ampoules (FSH 75 IU/LH 75 IU) daily for 3 days, followed by one ampoule daily for 3 days. It was hoped to slip into the cycle of development of the cohort follicles and perhaps rescue an additional one or two, but at best to obtain a predictable ovulation time for the dominant follicle and avoid hyperstimulation.

Although two and three dominant follicles with mature oocytes were obtained on occasion, in other cycles a single dominant follicle was found. In those cycles with single follicles, it seems to us that the post-aspiration progesterone values are low and require supplementation. When a number of mature oocytes are found the progesterone values are 2 to 3 times the expected values of a single pregnancy. This is in keeping with the findings during ovulation induction in women with abnormal ovulatory mechanisms.

Luteal defects can be observed when hyperstimulation is produced. Hyperstimulation is defined as oestradiol levels which are consistently 600 pg ml^{-1} or above, associated with four or more large follicles (above 20 mm) and usually in association with cystic follicles (30 mm or above) and no granulosa cells or oocytes obtained. If pregnancy does not occur, these cycles tend to show high progesterone values during the mid-portion of the luteal phase with a rapid fall and early menstruation at approximately day 10. However, one patient who became pregnant with this same syndrome was nevertheless able to rescue corpus luteum steroid function by the trophoblastic hormone HCG and the pregnancy progressed normally.

We would therefore suggest that ovulation induction by HMG followed by HCG does not produce an abnormal luteal function, although a short luteal phase may occur in the absence of HCG rescue. These findings are only currently being statistically evaluated and will be reported at a later date.

Conclusions

Although it can be shown statistically that aspiration of follicles may be associated with a decreased luteal function in both oestrogen and progesterone steroidogenesis, we do not believe that this is of clinical significance in the majority of patients. However, we do believe that a serum progesterone assay taken in the first six post-aspiration days of the cycle will determine if a luteal defect is present. If this is found, we believe it should be supplemented either in the natural cycle or in cycles where ovulation was induced. We have used 12.5 mg of progesterone in oil daily IM, or 25 mg progesterone suppositories vaginally twice a day. These amounts of progesterone will reproduce values found in the normal cycle. It can be concluded, therefore, that these dosages are within the normal physiologic range and do not induce luteolysis.

Once more, it should be emphasized that the average patient following in-vitro fertilization will not, in our experience, need supplementation of the luteal phase.

References

Abraham, G. E., Swerdloff, R., Tulchinsky, D. & Odell, W. D. 1971. Radioimmuno-assay of plasma progesterone. *Journal of Clinical Endocrinology and Metabolism*, **32**, 619.

Aksel, S. & Jones, G. E. S. 1974. Effect of progesterone and 17-hydroxyprogesterone caproate on normal corpus luteum function. *American Journal of Obstetrics and Gynecology*, **118**, 466.

Garcia, J., Jones, G. S. & Wright, G. L. 1981. Prediction of the time of ovulation. *Fertility and Sterility*, **35**, in press.

Garcia, J., Jones, G. S., Acosta, A. A., & Wright, G. L. in press. Corpus luteum function after follicle aspiration for oocyte retrieval. *Fertility and Sterility* (in press).

Jones, G. S., Aksel, S. & Wentz, A. C. 1974. Serum progesterone values in the luteal phase defects. Effect of chorionic gonadotropin. *Obstetrics and Gynecology*, **44**, 26.

McNatty, K. P., Smith, D. M., Makris, A., Sathanond, R. & Ryan, K. J. 1979. The microenvironment of the human graaffian follicle: interrelationship among the steroid levels in antral fluid, the population of granulosa cells and the status of the oocyte *in vivo* and *in vitro*. *Journal of Clinical Endocrinology and Metabolism*, **49**, 851.

Midgley, A. R. 1967. Radioimmunoassay of human follicle stimulating hormone. *Journal of Clinical Endocrinology and Metabolism*, **27**, 295.

Pauerstein, C. J., Eddy, C. A., Croxatto, H. D., Hess, R., Siler-Khodr, T. M. & Croxatto, H. B. 1978. Temporal relationships of estrogen, progesterone, and luteinizing hormone levels to ovulation in women and infrahuman primates. *American Journal of Obstetrics and Gynecology*, **130**, 876.

Soules, M. R., Sutton, G. P., Hammond, Ch. B. & Haney, A. F. 1980. Endocrine changes at operation under general anesthesia: reproductive hormone fluctuations in young women. *Fertility and Sterility*, **33**, 364.

Steptoe, P. C., Edwards, R. G. & Purdy, J. M. 1980. Clinical aspects of pregnancies established with cleaving embryos grown *in vitro*. *British Journal of Obstetrics and Gynaecology*, **87**, 757.

Wramsby, H., Kullander, S., Liedholm, P., Rannevik, G., Sundstrom, P. & Thorell, J. 1980. The success rate of *in vitro* fertilization of human oocytes in relation to the concentrations of different hormones in follicular fluid and peripheral plasma. *World Conference on Instrumental Insemination, in-vitro Fertilization and Embryo Transfer*, Kiel, West Germany. September, 1980.

The Luteal Uterus: Cellular Interactions with Blastocysts, and the Damaging Effects of Catheters

I. W. H. Johnston

I would like to describe briefly two aspects of the uterus during the luteal phase. We believe these are essential to the improvement in knowledge of the changing properties of the uterus during the period of embryo implantation. First, I will describe the nature of interactions between the different cell types in the uterus and between them and the blastocyst, and secondly comment on the damaging effects on the epithelium and endometrium of the canulae used for replacing embryos.

Interactions Between the Different Cell Types of the Uterus and the Blastocyst

My comments are based on the work of Glasser and McCormack (1981). They have worked with rats, to establish a model for the interactions occurring between the different types of cell in the uterus during the follicular and luteal phase of the cycle, and to study the effects of blastocysts on various aspects of cellular metabolism in the uterus. They have identified and separated myometrial, endometrial, and epithelial cells, and obtained pure cultures of them. Interrelationships between these three cell types and between them and blastocysts could then be analysed *in vitro*.

In rats, levels of oestrogen rise after mating, and progesterone increases from very low levels as luteinization begins. Later, levels of oestrogen decline. The number of oestrogen receptors in the total cell population of epithelial and stromal cells increased thirty-fold during the first one or two days after mating, and then decline. This was somewhat surprising, because in the uterus primed with oestrogens,

Department of Obstetrics and Gynaecology, Royal Women's Hospital, Melbourne.

and about to undertake a pregnancy, a steady increase in receptor numbers might be expected. Accordingly, they examined the number of oestrogen receptors during each hour, and discovered a diurnal rhythm existed in various types of cell. The maximum number of receptors occurred between 10 p.m. and midnight, and the minimum around noon, with a four-fold difference in numbers per cell at these two different times of day. There are also variations between the different types of cell. In epithelial cells, oestrogen receptor activity diminished with the onset of pregnancy, whereas in stromal cells the number of receptors increased during early pregnancy to provide the major source of receptors in the uterus.

They also studied decidualization during early pregnancy. Before oestrus, epithelial cells displayed a considerable mitotic and biochemical activity. As pregnancy began, activity reached to stromal cells, perhaps under the influence of progesterone, followed later by a massive increase in the number of decidual cells. There was a six-fold increase in numbers, resulting in a high ratio between decidual cells: epithelial cells at the time of implantation. In effect, epithelial cells represented only about 10% of the cellular mass in the uterus excluding myometrium.

The effect of a temporary withdrawal of progesterone was studied on the uterus of the immature rat. Interruption of the progesterone supply for one day, without changing the availability of oestrogens, caused a rapid decline in uterine sensitivity. When progesterone was reintroduced, uterine sensitivity was not recovered, as shown by analyses of the turnover of DNA in uterine cells. When progesterone was interrupted for 48 hours, the uterus could be reactivated.

Decidual cells are credited with two functions. One is nutritional, to sustain the early embryo as it implants, and uterine secretions are known to be rich in glycogen. Their second function may be to modify the invasion of the trophoblast into the mother's tissues, because trophoblast is more invasive in extrauterine sites than in the uterus. Glasser and McCormack co-cultured blastocysts with epithelial or stromal cells, and found that this modified the production of progesterone by blastocysts. In isolation, blastocysts produce increasing amounts of progesterone from day 5 until day 10, but this is reduced by half in co-cultures with epithelial cells, and totally inhibited by stromal cells. The progesterone might have been absorbed or utilized by the stromal cells.

Specific interrelationships are established between uterine cells and blastocysts during implantation. During pregnancy, the mitotic activity of the uterine epithelium is considerably increased, evidently by a local interaction with the blastocyst. There is also a marked local increase in the tenacity of the epithelium, in the region of the blastocyst, and it is difficult to withdraw the embryo from its surface. Other localized changes occur in the uterus, especially in the endometrium.

Likewise, the activity of the trophoblast is modified during implantation. It produces large amounts of plasminogen activator during implantation, as it moves through the epithelium and stroma, but this activity declines to almost zero as it approaches the maternal sinuses. This may be another mechanism which assists the movement of trophoblast through the stroma, ending as it approaches the sinuses so that the vasculature of the uterus remains intact.

The Effect of Catheters on the Uterus During Replantation of Embryos

We have noticed various effects of implantation catheters on the human endometrium. For these studies, we have examined uteri removed at various stages of the menstrual cycle. A small window was cut in the anterior wall of the excised uterus, and the surface of the endometrium was then examined microscopically as various catheters were passed through the uterus.

Small, straight, fine catheters, without any enlargement on the tip, tended to burrow under the endometrium. This occurred irrespective of the presence of an end- or side-aperture. The catheters were definitely submerged beneath the endometrium as they emerged from the internal cervical os into the uterus. They then rose to the surface of the endometrium as they entered the uterine cavity. In some cases, a furrow, rather like a plough, was created along the whole length of the endometrium.

Catheters of a larger size, or with an expanded bulb on the tip, caused much less damage. They would induce the furrow in the endometrium, but they did not disturb the surface or at least they did not penetrate through it. Stiffer catheters were more likely to create a furrow than were flaccid catheters. The curvature of the catheter in relationship to the curvature of the uterus was also important. Damage was less if these two curvatures coincided, but a great deal of damage could be caused along the whole length of the uterus if they were not coincident. The best compromise appeared to be a malleable catheter, perhaps made of Teflon, with a small bulb at the tip.

Histological sections were prepared of the uteri, to study the tracks made by the catheters. All the catheters disrupted the surface epithelium to a greater or lesser extent. Damage could be minimal, but occurred in every case. If the catheter was passed two or three times across the uterine surface, the whole of the epithelial cells could be removed, exposing the stroma.

Finally, we tested the effects of injecting specific amounts of fluid as if we were replacing an embryo. A volume of 0.05 ml was injected, although perhaps less than this, 0.03–0.04 ml, actually entered the uterus. Indigo carmine was used to label the fluid, and this volume of medium diffused through the interstices of the endometrium. It did not pass through the cornua, nor did it track backwards along the depression or furrow created in the endometrium. It would pass halfway down the uterine cavity, and did not backtrack anywhere near the internal os, provided it was deposited near the fundus.

We are therefore confident that, under these conditions *in vitro*, the fluid and the embryo would not be expelled from the uterus. These observations might also provide a guide to events occurring *in vivo* during replacement of the embryo.

Reference

Glasser, S. R. & McCormack, S. A. 1981. In: *Cellular and Molecular Aspects of Implantation*. Ed. S. R. Glasser and D. W. Bullock. Plenum,

Discussion on the
Replacement of Human Embryos

Uterine Trauma Using Catheters

Jones, G: The rat model is fascinating, it is not a good copy for man. The corpus luteum in the rat does not produce oestrogen and there could be a different interrelationship between the blastocyst and the endometrium. Information on this point will be gained from cultures of human endometrium, as Redick has shown; under these conditions the decidua will produce prolactin.

Questions must also be asked about mechanical interference with implantation. Is it a bad thing to produce a furrow in the endometrium? For many years, we thought that scraping the endometrium would raise the rate of implantation. In other words, a decidual reaction was believed to enhance implantation.

Johnston: I believe that some progesterone is needed in order to produce a decidual reaction. It is possible to invoke it in all sorts of ways, with chemicals and stimuli. We do not know what is happening in the furrow caused by the catheter, whether decidualization is invoked or not.

Jones, H: Histological examination could help to decide on the nature of the damage. Was there any evidence that the interstitial cells were different in the region of the furrow to the other areas of the uterus?

Johnston: No, not in our studies. Remember that the work was carried out on hysterectomized uteri, so dynamic changes were not possible. The experiment should be repeated, passing catheters into the uterus 24 hours before hysterectomy to find out if decidual or any other changes occurred.

Trounson: We did similar studies in cattle, and found it was essential to examine the uterus immediately after removing it. The uterus had then to be kept on ice. Otherwise, the endometrium, which is very fragile, degenerated within 30 minutes. Burying the catheter in the endometrium, as Johnston described, might have had more severe effects because the uterus had been removed for 2–3 hours.

Johnston: That is true. We found such damage in one uterus removed for 3–4 hours before the work was done. After this study, the uteri were removed immediately prior to the work. There was no significant time gap, and the endometrium appeared to be stable under those circumstances.

Conti: We have studied changes in uteri at about mid-cycle, following the passage of catheters through it, and the injection of media into it. Several different types of catheters were passed by hysteroscopy into the uterine lumen. With the stiffer catheters, the chance of bleeding was higher when it touched the fundal region, just as Johnston described. Even if the endometrium was not penetrated, the contact between a stiff catheter and the surface of the uterus caused small bleeds. As a result, there was a lot of subepithelial haemorrhage, even though the surface was not disturbed.

Distribution of Fluid After an Injection into the Uterus

Conti: We have studied the effects of injecting small amounts of fluid similar to those used for replanting embryos. Varying amounts were injected when the catheter was close to the fundus. Varying results were obtained, according to the volume injected. With 0.2 ml or more, the fluid always returned towards the internal os. This amount appeared to be too great to use for replanting embryos, because the embryo could be carried back towards the internal os. Likewise, 0.10 ml was also serious in small uteri. With quantities as low as 0.05 ml, this movement back towards the internal os was never seen, and these are the volumes that should be used. If the solution was injected too quickly, it would even penetrate into the oviducts, but when injected gently, this did not happen.

Edwards: These data are invaluable in giving some idea of what happens to injected fluid. Entering the uterus, especially the internal os, may not be easy, and could lead to damage. We use about 0.02–0.03 ml, and even less if we can, and have always been concerned about this volume and its distribution in the uterus. Johnston and Conti have reassured us on this point today.

When the catheter is withdrawn from the uterus, the embryo could be withdrawn with it, especially if small amounts of cervical mucus are carried in with the catheter. This is another reason why the design of the catheter is obviously important, because the aperture must not be covered with cervical mucus. The shape of the catheter must also be considered in relation to its withdrawal, because sharp projecting points might pull out endometrium and cervical mucus. It is important to have both a smooth entry and a smooth withdrawal.

Conti: We have not had any problem in entering and leaving, because in our work we had to dilate the cervical canal. This was necessary to introduce the hysteroscope.

Feichtinger: Other people have described how sometimes there is a leakage of fluid when they withdraw the catheter. In some cases, we have injected 0.05 ml, and have watched the cervix for 3–5 minutes after the replacement of the embryo. With a catheter of 4 French gauge, the uterus appeared to contract because the cervix moved distinctively, and a droplet of medium was expelled. Once, this droplet was sieved off and the embryo was found in it. Now, we always examine the cervix for 4–5 minutes after replacement, and collect any fluid. We use a 3 French gauge catheter. Even so, we suspect that a contraction of the uterus could expel many embryos as the patient is being moved back to the ward, or even placed in her bed.

Trounson: I doubt that the expulsion of fluid was due to contractions of the uterus. There may have been a plug of mucus on the end of the catheter and, as it was withdrawn, the embryo was left in the cervical mucus on the external os.

It is necessary to be very careful about attributing expulsion to uterine contractions, unless the point can be proved. It is difficult to see how uterine contractions can expel an embryo lying in 0.05 ml of medium near the fundus.

Interrelationships Between the Tissues of the Uterus

Edwards: The close relationship between epithelium and endometrium has been well characterized. Interactions between them begin even when the reproductive tract is differentiating in the fetus (Cunha, 1976). Such interacts establish and maintain the structure of the uterus during adult life, and during the rapid changes occurring during the menstrual cycle.

Obviously, any trauma caused by a catheter could cause considerable distortion to such interactions, quite apart from its effect on uterine secretions or inducing inflammatory changes. The histological pattern of damage caused by catheters is merely the tip of the iceberg — the biochemical lesions could be considerable.

Fishel: The experiments of Glasser and McCormack are elegant, but I am uncertain about their significance both to our work, and also to implantation in the rodent. A withdrawal of progesterone clearly makes the tissues very refractory and, moreover, studies *in vitro* which are two-dimensional may not relate to three-dimensional studies in the uterus itself. It is essential to remember too that in rodents, decidualization occurs at the site of implantation only, which is very different from man, where it is extensive along the uterus.

Johnston: Obviously, extrapolations must be carefully made from rodents to man. Nevertheless, the experiments showed how interrelationships between the uterine tissues might be effected.

Does a Weak Luteal Phase Arise after Aspirating Preovulatory Follicles?

Spiers: I was interested in Jones's conclusions that the aspiration of granulosa cells will not in general cause a decreased luteal function of any clinical significance. What were the size of follicles that were aspirated, and were they examined during stimulated or natural cycles?

Jones, G: On internal observation, the ovulatory follicle measured 1.8 cm or more, and a mean of 4.72×10^{-6} cells were aspirated from each follicle, varying from a low of 100,000 to a high of 12,000,000. In nine cases, the follicle was reported as 1.7 cm, and the range was between 6×10^3 and 6×10^6 cells.

It is difficult to make comparisons between follicular size and the number of cells without describing the collection and appearance of the egg. For example, if the follicle was atretic, the egg may not have matured normally and the cell number may vary considerably.

Trounson: We have been trying to control the luteal phase by giving some patients one form of treatment and others a different one as a control. Proluton depot, which is 17-hydroxyprogesterone, had no effect, the patients becoming pregnant in about the same ratio as with no treatment. Nor has progesterone given immediately after oocyte recovery until transfer, or after transfer, had any effect; if anything, progesterone given immediately after recovery has had a deleterious effect. At the present moment, numbers are not high, and we have to make our comparisons on the embryos which implanted. We have also tried HCG, but this has not been of any help in increasing the pregnancy rate.

Jones, G: I doubt that progesterone supplements will be of any value, especially during the natural cycle. The situation may be different in patients with stimulated cycles, because our treatments may have produced some defects in the luteal phase. For example, some of them had low levels of oestradiol-17β and these patients may need some form of supplementation in the luteal phase. But many more studies are needed before we can decide.

Hamberger: I believe the problem of progesterone deficiency mostly exists during the natural cycle. Even if many of the granulosa cells are aspirated, there will be enough progesterone if two or more follicles are present in the ovary. The single follicle could lead to a major problem for the natural cycle.

Testart: In farm animals, the rates of embryo cleavage vary in relation to the number of corpora lutea. Such an effect could be very important for our studies on implantation and pregnancy. The embryos appear to cleave faster if there are several corpora lutea, but there is no information on the rate of implantation and pregnancy.

Trounson: These data have been disputed, especially when large doses of progesterone were given without any effect. The administration of progesterone did not mimic the results claimed to be due to the presence of extra corpora lutea.

So far, we are quite disappointed in all the methods currently used to sustain the luteal phase in patients. Luteal phase support does not seem to assist in increasing the rate of implantation.

Edwards: We have also been testing the value of progesterone to support the luteal phase, to decide if luteal phase defects are causing embryonic loss after replantation. Our results agree with Trounson's remarks. Based on our preliminary work, the use of progesterone after oocyte recovery does not appear to enhance the rates of implantation.

Steroid Imbalance and the Luteal Phase

Hamberger: I get concerned when progesterone is given to support the luteal phase. Our studies on human corpora lutea grown *in vitro* have shown how the administration of progesterone may actually induce luteolysis, and prolonged treatment for ten days or so may impair the corpus luteum considerably. There is a long period of pregnancy before the placenta takes over the secretion of progesterone, hence if progesterone is given early after oocyte recovery, it may be necessary to carry on until the placenta is fully active 8 or 9 weeks later. There are problems then with the amount to give. In other words, progesterone for a short time can be dangerous, and would be best avoided.

Other progestins are probably not satisfactory either. Some of them carry the risk of fetal damage, and similar effects may also occur on the corpus luteum as happens with progesterone. It would be far better to give gonadotrophins to support the corpus luteum.

Jones, G: I find it difficult to accept those comments. We have many studies to show that progesterone given in the dosage and manner that we have described is very effective. I must stress here that we used progesterone and not progestogens, which does not cause luteolysis. Progesterone is rapidly cleared from the circulation, and it does not penetrate into the cells of the corpus luteum in sufficient amounts to cause damage. In tissue culture, I know that progesterone will interfere with its synthesis by the luteal cells but, by using the amounts that we describe, the levels in serum are raised, biological effects on the endometrium are caused, and there is no decrease in the function of the corpus luteum. We have been doing this for 35 years, and have followed over 500 pregnancies using this treatment! We have no evidence of biological or teratogenic effects with this treatment (Jones, 1976).

Edwards: I feel there could be a problem of progesterone deficiency, especially after treatment with HMG and HCG. In one the patients described by Jones, levels of progesterone showed a very sharp decline at approximately day 10 after ovulation. Other patients menstruated at day 10, especially if hyperstimulated. We always ascribed our failures in Oldham to the induction of short luteal phases as a result of high levels of oestrogen following hyperstimulation with HMG and HCG. No matter what we did in the luteal phase, we found it almost impossible to correct the deficiency. In the pregnancy cycle described by Jones, the corpus luteum almost failed, as judged by the massive decline in progesterone, and it recovered just in time, presumably as the embryo implanted.

Jones, G: We expect a similar decline in the natural cycle. The level to which progesterone declined in the pregnant patient was still far higher than in the normal luteal phase. It declined relative to an extraordinary increase in progesterone in the earlier luteal phase.

Johnston: Did levels of prolactin change in patients with hyperstimulation?

Jones, G: No, we did not measure it. Other investigators have shown how it is elevated in hyperstimulated cycles.

Feichtinger: We have studied a patient in the luteal phase, during the natural cycle. Taking blood regularly there is a sharp decline on day 10 to very low levels in one patient. Levels then started to rise, and the patient was found to be pregnant. This occurred during a spontaneous pregnancy, showing the typical decline in progesterone at about day 10 may be perfectly normal.

Effects of HCG on the Luteal Phase

Hamberger: Hypophysectomized patients who are treated with HMG and HCG require only a single shot of HCG to induce a normal luteal phase, both in length and other characteristics. This evidence confirms that the use of HCG is satisfactory in inducing the luteal phase, and the ovarian situation will probably be quite suitable after oocyte aspiration. When ovulation is induced with HCG, the nature of the luteal phase is changed. In effect, we have already given the supplement. Groups of patients given HCG, and those without, must be compared in order to find out if this treatment does exert influences in patients who have had stimulated cycles.

Jones, G: In Clomid-treated patients, there may be a problem if ovulation depends on their own natural LH surge. If they are given HCG, I cannot believe there is any problem, even if there is only one follicle.

Conti: Is it possible to give an optimal level of HCG for inducing the luteal phase? Many investigators give between 3 and 5,000 IU, and there may be dose-related effects of this hormone.

Jones, G: I do not know if there are any such effects.

References

Cunha, G. R. 1976. Alterations in the developmental properties of stroma during the development of the urogenital ridge into ductus deferens and uterus in embryonic and neonatal mice. *Journal of Experimental Zoology*, **197**, 357–380.

Jones, G. E. S. 1976. The luteal phase defect. *Fertility and Sterility*, **27**, 351.

A discussion on embryo transfer in animals and its relevance to man is given on page 289.

Part 5

ESSENTIAL TOPICS

Application of in-vitro Fertilization to Idiopathic Infertility

J. F. Leeton and A. O. Trounson

Introduction

Although the use of in-vitro fertilization for treatment of tubal infertility is well established, its use for the treatment of idiopathic infertility has yet to be fully evaluated. Spontaneous pregnancy occurs in this type of infertility so that the success rate of in-vitro fertilization will have to be carefully assessed by comparing it with the spontaneous pregnancy rate. Control studies are essential.

Trounson *et al.* (1980) proposed that in-vitro fertilization could be used in cases of idiopathic infertility to evaluate the capacity of the gametes to fertilize. As the method is currently difficult with a long waiting list, the fertilizing capacity of the husband's sperm in cases of idiopathic infertility can be tested prior to in-vitro fertilization by using either zona-free hamster eggs (Yanagimachi *et al.*, 1976) or human zonae (Yanagimachi *et al.*, 1979).

Hamster ova are not available in Australia. Preliminary studies of salt-stored human zonae in our laboratories have been encouraging. Sperm from fertile specimens can be found within the zona within 15 minutes. Binding and penetration curves are being established to determine optimum assay conditions. This test assesses only the capacity of spermatozoa to bind to and penetrate the zona. In cases of normal sperm penetration one or both of the following tests would be carried out to assess the capacity of the sperm to form pronuclei and initiate normal embryonic development.

(a) Fertilization of immature human oocytes matured *in vitro*. Studies in our laboratory have shown that >90% of oocytes obtained from follicles <2 cm diameter, mature to metaphase-II with extrusion

Department of Obstetrics and Gynaecology, Monash University, Queen Victoria Medical Center, Melbourne, Victoria, Australia.

of the first polar body, after 48 hours culture *in vitro*. These oocytes can be fertilized *in vitro* although normal embryonic development cannot be initiated further. This tests fertilization only.

(b) The ultimate test for the fertilizing capacity of a husband's sperm with his wife's oocytes (short of an in-vivo pregnancy) is to confirm fertilization and normal embryonic development of the wife's oocyte with her husband's spermatozoa *in vitro*. This means that at least two oocytes (and preferably four) are needed.

The Diagnostic Test Using in-vitro Fertilization

The diagnostic test for idiopathic or suspected male infertility has been described by Trounson and Wood (1981) and Trounson *et al.* (1981). In summary, fertilization with both the husband's and donor's spermatozoa establishes the fertilizing capacity of the gametes. Pregnancy after transfer of embryos would suggest undiagnosed problems of oocyte or sperm transport. Failure to achieve pregnancy by repeated embryo transfer would suggest undiagnosed genetic uterine abnormalities. Failure of husband's spermatozoa to fertilize, but normal fertilization with donor's spermatozoa would indicate abnormalities of husband's spermatozoa. Failure of both donor and husband's spermatozoa to fertilize the oocytes would suggest abnormalities of the oocytes or the presence of fertilizing inhibitors.

The use of donor sperm in the in-vitro fertilization programme for the investigation of idiopathic and male infertility is discussed months ahead of the procedure and is an integral part of our protocol. A formal consent form explaining the reason and choice of transfer is discussed and signed by both parties. The couple then have the final choice of deciding which embryo, and the number of embryos (1 or 2), are to be transferred.

The Effectiveness of in-vitro Fertilization in Treating Idiopathic Infertility

A few words are required about controlled studies for defining the effectiveness of fertilization *in vitro* for the treatment of idiopathic infertility, because a spontaneous pregnancy rate exists in the untreated cycle. I am indebted to Dr. Gordon Baker and Dr. Bryan Hudson of Melbourne who have computed the following data.

In the idiopathic group, can we predict the chance of pregnancy in a single cycle? This question must be answered if we are to compare pregnancy rates achieved by natural insemination versus those from in-vitro fertilization in such cases (as well as with men with oligo-spermia or reduced sperm motility).

This comparison is essential if we are to conduct controlled clinical trials to define the role of in-vitro fertilization in couples with idiopathic infertility. If we can devise techniques for such predictions, then it follows that we shall know how large a sample size will be required to show better than natural pregnancy rates.

Baker and Hudson approached this problem of predicting pregnancy-rates by an analysis of the outcome of 775 couples with either idiopathic or male infertility, in whom there were 250 pregnancies. The statistical procedure used to analyse this group was the method of life table analysis, using the log rank test as the test of significance of difference. A mean value for the whole group of 775 couples was calculated to produce a profile of what they chose to call the "average infertile man". They also calculated the mean value for the "worse than average" (severe oligospermia) and "better than average" (normal semen analysis) or idiopathic group.

In the idiopathic group (two years infertility with normal fertility parameters) the chance of pregnancy in the next cycle was calculated to be 15%, a figure which is less than the pregnancy rate in the general community. In order to compare this natural conception rate with that of in-vitro fertilization, they took the current success rate of our 1980 programme as a bench mark. This was 16 pregnancies from 112 laparoscopies, i.e. 14.3%.

As the situation stands at present, it would not be practical to conduct a controlled trial of in-vitro fertilization versus natural insemination in couples with idiopathic infertility of two years duration, since the pregnancy rate is approximately the same in each group. If for example, the pregnancy rate was 30% after fertilization *in vitro*, 90 couples would be required in each group to give an even chance for a significant result, for couples with two years idiopathic infertility.

However, in a couple complaining of idiopathic infertility for nine years duration, the pregnancy rate in the next cycle was calculated as <2%. In this situation, fertilization *in vitro* might offer a major advance, as there is a seven-fold increase over the chance of natural insemination. Under these circumstances to achieve an even chance of a significant difference would require only about ten pregnancies (8 or 9 *in vitro*, and 1 or 2 with natural insemination). Such a trial would still require 66 couples in each group.

Controlled trials will be necessary to establish the usefulness of in-vitro fertilization in idiopathic infertility. The number of couples required to establish that it is a better alternative treatment will be large, because it has a relatively low success rate and there is a background spontaneous rate of pregnancy. All groups studying in-vitro fertilization and investigating idiopathic infertility should start to plan such controlled trials on a collaborative basis because of the large number of couples involved.

Current Results of in-vitro Fertilization with Idiopathic Infertility

In our initial studies (Trounson *et al.*, 1980) there was a marked difference between tubal and idiopathic patients in the proportion of oocytes which were fertilized and developed to normal embryos. Among the abnormalities seen were polyspermia, failure of sperm attachment to oocytes, abnormal cleavage and a high incidence of failed fertilization. Subsequent studies (Trounson *et al.*, 1981) showed that the rate of fertilization and development was lower in the idiopathic group although not that remarkably different to the group with tubal infertility. The comparison revealed that 70% versus 83% of recovered oocytes developed to normal embryos in the idiopathic and tubal groups respectively. In addition, this study showed that of those patients with transferred embryos, the pregnancy rate (15.5%) was exactly the same.

In our more recent work we have found no significant difference in any of the parameters of oocytes recovery rate, fertilization and cleavage rate or pregnancy rate between the two groups, even though a lower success rate occurs in idiopathic infertility at each stage. This leads to very different conclusions than those made previously. Idiopathic infertility does not appear to be an abnormality of the gametes because of the high fertilization rate *in vitro*, nor one of implantation failure because pregnancy rate of transferred embryos is equivalent to that of the tubal infertility group. There may be undiagnosed problems of gamete transport or association *in vivo* which cause prolonged infertility.

In isolated cases we have found sperm abnormalities such as failure of the spermatozoa to bind to the zona pellucida, and a patient who appears to have no cortical granules in her oocytes, so that polyspermy occurs each time fertilization *in vitro* is attempted. However, these tend to be isolated and unusual situations.

We must conclude that, at the present time, in-vitro fertilization is a possible treatment for idiopathic infertility, but that some attempt should be made to determine the cause(s) to enable less heroic procedures to be developed.

References

Trounson, A. O. & Wood, C. 1981. Extracorporeal fertilization and embryo transfer. *Clinics in Obstetrics and Gynaecology*, **8**, 681–713.

Trounson, A. O., Leeton, J. F., Wood, C., Webb, J. & Kovacs, G. 1980. The investigation of idiopathic infertility by in-vitro fertilization. *Fertility and Sterility*, **34**, 431–438.

Trounson, A. O., Leeton, J. F., Wood, C., Buttery, B., Webb, J., Wood, J., Jessup, D., Talbot, J. Mc. & Kovacs, G. 1981. A programme of successful in-vitro fertilization and embryo transfer in the controlled ovulatory cycle. In: *Proceedings III World Congress of Human Reproduction*, Berlin, 1981. Excerpta Medica, Amsterdam.

Yanagimachi, R., Yanagimachi, H. & Rogers, B. J. 1976. The use of zona-free animal ova as a test system for the assessment of the fertilizing capacity of human spermatozoa. *Biology of Reproduction*, **15**, 471–476.

Yanagimachi, R., Lopata, A., Odom, C. B., Bronson, R. A., Mahi, C. A. & Nicholson, G. L. 1979. Retention of biological characteristics of zona pellucida in highly concentrated salt solution: the use of salt-stored eggs for assessing the fertilizing capacity of spermatozoa. *Fertility and Sterility*, **31**, 562–574.

Discussion on Idiopathic Infertility

Definition of Idiopathic Infertility

Steptoe: Could you please define what you mean by idiopathic infertility? It is essential to work from a baseline when we consider this situation. Would you regard it as six years in which they have constantly been investigated but without successful pregnancy?

Trounson: The best definition is that of the World Health Organization, namely of two years' infertility. The analysis of semen should show normality, e.g. above 20,000,000 spermatozoa, with good motility, and the woman must have passed various other tests. In our group, we classify women as having idiopathic infertility if they have at least one open tube. This means that we have perhaps included genuine cases of tubal infertility, but if they have one open tube, the fimbria is effective and the woman is ovulating regularly, then this would lead us to classify the patient as idiopathic. We also ensure that there are no lesions or other factors which may prevent conception.

We also do three tests on the husband, and these must show that his sperm count is above 20,000,000, and motility about 30%. We may pick up a few cases of male infertility, and this may explain the difference in our fertilization rates beween tubal and idiopathic infertility.

Cohen: Before selecting patients, has Leeton tried to induce ovulation in them in case there are problems in this respect?

Leeton: We try to induce ovulation in these patients. We test them with six months of clomiphene, and also six months of AIH in most cases.

Johnston: What is the diagnostic criteria of tubal function? I assume that all these patients have had a laparoscopy to examine tubal patency. How far are the tests carried on?

Trounson: All the standard tests have been carried out. Nevertheless, we would expect that in our idiopathic group, some women with antibodies against spermatozoa would be included although our evidence implies that fertilization still occurs despite the presence of antibodies. And this too, despite the fact that the wife's serum is being used to culture the embryos. Perhaps it depends on the method of classification of men with antibodies, because the way that John McBain classifies his patients may raise the incidence slightly.

Steptoe: One problem here is that many patients are referred without complete investigation. It is very difficult to decide if they have idiopathic infertility or anything else, and it also depends very much on their country of origin. In some countries, previous investigations would probably have clarified a great deal of the causes of infertility, but in others there may be no information whatsoever. One has to make an arbitrary decision about a patient when they arrive, and it is not always easy.

Edwards: Our data were given earlier (Fishel & Edwards, in Part 3). Our rates of fertilization *in vitro* are identical in idiopathic and tubal patients. Fertilization rates are low only in patients who also have spermatozoa of poor motility, but not in others, whatever the description of the cause of infertility. This could well be one cause of the idiopathic infertility, but there is often not enough time to decide on the true causes of infertility in the couple.

Jones, H: I must stress again the importance of defining idiopathic infertility. I am not convinced that many of the patients listed by Leeton were actually in the category of idiopathic infertility. They included endocrinological, surgical, pathological and other types of causes. It is misleading to imply that idiopathic infertility can be treated by fertilization *in vitro* using figures that are a mixture of identifiable types of infertility.

Trounson: Hudson's data showed that it does not matter too much if the patients have different types of infertility. The data are still relevant and the expectations of patients would be much the same as those with true idiopathic infertility. The whole point is that, whatever the type of patient, given the mean value and its confidence limits for the factors described, each clinic can decide what it wants to do with an individual patient. Moreover, while the tests are being carried out to determine idiopathic infertility if the patient is placed on the waiting list, they may be treated as soon as possible once the final decision is made about the causes of their infertility.

Fertilization *in vitro* and Idiopathic Infertility

Edwards: The pregnancy rates in the tubal and idiopathic patients described by Trounson are remarkably similar. Presumably, there are some idiopathic patients in the tubal group, but this will not affect the results if, overall, the idiopathic patients have the same rate of implantation as the others. The great similarity between pregnancy rates in the two groups implies that there may be common factors at work in causing their infertility. Perhaps fertilization and/or tubal transport are the factors deficient in the idiopathic groups, i.e. they may be very similar to the tubal group. Obviously more data are needed, because it is important to have many more pregnancies in each group to confirm the similarities.

Trounson: I would agree that the similarity between the idiopathic and tubal groups implies that there is some form of deficiency in fertilization or transport of the embryo. Some deficiencies may not be identified by current gynaecological tests.

Mettler: The fertilization rates described by Trounson in some of these patients with idiopathic infertility are much higher than he described earlier. Is there any special reason for this? It seems to me that the fertilization rates are similar in both groups.

Trounson: The data on fertilization in patients with tubal or idiopathic infertility has accumulated since we first opened the clinic. We have improved our fertilization rates recently, so the earlier data may be slightly low. There is no significant difference between the two groups at present, even though the idiopathic group is slightly lower. We now expect to fertilize 90% or more of eggs from patients with tubal occlusion, and more than 80% of those from patients with idiopathic infertility.

Edwards: The data from Britan Hudson seemed very useful. It seems to give a "score" for each idiopathic patient, to indicate the value of doing in-vitro fertilization.

Trounson: Yes, that is the idea of Hudson's system. There is a confidence range in the value of the statistics, which must be accepted. But it enables us to advise each couple with idiopathic infertility what the increase chance of pregnancy would be if they entered the programme of in-vitro fertilization. The method could also be used for introducing patients into the in-vitro fertilization programme, by stating that the chance of pregnancy must be below a certain level before patients are brought into the clinic. We have not used any criteria yet, but with over 1,000 patients on the waiting list, we have to include one sooner or later.

Edwards: In relation to the score for idiopathic infertility, there must come a time as rates of implantation improve when virtually all idiopathic patients will be introduced into the programme within, say, 3-6 months of their condition being diagnosed. Do you have such a figure in mind, i.e. on the success rate of in-vitro fertilization in relation to implantation before this stage would be reached?

Trounson: Yes, we do not know at the moment where our techniques will optimize. This was a difficulty for Hudson, and all he could do was to produce a mean range. But it is clear that large numbers of pregnancies are needed from in-vitro fertilization before we can come to any meaningful assessment of the Hudson score.

Spiers: Even when we know the mathematical prediction of the best time to treat patients with idiopathic infertility by in-vitro fertilization, the waiting list is going to be so long that the benefit will have to be enormous before tubal patients can wait longer. There is no chance of pregnancy in a tubal patient by any other means, whereas the idiopathic patients may, of course, become pregnant spontaneously or by the use of other forms of treatment.

Amniocentesis in Precious Pregnancies

B. A. Lieberman and P. Dyer

Introduction

The decision to undertake an amniocentesis in a pregnancy following in-vitro fertilization and embryo replacement should largely be governed by the parental wishes, as it would surely be an unhappy event if the replacement of an embryo led to the birth of a living child with severe handicap which could have been diagnosed prenatally. The case for amniocentesis is based upon the risk category of the individual woman, the hazards of amniocentesis, the information that the procedure yields, and to these should be added the as yet undetermined incidence of chromosomal and other diagnosable defects peculiar to in-vitro fertilization.

The dilemma lies in deciding what value should be placed on the gains of terminating affected fetuses and the losses of killing normal fetuses. These simply cannot be weighed against each other in numerical terms. The value of terminating affected fetuses must depend on a likely degree of handicap and its effects on the parents, their family, and society; some fetuses will be so severely affected that they will be stillborn or die shortly after birth, in which case amniocentesis and termination cannot be said to have averted the handicap. At the other end of the scale, some will be only mildly affected and have a prospect of almost normal life. Between these two extremes lies a full range of physical and mental disability (Lancet, 1978).

The National Registry of Amniocentesis study group of the N.I.C.H.D. (1976) and Simpson et al. (1976) were the first substantial reports concerned with the risk/benefit of amniocentesis. Polani et al. (1979) have reported their extensive experience in the counselling, diagnosis and prenatal detection of genetic defects, Golbus et al. (1979) the results in three thousand amniocenteses and Webb et al. (1980) the

St. Mary's Hospital, Manchester, England.

results in a further one thousand amnioceteses. The Medical Research Council Working Party on amniocentesis reported its findings in 1980.

Risk Category of Individual Women

Several criteria are used to assess this risk. They include the maternal age and previous reproductive history (previous neural tube defects, congenital abnormalities, recurrent abortion, premature rupture of membranes, growth retarded fetuses). The results of the physical and chromosomal examination of the mother and father include particularly evidence of a balanced translocation, spina bifida occulta, impaired maternal glucose tolerance and the evidence of non-invasive assessments including ultrasound and maternal serum α-fetoprotein (MSAFP).

The Hazards

The two North American studies (N.I.C.H.D., 1976; Simpson et al., 1976) concluded that the risks of fetal loss after mid-trimester amniocentesis were very small and not easily quantified. These studies were not without imperfections and the M.R.C. Report (1980) has also been criticized (Milunsky, 1979; Parkin, 1979).

The M.R.C. Report compared the outcome of pregnancy and infant welfare up to the age of ten months, in 2,428 women who underwent a diagnostic amniocentesis before the twentieth week of pregnancy to the same number of matched controls. The amnioceteses were undertaken in nine British obstetric units before ultrasound was generally available, and on a substantial number of women no attempt was made to localize the placenta. The report is detailed and complex. Half-way through the study the criteria governing selection of controls had to be widened because of delay and difficulty in obtaining such women and because of possible bias introduced with the initial selection of earlier controls. The survey is sub-divided into a main study (1,402 control women) and a supplementary enquiry of 1,206 controls; some conclusions relate to one study while others are based on information from both. Bias may have been introduced at a number of stages during the study; the subjects were often referred for amniocentesis to these centres whilst the controls were largely selected from women who had booked at these hospitals.

These difficulties, which the report discussed in considerable detail, are highlighted by the fact that 19% of amniocentesis subjects were excluded from the analysis because of the lack of suitable controls. The control group contained more women from 25 to 34 age range and fewer at the extremes, 25% of the controls were primipara compared to 19% of the subjects; 31.9% of controls were social class 1 and 2 compared to 37.8% of subjects.

The report showed an excess risk of abortion estimated to be between 1 to 1.5%. It revealed an excess risk of serious antepartum haemorrhage of about 1%, the risk being related to both placenta praevia and placental abruption, an excess risk of about 1% of unexplained respiratory difficulties at birth lasting for more than 24 hours, a similar excess of major orthopaedic postural deformities largely consisting of talips equinovarus and congenital dislocation of the hip and an increased risk of rhesus isoimmunization. The perinatal mortality was 20 in the amniocentesis group and 11 in the controls. All of these findings were unexpected except for the increased risk of abortion and rhesus isoimmunization.

The findings not only reflect the relationship between the procedure and the outcome of pregnancy, but it is likely that the selection of controls also contributed to the final analysis. The increased risk of antepartum haemorrhage and in particular placenta praevia requires substantiation, while respiratory difficulty may be related to the increased incidence of caesarean section amongst the subjects. Parkin (1979) noted that the birth prevalence of infants requiring treatment for congenital dislocation of the hip in the controls was very low (0.8 per 1,000) the rate being 3.8 per 1,000 in the subjects which is more in keeping with the expected figures of 2.5 to 20 per 1,000 (Place *et al.*, 1978) in the general population.

It has been estimated that in England and Wales to prevent the 555 or so neural tube births a year, most of whom would die in early life, would result in 120 dead or damaged *normal infants* (Chamberlain, 1978). Kennedy (1978) judged that the cost benefit in human terms would be even less advantageous in that *95* healthy *fetuses* and *110* handicapped but not hopeless children would be aborted to prevent 329 seriously affected babies with a neural tube defect, many of whom would not survive.

In the M.R.C. Report an amniocentesis had a good chance of detecting a fetal abnormality in those instances where there had been a previous child with a single autosomal gene defect (25%), a raised maternal serum α-fetoprotein (20%), a previous child with a neural tube defect (3% after one and 14% after two or more) and maternal age of 40 or over (Downs Syndrome in 5% of the mothers aged 40 to 41, 8% in those 42 to 43 and 11% in those aged 44 to 47). Bennett *et al.* (1978) stated that there is a 6 to 8% fetal loss following amniocentesis when the indication is a raised maternal serum α-fetoprotein. These figures include a group of accidental abortions and a smaller group of normal babies aborted because of a false positive in amniotic fluid α-fetoprotein.

Read *et al.* (1980) compared the outcome of pregnancy after an amniocentesis for previous neural defect to that of a raised maternal serum α-fetoprotein. They concluded, as have many other workers, that maternal serum α-fetoprotein screening defines a group of high risk pregnancies. The greater fetal loss and low birth weight associated with high α-fetoprotein levels in maternal serum were not the result of amniocentesis but were an inherent feature of these pregnancies. These findings are in keeping with the experience of Milunsky (1979) who noted that women with a raised maternal serum α-fetoprotein have without amniocentesis a sixfold increased likelihood of spontaneous abortion and the risk in excess of 11% for having a low birth weight rate. Read *et al.* (1980) reported that spontaneous abortion occurred in four of 219 pregnancies (1.8%) where the procedure was undertaken because of a previous neural tube defect and in nine of 212 pregnancies (4.2%) with a raised maternal serum α-fetoprotein. Golbus *et al.* (1979) also report a spontaneous abortion rate of 1.5% following an amniocentesis, which is similar to that reported by Simpson *et al.* (1976) in Canada and Galjaard (1976) in Europe. Golbus (1979) noted with interest that 1.2% of patients who made appointments for counselling and amniocentesis had spontaneous abortions during the time before the appointment.

The Danger of Abortion After Amniocentesis

One of the difficulties of carrying out an amniocentesis following in-vitro fertilization concerns the possible risk of an induced abortion. The parents have already gone to considerable trouble and expense to establish a pregnancy, and any additional risks of amniocentesis threatening its survival must be carefully assessed.

The data in Fig. 1 was obtained by courtesy of Dr. Andrew P. Read. It gives the distribution of all the spontaneous abortions occurring within 99 days of amniocentesis. It consists of data from patients for whom a sample of amniotic fluid was received by the Department of Medical Genetics in St. Mary's Hospital, Manchester, between

October 1975 and December 1980. Overall, 108 spontaneous abortions were identified in 3,062 pregnancies which were followed. This gives an overall incidence of 3.71%.

It must be remembered however that these figures refer to women who required amniocentesis because of high maternal age, past reproductive disasters or raised serum α-fetoprotein (which may indicate a pregnancy at risk). Data are not available on the risk of amniocentesis in young healthy women without unfavourable risk factors; however the three studies of mid-trimester amniocentesis concluded that the risk of fetal loss attributable to amniocentesis was not greater than 1%.

The Procedure

Golbus *et al.* (1979) report that amniotic fluid was obtained on the first attempt in 99.3% of the last 1,000 cases but in six of their first 100 amniocenteses sufficient amniotic fluid was *not* obtained. Webb *et al.* (1980) report a failed amniocentesis in 46 of 531 (8.6%) pregnancies at the Birmingham Maternity Hospital and 6 of 549 (1.1%) at the East Birmingham Maternity Hospital. Greenish-brown discoloured fluid

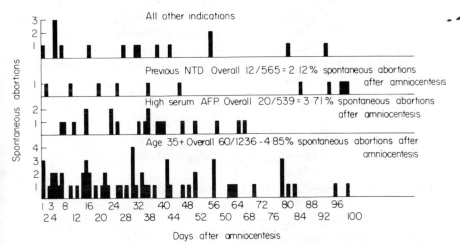

FIG. 1. Spontaneous abortions subsequent to amniocentesis at ~16–20 weeks. Distribution of all spontaneous abortions occurring within 99 days of amniocentesis for patients from whom amniotic fluid samples were received by Medical Genetics, Oct. 75–Dec. 80 inclusive. Overall, 108 spontaneous abortions in 3,062 followed up pregnancies = 3.53%. By courtesy of Dr. Andrew P. Read. NTD = neural tube defect.

was obtained in 36 of 3,000 (1.2%) of the patients reported by Golbus *et al.* (1979). Two-thirds of the pregnancies with this discoloured fluid resulted in normal neonates but in the remaining one-third the fetus was abnormal or dead. They performed spectrophotometric analysis on the discoloured samples and concluded that the discoloration of the amniotic fluid was due to aged blood pigments.

Golbus *et al.* (1979) reported that cultures were established from 99.7% of patients (98.3 at first attempt) attending the clinic whilst Webb *et al.* (1980) reported that chromosome studies were completed in only 85% of the pregnancies in the West Midlands study. Golbus *et al.* (1979) regard the most important problem as obtaining and communicating correct results. In 3,000 amniocentesies *eight errors* regarding fetal sex were made which *did not* affect the outcome of the pregnancy. Two of the six resulted from mixing of slides of two patients, one fetus was miskaryotyped, cultures in three male fetuses showed only 46 XX cells which in retrospect were due to maternal contamination, and two secretarial typing errors occurred. In addition three cultures mosaics 46XX/46XY were interpreted correctly as male fetuses with maternal contamination.

Six more serious errors occurred. A fetus with an α-fetoprotein concentration between three and four times greater than the standard deviation of the mean had a small meningomyelocele. There was one failure to diagnose argino-succinic aciduria and the incorrect identification of a fetus with possible osteogenesis imperfecta. An error resulting in the exchange of two fluids resulted in the continuation of the pregnancy with an anencephalic fetus and the termination of an unaffected fetus at risk for the Meckel–Gruber syndrome. Misinterpretation of a variant 22 chromosome led to the termination of an unaffected fetus.

Ultrasound of the Placental Site

Ultrasound determination of the placental site is of unquestionable value at the time of amniocentesis. Ultrasound is an important diagnostic procedure when the indication for the amniocentesis is a raised maternal serum α-fetoprotein as multiple pregnancies and missed abortions are easily seen, and a thorough ultrasound examination is necessary to exclude a neural tube defect, renal abnormalities and gastroschisis. Furthermore, most failures to obtain sufficient amniotic fluid are related to incorrect assessments of gestational length.

The optimum time for an amniocentesis corresponds to the 16th week from the first day of the last normal menstrual period (that is 14th week since conception). Golbus *et al.* (1979) found that ultrasound did not lower the incidence of multiple needle insertions or the incidence of blood-stained taps. It is surprising how often after 16 weeks the anterior-situated placenta appears to occupy the whole anterior wall of the uterus; delaying the amniocentesis by a week or two often results in a placenta-free space becoming visible.

Amniocentesis Following Successful in-vitro Fertilization

The decision to perform an amniocentesis should as with any pregnancy, be undertaken only after thorough discussion with the parents. The parents' advisors should recognize the risks inherent to the technique. These risks need to be carefully balanced against the benefit of knowing that the fetus is chromosomally normal.

The combination of maternal serum α-fetoprotein and detailed ultrasound may suffice to exclude the fetus with a neural tube defect. An amniocentesis is indicated in patients over the age of 38 and in those with a raised maternal serum α-fetoprotein.

The argument in favour of amniocentesis in all successful cases of in-vitro fertilization and embryo replacement is open to debate. Until it is known for certain that the incidence of chromosomal abnormalities is *not* increased, the case for amniocentesis is valid, although there is no evidence as yet to suggest an excess risk of triploidy or trisomy after in-vitro fertilization. It is also essential that the karyotypes of all fetuses aborted after successful in-vitro fertilization are examined.

References

Bennett, M. J., Johnson, R. D., Blau, K., & Chamberlain, G. V. P. 1978. Some problems of alpha-fetoprotein screening. *Lancet*, **ii**, 1296.

Chamberlain, J. 1978. Human benefits and costs of a national screening programme for neural-tube defects. *Lancet*, **ii**, 1293.

Galjaard, H. 1976. European experience with prenatal diagnosis of congenital disease, a survey of 6121 cases. *Cytogenetics and Cell Genetics*, **16**, 435–467.

Golbus, M. S., Loughman, W. D., Epstein, C. W., Halbasch, G., Stephens, J. D. & Hall, B. D. 1979. Prenatal genetic diagnosis in 3000 amniocenteses. *New England Journal of Medicine*, **300**, 157.

Kennedy, I. The Defect. BBC Radio 3, October 25th, 1978.

Lancet, Editorial. 1978. The risk of amniocentesis. *Lancet*, 1287.

Medical Research Council Working Party on Amniocentesis. 1978. *British Journal of Obstetrics and Gynaecology*, **85**, suppl. 2.

Milunsky, A. 1979. Hazards of amniocentesis. *Lancet*, **i**, 546.

N.I.C.H.D. National Registry for Amniocentesis Study Group. 1976. *Journal of the American Medical Association*, **236**, 1471.

Parkin, D. M. 1979. Hazards of amniocentesis. *Lancet*, **i**, 733.

Place, M. J., Parkin, D. M. & Fitton, J. M. 1978. *Lancet*, **ii**, 249.

Polani, P. E., Alberman, E., Alexander, B. J., Benson, P. F., Berry, A. C., Blunt, S., Daker, M. G., Fenson, A. H., Garrett, D. M., McGuire, V. M., Fraser Roberts, J. A., Seller, M. J. & Singer, J. D. 1979. Sixteen years' experience of counselling, diagnosis and prenatal detection in one Genetic Centre; progress, results and problems. *Journal of Medical Genetics*, **16**, 166–175.

Read, A. P., Donnai, D., Harris, R. & Donnai, P. 1980. Comparison of pregnancy outcome after amniocentesis for previous neural tube defect or raised maternal serum alphafetoprotein. *British Journal of Obstetrics and Gynaecology*, **87**, 372–376.

Simpson, N. E., Dallaire, L., Miller, J. R., Siminovich, L., Hamerton, J., & McKeen, C. 1976. Prenatal diagnosis of genetic disease in Canada: report of a collaborative study. *Canadian Medical Association Journal*, **115**, 739–746.

Webb, T., Edwards, J. H., Cameron, A. H., Crawley, J. M., Hulten, M. A. J., Rushton, D. I., & Thompson, R. A. 1980. Amniocentesis in the West Midlands: report on 1000 births. *Journal of Medical Genetics*, **17**, 81–86.

Discussion on Fetal Growth and Amniocentesis after Fertilization *in vitro*

Chromosome Numbers Found at Amniocentesis after Fertilization
in vitro

Mettler: Could we please know the number of fetuses that have proceeded as far as amniocentesis after fertilization *in vitro*, and which have been shown to have chromosomal anomalies?

Steptoe: All three of the patients who reached this stage of pregnancy in our Oldham work had an amniocentesis, and everything was normal. Two patients here in Bourn Hall had amniocentesis, and a similar discovery has been made. Many of the others who are now pregnant have declined to have amniocentesis. Our attempts at obtaining material for karyotyping from the fetuses which aborted, have been largely frustrated. It is very difficult when patients have left our care to arrange to collect tissue from an abortion. One recent report gave a chromosomal complement of 46 XX on an aborted fetus, although contamination with maternal cells could not be excluded. We hope to confirm this data in the near future.

Johnston: We have a similar situation in Australia. Our first pregnancy had an amniocentesis, which was normal, and the second one aborted after we had presumably damaged the bowel on the way to collect the amniotic fluid. The fetus was normal too. Since then, not a single patient, in either of our two teams, has elected to have an amniocentesis. In a sense, this is the doctor's responsibility, because in our discussions we tend to stress against having amniocentesis, because we have become less than enthusiastic about the exercise. With a high-risk patient, the technique may be made safer by consulting the notes on laparoscopy, because this patient of ours had a loop of bowel adherent to the uterus. This information was not available when the amniocentesis was performed. The surgeon had to enter her high in the uterus, because she had an anterior placenta praevia, hence a combination of accidents produced that bad result.

Steptoe: One of the three babies in our series in Oldham was lost through amniocentesis, or at least we believe this was the case. The amniocentesis was carried out at 15 weeks, and she aborted at 20 weeks. Is it a general experience that, if an abortion is to occur after amniocentesis, it will occur very quickly? Our patient had a nice clear space for amniocentesis, and the fluid was aspirated at the first collection.

Lieberman: In general, abortion occurs shortly after the amniocentesis. Only if we can postulate a low-grade infection, or bleeding, can we expect such a delayed problem.

Jones, G: Did this patient who aborted in Oldham have a fetus with a normal karyotype?

Edwards: The fetus had a normal karyotype. The Y chromosome was slightly elongated, and there was pleomorphism in chromosome 15. Both of these chromosomal conditions were present in the husband, who was perfectly normal. In other words, the karyotype was perfectly normal, and the child was perfectly normal at delivery, as extensive tests showed. A long Y has been associated with various factors, including a high risk of abortion, but also with so many others that it is hard to decide if any of them are significant (Makine, 1975). The karyotype was normal; there was no chromosomal imbalance and the long Y and the satellite were exactly as present in the father.

Jones, G: There must have been some misinterpretation about this fetus. My ascertation that this was normal at a recent meeting in Norfolk was challenged and reports have been circulating that the chromosomal analysis was abnormal.

Edwards: Let me stress once again that the fetus was normal. There is some debate about what a long Y does, but nothing is known for certain, to the best of my knowledge. Likewise, the satellite on the chromosome 15 was perfectly normal, because it was present in the father too.

Dyer: The fact that the long Y and the satellite were inherited from the father shows that the fetus was probably quite normal too.

Edwards: There is absolutely no doubt that everything was normal. Many people have studied individuals with similar satellited chromosomes, which have no effect whatsoever on the phenotype. Likewise, many men have a long Y, and there is no condition that can be specifically attributed to it. The chromosomes in this child represented normal Mendelian inheritance, inheriting one set from the father and another from the mother. There were no abnormalities in the anatomy or physiology of this child. He was born, lived for 24 hours or so, and was perfectly normal. Being born premature, there was no chance of survival. The whole pregnancy was marvellous until the tragic moment.

We always blamed amniocentesis for the loss of this fetus 4–5 weeks later. The patient reported pain after amniocentesis, and I believe she had a slight bloody discharge on occasions. Lieberman has pointed out how most abortions occur early after amniocentesis, but I would certainly attribute the loss of this fetus to the technique, perhaps to bleeding. The abortion began while the patient was taking a walking holiday in the Pennines, which may not have been the most advisable thing to do under the circumstances. We believe that something went wrong after amniocentesis, was never put right, and this precipitated the abortion when the couple went for their holiday.

Jones, G: I think it is very important to get this in the literature as a normal karyotype. It has been misinterpreted by many people, and I believe that it has misled many people about the pregnancies that were established during the Oldham work.

Edwards: I have never referred in any way to this fetus or karyotype as being abnormal. The baby was fully normal. It was a great tragedy that the couple lost it.

Amniocentesis and Abortion

Jones, H: Is there any information on the delivery of the Oldham abortus? Was there a partial placenta praevia, or any other condition which predisposed to the loss of the fetus? This could be a very important case to clean up. Was there any evidence of haemorrhage behind the placenta?

Steptoe: I actually delivered the child. We held on to the baby for 24 hours, and tried to save it, but it was impossible. The placenta came first, as it so often does with abortions at 20 weeks. There was no evidence of haemorrhage. From my memory, the placenta was rather a thin, membranous type.

Lieberman: In my paper, I have given the data from Manchester on the interval between amniocentesis and abortion. This is especially relevant since the chromosomal examination of this fetus, and of Louise Brown, was done in our department at St. Mary's.

Edwards: The one fetus that was abnormal in our first series was triploid, the only one of the four babies established in Oldham with an abnormal karyotype. We were able to photograph the fetus, save some tissue, and obtain the karyotype. Unfortunately, there were no chromosome markers in the parents to show the origin of this triploid.

Cohen: We must recall data by, for example, Boué and Philip who describe the anatomy of abortion and show how it can be used to gain a great deal of information, and sometimes knowledge on the chromosomal complement. An idea of the state of the fetus could be gained if patients could bring the tissue back, but, of course, it is very difficult asking them to do this. Histology is sufficient to give a clear indication, concentrating on tissues such as the villi, vascularization, etc. This was done in a double-blind experiment, where Boué did the karyotyping and Philip did the histology.

Fetal Hormones and
Normal and Abnormal Embryonic Growth

Jones, H: I would like to discuss further the two abortuses in the Oldham series. The values of HCGβ in the triploid case were low. This clearly indicated that it was a "bad" pregnancy. In the second case, those values were not taken so frequently. It is very important to have excellent HCGβ values, because the hormones are produced by fetal tissue and give some idea of the competence of the embryo. I would like to know, for example, what the values were on the G22 trisomy case reported by Cohen.

Cohen: The hormone assays were carried out by our colleagues. During pregnancy, levels of HCG stay high, unless there is a chance of abortion when they decline.

Frydman: Three pregnancies were followed by hormonal and chromosomal data. Levels in our normal pregnancy rose nicely, but they also did in the two others with a chromosomal imbalance (an X monosomy and a 22 trisomy respectively). Perhaps oestradiol-17β is more indicative in the early stages of pregnancy, because it was lower in both of the fetuses that aborted. Later, the levels of HCGβ declined in the two abnormal fetuses, after the initial rise, declining to very low levels by day 70 after fertilization and so indicated troubles with pregnancy.

Cohen: In the initial stages of this pregnancy, the endocrinologists reported that everything was satisfactory. It was impossible to predict that the fetus was abnormal. As the levels of HCG turned down later, then we knew something was wrong. But the levels of hormone were absolutely normal until about day 40.

Jones, H: I still suggest that levels of HCGβ may indicate abnormalities in early pregnancy, and can be used after the pregnancy is established as an indication of how the fetus is progressing. A sharp decline after 50–60 days, as in this case, indicates something is very wrong, because levels should never be that low.

Edwards: The values on our third pregnancy in Oldham were taken less frequently than the earlier two, because I was satisfied that the levels were rising satisfactorily. The endocrine evidence was very convincing, and we had more data using Hi-Gonavis as a rapid assay. There was no problem with the levels of HCG, and this was fully justified, because the pregnancy was proceeding excellently until after amniocentesis.

Jones, H: It would have been worthwhile taking a few more samples, to follow the levels of HCG more carefully. This would have given a better indication of the progress of the pregnancy, although it was obvious that everything was proceeding normally.

Cohen: There would be a benefit in knowing when a pregnancy begins, that some idea of the quality of the pregnancy can be gained. From our data on HCG we must wait until day 60 before some ideal of the normality of fetus can be obtained, at least as regards monosomy ·and trisomy.

Jones, H: The use of HCG as a marker might even preclude the need for amniocentesis. The indications of a sharp fall in HCG in both the monosomy and the trisomy could be diagnostic. It could warn us of an impending abortion, and might even warn us that amniocentesis is necessary to prove what we fear. For example, data could be compared with a diploid fetus at 70 days, with good levels of HCG, and if the comparison was satisfactory we could be confident there was no serious problem with the fetus at this stage. The assay of HCG regularly throughout pregnancy must be considered to be essential as a monitor, provided it can be done easily.

The Origin of Monosomy and Trisomy

Edwards: We would like to know if any other groups have had evidence of trisomy or monosomy in fetuses examined during gestation. By now, there must be sufficient pregnancies to provide an indication of the incidence of chromosomal imbalance, and to know if it was a serious factor in our work. More than 15 children have been born, all diploid, including the two who were unfortunately lost after amniocentesis. The numbers of children are now beginning to be quite substantial. Does any one have data on amniocentesis at this stage?

Johnston: We have had none, apart from the baby lost earlier. Our attempts to culture tissue from abortuses have been somewhat disappointed, only one sample grew, and that proved to be dominated by maternal tissue. No evidence was gained on the fetus itself. Like everyone else, we have had the same problems in obtaining material from aborted fetuses. One sample was treated with formalin before we could get hold of it, and the other one discarded.

Edwards: We have had one abortus karyotyped, and it was reported to be XX. But maternal tissue could not be excluded from the preliminary investigation. We are still hoping to find markers in the mother and father which will indicate whether one of the two X chromosomes in the fetus was paternal and the other maternal. The chances of finding bands or other markers do seem to be low.

Johnston: Concerning the inheritance of specific chromosomes, our first child born inherited a chromosome with a somewhat unusual banding pattern. When we examined the parents, we found that both of them had it, which did not help much with identifying its origin in the fetus!

Edwards: I would like to make a comment on the origin of monosomies and trisomies, especially in relation to the two reported by the French group. It is very important to consider whether these arose through fertilization *in vitro*, or through factors totally unrelated to it. A fetus with 47 chromosomes and trisomy 22 could almost certainly have arisen in the ovary even before the laparoscopy for oocyte recovery was performed. The mother was aged 40 years, and age-related trisomy is a situation which faces us all together, not only during fertilization *in vitro*, but also during fertilization *in vivo*. Ultimately, we are all going to get such fetuses with trisomic conditions in our older mothers, and the French group happen to be the first. Nothing could have been done about it, because such trisomies are bound to arise when older mothers are appealing to us for treatment to alleviate their infertility.

The 45 X was also almost certainly due to factors other than fertilization *in vitro*. The inheritance of X chromosome monosomy differs from autosomal monosomy and trisomy. Many XO's arise in the testis (Polani, 1981). This 45 X fetus could have arisen through the fertilization of an egg by a spermatozoon which had neither X nor Y chromosome, i.e. it was 22,0. Its origin may have had nothing to do with fertilization *in vitro*, except that this particular spermatozoon was able to fertilize the egg. We suspected that the triploid fetus in our Oldham work arose through fertilization by a diploid spermatozoon because dispermy is so rare during fertilization *in vitro*. We may ultimately have to debate as to whether fertilization outside the body gives spermatozoa with unusual chromosomal complements a greater chance of reaching and penetrating oocytes.

For this reason, it could be helpful if the French workers could gain information on the origin of the single X chromosome in the XO abortus. If it proves to be maternal, then the most likely explanation is that the paternal X chromosome was lost during spermatogenesis. We will have to await the collection of data from Paris or elsewhere, and the combination of data from several sources might help to decide on the origin of any trisomies and monosomies arising after fertilization *in vitro*.

References

Makino, S. 1975. *Human Chromosomes*. Igaku Shoin, Tokyo.
Polani, P. E. 1981. Abnormal sex development in man. I. Anomalies of sex-determining mechanisms. In: *Mechanisms of Sex Differentiation in Animals and Man*, p. 465. Eds. C. R. Austin & R. G. Edwards. Academic Press, London.

The Ethics of in-vitro Fertilization — 1981

H. W. Jones, Jr.

Introduction

In-vitro fertilization is one of many methods for the treatment of infertility. Each method has its special application depending on the cause of the infertility. It happens that in-vitro fertilization is the only available method to treat certain problems. If the treatment of infertility is ethically acceptable, we hold that there can be no ethical objection to the use of in-vitro fertilization for this purpose.

Although this position seems simple, clear, and self-evident, there are those who have voiced objections. These objections are so diverse and put forth with such varied scholarship, motives, and prejudices that they do not easily lend themselves to classification. Walters in 1979 in a comprehensive review of 240 published articles comprising the ethical literature to that date discussed them under 16 major headings and additional sub-headings. With this vast literature, it seems impossible to say anything new. Nevertheless, those opposed to in-vitro fertilization are so organized and repetitive that comments limited to each of the most frequently voiced objections might be appropriate.

Rejoinders to Frequent Objections

Comment: in-vitro fertilization is unethical because large numbers of embryos are lost after transfer

It is true that only a minority of embryos survive after transfer. The exact figure remains tentative and can be expected to improve but a report in May, 1981 recorded nine pregnancies after laparoscopies in 103 cycles, although the number of embryos transferred is not stated (Wood et al., 1981). However, there are unpublished data which

Eastern Virginia Medical School, 603 Medical Tower, Norfolk, Virginia 23507, U.S.A.

indicate that the pregnancy rate after transfer is in the range of 10–20%. Thus, the success rate after transfer has already improved over the original experience of Edwards *et al.* (1980) who transferred over 100 embryos before their first success.

These embryonic losses are regrettable for various reasons, but except in present magnitude are a phenomenon of human reproduction. In various studies recently reviewed by Biggers (1981), it has been shown that unprotected intercourse through a single menstrual cycle resulted in a viable pregnancy in between 20 and 31% of cycles depending on the method of study. The non-fruitful cycles were found to be the result of failures of implantation or early abortions of abnormal embryos. Thus, the concern about early embryonic loss cannot be related only to in-vitro fertilization. It is a phenomenon of nature. The only way to stop such losses is to stop human procreation.

Comment: in-vitro fertilization is unethical because embryos are destroyed instead of being transferred

Ethical concern has been expressed about the loss of embryos which are not transferred for whatever reason or the use of such embryos for investigation. It happens that this concern is not applicable to many programs of in-vitro fertilization. However, this non-applicability only begs a question of the greatest significance to the quality and quantity of human life. Proper investigation of early embryogenesis might aid in the understanding and prevention of the large embryonic loss which now occurs naturally. An attempt to carry out such an investigation by Pierre Soupart was thwarted and led to the appointment of a special ad hoc committee of the Department of Health, Education and Welfare to determine if such investigations were ethically acceptable. In spite of the finding that such studies were ethically acceptable, the report of the committee has never been implemented.

Society has promulgated laws to protect the individual. The real question at issue is when in the development of a conceptus should such laws for the procreation of the individual be applied.

Parenthetically, various other types of laws are applied to the individual at various other times in development. For example, it is illegal to vote prior to the age of 18 years. It is illegal to drive a car until age 16. An income tax deduction is not allowed until birth; if it were really thought that an individual person existed from conception, every pregnant woman should be allowed two income tax deductions. Furthermore, the census-taker counts only those individuals capable of individual existence.

Some theologians, philosophers, and professional ethicists, as well as some scientists, have tried to simplify the problem of individual protection by claiming that conception is an identifiable event from which a human individual person begins and that therefore the man-made laws pertaining to the protection of the individual should be applied from that moment.

There are many things wrong with this concept.

To say that life, or a life, or personess, begins at conception is to imply that what existed before is not life. On the contrary, the sperm and egg are very much alive. Indeed, prior to fertilization, the egg undergoes an active process of maturation without which fertilization is impossible. Fertilization is but one phase of embryonic development. Incidentally, fertilization is easier to define than precisely identify.

Long ago, theologians particularized the human desire to identify personess by speaking of ensoulment; i.e. the moment when the soul (apparently a quality not shared by other species) enters the embryo. There is a long and interesting history of the theological wrestle with this problem and at various times it has been thought to occur at conception, at implantation, at quickening, at birth, and so forth.

However, fertilization with or without ensoulment does not necessarily result in a human individual. Reference has already been made to the large number of chromosomal abnormalities which occur at this time. In addition, in monozygotic twins, the formation of two embryos occurs much later than fertilization. What about ensoulment in this circumstance?

Again, fertilization may result not in a human embryo but in a tumour — a hydatidiform mole. Can this tumour be a person?

Even under normal circumstances, fertilization does not result in an individual but in a cell mass which ultimately divides into two major components: the embryoblast and the trophoblast. The embryoblast becomes the fetus and the trophoblast becomes the extraembryonic membranes, the placenta and umbilical cord. The trophoblastic derivates are alive, are human, and have the same genetic composition as the fetus and are discarded at birth. Are they a person?

The fact is that life is a continuum. Indeed, an individual life is a continuous process of development beginning well before conception and extending long afterwards.

The assignment of a time to apply laws to protect the individual must of necessity be arbitrary. Just as the times are arbitrary when laws are applied assigning a time to vote, or to drive a car, or to be eligible for an income tax deduction, or to be counted in the census. There simply is no identifiable biological event to make easy the determination of a time to apply laws to protect the individual.

It is sometimes said that the embryo, if not a human person is potentially a human person, and therefore should be treated as such. But, in this sense, so is the egg, or sperm. A chassis with four wheels attached at the beginning of the assembly line is potentially an automobile, but no one would buy it for such until it was developed into an object which could be driven away from the end of the line. At the beginning, it is only potentially an automobile, just as is the iron ore from the mountains.

What has all this to do with the clinical application of in-vitro fertilization? Nothing really, but ethicists intermingle these considerations with those thought to apply to such a process. However, some scientific questions of early reproductive biology of intense interest and important to those who treat infertility including those who apply in-vitro fertilization might be answered by studying early embryos.

The biological facts as now known need to be understood and not selectively applied by those who wish to assign moral values to this field.

Comment: in-vitro fertilization is unethical because it entails unknown risks to a potential child who cannot give consent

This objection is less pertinent now than it was prior to the birth of the first child after in-vitro fertilization. While abnormalities will undoubtedly be associated with this process, it now seems unlikely that the risk will be substantially greater than the risk following normal fertilization. Furthermore, this view is supported by the animal data which have failed to show any increased risk to either those animals born after embryo transfer or as the result of in-vitro fertilization and embryo transfer.

In addition, this ethical argument, as originally applied, could equally well be applied to a couple, the female of which is above the age of 35 where the expectancy of an abnormality is measurable and substantial for the creation of an individual with the G-21 trisomy. The ethics of such a couple could be ever so much more questionable especially if they were unwilling to use contemporary methods of diagnosis with abortion in the event an affected fetus were discovered.

Comment: in-vitro fertilization is unethical because it violates the sanctity of marriage and a proper family environment for child rearing

Sexual intercourse might well be an act of love and sanctify marriage but it certainly does not guarantee a happy family environment. This is too self-evident to require documentation. The process of in-vitro fertilization demands sacrifice on the part of both husband and wife far beyond anything required for normal procreation. Sacrifice is possible only by stable couples who would create an ideal family environment for the rearing of children. To hold otherwise is to be unfamiliar with couples who are infertile and who are willing to go the last mile to overcome this physical handicap.

Comment: in-vitro fertilization is unethical because the risks of publicity to a child so conceived would not allow normal development for that child

This is indeed a concern, particularly for the first few children born by this process. However, there is every reason to believe that with the wider application of the programme the number of children so born will tend to mitigate and indeed eliminate undue publicity surrounding the event. In the meantime, the tenets of medicine emphasize the desirability of confidentiality and if it were possible to maintain this usual standard of medical practice publicity would not be a problem.

It needs to be pointed out that the pressure of the media is in no small measure stimulated by the statements of alarm issued by ethicists of all stripes who oppose the programme for whatever reason and thereby create the environment which causes the problem to which they object and in which it is difficult to maintain the usual standards of medical confidentiality.

Comment: in-vitro fertilization is unethical because the perfection of this technique might lead to several subsequent procedures

This domino-effect-reasoning concerns many procedures which really have little relation to in-vitro fertilization. The items concerned are those of genetic manipulation; i.e., embryo modification, surrogate motherhood, cloning, and such. Without prejudging the ethics of such programs, it is only logical that a discussion of the ethics of in-vitro fertilization be confined only to a discussion of the ethics of in-vitro fertilization.

Comment: in-vitro fertilization is considered unethical because it is thought that science does not have the right to manipulate nature

Curiously enough, this argument is set forth apparently in good faith by some theologians. Actually, every request of a physician to diagnose and treat disease is a request to manipulate nature. If it is ethically acceptable to seek medical care for a reproductive disorder, it is ethically acceptable to seek care which requires in-vitro fertilization.

The Separation of Civil and Religious Authority: A Most Serious Consideration

There are two separate issues which have become intermingled and confused. They need to be clearly separated.

First is the civil issue of when laws for the protection of the individual should be applied. As already noted, various laws applying to the rights and responsibilities of the individual specify certain developmental ages for such items as driving a car, voting, and so forth. The Supreme Court decision of 1973 defines our current legal position with respect to one aspect of abortion. This ruling clearly provides that protection does not apply to the first trimester of pregnancy under any circumstance. It needs to be added that other laws delay protection under other circumstances, such as when an abnormal conceptus is identified.

A second and completely separate issue is the question of ensoulment or personess. As indicated in the above discussion, there is no biological indication of such an event. Indeed, this is not a biological matter but a concept which has been of concern to scholars of various philosophies and religions through the ages. As mentioned above, it has been considered to occur at various times in various eras.

A keystone of contemporary societal organization is the separation of the civil and religious authority. Failure to maintain this separation is to invite tyranny. Through the ages, one of man's greatest struggles has been the attempt to eliminate tyranny of all kinds. In the political arena, one of the best known attempts can be found in the Bill of Rights of the Constitution of the United States. This Bill of Rights guarantees several freedoms. It attempts to prevent the imposition of the religious or ethical beliefs of one individual or group on another individual or group.

No one is required to seek such benefits as may be available from abortion or from in-vitro fertilization which in no way encompasses abortion and which in concept and purpose is the complete opposite from abortion. It is fundamental to our freedoms that the right of those who wish to participate in these programmes not be compromised.

References

Biggers, J. D. 1981. In-vitro fertilization and embryo transfer in human beings. *New England Journal of Medicine*, **304**, 336.

Edwards, R. G., Steptoe, P. C. & Purdy, J. M. 1980. Establishing full-term human pregnancies using cleaving embryos grown in vitro. *British Journal of Obstetrics and Gynaecology*, **87**, 737.

Walters, L. 1979 Human in-vitro fertilization: A review of the ethical literature. *The Hastings Center Report*, **9**, 23.

Wood, C., Trounson, A., Leeton, J., McKenzie Talbot, J., Buttery, B., Webb, J., Wood, J. & Jessup, D. 1981. A clinical assessment of nine pregnancies obtained by in-vitro fertilization and embryo transfer. *Fertility and Sterility*, **35**, 502–508.

Discussion on the Ethics of
Fertilization *in vitro*

Donor Spermatozoa and Donor Oocytes

Mettler: One of the ethical problems facing us concerns the donation of spermatozoa and oocytes from one person to another. Some groups have started to use donor spermatozoa, and others are now contemplating the use of donor oocytes. We are, in effect, taking the couples out of their own "boundaries", and this is an issue which should be discussed.

Johnston: We have commenced using these treatments, and I would like to comment on them. Each society will have its own social standards and norms, and changes will be introduced at different rates according to the social outlook in each country. I feel it is not right for an international group debating the science and techniques of in-vitro fertilization to discuss the social norms of each individual country. In many Western countries, A.I.D. has now been accepted by many couples. It has also been accepted in a social context, and even legally in some countries. In Australia, A.I.D. is socially acceptable, although oocyte donation is not acceptable at the moment because people do not really consider it. I believe that we will begin the debate about it soon in the future. Our argument will rest simply on the basis that if A.I.D. is acceptable then oocyte donation should be equally acceptable. All it involves is transfer of one of the two gametes to help an infertile couple. In Australia, we have evolved socially to the point of accepting A.I.D., but in countries where this has not been attained, or desired, then oocyte donation may not be acceptable.

Fishel: There is one difference between sperm and oocyte donation. With a donor oocyte, the woman is not carrying her own child. With donor spermatozoa, the oocyte is hers. There may be a difference here between the two situations in that she may feel more related to her own egg and child than to a donated egg.

Johnston: This is a fine legal point. Most law accepts the mother of the child as the person who carries the child. In medicine, I doubt there is much difference, since we know that embryo transfer is widely used in animal species.

Edwards: If a woman goes to the lengths of accepting an oocyte, then I believe that, in law, she would be considered to have accepted the oocyte willingly, and to have accepted the fetus. It is unlikely that she was not aware that an oocyte had been donated, and the very act of acceptance would provide a suitable legal basis for "prenatal adoption". This situation could not occur until preovulatory oocytes were available and it will be interesting to see if any debate arises in the near future from any of the groups present at this meeting.

Lopata: An unusual point of view was presented at a recent meeting in Basle by a Swiss lawyer. According to Swiss law, a difficult situation would arise if the husband dies while a preimplantation embryo from him and his wife is being incubated, and his wife knows the embryo is present. She is no longer married when the embryo is replaced in her. If she conceives, then the child will be illegitimate. This could be very important because the father's inheritance to the child could possibly be disputed by another claimant.

Cohen: Only recently has it been accepted in France that babies born through A.I.D. have a special status. The law has been recently changed during the last two years. But I think times are changing, and we will have to wait and see what happens.

The "Spare" Embryo

Feichtinger: There is also another ethical problem that we have to face, and which we have not mentioned so far. This concerns the replacement of triplet embryos. We have replaced some triplets, and I believe that other groups have done so too. We all realize there may be obstetric risks, and these were discussed in our group in relation to the chance of the pregnancy, and to the saving of all the embryos that we had from particular patients. We replaced them all into the mother. Fortunately, we have not yet had four embryos, so we have not had to face this difficulty! We did not wish to experiment with the third embryo, so replaced it in the mother in the knowledge that the chance of a triplet pregnancy was very slight, while the chance of implantation may be raised by having three rather than two embryos in the uterine cavity.

Edwards: Could the people who are actually doing experimental studies on embryos inform us of the feeling within their own country? I am specifically interested here in grant applications, and in social responses to the use of human embryos for investigative purposes. I believe our work is fully acceptable when we grow human embryos which are to be replaced into the mother. But what is the social response when we take, quite deliberately, a spermatozoon and an oocyte to establish an embryo which will be used for scientific analyses? My own view is that such studies would be justified, provided they were of immediate help to clinical problems facing us, including problems in areas of medicine other than our own. I wonder if other groups have considered this point, and what is their attitude.

Jones, H: This topic prevented at least one grant application in the United States from being funded. A report by a committee had no problem in accepting in-vitro fertilization, and they also believed that analyses on human embryos were quite justifiable with embryos aged up to 15 days after fertilization. This recommendation was incorporated into a report which is available (Federal Register, 1979). This view was supported by Father McCormick from the Kennedy Center in Washington, and by other theologians. Other people do not agree, and although the report has been published it has never been formally accepted by the National Institutes of Health.

Edwards: Could I make an appeal that we now use the stages of growth of human embryos which have been so clearly defined by embryologists, especially those at the Carnegie Institute (O'Rahilly, 1973, 1981). We should now conform to this practice, since we are entering the stages of growth after implantation. Growth for 15 days is approximately Stage 7, when the amniotic cavity, primitive groove, notochordal process, prechordal plate and haematopoetic cells are differentiating. Using these identified stages would be more meaningful, since the developmental age of any fetus could be interpreted in terms of its organogenesis. This would also be much more suitable in ethical debates because organ differentiation must be an essential point to bear in mind when we are growing embryos *in vitro*, especially the differentiation of neural tissue.

Jones, H: The report from the National Institutes of Health stressed 15 days. It would be useful to use stages, but it was not done in this case. Even today, the N.I.H. will not fund work on fertilization *in vitro*. At a recent meeting, studies on fertilization *in vitro* were confined to animal work, and all references to human fertilization *in vitro* were rigorously excluded.

Lopata: My application to the National Health and Medical Research Council of Australia to study the electron microscopy of human blastocysts grown *in vitro* was submitted 3 years ago. There was no objection from the Council, and I obtained a grant. My argument in the application stressed that it was essential to maintain the quality control of culture media and other conditions using human embryos. We believed it was essential to show that the embryos we were growing were normal, and these arguments were apparently accepted, and the grant was approved.

Trounson: The use of embryos, as indeed other human tissues, for research purposes must be accompanied by reasonable argument for the alleviation of human suffering. For instance, our Ethics Committees consider the development of embryo freezing more acceptable than their disposal or use for morphological or biochemical study. The production of excess embryos for immediate replacement would be more acceptable if freezing succeeds because the patient does not need or suffer the risks of additional treatment by in-vitro fertilization. Similarly, other arguments can be developed for new advances or new techniques, provided this is within the framework of what society considers justifiable. Indiscriminate or secret research, or work based on dishonest arguments, is dangerous and will affect us all. Our work must be under scrutiny by everyone including those who disagree. Rational argument for honourable purpose is a strong ally. This is the basic philosophy of our group and to date we carry the majority of society's support (Survey on Test-Tube Babies, 1981).

Conti: There is a great deal of unease about the spare embryos. There is disquiet about the embryological studies being carried out on them, and the doubts about this aspect of the work then result in ethical doubts about the whole form of treatment, including the cure of infertility. It would be in our own interests to keep the two things completely separate.

Parental Consent and the "Spare" Embryo

Fishel: The embryos belong to the patients. How is consent obtained from the parents about spare embryos? What is the current method of requesting; are the parents asked formally to give permission to use the embryos once they are obtained?

Conti: Consent from parents is only one of the issues. Even with their consent, there is no consent from those people who are critical about embryological studies with spare embryos.

Fishel: There are several overtones about this question of consent. If we ask a patient for permission to use the third embryo, even for freezing, how do we know that this may not be the one that might have implanted? What is the practice currently being carried out—are patients being requested to donate their spare embryos for research?

Jones, H: If we intend to do embryological studies on embryos, then the Ethical Review Board of our hospital would insist that we had the patient's consent first. The method of institutional review or ethical committee must give their consent first, and we have a duty to ask them about the use of tissues, including embryonic tissue. So far, we have not asked that permission, because it could cause trouble. We have had one case where three embryos were obtained from a couple, and all of them were replaced in the mother.

Edwards: We are possibly trying to dodge an issue that must be faced. Each of us has some spare embryos, after the great majority are replaced in the mothers. We must accept that spare embryos are there, and any studies on them may help considerably with our treatments. It may also help with other forms of medicine. I am very much in sympathy with Lopata's point of view, where he used embryos for quality control.

I feel in a very invidious position about requesting parents for permission to use their spare embryos. If it is decided later that growing embryos for 3–4 days *in vitro* is unethical, or unlawful, then I do not see how patients can be asked to consent. We cannot ask them to agree to potential unethical or unlawful acts. We would be in double jeopardy; asking a patient to consent to something that was intrinsically wrong, and then doing the work on the embryo too. It is no defence for us to say that we have asked the patient's consent before doing studies on the embryo, because it might give us the feeling of a protection that actually does not exist.

This debate reminds me of an article on the use of fetal tissue and the in-vitro growth of fetuses aborted in mid-gestation (Tiefel, 1976). The author pointed out that the mother is often asked for consent to use her fetus, yet this is a double moral wrong. It is hardly the right of the mother, who has condemned her fetus to be aborted, to then give her consent for it to be experimented upon. Nor does it justify the doctors doing the work to gain consent from the mother, and then to state that the situation is correct ethically.

Obviously, the ethics of growing mid-term fetuses in incubators is greatly different to growing preimplantation embryos *in vitro*. But I believe it is naive for us to believe that we can ask the parents for consent to use the embryo, and then assume that everything is fine. We have to make a decision as to whether human embryology should be pursued for its own sake.

Jones, H: We would have to get consent for any tissue, even if it was the uterus. This is an aspect of our law which says that we must get consent.

Edwards: A further difficulty about parental consent is that it cannot be knowledgeable. In many cases we ourselves may not know what we could use the embryos for. Obviously, the parents must be asked, but it is almost impossible to expect them to understand the purposes of the investigation. Suppose we wish to grow an embryo to 16 days of gestation, to study organogenesis. How can the patients understand what value this would be, especially if to a field not related to the cure of their infertility? In some of the studies I have outlined earlier, fetuses of 16 weeks gestation were exposed to various shocks and stimuli after they had been aborted. How can the parents understand the need for this? Would we accept the need for this? And would the parents know their rights within the law, or the standards of ethical committees or whatever?

Fishel: As I understand it, there is no law which says that we can or cannot go ahead and carry out experiments on early human embryos. Consent is merely one step. It may not be the correct step, or the only step, but it would be better to have this, than to have nothing.

Steptoe: How about the fetus which is not growing satisfactorily, or which is cleaving abnormally? Do we regard this embryo as having condemned itself to death, and do we merely watch it, or use it as a control? Is it not time that we started regarding these early embryos as collections of cells, and not as fetuses? Those that are not replaced in the mother are condemned to death, just as sperm that is spilt on the floor is condemned to death.

Szalay: Similar problems arose during donors in organ transplantation. In that case, when the donor had just died, the relations had to be asked very quickly to give their consent. I believe we are in the same situation and the donors must be asked if we may use the embryo for various purposes.

Edwards: There is no doubt that one must ask the patients. And it must be clear that in most cases, although not all, the spare embryos arose because three or more were collected during laparoscopy, when only two were needed for replacement. Freezing embryos, of course, solves these problems, because the intent is to replace the embryo in the mother at a later cycle.

The problem of the spare embryo is even greater if it is not intended to replace it in the mother, i.e. if a woman being sterilized, for example, is asked to take Clomid and HCG so that she can donate preovulatory oocytes for fertilization *in vitro*. This is entirely experimental, and some people may consider it to be a cynical disregard of human life, i.e. to establish it in order to examine it later.

Jones, G: I believe it essential that these issues are discussed with the patients long before they happen. The explanation must be clear, so that if three eggs are obtained, two are replaced, and one is retained and used for a specific purpose. It should not be for a trivial purpose. The Review Committee should examine the proposals, to ensure that essential information will be gained from the study of the spare embryo. Patients could then understand what was intended, and I am sure that most of them would accept willingly to donate the embryo.

Purdy, J: There is obviously no easy solution to this problem, when we have to stimulate the ovary to get embryos for replantation. There is, however, an alternative, and that is to use the natural cycle. And in many ways, this is an easy solution; the problem of the spare embryo simply does not arise. If, for example, Conti could use the natural cycle in his own country, and get the work accepted, then the whole attitude to the work would change and there would be a much better background for discussion about the other aspects of the work. We ourselves have seen considerable changes over the years in acceptance of the work on fertilization *in vitro*. Much of the opposition departed when we abandoned superovulation with gonadotrophins and went to the natural cycle. This would avoid problems, especially with those groups that are just starting. Why start with all the difficulties of facing Ethical Committees, when a much easier beginning can be made?

Trounson: I agree with Edwards that it is impossible for a patient to give "informed consent" about the use of spare embryos. They cannot know the purpose of the research, and our legal advisers tell us that consent forms have limited value. The patients might consent to please the doctor, or because they fear that a refusal might prejudice their further treatment. Moreover, technical negligence is not protected by any consent, although it would be evaluated in relation to an expected level of accidental error. An honest and open approach to patients, within the law and our knowledge, is best. We have consent forms because our medical research committees prefer this, but the deficiencies of the forms in law mean there is little protection for the operators if patients change their mind.

Using the natural cycle does not escape from the dilemma of the spare embryo. Sooner or later the problem will arise.

Edwards: Some of the difficulties facing us over the years have concerned the absence of any law in this field of study. There was literally nothing to cover the work we were doing; we were not carrying out illegal work, but we were simply outside any accepted framework of law (Wolstenholme & Fitzsimmons, 1973; Edwards, 1974, 1980). There was no legislation, nor any court decisions, which could help us in any way, and we had to make decisions against this vacuum in law. In my country, we have recently been faced with legislation on congenital injuries, which gives tort compensation to children for any injury inflicted before conception (under some circumstances), at conception, or during gestation (U.K. Congenital Disabilities Act, 1976). We find ourselves in conflict with many aspects of this Act, especially the need for the child to claim compensation in tort, and others of its clauses, e.g. excusing the wife for certain forms of behaviour whereas in similar circumstances the husband may be considered guilty of inflicting damage on his own child (Kennedy & Edwards, 1975).

I cannot see the problem of the spare embryo in the natural cycle arising to the same extent as with induced cycles. There will be one embryo in most women, two in a few, and three or more extremely rarely. For groups just starting this work, I agree with Purdy that the use of the natural cycle would alleviate many objections in the initial phase of the work.

Fishel: I would like to have a comment about the freezing of embryos. We know that the Australian groups are now freezing embryos, with the intention of replacing them into the mother. Could I ask if this is done with all embryos obtained from a couple, and if there is any request to use any spare embryos for experimental purposes?

Lopata: We are not freezing embryos, but we have considered the effects of replacing three embryos. There is an additional factor to be considered here. If three are replaced, there may be a greater risk of losing the pregnancy, i.e. all three embryos, than if only two or one are replaced. In other words, it may be ethical to replace two and leave the third *in vitro*. Fishel pointed out earlier how the embryo not replaced might have implanted, but it is equally relevant that replacing all three may be the wrong thing to do under these circumstances.

Steptoe: Even replacing two embryos increases the hazards to mother and to the children if they both implant. Therefore one must be very careful about replacing three embryos.

Fishel: Yet, the Australian data has shown that replanting two embryos gave a higher chance of obtaining a singleton pregnancy.

Trounson: We are in no two minds at all about the destination of the embryos we obtain. The majority are replaced immediately and the others preserved at low temperature for replacement in later ovulatory cycles. The embryos belong to the parents, and we have no licence to research on them except by consent for freezing. Initially, we had to use a few embryos to establish our system was working. We asked the patient to decide on the destiny of their embryos, given the appropriate information of risks associated with multiple fetuses, pregnancy rates and the likely failure of freezing to establish pregnancy at the moment. To date, they all request immediate replacement of one, two or three embryos, and the others are frozen. In this way, the patients retain "control of their destiny".

The "Quality" of Babies Following Fertilization *in vitro*

Cohen: There must be some discussion about the qualities of the babies produced by in-vitro fertilization. It is a topic which is likely to arise in France. The criticism is that we are unsure of how normal the babies will be. There is some doubt as to whether there will be an increased number of abnormal babies born after the treatment, and this is a very important consideration.

Jones, H: We have discussed already the normality of children born following in-vitro fertilization. Virtually all of them appear to be normal, and the risks do not appear to be any greater than with conception *in vivo*. There has been an argument that the fetus cannot consent to an unknown risk to itself, i.e. any risk cannot be justified later.

Steptoe: Yet there is no country that I am aware of which says that a retarded boy or girl cannot have intercourse, and many countries accept that people with a risk of producing an abnormal child can attempt to conceive. There are many individuals with inherited conditions which can be transmitted, yet there is no law that I know which prevents them establishing their family.

Conti: As far as Switzerland is concerned, my impression is that the majority of people would accept fertilization *in vitro* for the treatment of infertility. The technique is respected and accepted, and there is sympathy for those who cannot have their own child except by these means.

Cohen: There is an important general question to be answered. Suppose we advise the patient to have amniocentesis, but she refuses. Then she delivers a baby with a trisomic condition. Would this be disastrous for programmes of in-vitro fertilization? Would the criticism be so great that we would have to reanalyse our point of view about the work?

Johnston: We regard the situation as a team situation, and the patient discusses it with us. In other words, should a mistake arise like that, we would regard the parents as part of the team in this case. I do not think this would have any deleterious effect on the programmes for in-vitro fertilization. In contrast, if the mother was forty years old and we had advised against amniocentesis, then the situation would be very different. That would be bad medicine. A lot depends on the situation.

Cohen: I would like to discuss with the Bourn Hall group the quality of their embryos. They had nine abortions and 28 continuing pregnancies. I have omitted the "biochemical" pregnancies. Is this rate high, or is it normal? I would like to have the opinion of the team in view of the acceptability of this work. Remember that most early abortions are probably genetic abortions.

Edwards: From the data I know, the estimates of the abortion rates in pregnancy vary widely. According to O'Rahilly, the figure varies about 25%, but there are considerable variations in published data. He is concerned with the clinical abortions, and not the "biochemical" abortions that we have been discussing at this meeting. I have seen some other figures rising as high as 33% of embryos aborted during pregnancy. I think we are, on average, within these ranges.

Cohen: The figures quoted by the Boués in Paris is 15%. This is done after the time of the first missed period. They believe that many more, up to 50% of the total, die before the first menstrual period.

Edwards: The difficulty here is with factors such as maternal age, which can greatly influence abortion rates. We must obviously study the detailed analyses on abortion following conception *in vivo* to find out if our figures are higher in relation to factors such as maternal age, smoking, etc. At present, the estimates after fertilization *in vitro* are very crude because numbers are so small, and no one has looked at these extraneous factors.

Mettler: At a recent meeting in Berlin, Gropp gave a figure of 37% of abortions during pregnancy. His figures were based on a very large sample.

Edwards: Are we obtaining a high rate of abortion on all these data? It is noticeable that some groups do not have any births, and the number of continued pregnancies is low. In our data, we are losing approximately 25% by clinical abortions, if we exclude the biochemical abortions, which are obviously of dubious merit. We need to know a lot more about them.

Jones, H: I am not sure the biochemical abortions can be included, because women in natural pregnancy are not followed by monitoring as closely as in this work. Many of them may abort, but are not recorded. Patients could go two weeks over their expected RTM and it is never known if they were pregnant or not.

Edwards: Many people have described very high rates of embryonic loss in man before implantation. Much of the data are based on known abortion rates in later pregnancy, and extrapolating to early pregnancy, so the values get very high indeed. We must be very careful about such data.

Cohen: I agree. If we exclude the biochemical abortions from our data, we end up with approximately 25% of abortions, which is much better.

Jones, H: It would be very valuable to have quantitative data on patients who show a clinical abortion. This would indicate if the pregnancy was continuing normally from the beginning, or if it was always threatened with abortion. This is something we should decide to do, because we have a unique opportunity to learn a great deal about early human conception.

Edwards: We do not have good data at present. Our patients go home, and we merely ask them to send urine samples. We do not ask for blood.

Mettler: A great deal of knowledge can be gained on the timing of implantation in man. Several samples of blood could be taken from our patients, knowing exactly the stage of implantation, to find out when the rise in HCGβ occurred. We may even be able to find some markers before implantation.

Edwards: I am astonished at the high levels of HCGβ during early implantation, and how such a small embryo can produce such vast amounts of hormone. I would be dubious about the possibility of finding markers before implantation. Even some of our biochemical pregnancies may not be genuine because injecting medium into the uterus, possibly stimulating the stroma by the catheter and releasing locally active agents, could stimulate the local production of HCGβ. We know the decidual cells produce prolactin; can they also produce HCGβ under certain circumstances?

Jones, G: The data we obtained showed that HCGβ was not high in plasma until ten days after retrieval of the oocyte. This is the earliest time we could detect the rise in HCGβ.

References

Edwards, R. G. 1974. Fertilization of human eggs in vitro: morals, ethics and the law. *Quarterly Review of Biology*, **49**, 3–26.

Edwards, R. G. 1980. *Conception in the Human Female*, Chapter 14, Academic Press, London.

Federal Register, June 18 1979. U.S. Department of Health, Education and Welfare.

Kennedy, I. & Edwards, R. G. 1975. A critique of the Law Commission report on injuries to unborn child and the proposed Congenital disabilities (Civil Liability) Bill. *Journal of Medical Ethics*, **1**, 116–121.

O'Rahilly, R. 1973. *Developmental Stages of Human Embryos, Part A.* Carnegie Institute, Washington.

O'Rahilly, R. 1981. *Wallchart on Human Embryology.* International Planned Parenthood Federation, London.

Survey on Test-Tube Babies. 1981. *The Roy Morgan Research Centre,* June 1981.

Tiefel, H. O. 1976. The cost of foetal research: ethical considerations. *New England Journal of Medicine*, **294**, 85–90.

U.K. Congenital Disabilities (Civil Liability) Act, 1976.

Wolstenholme, G. E. W. & Fitzsimmons, D. W. (editors). 1973. *Law and Ethics of A.I.D. and Embryo Transfer.* Ciba Foundation Symposium, no. 17. Elsevier, Amsterdam.

The Case for Studying Human Embryos and their Constituent Tissues *in vitro*

R. G. Edwards

Introduction

Human embryos have now been grown *in vitro* through cleavage to the blastocyst stage for more than 10 years (Edwards *et al.*, 1969; Steptoe *et al.*, 1971). Some of them escape from the zona pellucida and develop for several days until Stage 5a (Edwards, 1980). They can be grown through cleavage with less difficulty than in the case of embryos of virtually all animal species, as testified by the contents of this book, and there seems little doubt that many will be grown through post-implantation stages in the near future. Sometimes, ovarian stimulation will result in three, four, or more embryos, and two will be replaced in the mother, leaving two others to be studied *in vitro*. Should the ''spare'' embryos be used for this purpose? My own views of some of the potential advantages of studying human embryos in vitro are presented in this paper. I will also comment briefly on the underlying ethical situation; detailed comments have been made elsewhere (Edwards, 1974; 1980).

I will not discuss the advantages and disadvantages of methods such as oocyte or embryo donation, and of the frozen storage of embryos for replacement into the mother during successive cycles, as these subjects have been discussed extensively elsewhere (Edwards, 1974; 1980; Ciba Foundation, 1973; Jones & Bodmer, 1974). I wish to concentrate on the need to study growth *in vitro* for improving the alleviation of infertility and inherited disorders and for investigating other scientific and clinical problems.

Physiological College, Cambridge University, and Bourn Hall, Cambridge.

Improving Methods to Alleviate
Infertility or Inherited Disorders

Every group beginning clinical studies on in-vitro fertilization has passed through an initial stage when methods were established for successfully culturing embryos. Oocytes and embryos were grown during these early investigations, without any intention of replacing them in the uterus, so that a minimum standard of success compatible with the introduction of a clinical programme to cure infertility could be attained.

This preliminary period is by no means completed, even in hospitals and clinics where many pregnancies have already been established through in-vitro fertilization. Improved methods are needed to assess the normality of growth of the embryos, and to sustain or monitor their development without impairing the development of those which are to be replaced in the mother.

Most of the available data on the growth of human embryos *in vitro* is empirical, gained by culturing embryos in various defined media, adding serum albumin, pyruvate, and other compounds. These methods have resulted in many successful pregnancies, yet no knowledge exists on such fundamental factors as intermediary metabolism, or the synthesis of macromolecules in human embryos. There are obviously reservations about using human embryos for biochemical studies, but some minimal information is essential on these early stages of growth if the methods of culture are to be improved. Tests are also needed on variations in culture media, e.g. pH, osmotic pressure, the addition of increased amounts of proteins during later cleavage. The overall pattern of growth appears to be similar in most mammalian species, but differences exist between animal species, e.g. between rat, mouse and monkey (Brinster, 1972), and we must be cautious about concluding that the "correct" conditions for human embryos can be gained from the study of animal embryos. Even today, we do not know if replacements at $4\frac{1}{2}$ or 5 days will give better results than at 2–3 days, because most groups replace embryos in early cleavage.

A positive approach to avoiding inherited defects through in-vitro fertilization could be established by identifying embryos carrying deleterious genes or other defects. Animal embryos can be screened for certain characteristics by forming duplicate embryos after disaggregation of the blastomeres, or by excising pieces of trophoblast. Most success has been gained in sexing embryos, which might one day help to avert sex-linked disorders (Edwards, 1980). Screening may be possible using DNA probes for specific gene sequences or restriction analyses. Gene analysis has been carried out on single chorionic villi removed from fetuses aged 8–14 weeks (Chang & Kan, 1980; Williamson *et al.*, 1981). At present, it is doubtful that sufficient tissue can be obtained from preimplantation embryos for this purpose, even if "replicates" are cultured *in vitro* to produce cell colonies. But methods are advancing so quickly that analyses on a few cells or mitoses might well become possible in the near future, using fluorescent-labelled or radio-labelled DNA probes (Langer *et al.*, 1981). If I understand this approach correctly, it may permit the identification of heterozygous "carrier" embryos as well as homozygous afflicted embryos. Examining embryos for gene products provides another approach, which is feasible for some genes with the recognition that paternal genes can be detected from the 2-cell stage, e.g. in mice (Sawicki *et al.*, 1981). Replicate embryos might also help in alleviating infertility, two embryos raising the chances of implantation, especially if identical twins were desired by the parents.

Identifying embryos with genetic abnormalities would offer an alternative to amniocentesis during the second trimester of pregnancy, and the "abortion *in vitro*" of a defective preimplantation embryo, still free-living, minute and undifferentiated, would be infinitely preferable to abortion *in vivo* at 20 weeks of pregnancy or thereabouts as the results of amniocentesis are obtained. It would also be less traumatic for parents and doctor to type several embryos and replace or store those that are normal, rather than having the threat of a mid-term abortion looming over each successive pregnancy. Aborting defective embryos *in vitro* would be preferable to repairing them by the techniques of genetic engineering, with its unknown and uncertain consequences.

Assessing the Normality of Embryos Growing *in vitro*

Any information on the growth of embryos in culture is urgently needed. The relatively low rates of implantation after replacement reported by some groups of workers could be due to the anomalous growth of embryos with trisomy, triploidy, or other chromosomal defects. Large numbers of heteroploid and polyploid fetuses arise after conception *in vivo*, trisomic fetuses accounting for more than half, triploids for 20%, monosomics for 5%, and tetraploid embryos for 5% (Boué *et al.*, 1975).

Triploidy arises *in vivo* mostly through dispermy, or the fertilization of an oocyte by a diploid spermatozoon (Jacobs *et al.*, 1978). Too many active spermatozoa in the insemination droplet, or disorders in the first or second meiotic divisions *in vitro* could be additional factors predisposing to triploidy. Nevertheless, very few eggs with three pronuclei (1–2%), and no triploid embryos were found during culture *in vitro* (Edwards & Steptoe, 1973; Edwards *et al.*, 1981), although a triploid fetus aborted early in gestation after the replacement of an embryo (Edwards *et al.*, 1980). More information is obviously needed on the karyotypes of cleaving embryos.

Trisomy occurs more commonly in older women, rising from a frequency of 1.6% to 25% in mothers between the ages of 35 and 49 (Tsuji & Nakano, 1978). Most autosomal trisomies arise *in vivo* through non-disjunction in the first meiotic division of the oocyte, rarely in the second meiotic division, and very infrequently during a cleavage division of the embryo (Hassold & Matsuyama, 1978; Niikawa *et al.*, 1977). In contrast, monosomy and trisomy for the sex chromosomes can also arise in spermatogenic cells (Polani, 1981).

Why should most autosomal trisomies arise during the first meiotic division in the oocyte? Homologous chromosomes may separate during the long dictyotene period (desynapsis), so leading to a disordered segregation of chromosomes into the first polar body, but there is very little evidence to support this hypothesis. Alternatively, autosomal trisomy may arise during oogenesis in the fetal ovary, as oocytes are formed successively in the fetus (Henderson & Edwards, 1968; Jagiello & Fang, 1979). Oocytes with few chiasmata may be conserved until late in reproductive life, so that non-disjunction would arise mostly in oocytes of older mothers. If this hypothesis is correct, the risks of monosomy and trisomy would be determined in the fetal ovary, long before ovulation occurred, and would presumably be similar during fertilization *in vitro* or *in vivo*.

The autosomal trisomics surviving to birth might perhaps have arisen through non-disjunction during the cleavage division in the embryo. In this case, they would be mosaics. There is no information on the risk of non-disjunction during cleavage *in vitro*, an important reason for studying the chromosome complement in preimplantation and postimplantation embryos. Any information gained on disorders in chromosomal movements in oocytes or embryos could obviously help to understand the etiology of abortion and malformations arising *in vivo*.

Likewise, studies on rates of cleavage, the formation of small nuclei, fragmentation, disorders in blastulation, etc. will clarify the incidence of these anomalies *in vitro* and *in vivo*. There are no teratological dangers associated with fertilization and cleavage *in vitro* in several animal species (Edwards, 1980; Testart & Renard, 1982). One reported exception, microphthalmia in rat offspring, actually arose through a segregating gene (Chang, personal communication), and limb defects found in one group of rabbit offspring have not been found subsequently. Moreover, many normal animal offspring have been born after astonishing manipulations on preimplantation embryos, including exposure to drugs, freezing, separating blastomeres and microdissections of blastocysts. There is barely a single report of anomalies, confirming the resistance of preimplantation embryos to teratogenic agents (Wilson, 1977).

It may even be possible to monitor some forms of anomalous growth *in vitro*. Androgenetic embryos can form hydatidiform moles (Kajii & Ohama, 1977). They may be detected by the extrusion of a female pronucleus in a tripronucleate embryo (Trounson, 1982), or the premature growth of the male pronucleus (Edwards, 1981). Choriocarcinoma can be a sequel to a hydatidiform mole, and studies *in vitro* could help to elucidate causative factors such as the expression of antigens on trophoblastic tissue and disorders in the formation of chorionic villi (Brewer *et al.*, 1978). Numerous other opportunities arise for studying normal and abnormal human growth *in vitro*. For example, the selective inactivation of the paternal X chromosome in trophectoderm might be critical for establishing normal materno-fetal relationships in mice (Takagi & Sasaki, 1975). Several X-linked human genes could be used for similar studies on human embryos. A second example concerns the unusual antigens expressed on cleaving embryos, many being shared with tumours (Allison, 1975; Ruoslahti & Seppälä, 1979); such carcinoembryonic and oncofetal antigens may be "incomplete" histocompatibility antigens or differentiation antigens expressed on tumour cells as they are derepressed (Jacob, 1977; Uriel, 1979). The expression of histocompatibility antigens on trophectoderm is very restricted (Cozad & Warner, 1981).

All the evidence on the normality of embryonic growth in culture does not obviate the need to record any cases of abnormal growth after in-vitro fertilization. In one sense, many observations on animals cannot be compared with clinical work on human embryos, in which oocytes are collected before ovulation and all subsequent growth occurs *in vitro*. Animal eggs are usually collected after ovulation, or even after fertilization, to be cultured only briefly for a highly restricted period of growth, e.g. in non-human primates (Marston *et al.*, 1977).

More than 30 children have now been born after conception *in vitro*, all evidently fully normal, although heart defects were found in one twin boy. Between 3 and 8% of children are born with various anomalies after conception *in vivo* (Fraser, 1977), so a similar percentage must be expected after conception *in vitro*, although not attributable to the procedures involved. Pregnancies established through in-vitro fertilization are subject to the usual hazards of in-vivo pregnancy, including teratogenesis and intrauterine death. Many teratogens have been identified, including alcohol, smoking, insecticides, defoliants, vitamin deficiency, etc. (Wilson, 1977). Some embryos will die *in utero*, through conditions similar to those arising *in vivo*. These will include blighted ova (Hertig, 1975), hydatidiform moles which are androgenetic in origin (Kajii & Ohama, 1977), and perhaps some with placental anomalies (Torphin, 1969). Additional problems might arise after conception *in vitro* if the replacement of embryos leads to trauma, infection, or an inadequate site of implantation in the uterus.

It is obviously desirable to gain as much information as possible on chromosome complement, cleavage rates, conditions of reimplantation, etc. from human embryos grown *in vitro*, and to carry out detailed analyses on abortuses and full-term infants following conception *in vitro*. We have proposed that a Register of Births and Abortions be established, with contributions from each group practising in-vitro fertilization. We hope to publish details of this Register in the near future.

Analyses on the Growth of Post-Implantation Embryos *in vitro*

Knowledge of normal and abnormal organogenesis could arise from the study of human embryos in culture through their preimplantation and immediate post-implantation stages of growth. In the U.S.A., one committee has suggested that the limit should be 14 days (Federal Register, 1979). A classification of stages of growth of human embryos *in vivo* given in Table 1 (O'Rahilly, 1973).

It is worth noting some landmarks in the growth of the human fetus *in vivo*. Embryonic ectoderm forms in Stage 6. Extraembryonic endoderm has formed a single layer on the inner aspect of the inner cell mass by Stage 5 at 7½ days. The primitive streak is present as a group of cells at the caudal end of the embryo by 15 days (Stage 6b). The segmentation of somites begins on day 21 (Stage 9), extending to the 30th day, and by day 26 the forebrain projects markedly. The notochord extends along the entire length of the embryo between the endoderm and the roof of the yolk sac, and the ventral aspect of the neural groove by 28 days.

The major challenges in this field almost certainly arise in relation to

Table 1
Organ primordia in human embryos[a]

Carnegie Stage		Length (mm)	Age (days)	Embryogenesis
1		,,	1	Fertilization
2		,,	2–3	Cleaving embryos
3		,,	4–5	Free blastocyst. Inner cell mass and trophectoderm
4		,,	5–6	Attaching blastocyst Syncitiotrophoblast?
5		,,	7–12	
	5a			Bilaminar embryonic disc. Extra-embryonic mesoblast. Amniotic cavity. Solid trophoblast
	5b			Trophoblastic lacunae. Primitive yolk sac
	5c			Utero-lacunar circulation. Maternal blood in lacunar spaces
6		0.2	13–15	
	6a			Chorionic villi. Extra-embryonic coelom.
	6b			Embryonic ectoderm. Primitive streak (embryonic mesoblast)
7		0.4	15–17	Notochordal process. Primitive node. Angiogenesis (modified mesenchymal cells, haemocytoblasts, primitive erythroblasts) Primordial germ cells
8		1.0–1.5	17–19	General area of neural plate. Neural groove. Neural folds. Primitive pit. Notochordal and neuroenteric canals. Pericardial cavities. Prechordal plate. Blood islands in yolk sac
9		1.5–3.0	19–21	Somites. Forebrain and midbrain regions. Foregut. Coelom. Vascular system.

[a]Modified from O'Rahilly, 1973.

the growth of organ primordia, and their constituent cells in culture. Studying embryos in postimplantation stages of growth would provide an opportunity to obtain and analyse the stem cells and primordia of many organ systems. Broadly speaking, there are two methods of organ formation and maintenance. In one group, stem cells remain proliferative throughout fetal and adult life, e.g. skin, bone marrow and testis, and constantly repopulate the tissues. In the other groups, e.g. brain and neural system, myocardium, ovary and perhaps Islets of Langerhans, stem cells cease dividing and may become totally depleted during fetal or juvenile life (Ham & Cormack, 1979), so that proliferation and repair cannot occur. The widest opportunities perhaps relate to the primordia of those organs without a renewal of stem cells in adults, and I will briefly describe the early embryogenesis of the nervous system, myocardium and primordial germ cells.

The differentiation of the neural system is evidently tightly programmed in the very early embryo. Neural tissue differentiates under the influence of mesodermal inducers which regulate the differentiation of the neural plate, and the cells of the neural crest (Jacobson, 1978). The mitotic cells of the neural plate and neural tube are polarized in the sense that cell division occurs close to the lumen, and daughter cells move to the outer half of the tube. In the human embryo, the neural groove is present in embryos in Stage 8 (O'Rahilly, 1973), and neural cells presumably differentiate before this time.

Myocardial cells do not divide in adults (Ham & Cormack, 1979). These cells are also formed early in the fetus during the differentiation of the heart. The myoepicardial mantle is formed between Stages 9 and 10, i.e. between 18 and 19 days after fertilization, and contractions of the heart are apparent on day 22 (Moore, 1977; O'Rahilly, 1973). Primordial germ cells also appear early in the growth of the fetus. They differentiate by day 7, when they are found in the yolk sac. In males, stem cells colonize the testis and continue to divide mitotically throughout the life of the adult. In females, the final mitoses in primordial germ cells and oogonia occur in the fetal ovary; there is no replenishment after birth when the total pool of oocytes is already established (Edwards, 1980).

The primordia of many other organ systems are also established during very early stages of growth, and could be studied *in vitro* (Table 1). The pluripotential colony-forming cells of the haemopoietic system are present in the yolk sac, in blood islands, and are precursors of erythrocytes, leucocytes, megakaryocytes, and lymphocytes (Becker *et al.*, 1973; Moore & Metcalfe, 1970). They seed the liver, spleen, and bone marrow, which then supercede the yolk sac as haemopoetic centres. Fetal haemoglobin is synthesized in blood islands of the yolk sac.

Information on the immune system and the development of self-tolerance in the early embryo is very limited. Fetuses can mount immune responses from the earliest stages of growth (Gathings *et al.*, 1981; Hayward, 1981; Toivanen *et al.*, 1971). At 7–10 weeks, liver cells bind antigen and respond to allogeneic or xenogeneic cells in mixed lymphocyte cultures, and thymocytes respond to phytohaemagglutinin after the thymus gland has differentiated. Pre-B cells in the fetal liver at 7½ weeks gestation express HLA antigens, but lack surface immunoglobulins. Natural killer (NK) cells are active by 9 weeks in the fetal lives, and are highly developed by 19 weeks (Toivanen *et al.*, 1981); they may be involved in the immune surveillance of tumours, virus infected cells, and the homeostatic regulation of tissues (Cudkowicz & Hochman, 1979; Kiessling & Wigzell, 1979). Current theories suggest that clones of lymphocytes reactive with self are deleted during fetal life, or their activity is held in check by suppressor cells (Burnet, 1959; Naor, 1980). Embryonic lymphoid cells may be incapable of responding to self-antigens until later in life, e.g. after the histocompatibility antigens have differentiated and the thymus gland has developed.

Many other organ primordia could be studied *in vitro*, e.g. derivatives of the neural crest which differentiate and migrate through the fetus during these early stages of growth, colonizing various neural and neuroendocrine centres in the body (Jacobson, 1978). The early stages of fetal growth are obviously of crucial importance in organ differentiation, the establishment of symmetry in the body, and the migration of cells from their point of origin to their final site in the adult.

I will discuss below the potential medical value of cells and tissues from postimplantation embryos. What are the chances of growing embryos *in vitro* through these early stages of growth or of obtaining tissues such as kidney, heart, nerve in sufficient amounts for grafting? At present, the culture of postimplantation fetuses, and their constituent tissues, is still rudimentary. There is no doubt that human blastocysts will migrate from their zona pellucida *in vitro* and develop through their earliest postimplantation stages of growth. To my knowledge, details have been published on only one embryo, which developed to Stage 5a, growing for 9 days in culture (Edwards & Surani, 1977; Edwards, 1980). This embryo was growing actively, with numerous mitoses when prepared for examination, and it would undoubtedly have developed further. Trophoblastic lacunae had not appeared, indicating that it had not yet reached Stage 5c. This assumption may not be justified, because it is possible that these lacunae will not develop *in vitro* in the absence of maternal blood vessels. Growth could be stunted by inadequate placental function, although the yolk sac may sustain the early stages of fetal development. Increasing success is being achieved with the culture of animal embryos through various stages of their postimplantation growth (Hsu, 1979; New, 1978; Wu *et al.*, 1981).

There can be little doubt that analyses on differentiation and early organogenesis in the human embryo are now feasible. Will they be ethically acceptable? Should they be carried out at all? These are difficult questions to answer. I have indicated the considerable scientific possibilities that could accrue from such work. I now wish to become highly speculative indeed, and indicate some of the potential clinical opportunities.

The Grafting of Cells and Tissues from Postimplantation Embryos

There should be no difficulty in obtaining the primordia of organ systems which differentiate early in the embryo, e.g. the neural system and cells of the neural crest. What are the potential clinical advantages in studying organ primordia from human embryos? I will discuss one aspect only, the potential use of embryonic tissues and cells for grafting into adults.

It is now possible to contemplate the use of "tailor-made" embryonic tissue grown *in vitro* for grafting into adults. Grafts of embryonic tissue may offer a wider scope than those taken from neonates or adults, because tissue could be obtained from organs which do not regenerate in adults, and the risks of graft rejection can probably be eliminated.

This approach is novel, although there are various indications of the potential benefits of using fetal tissue. Grafts of adult tissue have long been used to replenish bone marrow in animals or patients previously exposed to radiation, and fetal tissue can be used for this purpose (Till & McCulloch, 1961; Metcalf & Moore, 1971). Haemopoetic tissue from sheep fetuses was transplanted into adults, and adult-type haemoglobin was synthesized in some recipients (Zanjani *et al.*, 1982), and injections of normal fetal liver cells into the placenta prevented the expression of inherited anaemia in mouse offspring (Fleischman & Mintz, 1979). Bone-marrow grafts restore mast cells in irradiated mice (Kitamura *et al.*, 1977).

Grafting using neonatal tissue has been proposed as a method to restore immune deficiencies in old people, and practised in rodents by transferring bone marrow stem cells and thymic tissue from newborn mice into old recipients (Makinodan & Kay, 1980). Immune functions in the old mice were reportedly restored to levels approaching those of younger mice, the restorative effect lasting for at least 6 months. A practical approach to controlling immunological aging may involve a combination of dietary manipulation, chemical therapy and cell grafting (Makinodan & Kay, 1980). Other recent reports have indicated that pancreatic cells may be used to repair diabetes, and cultured skin cells grafted to repair lesions (Stoker, 1981). Some cell types may be valuable for repairing inherited disorders. Human amniotic epithelial cells can be grafted into recipients because they do not express HLA antigens or β_2-microglobulins, and they could be useful in repairing inherited enzyme defects in recipient children and adults (Adinolfi et al., 1982).

Fetal brain tissue has been transplanted into recipient adults in rats, and shown to be capable of repairing neural defects. Motor asymmetry and a contralateral sensory neglect were induced experimentally in adult rats by unilaterally destroying the nigrostriatal dopamine pathway. Grafts of ventral mesencephalic tegmentum removed from rat fetuses aged 16–17 days were then inserted into the lesion 2–3 weeks later. Large parts of the dorsal neostriatum were reinnervated by axons containing dopamine, which could fully compensate for the motor asymmetry although the associated sensory neglect remained in the recipients (Björklund et al., 1980). Deficits in consummatory behaviour following bilateral lesions were not restored by the grafts. There are reports that kidney cells may be transplanted into the human brain, in order to cure illnesses such as Parkinson's disease by the production of dopamine (ascribed to Backlund, 1981).

Embryonic tissue and cells might one day be valuable for similar studies on other organs. Autografting of tissues will come as no surprise to cardiologists using the method to repair the major vessels. Myocardial tissue differentiates in Stage 9 or 10, and should be obtainable from embryos growing in vitro without great difficulty. There seems to be no information available on the potential value of these tissues to restore diseased or damaged tissues in animals. Fetal pancreas and Islet cells have been used in attempts to cure human diabetes, apparently with little success because the grafts were rejected rapidly (Sutherland, 1980). A primary need in this field of medicine is to obtain grafts of tissue genetically identical with the patient. This principle has been applied in the treatment of chronic granulocytic leukemia, where the use of chemoradiotherapy and the transplantation of tissue from an identical twin has proved of considerable value in combating the malignancy (Fefer et al., 1982). Obviously, very few patients have an identical twin to serve as a donor.

Embryonic cells could offer an unique advantage, because graft rejection could be completely avoided. This could be achieved by using experimental methods to tailor embryos to suit a particular recipient. Replica tissues without any histoincompatibility for a woman could be formed by inducing parthenogenesis in her oocytes. Organogenesis occurs in parthenogenetic animal embryos (Kaufman *et al.*, 1977), although there is no knowledge on the growth of human partheno-genones. The gynogenetic activation of oocytes also offers a method of obtaining embryonic cells fully compatible with the woman, and androgenesis would offer the same benefit for men. In mice, andro-genetic embryos develop to full term and into adults (Hoppe & Illmensee, 1977). Tissues compatible with an adult host might also be obtained through cloning, and this might perhaps be one of the few potential advantages of introducing this method into experimental human embryology. There is another possible advantage in using fetal tissue, because it might not be rejected by incompatible donors as strongly as adult tissue (Billingham & Silvers, 1964). Unfortunately, this principle did not seem to apply to fetal pancreatic tissue, as described above.

Can we contemplate grafts of embryonic cells to repair defects in adults? Are there too many difficulties in obtaining sufficient amounts of tissue for grafting, or in applying grafts locally to effect a repair of damaged tissues? Could organogenesis begin in embryos cultured *in vitro* and continue in tissue isolates? Isolated neural tube tissue apparently continues to grow in ectopic sites (Jacobson, 1978), and might continue *in vitro*. A few hundred or thousand cells would be insufficient to make much difference in organs where massive numbers of stem cells are in active division. But such grafts may be highly effective in organs such as the brain or myocardium, where there are no stem cells and where they may be applied locally. The deliberate production of fetal tissue for the repair of adult organs could not be seriously contemplated until methods became possible to grow human embryos through the early stages of organogenesis, i.e. beyond Stage 5. The rabbit advances in the culture of embryos *in vitro* suggest it is perhaps time to consider the ethical issues involved, because the therapeutic benefits could be considerable (Edwards, 1980).

Establishing Embryonic Cells *in vitro*

As indicated in the previous sections, there could be considerable potential in obtaining and using tissues from post-implantation human embryos. The ethical dilemma is simple: should embryos be grown *in vitro* for their constituent tissues perhaps after some genetic tailoring to match the recipient?

There may be an alternative approach for obtaining cells and tissues *in vitro*, by obtaining cell lines from embryos in earlier stages of growth, and allowing their differentiation to occur in culture. The cells of preimplantation embryos are undifferentiated, whereas those taken from implanting, or immediate post-implantation fetuses may be committed to particular embryonic pathways.

It has proved difficult to establish lines of cells from fertilized eggs, and even from embryos in early cleavage. After disaggregation into component cells, the blastomeres survive only briefly (Edwards, 1964). Accordingly, blastocysts have been mostly used as a source of undifferentiated cells, since the cells of the inner cell mass retain a considerable degree of flexibility.

Our own studies began with rabbit embryos (Cole, Edwards & Paul, 1966). Initial attempts to disaggregate cleaving embryos into component cells, and grow them into colonies were unsuccessful, but cell colonies could be established from outgrowths of blastocysts. The trophoblast cells adhered firmly to plastic, and considerable differentiation occurred as the embryonic cells grew over them. Blood islands, cells resembling muscle fibres, and other types of tissues could be identified in outgrowths of cells. The addition of mesodermal inducers did not appear to switch the nature of differentiation to any significant extent. Lines of cells could be obtained from these outgrowths, and passaged *in vitro* through many generations. Only one persisted permanently and it was stored at low temperatures. It has recently (1981) been thawed, and found to be viable (Paul, personal communication).

Another successful attempt has now been made to grow embryonic cells *in vitro*, from mouse blastocysts undergoing delayed implantation. Embryoid bodies were formed *in vitro*, and could be disaggregated and passaged. Their constituent cells retained sufficient developmental potential to develop into various tissues, shown by the production of mosaic embryos when they were injected into recipient blastocysts (Evans & Kaufman, 1981). These lines of embryonic cells may resemble teratocarcinoma cells.

At present there is no information on outgrowths of stem cells and tissues from human embryos *in vitro*. It should not prove too difficult to obtain them from embryos in Stages 6 or 7, which are still very early in the formative period of the embryo, before neural tissue has become highly organized. There is little doubt that these studies could be undertaken now.

Conclusions

I have discussed some potential advantages of studying early human embryology *in vitro*. Current methods of treating infertility through in-vitro fertilization could be improved. Better methods may be devised for culturing embryos *in vitro*, and the nature of normal and abnormal growth could be analysed. Methods might be introduced to use embryonic tissues for the cellular repair of damaged tissues in adults, especially for organs without a renewal of stem cells. Fundamental knowledge may be gained in other areas of medicine, e.g. the relationship between embryonic and tumour cells.

I believe that such studies must be carried out. Their advantages could be too great to be neglected or ignored. The ethical issues involved in establishing and studying early embryos *in vitro* should be acceptable in view of the potential advantages of the work. These issues seem to be minor in relation to other ethical dilemmas involving embryos and fetuses, e.g. the accepted and widespread use of I.U.D.s and abortion for family limitation.

Acknowledgements

I wish to thank Walter Bodmer, Simon Fishel, Ruth Edwards and Jean Purdy for their helpful comments.

References

Adinolfi, M., Akle, C. A., McColl, I., Fensom, A. H., Tansley, L., Connolly, P., Hsi, B.-L., Faulk, W. P., Travers, P. & Bodmer, W. F. 1982. The human amniotic epithelial cell: HLA antigens and enzyme production. Potential use for the correction of enzyme deficiences. *Nature* (in press).

Allison, A. C. 1975. Antigens shared by tumour cells and fetal or gonadal cells. In *Immunobiology of Trophoblast*, p. 19. Ed. R. G. Edwards, C. W. S. Howe & M. H. Johnson. Cambridge University Press, Cambridge.

Backlund, E.-O. 1981. The Times, London, Nov. 21.

Becker, A. J., McCulloch, E. A. & Till, J. E. 1963. Cytological demonstration of the clonal nature of spleen colonies derived from transplanted mouse marrow cells. *Nature*, **197**, 452.

Billingham, R. E. & Silvers, W. K. 1964. Studies on homografts of foetal and infant skin and further observations on the anomalous properties of pouch skin grafts in hamster. *Proceedings of the Royal Society, B*, **161**, 168.

Björklund, A., Dunnett, S. B., Stenevi, V., Lewis, M. E. & Iversen, S. D. 1980. Reinnervation of the denervated striatum by substantia nigra transplants: functional consequences as revealed by pharmacological and sensorimotor testing. *Brain Research*, **199**, 307–333.

Boué, J., Boué, A. & Lazar, P. 1975. The epidemiology of human spontaneous abortions with chromosomal anomalies. In *Agine Gametes, Their Biology and Pathology*, p. 330. Ed. R. J. Blandau. Karger, Basle.

Brewer, J. I., Torok, E. E., Kahan, B. D., Stanhope, C. R. & Halpern, B. 1978. Gestational trophoblastic disease: origin of choriocarcinoma, invasive mole and choriocarcinoma associated with hydatidiform mole, and some immunological aspects. *Advances in Cancer Research*, **27**, 89-147.

Brinster, R. L. 1972. Developing zygote. In *Reproductive Biology*. Ed. H. Balin & S. Glasser. Excerpta Medica, Amsterdam.

Burnet, F. M. 1959. *The Clonal Selection Theory of Acquired Immunity*. Cambridge University Press, London.

Chang, J. C. & Kan, Y. W. 1981. Antenatal diagnosis of sickle-cell anaemia by direct analysis of the sickle mutation. *Lancet*, ii, 1127-1129.

Ciba Foundation. 1973. *Law and Ethics of A.I.D. and Embryo Transfer*. Symposium No. 17.

Cole, R. J., Edwards, R. G. & Paul, J. 1966. Cytodifferentiation and embryogenesis in cell colonies and tissues cultures derived from ova and blastocysts of the rabbit. *Developmental Biology*, **13**, 385-407.

Cozad, K. M. & Warner, C. M. 1981. Specificity of H-2 antigens expressed in mouse blastocysts. *Journal of Experimental Zoology*, **218**, 313-320.

Cudkowicz, G. & Hochman, P. S. 1979. Do natural killer cells engage in regulated reactions against self to ensure homeostasis? *Immunological Reviews*, **44**, 13-41.

Edwards, R. G. 1964. Cleavage of one and two-celled rabbit eggs *in vitro* after removal of the zona pellucida. *Journal of Reproduction and Fertility*, **7**, 413-415.

Edwards, R. G. 1974. Fertilization of human eggs in vitro: morals, ethics and the law. *Quarterly Review of Biology*, **49**, 3-26.

Edwards, R. G. 1980. *Conception in the Human Female*. Academic Press, London and New York.

Edwards, R. G. 1981. Test-Tube Babies, 1981. *Nature*, **293**, 253-256.

Edwards, R. G., Bavister, B. D. & Steptoe, P. C. 1969. Early stages of fertilization *in vitro* of human oocytes matured *in vitro*. *Nature*, **211**, 632-635.

Edwards, R. G., Purdy, J. M., Steptoe, P. C. & Walters, D. E. 1981. The growth of human preimplantation embryos *in vitro*. *American Journal of Obstetrics and Gynecology*, **141**, 408-416.

Edwards, R. G. & Steptoe, P. C. 1973. Biological aspects of embryo transfer. In *Law and Ethics of A.I.D. in Embryo Transfer*, p. 11-18. Ciba Foundation Symposium, no. 17.

Edwards, R. G., Steptoe, P. C. & Purdy, J. M. 1980. Establishing full term human pregnancies in cleaving embryos grown *in vitro*. *British Journal of Obstetrics and Gynaecology*, **87**, 737-756.

Edwards, R. G. & Surani, M. A. H. 1977. The primate blastocyst and its environment. *Upsala Journal of Medicine*, **522**, 39-50.

Erikson, B. G., Hamberger, L., Hillensjö, T., Janson, P. O., Löfman, C. D., Nilsson, L., Nilsson, L., Sjögren, A. & Wikland, M. 1982. Microcinematographic recordings as a tool for monitoring the development of the human embryo in culture. In *Human Conception in Vitro*, pp. 213-218. Ed. R. G. Edwards & J. M. Purdy. Academic Press, London. (This volume)

Evans, M. J. & Kaufman, M. H. 1981. Establishment in culture of pluripotential cells from mouse embryos. *Nature*, **292**, 154.

Federal Register, June 18, 1979. U.S. Department of Health Education and Welfare.

Fefer, A., Cheever, M. A., Greenberg, P. D., Appelbaum, F. R., Boyd, C. N., Buckner, C. D., Kaplan, H. C., Ramberg, R., Sanders, J. E., Storb, R. & Thomas, E. D. 1982. Treatment of chronic granulocytic leukemia with chemo-radiotherapy and transplantation of tissue from an identical twin. *New England Journal of Medicine*, **306**, 63–68.

Fleischman, R. A. & Mintz, B. 1979. Prevention of genetic anaemias in mice by microinjection of normal hematopoietic stem cells into the fetal placenta. *Proceedings of the National Academy of Sciences*, **76**, 5736–5740.

Fraser, F. C. 1977. Interactions and multiple causes. In *Handbook of Teratology*, Vol. 1, p. 445. Ed. J. G. Wilson and F. C. Fraser. Plenum Press, New York.

Gathings, W. E., Kubagawa, H. & Cooper, M. D. 1981. A distinctive pattern of B cell immaturity in perinatal humans. *Immunological Reviews*, **57**, 107–126.

Ham, A. W. & Cormack, D. H. 1979. *Histology*. J. P. Lippincott, Philadelphia.

Hassold, J. J. & Matsuyama, A. 1978. Origin of trisomies in human spontaneous abortions. *Human Genetics*, **46**, 285–294.

Hayward, A. R. 1981. Development of lymphocyte responses and interactions in the human fetus and newborn. *Immunological Reviews*, **57**, 39–60.

Henderson, S. A. & Edwards, R. G. 1968. Chiasma frequency and maternal age in mammals. *Nature*, **218**, 22–28.

Hertig, A. T. 1975. Implantation of the human ovum: the histogenesis of some aspects of spontaneous abortion. In *Progress in Infertility*, p. 411. Ed. S. J. Behrman and R. W. Kistner. Little Brown and Company, Boston.

Hoppe, P. C. & Illmensee, K. 1977. Microsurgically produced homozygous-diploid uniparental mice. *Proceedings of the National Academy of Sciences*, **74**, 5657–5661.

Hsu, Y. C. 1979. In-vitro development of individually cultured whole mouse embryos from blastocyst to early somite stage. *Developmental Biology*, **68**, 453–461.

Jacob, F. 1977. Mouse teratocarcinoma and embryonic antigens. *Immunological Reviews*, **33**, 3–32.

Jacobs, P. A., Angel, R. R., Buchanan, I. M., Hassold, T. J., Matsuyama, A. M. & Manuel, B. 1978. The origin of human triploids. *Annals of Human Genetics*, **42**, 49–57.

Jacobson, M. 1978. *Developmental Neurobiology*. Plenum, New York.

Jagiello, G. & Fang, J. S. 1979. Analyses of diplotene chiasma frequencies in mouse oocytes and spermatocytes in relation to ageing and sexual dimorphism. *Cytogenetics and Cell Genetics*, **23**, 53–60.

Jones, A. & Bodmer, W. F. 1974. *Our Future Inheritance, Choice or Chance?* Oxford University Press, Oxford.

Kajii, T. & Ohama, K. 1977. Androgenetic origin of hydatidiform moles. *Nature*, **268**, 633–644.

Kaufman, M. H., Barton, S. C. & Surani, M. A. H. 1977. Normal post-implantation development of mouse parthenogenetic embryos to the forelimb bud stage. *Nature*, **265**, 53–55.

Kiessling, R. & Wigzell, H. 1979. An analysis of the murine NK cell as to structure function, and biological relevance. *Immunological Reviews*, **44**, 165–208.

Kitamura, V., Shimada, M., Hatanaka, K. & Miyano, Y. 1977. Development of mast cells from grafted bone marrow in irradiated mice. *Nature*, **268**, 442–443.

Langer, P. R., Waldrop, A. A. & Ward, D. C. 1981. Enzymatic synthesis of biotin-labelled polynucleotides: novel nucleic acid affinity probes. *Proceedings of the National Academy of Sciences*, **78**, 6633–6637.

Makinodan, T. & Kay, M. M. B. 1980. Age influence on the immune system. *Advances in Immunology*, **29**, 287–330.

Marston, J. H., Penn, R. & Sivelle, P. C. 1977. Successful autotransfer of tubal eggs in the rhesus monkey (*Macaca mulatta*). *Journal of Reproduction and Fertility*, **49**, 175–176.

Metcalf, D. & Moore, M. A. 1971. *Haemopoietic Cells*. North-Holland, Amsterdam.

Moore, K. L. 1977. *The Developing Human*. Saunders, Philadelphia.

Moore, M. A. S. & Metcalfe, D. 1970. Ontogeny of the haemopoietic system: yolk sac origin of in vivo and in vitro colony-forming cells in the developing mouse embryo. *British Journal of Haematology*, **18**, 279.

Naor, D. 1980. Unresponsiveness to modified self antigens — a censorship mechanism controlling autoimmunity? *Immunological Reviews*, **30**, 187–226.

New, D. A. T. 1978. Whole-embryo culture and the study of mammalian embryos during organogenesis. *Biological Reviews*, **53**, 81–122.

Niikawa, N., Merotto. E. & Kajii, T. 1977. Origin of acrocentric trisomies in spontaneous abortuses. *Human Genetics*, **40**, 73–78.

O'Rahilly, R. 1973. *Developmental Stages in Human Embryos*. Carnegie Institute, Washington.

Polani, P. E. 1981. Abnormal sex development in man. 1. Anomalies of sex-determining mechanisms. In *Mechanisms of Sex Differentiation in Animals and Man*. Ed. C. R. Austin & R. G. Edwards. Academic Press, London and New York.

Ruoslahti, E. & Seppälä, M. 1979. α-foetoprotein in cancer and fetal development. *Advances in Cancer Research*, **29**, 275–346.

Sawicki, J., Magnuson, T. & Epstein, C. J. 1981. Evidence of expression of the paternal genome in the two-cell mouse embryo. *Nature*, **294**, 450.

Steptoe, P. C., Edwards, R. G. & Purdy, J. M. 1971. Human blastocysts grown in culture. *Nature*, **229**, 132–133.

Stoker, M. 1981. The manipulation of cell growth. Annual Meeting, British Association for the Advancement of Science, York.

Sutherland, D. E. R. 1980. International human pancreas and islet transplant registry. Transplantation Proceedings, **12**, No. 4, Supplement 2, 229–236.

Takagi, N. & Sasaki, M. 1976. Digynic triploidy after superovulation in mice. *Nature*, **264**, 278–287.

Testart, J. & Renard, J.-P. 1982. Animal studies in embryo transfer and storage. In *Human Conception in Vitro*. Ed. R. G. Edwards & J. M. Purdy. Academic Press, London and New York. (This volume.)

Till, J. E. & McCulloch, E. A. 1961. A direct measurement of radiation sensitivity of normal bone marrow cells. *Radiation Research*, **14**, 213.

Toivanen, P., Uksila, J., Leino, A., Lassila, O., Hirvonen, T. & Ruuskanen, O. 1981. Development of mitogen responding T cells and natural killer cells in the human fetus. *Immunological Reviews*, **57**, 89–105.

Torpin, R. 1969. *The Human Placenta, Its Shape, Form, Origin and Development*. C. C. Thomas, Springfield.

Trounson, A. O. 1982. Comment in Discussion on the Growth of Human Embryos in Vitro. In: *Human Conception in Vitro*. Ed. R. G. Edwards & J. M. Purdy. Academic Press, London and New York. (This volume)

Tsuji, K. & Nakano, R. 1978. Chromosome studies of embryos from induced abortions in pregnant women aged 35 and over. *Obstetrics and Gynecology*, **52**, 524–544.

Uriel, J. 1979. Retrodifferentiation and the fetal patterns of gene expression in cancer. *Advances in Cancer Research*, **29**, 127–174.

Williamson, R., Eskdale, J., Coleman, D. V., Niazi, M., Loeffler, F. E. & Modell, B. M. 1981. Direct gene analysis of chorionic villi: a possible technique for first-trimester antenatal diagnosis of haemoglobinopathies. *Lancet*, **ii**, 1125–1127.

Wilson, J. G. 1977. Current status of teratology. General principles and mechanisms derived from animal studies. In *Handbook of Teratology*, Vol. 1, p. 47. Ed. J. G. Wilson and F. C. Fraser. Plenum Press, New York.

Wu, T-C., Wan, Y-J., & Damjanov, I. 1981. Rat serum promotes the in-vitro development of mouse blastocysts during early somite stages of embryogenesis. *Journal of Experimental Zoology*, **217**, 451–453.

Zanjani, E. D., Lim, G., McGlave, P. B., Clapp, J. F., Mann, L. I., Norwood, T. H. & Stamatoyannapoulos, G. 1982. *Nature*, **295**, 244–246.

Appendix

GROUP REPORTS ON
METHODS AND RESULTS

I. Patient Selection and Monitoring

Methods of Each Group

The methods used by each group are given in Table IA. These details are amplified in the following discussion.

Detailed Reports

Basel (Conti): Our programme has hardly begun. We have merely monitored some cycles to gain experience of the necessary methods. Most of our patients are undergoing laparoscopy for other purposes, and they are willing to be included for our monitoring studies.

In the natural cycle, we carry out an ultrasonic examination only between days 7 and 8. We continue examining the ovary with ultrasound until the moment of ovulation and we place an intravenous cannula in our patient on day 11, in order to reduce the distress of repeated blood collection. We usually collect samples of blood every 4–6 hours for estimating LH, although in some patients this is done more frequently.

Most of our patients discharge their LH during the night-time, mostly between 1 a.m. and 5 a.m. We have made very careful ultrasonic measurements during these cycles to find out when the follicle was ruptured. We have never found a patient who had ovulated 30 hours after the rise of the LH in plasma, and there was no correlation between the diameter of a follicle and the moment of spontaneous ovulation. Some large follicles showed a spontaneous ovulation some 14–15 hours after the LH rise, and others never ovulate. Most follicles seem to ovulate by 38 hours, although it is difficult to continue examining them for long periods.

We have examined some of our patients given clomiphene and HCG, and by 36–38 hours it appears that about 10% of follicles are beginning to ovulate spontaneously. The last ovulation we have witnessed is 44 hours after the injection of HCG; the majority were ovulated by 40 hours.

Table IA
Patient selection and monitoring

		Basel	Bourn Hall	Gothenburg	Kiel
Patients	Volunteers	Irregular cycle	Tubal (90%) Idiopathic Oligospermia (10%)	Various	Tubal & idiopathic
Cycle	Natural	Clomiphene, HCG	Natural	Clomiphene, HCG	Clomiphene, HCG
Clomiphene treatment	—	—	Clomiphene, HCG or LH surge 50–100 mg day 2 for 5 days	100 mg, day 2 or 3 for 5 days	100 mg, days 5–9
Gonadotrophin treatment	—	—	—	—	—
Monitoring					
Ultrasound	Day 7–8 and after		Difficult cases	From 8 mm continuously	Yes
Oestrogens			Urinary, 24 hr	—	Plasma E_2
LH			Urinary, every 3 hr	—	—
Mucus, smear			—		
Decision to give HCG			Clomid only, urinary, E $>100\ \mu g\ day^{-1}$	Follicles 2.0–2.3 cm	Follicles 1.8–2.0 cm
Dose of HCG			5,000	4,500	10,000
Natural LH surge used	Natural cycles		Urinary	No	No
Laparoscopy					
Hr after HCG			32–34	34–36	
Hr after LH surge			26		

Table IA (continued)

	Melbourne—Monash	Melbourne—Royal Women's Hospital	Norfolk	Paris—Clamart	Paris—Sèvres	Vienna
Patients	Tubal & idiopathic	Tubal (60%) Others (40%)	Tubal	Tubal (66%) Idiopathic (34%)	Tubal (80%) Idiopathic (20%)	Tubal & idiopathic
Cycle	Clomiphene, HCG. Some patients also given HMG	Clomiphene, HCG	HMG, HCG	Natural, clomiphene, HMG, HCG	Natural, clomiphene, HMG, HCG	Clomiphene, HCG
Clomiphene treatment	150 mg days 5–9	100 mg days 5–9	—	150 mg days 5–9	150 mg days 5–9	100 mg days 5–9
Gonadotrophin treatment	300 IU, days 6, 8 & 10	—	2 amps days 3–5 then 1 amp daily if needed	3 amps, days 5–8	3 amps days 5–8	—
Monitoring Ultrasound	Day 9 only	Day 11 and alternate days	From day 7	Days 9–11	Days 8–10	Yes
Oestrogens	Plasma E$_2$	Urinary, 24 hr	Plasma E$_2$	Plasma E$_2$	Plasma E$_2$	—
LH	Day 9, plasma, LH every 3 hr	Plasma LH when HCG given	Plasma LH when HCG given	Plasma LH, 4 times daily	Plasma LH, every 6 hr	Urinary, 4 hr
Mucus, smear	Day 9 onwards	—	From day 7	—	—	—
Decision to give HCG	400 pg E$_2$ per follicle. Also if E$_2$ declining	Follicles 2.0 cm	Follicles 1.7 cm 12 hr earlier, E$_2$ > 250 pg ml^{-1}	Follicles >1.8 cm, E$_2$ > 300 pg per follicle	Follicles 1.8–2.0 cm, E$_2$ > 300 pg ml^{-1}	Follicles 1.8–2.0 cm
Dose of HCG	4,000	5,000	10,000		10,000	5,000
Natural LH surge used	Emergency	Emergency	Emergency	Plasma		Emergency
Laparoscopy Hr after HCG	36	36	36	34	34	36
Hr after LH surge	26			34 (after LH S.I.R.)*	34 (after LH S.I.R.)*	28

*See paper by Jean Cohen et al. (p. 3).

Bourn Hall (Webster): About 90% of patients have occluded tubes or have had both tubes removed because of ectopic pregnancies or pelvic infection. Many have been operated on more than once, to restore tubal function, and multiple abdominal scars may be present but these do not necessarily preclude treatment. The remaining 10% have damaged but patent tubes or apparently healthy tubes and idiopathic infertility of several years duration. Other patients are offered in-vitro fertilization because of oligospermic husbands or cervical mucus hostility.

Patients over the age of 40 are not usually accepted. We try to ensure that each patient is ovulating regularly, using basal temperature charts, endometrial biopsies, serum progesterones and prolactin levels. Serum FSH and LH levels may also be measured. Ideally, both ovaries should be accessible at laparoscopy. All patients should have a normal, healthy uterus and should be free from any disease which would be a contraindication to pregnancy.

We plan to admit patients 2–3 days prior to ovulation, as determined from recent temperature charts. Most patients are in their natural cycle, some are on Clomid. On admission the patient is instructed in collecting three-hourly specimens of urine during the day and four-hourly specimens at night. These specimens are assayed for LH using the Hi-Gonavis test. Daily 24-hour total urinary oestrogens are also determined. If we fear there are adhesions or other problems, we give 50 mg Clomid daily for 5 days. In the absence of a natural LH surge patients on Clomid are given 5,000 IU HCG IM whenever their daily oestrogen output rises well above 100 mg, and laparoscopy is performed 32 hours later. In all patients with a natural LH surge we plan oocyte recovery 26 hours after the start of the natural surge. The patients on Clomid are given 5,000 IU HCG IM whenever their daily oestrogen output rises well above 100 mg, and laparoscopy is routinely followed follicular development using ultrasound.

The husband must wash thoroughly to prevent contamination. All samples of semen are tested for infection 4–6 weeks prior to admitting patients. This helps but may not always prevent infected semen from entering the culture laboratory.

Edwards: We miss the LH surge during the natural cycle in very few patients, perhaps as low as 2–3%. In some patients the LH surge has begun when the patient enters the clinic. This occurs in approximately 3% of patients (see paper by Edwards *et al.* on the use of Hi-Gonavis in this symposium). We are satisfied with our methods of assaying oestrogens and urinary LH by Hi-Gonavis, which provide a very close monitoring system in all our patients. We do not use ultrasound routinely; I am dubious about using ultrasound on a preovulatory follicle when the oocyte is in meiosis and the chromosomes are segregating, in case chromosomal segregation is disturbed.

In patients given clomiphene, we monitor the cycle by the same methods. If the natural LH surge has not begun when oestrogens reach well above 100 μg 24 hr^{-1}, we give 5,000 IU HCG to induce ovulation. Urine samples for LH assays are continued until the HCG is given; the time of the operation can be adjusted retrospectively if the LH surge begins before HCG was administered.

We are taking increasing numbers of couples with infertility due to oligospermia, antibodies against spermatozoa, hostile cervical mucus, etc.

We have pregnancies from patients with severe oligospermia. Fertilization *in vitro* is successful even when the total sperm count is very low: as low as 2×10^6 in one man. We are on guard if patients have viscous seminal plasma, sperm agglutination due to antibodies, considerable cellular debris in the semen, and erratic movement of spermatozoa (Fishel & Edwards, this symposium).

Gothenburg (Hamberger): We use HMG or clomiphene in various doses, and have now settled on our treatment. We examine the follicles by ultrasound, and monitor their growth continuously (2–4 times daily). We inject HCG in the evening in order to induce ovulation and carry out oocyte recovery 24–34 hours later, collecting 2–3 oocytes per patient. We do not like to overstimulate because we fear that many corpora lutea will then be formed, and this may damage the ovary. Evidence from our earlier work has suggested that we have induced precocious menopause by overstimulating the ovary.

We used various doses of HCG, between 3,000 and 9,000 IU, and we now use 4,500. We fear 9,000 is too much and believe that 3,000 IU is too little. We also fear that some of our patients may have an LH peak before we give HCG and, under these circumstances, we would prefer to wait until the next cycle before treating the patient. At present, we cannot monitor hormone levels in our patients too closely, because we do not have the facilities.

We believe the optimum follicular diameter in patients given clomiphene and HCG, or monitored during the natural cycle should be between 2.0 and 2.3 cm, and this is the time when we inject HCG. Follicular diameters are approximately the same after gonadotrophin treatment and in the natural cycle. We have no difficulty in finding out if a follicle has collapsed by using ultrasound. So far, we fertilize approximately 50% of the oocytes and have carried out one transfer without success, but we intend to develop our programme this Autumn.

Kiel (Mettler): In 1978 and 1979, we studied a total of 114 patients given HMG and HCG. The cleavage rate of oocytes collected from these patients was about 39%. We then turned to the natural cycle, where we studied about 30 patients. Many of these patients were undergoing adhesolysis or other forms of treatment to repair the ovary or the oviduct. In some of these cases, it was not possible to find the ovary and puncture a follicle, and the results must be judged on this basis.

We assay urinary and plasma oestrogens during the natural cycle, and measure follicular diameter. We use a rapid method of LH assay in urine or plasma. We also assess the viscosity of cervical mucus, and the cervical score as a guide to estimate the timing of follicular puncture. During the natural cycle, the oocyte was found in approximately 61% of the patients examined, and the cleavage rate was 41%.

We now use clomiphene stimulation and HCG as shown in Table IA. We ask our patients for temperature records for three cycles before administering clomiphene and admitting them. We have been using ultrasound and assays of LH, and have now incorporated plasma oestradiol-17β into our monitoring system. When follicles reach 2 cm in diameter, and oestradiol-17β reaches a plateau, we give 10,000 IU HCG to induce ovulation, and try to set the time of follicular puncture for 36–37 hours later, during the afternoon. This is necessary to fit in with the programme of our clinic. The recovery rate of oocytes is now about 90%, which is very satisfactory. The cleavage rate is approximately 41% of all oocytes aspirated.

Melbourne — Monash (Leeton): We now use only the stimulated cycles, having abandoned the natural cycle. We observe a standard protocol for all patients as far as possible, and this is shown in Table IA. We admit patients to hospital when oestrogen levels rise to 400 pg ml^{-1} or when ultrasound shows a follicle of 1.8 cm or more in diameter. This is when we begin assaying urine for LH in 3-hourly collections. Patients are discharged for several reasons: if their levels of oestradiol-17β remain low, when they have a rising progesterone which indicates ovulation, if they have one follicle which is greater than 3 cm in diameter and which we fear may be atretic, and when the follicle is growing in the inappropriate ovary, i.e. in an ovary obscured by adhesions. HCG is given when the average output per follicle is 400 pg of oestradiol-17β; if levels are falling, we will often give the HCG in an attempt to induce ovulation. This treatment has worked in some cases.

I would stress that we discharge patients if they have a single large follicle of 3 cm in diameter. If several other medium sized follicles are associated with such a follicle, then we carry on with the preparations for oocyte recovery.

Melbourne — Royal Women's Hospital (Lopata): We now use clomiphene and HCG cycles entirely. We have recently changed our protocol. Until recently, we measured follicular size by sonar, and a diameter of 1.7 cm was the criterion to admit the patient. A sample of blood was taken for plasma LH and we then gave the patient 5,000 IU HCG. If plasma LH was elevated, the patient was sent home.

We time the injection of HCG at a convenient time of day to perform the laparoscopy for oocyte recovery 36 hours later, usually between 11 a.m. and 2 p.m. Our new criterion for administration of HCG is the size of the largest follicle amongst the cohort of follicles. Its average size on sonar must be 2.0 cm before HCG is given. The remainder of the treatment is the same as before.

Testart: What happens when there are different sized follicles in the ovary? If there is one follicle, say of 1.6 cm, would this be the follicle that would grow and ovulate? Do you wait for the others to catch up?

Johnston: We find that, although we work on the dominant follicle, at the time of laparoscopy we may have three or four follicles. Sometimes during the follicular phase, a small follicle can be much smaller in size than the dominant follicle, yet, by the time the laparoscopy is performed, it may have grown and overtaken the larger follicle.

Norfolk (Jones, G): We have recently changed our methods and now work with stimulated cycles. Pergonal is given to stimulate follicular growth and HCG to invoke ovulation. Details are given in Table IA. The response is monitored in several ways. We use the patients' own bioassay, by means of a maturation index of 30% of cornified cells in the vagina, an open external os, tests on mucus including an amount greater than 0.2 ml, spinnbarkeit of greater than 10 cm, and ferning of 4 + . Measurements are made of plasma oestradiol-17β, which should reach 250 pg ml^{-1} at least before the HCG is given, and over 670 pg ml^{-1} is considered to be excessive. When these requirements are satisfied, the HMG is stopped and HCG is given 60 hours later, usually in the evening. The HCG may be delayed if the oestradiol-17β remains below 80 pg ml^{-1}. Ultrasound is also used, and we like to see a follicle of 1.7 cm or more 12 hours before HCG is given, although we have been successful with 1.4 cm. More Pergonal may be given if the follicles are too small. Plasma LH levels are recorded before the HCG is given, to ensure that the endogenous LH surge has not begun.

We were using the natural cycle, but found it difficult to fit in with our regime, and had no pregnancies. It is also expensive to do repeated LH assays in plasma every 3 hours, and so we abandoned the method and used HMG-stimulated cycles. In my clinical experience with anovulatory patients, the pregnancy rate was better and there was a lower rate of miscarriage than with the use of Clomid.

Paris — Clamart (Frydman): We are testing several different methods. In some of our patients, we monitor the natural cycle; others are given clomiphene and HCG, and a third group HMG and HCG. We use a combination of plasma oestradiol-17β and LH assays, together with ultrasound to detect the growth of follicles. During stimulated cycles, we prefer to see levels of oestradiol-17β in plasma rise to more than 300 pg ml^{-1} per follicle. During stimulated cycles, HCG is given only when follicle size is 1.8–2.0 cm, whether stimulation is by HMG or clomiphene. We are using similar methods to those described by Trounson. We tend to use natural cycles in patients with tubal occlusion, and stimulated cycles in those with idiopathic infertility.

Paris — Sèvres (Cohen): For stimulated cycles, we use clomiphene, clomiphene plus HMG, or HMG alone. We have decided to abandon clomiphene alone, and use it with HCG. We could not understand what happened using clomiphene by itself. We would not find the right time when to give HCG and had very poor results from the fluctuating levels of hormones; this may have been due to the administration of HCG at the wrong time. We measure oestradiol-17β at 5 p.m. and give 10,000 IU HCG between 44 and 48 hours after reaching values of 800–1,000 pg. We then give no more HMG, which is usually omitted the day after the oestradiol result is found, and is usually 48 hours after the last injection of HMG.

Edwards: The gap in the assay of hormones in plasma by Frydman is actually nine hours on one occasion, between 11 p.m. and 8 a.m. This is probably the most important time for the discharge of LH to begin, most patients discharging at about 3 o'clock in the morning. Data is missing at the most important part of the cycle, the point when information is really needed. This is why we have turned to urine, because we can easily rouse a patient from bed at 03.00 a.m. for this purpose and have the result by 10.00 a.m. but it is more difficult to take a sample of blood from them and have the immunoassay result so quickly. An 8-hour gap is, in any case, far too wide to predict the beginning of the LH surge with any accuracy.

Frydman: We make an extrapolation to determine the beginning of the LH surge. From this, we know that the average beginning of the

Table IB
Vienna: indications for laparoscopic oocyte recovery and in-vitro fertilization

	No.
Periampullar adhesions	13
Bilateral hydrosalpinx	13
Cornual block on one side, hydrosalpinx on the other side	3
Hydrosalpinx on one side, organized periampular adhesions on the other side	1
Missing tube on one side, hydrosalpinx on the other side	5
Bilateral tubectomy	3
Clip-sterilization	1
Idiopathic sterility	11

LH surge is about 3 a.m. Most of our cases are therefore judged by the extrapolation of the shape of the curve, and steepness of the rise. Sometimes we have taken supplementary samples at 3 a.m. without benefit, since we found the same time for the beginning of the surge.

Vienna (Szalay): We have been working on two groups of patients in our programme on in-vitro fertilization. The majority suffer from obstruction of the Fallopian tubes; many others are now being introduced with idiopathic infertility (Table IB). The specific conditions for patient instruction are as follows: The couple must be married. The wife must be under 40 years of age. Spermatozoa of reasonable quality must be available from the husband, and the woman must have an ovulatory cycle. The man must have a normal spermiogram, and low bacteriology. We have found some cases where the husband has oligospermia despite these precautions, and the fertilization generally failed. We plan to extend this part of our programme. We have taken steps to exclude patients with sperm antibodies.

Initially we began using natural cycles, using Hi-Gonavis to assay LH. We made estimates of increasing LH between two sequential estimations, and we carried out laparoscopy approximately 22–26 hours after the mid-point of the interval to the first rising level of LH. We could estimate correctly the time of ovulation in 92% of our patients. We had problems with adapting to the natural cycle in our busy clinic, and we found that repeated estimations of LH were not possible. Moreover, we could not get an operating theatre just as and when we needed it.

We have accordingly changed to the use of clomiphene and HCG (see Table IA). We give HCG at a time determined by the individual's ovulatory history, based on the expected time of ovulation during her previous cycles.

We use ultrasound to measure the follicle but we do not use cervical mucus spinnbarkeit because of the antioestrogenic effects of clomiphene. Two patients were given HMG and HCG to induce follicular growth and ovulation, and in each of them a single embryo was replaced but without a pregnancy.

Our recovery rates of oocytes are increasing regularly. They are now as high as 80% of follicles from our patients, and on some occasions have reached as high as 90%.

II. Follicular Aspiration

Methods of Each Group

Details of the methods used by each group are given in Table II.

Detailed Reports

Bourn Hall (Steptoe): We have described our techniques in our earlier paper in this book. I would like to mention that in a difficult ovary, where the ovary is two-thirds or three-quarters covered, it is necessary to approach the follicle with a needle at a right angle. It is only by experience that the place to insert the needle is identified, and also how the trochar and the cannula should be passed through the body wall. We like to use a cannula to pass the needle through the body wall in order to avoid fat or other tissues from clogging its end.

We choose an avascular area of the abdominal wall, using transillumination, and we use Palmer forceps to hold or twist the ovary. We do not have to reinsert the trochar and cannula to replace the aspirating needle when we move to the opposite ovary. We may use a secondary ancillary instrument on the opposite side to push the bowel out of the way, to lift an adhesion, and to help choose the best side to insert the needle into the follicle.

We usually flush the aspirating needle with heparin solution before entering the follicle, and ideally use only a small amount of flushing medium if the aspiration is easy. If the case is difficult, we may have to flush many times. Under these circumstances, blood may be aspirated from the follicle, and we have a method for adding heparin to the collecting chamber to prevent clotting in it. The worst thing that can happen is to trap the oocyte in a blood clot, or in a clot forming within the needle. We have to take the needle out if a clot forms in it, and wash it out with heparin saline. If necessary, we have another needle ready which can be inserted quickly to carry on the suction.

We have a large dial facing the laparoscopist to indicate the suction

401

Table II
Follicular aspiration

	Bourn Hall	Gothenberg	Kiel	Melbourne — Monash
Needle	Double	Single	Double	Single
Material	Stainless steel	Stainless steel, siliconized	—	Stainless steel, Teflon lined
External diameter (mm)	—	1.2–1.6	—	1.4
Internal diameter (mm)	{ 1.4–1.6 (aspirating) / 0.7 (flushing)	0.9–1.4	{ 1.6 (aspirating) / 0.2 (flushing)	0.9
Length (cm)	18	25	28	19
Washing medium	2 IU ml^{-1} heparin in culture medium, 0.1 gm% bicarbonate	—	Culture medium	Heparin in culture medium
Suction control	Finger	Finger	Finger	Foot
Pressure (mmHg)	Up to 100	90 to 100	20 to 80	—

Table II (continued)

	Melbourne—Royal Women's Hospital	Norfolk	Paris—Clamart	Paris—Sèvres	Vienna
Needle					
Material	Single Stainless steel	Single Stainless steel	Single Stainless steel	Single Stainless steel	Single mostly Stainless steel
External diameter (mm)	—	—	1.5	1.8	—
Internal diameter (mm)	1.4	2.25	1.3	—	1.4
Length (cm)	23	43	22	25	—
Washing medium	1 IU ml^{-1} heparin in culture medium	Culture medium	Culture medium	Heparin in culture medium	Heparin in culture medium
Suction control	Foot	Hand Syringe	Hand Syringe	Hand Syringe	Hand
Pressure (mmHg)	100	—	—	—	100–120

pressure. This enables him to see exactly what the pressure is at any particular moment. This piece of apparatus has been especially designed for our team, and it enables a delicate control of the suction pressure to be maintained.

Gothenburg (Hamberger): We use similar methods to these described by other workers, but some additions include the ability to reverse the flow of medium in the aspirator, so that the needle can be cleared by pumping it back into the follicle. We suspend the oocyte in 2 ml of culture fluid, maintaining it at 37 °C, and work in darkness. We avoid exposing oocytes to any unnecessary light whatsoever. All our microscopical work is carried out in a temperature-controlled room. Our recovery rates are: 78% of follicles yield an oocyte, and we obtain at least one oocyte from 96% of our patients.

Kiel (Mettler): Our methods are similar to other groups. We aspirate the follicle into a tube containing a small amount of culture medium. The tube is maintained at 37 °C under sterile conditions. In cycles stimulated by HMG and HCG, we recovered 88 oocytes from 43 patients, a success rate of 44% of follicles. In spontaneous cycles and in cycles stimulated by clomiphene and HCG the success rate was 61% of follicles in a total of 30 patients.

Melbourne — Monash (Leeton): We have now improved our oocyte collection up to 90%. We have improved methods for carrying out a laparotomy on difficult patients, or by not doing them at all, excluding patients in whom ovulation has occurred, and using a special aspiration needle and good surgical technique. We actually assessed three needles, including a large one. The large needle had an internal diameter of 2.3 mm, and our collection rate even after repeated aspirations was only 34%.

We selected a narrow needle of 1.4 mm because the oocyte external diameter of the cumulus mass is 0.5 mm. The narrow needle gives a minimum space coefficient of friction in continuous flow. The needle is lined with teflon, the level of the needle is at 45 °C, and the point is checked on each occasion for sharpness and lack of burrs. For collection, we use culture tubes with silicon rubber bungs.

We collect oocytes only from follicles larger than about 1.7 cm in diameter. Early last year, when our systems were not optimal, and before we introduced oestrogen as a criterion to inject HCG, fertilization rates were lower than 30% with eggs taken from follicles with less than 4 ml of follicular fluid. Above 5 ml, the rate was 70%. Now, after the introduction of oestrogen assays, and aspirating only large follicles, our figures have improved.

Jones, H: Coupling the 2.3 mm needle on to a needle of 1.8 mm internal diameter, as you described for the larger needle, would vitiate any comparisons made according to the diameter of the aspirating needle itself. The movement from the large needle into a small needle means that the system was not being tested to full advantage. Estimates of recovery can only be based on the smallest diameter in the system, i.e. 1.8 mm. Data from the large needle should therefore be reconsidered quite separate from the others.

Trounson: It also had a dead space of 4 ml compared with the one we finally used. This deficiency should not be present in such an instrument.

Leeton: As we reduced the size of the needle, our recovery rate of oocytes increased. The inclusion of a teflon lining gives a 100% collection rate, but in some cases requires five aspirations.

Melbourne — Royal Women's Hospital (Johnston): We commence aspiration as the oocyte enters the follicle, because the operator can regulate pressure by means of a foot pump. We hand the clear follicular fluid to the laboratory, and wait to find out if the oocyte is recovered before proceeding further. Approximately 90% of our oocytes are collected in the first aspirate. If the oocyte is not recovered, we replace the single needle with a double-channelled needle, and flush the follicle with fertilization medium containing Hepes buffer in place of bicarbonate and heparin at a concentration of 1 IU ml^{-1}.

We obtain at least one preovulatory egg in 89% of our laparoscopies. We have too many junctions and dead space in our system and we are proposing changing it. We warm the collecting tube by surrounding it with bags containing warm distilled water, and the whole apparatus is clipped on to the drapes.

Spiers: The needle for the primary extract is sharpened, but for flushing, we use a double needle with a blunter end.

Webster: It must be very difficult changing needles once you have entered the follicle. Do you not get leakage or bleeding, which might interfere with the collection of the oocyte?

Johnston: It does not cause much difficulty. It is a problem when adhesions or other problems limit access to the ovary, because the follicle cannot be seen and it is difficult to know where to place the needle. We seem to be washing less and less as time goes on, and collecting the oocyte more and more quickly. Provided we can see some fraction of the ovary, we will make an attempt at oocyte recovery.

Norfolk (Jones, H): We use a laparoscope with an operating channel. We believe the needle should not be too sharp, so that it does not shave the oocyte as it is withdrawn from the follicle, although this makes penetration more difficult.

We support the ovary by the use of a second instrument. There should be no decrease in the diameter of the lumen of the needle and the aspirating tube at any point. A small band is placed 5 mm from the distal end of the needle, to indicate how deep we are into the ovary. A small hub is also placed on the needle to indicate which way the bevel is turned when it is out of sight in the follicle. In a series of 18 cycles, with 18 dominant follicles, we recovered the oocytes from seventeen of them. We almost always obtain the oocyte in the initial aspirate. In patients treated with HMG and HCG, 19 patients were examined, and at least one preovulatory oocyte was aspirated from each of them; of the 45 follicles aspirated, we obtained 32 preovulatory oocytes.

Steptoe: The flange on the needle described by Jones could present problems when it is difficult to locate the follicle deep in the ovary. Aspiration sometimes has to be done ''blind'', and sometimes quite deep, and a follicle might lie on the inferior surface of the ovary which cannot be manipulated.

Jones, G: We have a selection of needles available. Under those circumstances we use a slightly different needle for the aspiration. I have found the flange very helpful because when penetrating a follicle, it is possible to go too far and strike the opposite wall and so cause bleeding. The flange passes easily through the operating channel of the laparoscope, or we can use a third puncture wound, if necessary.

Paris — Sèvres (Cohen): We have modified our extractor from the mucus extractor used on newborn babies. We have so far used a syringe for aspirating oocytes, but are now changing this to use a controlled pressure for aspirating. When the oocyte is collected, it is placed in a thermos bottle and sent five kilometres to a laboratory for fertilization. Nevertheless, we do not notice any interference with the quality of fertilization. Our recovery rate at the moment is just about 50% of follicles but we hope to improve this in the near future.

Paris — Clamart (Frydman): We attach the syringe directly to the needle used for aspiration. We recovered approximately 60% of the oocytes per follicle during the natural cycle, and 80% in patients given clomiphene.

Vienna (Szalay): We use a general anaesthesia without any pre-medication. We insufflate with CO_2 and then change to a gas mixture used for oocyte culture, i.e. 5% O_2, 5% CO_2, and 90% N_2. With our single-bore needle, recovery rates are high, usually 80% of the follicles aspirated. We collect the oocyte into a specially-designed glass tube, which is round with a flat bottom, and this can be placed directly under the microscope. A double-bore needle has proved disadvantageous because it is too thick for penetrating the follicle early. Needles with diameters of 0.9 mm or 1.4 mm are more satisfactory than those with a diameter of 2 mm and no differences in oocyte collection were detected between the two smaller diameters. Our needle is inserted directly, with a trocar in it, so it can be passed through the abdomen without any contamination with fat or other tissues.

We first used the method of Edwards, Steptoe and Purdy using natural cycles, timing the laparoscopy 26–32 hours after the onset of the LH peak. The LH peak was determined by the Hi-Gonavis test (Mochida, Tokyo).

Of 67 laparoscopies, 45 were timed correctly, four were performed too early, and ten too late. Adhesions prevented the identification of the ovaries in eight patients. There were 48 follicles, and 27 mature oocytes were aspirated. During this work, the recovery rate of oocytes improved from 28% to 70%.

Recently, patients have been given 100 mg clomiphene citrate from day 5 to 9. Follicular growth was monitored by ultrasonics and 5,000 IU HCG given to induce ovulation. Laparoscopy was performed 36 hours later. There was an improvement in recovery rate to 80%, and in the 50 patients a total of 77 follicles yielded 62 oocytes. In 41 patients (82%) a sufficient or very good stimulatory effect was evident.

Edwards: I do not like the collecting bottle with its long arm. It can be easily carried from the theatre, but why do you have to examine the contents in the collecting pot itself? It must create difficulties in picking up the oocyte once it is identified. Manipulating pipettes down the long arm of the tube cannot be easy.

Feichtinger: Most of them can be seen macroscopically and picked up by pipette very easily. The volume of the container is 10 ml, so a great deal of fluid can be contained within it, although we do not like to fill it up completely.

Edwards: When working under the microscope, I like to have a dish which can be handled quickly and easily, decanted if necessary, have very rapid access to its contents, and be placed down without any problem. Then I am free to handle the oocyte, or the next collecting vessel. Placing down the particular bottle you describe would cause difficulties for me, because it would have to be done so carefully to ensure it did not tip over. There could also be time wasted ensuring the bung was in place. Our containers are not sealed because they are brought from the theatre and decanted into a Petri dish within one or two seconds. Any sort of seal, bungs or others are suspect because even though they are sterile, there is danger in the liquid touching the lid of the vessel and so introducing contaminants into the culture medium.

III. Fertilization and Embryonic Growth

Methods of Each Group

The methods used for fertilization and embryonic growth *in vitro* are presented in Table III.

Table III

Group methods on fertilization and embryonic growth *in vitro*

	Bourn Hall	Gothenberg	Kiel	Melbourne— Monash	Melbourne— Royal Women's Hospital
			Fertilization		
Medium					
Type	Earle's	Tyrode's	F10	F10, Earle's, T6, Hoppe/Pitts	F10 + Ca lactate
Conditions in medium	pH 7.3, 285 mOsmol Kg^{-1}	pH 7.4, 285 mOsmol Kg^{-1}			pH 7.35, 280 mOsmol Kg^{-1}
Macromolecule	Patient's serum (8%)	Patient's serum (15%)	Serum (15%)	Serum (7.5%)	Serum (10%)
Spermatozoa					
Time obtained	Before laparoscopy	Before laparoscopy	3 hr before insemination	2 hr before insemination	2 hr before insemination
Wash	Culture medium	Culture medium			2 washes in culture medium
Treatment of oocyte before insemination	Incubated 1–12 hr	Incubated 2–6 hr	Incubated 5–6 hr	Incubated 5–6 hr	Incubated 4–6 hr
Conditions of culture					
Incubation	Paraffin/tube	Paraffin/tube	Tube	Tube	Tube
Gas phase	5:5:90	5:5:90	5:5:90	5:5:90, 5:10:95 or 5:95	5:5:90
No. sperm/ml	1–2 × 10^5 living	5 × 10^5 total	2–5 × 10^5		2–5 × 10^5
			Cleavage		
Time of transfer to growth medium	12–24 hr	20 hr	15–20 hr	16 hr	18 hr
Medium					
Type	Earle's	F10	F10	As above	F10 + Ca lactate
Conditions in medium	As above		As above		As above
Macromolecule	Patient's serum (15%)	Serum (15%)	Serum (15%)	Serum (15%)	Serum (15%)
Conditions of culture					
Incubation	Tube usually		Tube	Tube	Tube
Gas phase	5:5:90	5:5:90	5:5:90	As above	5:5:90
Observed development	Cleavage usually	Cleavage	Cleavage	Cleavage usually	Pronuclei and cleavage
Stage when embryo replaced	4 cell-blastocyst	2–8 cell		2–8 cell	4–8 cell

	Norfolk	Oldham Kershaws	Paris—Clamart	Paris—Sèvres	Vienna
			Fertilization			
Medium					
Type	F10	Tyrode's, Earle's	B2	B2	F10 + lactate + K$^+$
Conditions in medium		pH 7.3, 285 mOsmol Kg^{-1}	pH 7.5, 265–280 mOsmol Kg^{-1}	pH 7.4, 280 mOsmol Kg^{-1}	pH 7.4–7.5, 276 mOsmol Kg^{-1}
Macromolecule	Albumin	Patient's serum (8%)	Albumin	Human serum albumin	Albumin
Spermatozoa					
Time obtained	2 hr before insemination	Before laparoscopy	Before laparoscopy	Before laparoscopy	Before laparoscopy
Wash		Culture medium	Culture medium	Culture medium	Culture medium
Treatment of oocyte before insemination	Incubated 5–6 hr	Incubated 0–15 hr	Not pre-incubated	Incubated 1–2 hr	Incubated 2–4 hr
Conditions of culture					
Incubation		Paraffin/tube	Tube	Tube	Tube
Gas phase	5:95	5:5:90	5:5:90	5:5:90	5:5:90
No. sperm/ml		10^6 total	2–10 × 10^5 living	5 × 10^5	10^6
			Cleavage			
Time of transfer to growth medium	6–8 hr	12–24 hr	6–23 hr	12–24 hr	12–16 hr
Medium					
Type	F10	Earle's, F10	B2	B2	As above
Conditions in medium		As above	As above	As above	As above
Macromolecule		Patient's serum (15%)	Albumin or serum (15%)	Patient's serum (15%)	Patient's serum (15%)
Conditions of culture					
Incubation		Tube/paraffin	Tube	Tube	Tube
Gas phase		5:5:90	5:5:90	5:5:90	5:5:90
Observed development	Cleavage	Pronuclei and cleavage	Cleavage	Cleavage	Pronuclei and cleavage
			Stage when embryo replaced			
	4 cell	8 cell-blastocyst	4–10 cell	6–12 cell	2–16 cell

IV. Embryo Replacement and Fetal Growth

Methods of Each Group

The results obtained by each group are given in Table IV. Some groups have included data gained during preliminary work, e.g. Kiel and Paris (Sèvres), hence the number of replacements is considerably less than the numbers of laparoscopies or of cleaving embryos. Data have also been included from the original work in Kershaws Hospital, Oldham.

In Table IV, "biochemical" pregnancies are those detected only by a rise in HCGβ or another marker specific for early fetal growth.

Since this table was compiled, clinical pregnancies (i.e. excluding biochemical pregnancies) have been established by the groups in Gothenburg and Vienna, and several more have begun in Norfolk and Paris. Forty clinical pregnancies, including deliveries, have been established by the two Australian groups combined, and more than 70 in Bourn Hall.

Detailed Reports

Bourn Hall (Steptoe): The lithotomy position was used initially and both lithotomy and knee–chest position are now employed depending on the uterine situation in each patient. A simple wedge cushion is placed on the end of the bed, and the patient can drape herself over it. The cushion allows her to exaggerate the downward position of her uterus. A simple 4 French catheter made by Portex was used initially. Difficulties occurred in passing this catheter through the cervix. A 6 French gauge cannula was then introduced as an outside sleeve to pass the smaller catheter, and a solid metal obdurator could be used within this outer sleeve to guide it through the cervical canal. The obdurator was removed, to allow the inner catheter to be threaded, once entry had been gained to the uterus. Suitable markings were made on the end of the catheter to ensure it was passed satisfactorily

Table IV

Group results on embryo replacement and fetal growth

Stimulation	Bourn Hall (Jan. 1981–July 1981) Natural and Clomid	Gothenberg (Sept. 1981) Natural	Gothenberg (Sept. 1981) Clomid	Kiel (Sept. 1981) Natural, Clomid and HMG	Melbourne—Monash (End Sept. 1981) Clomid	Melbourne—Royal Women's Hospital (July 1979–July 1981) Natural and Clomid
Laparoscopies						
Total no.	330	31	27	149	368	392
With ≥ 1 egg	263	3	15	98		293 (75%)
With ≥ 1 fertilization	203	0	3	70		202 (52%)
With ≥ 1 cleaving	197	0	2	29		
With ≥ 1 replacement	195 (59%)	0	0			152 (39%)
No. of preovulatory follicles aspirated		25	58			717
Eggs						
Preovulatory		11	32			517
Non-ovulatory		7	9			11
No. of eggs fertilized		7	23	ca 38%		300 (58%)
No. cleaving		2	18			282
Replacements						
Single	} 195	0	3	} 3		152
Double						39
Treble						0
Pregnancies						
Total (including deliveries)	44	0	0	0	40	8
Biochemical	6				12	1
Aborted before 10 weeks	9				7†	3
Aborted after 10 weeks	0				1	1
Continuing, less than 10 weeks	} 29				‡	
Continuing, more than 10 weeks					10	
Twin (included in continuing)	2				1	1
Deliveries						
Single	2				9	
Twin					1	2

Table IV (continued)

Stimulation	Norfolk (1980–1981)	Oldham Kershaws (1970–1978)		Paris Clamart (Sept. 1981)	Paris Sèvres (Sept. 1981)	Vienna (Sept. 1981)	
	HMG	HMG	Natural	Natural, HMG, Clomid	Various	Natural	Clomid
Laparoscopies							
Total no.	31		65	139	77	25	50
With ≥ 1 egg	27		45	92 (66%)	38		
With ≥ 1 fertilization	16			59 (42%)	16		
With ≥ 1 cleaving			35	39	9		
With ≥ 1 replacement	12 (39%)		32 (49%)	24 (17%)	5		
No. of preovulatory follicles aspirated				181	115	22	77
Eggs							
Preovulatory				92	40	15	62 (43 for IVF)
Non-ovulatory	16		35	17	12	8	22
No. of eggs fertilized	} 12	} 77	35	59* (64%)	16	5	18
No. cleaving				33/54	9		
Replacements							
Single	} 12		} 32	24	5	} 5	11
Double				0			2
Treble				0			1
Pregnancies							
Total (including deliveries)	2	3	4	5	2		4
Biochemical		3		1	1		4
Aborted before 10 weeks			1	1	1		
Aborted after 10 weeks				2			
Continuing, less than 10 weeks	1			0			
Continuing, more than 10 weeks	1			1			
Twin (included in continuing)							
Deliveries							
Single			3				
Twin							

* Some oocytes fixed before or after fertilization.
† Before 12 weeks.
‡ Approx. 5, data being analysed.

beyond the end of the outer sleeve which was withdrawn, leaving only the inner catheter within the uterine cavity. Our first successful pregnancies in Oldham were obtained with these methods.

The use of double catheters was then abandoned for a single catheter 12 cm long, 4 French gauge, made by Portex. It had sharp ends, which were not sufficiently rounded, but two pregnancies were obtained in Oldham by this method. Sometimes a tenaculum was placed on the cervix, and occasional attempts were made to reduce levels of prostaglandins, or to try the use of Ritodrine, but without much success.

In Bourn Hall, attempts are made to get the fundus uteri as low as possible, using the cushion described above. If the uterus is very sharply anteverted, which causes great difficulty in getting through the internal os, or markedly retroflexed, the knee–chest position or dorsal position are used respectively. Sometimes the patients must be turned over during replacement.

We have designed a new catheter, with an outer sheath terminating 5 cm from the tip. The last 5 cm are 4 French gauge, marked in centimetres to indicate the distance through the cervical canal. The end is smoothed off, and it is produced by Portex. It can be used in the majority of cases, but again difficulties may arise at the internal os, even though the position of the uterus and the condition of the canal are noted beforehand, and despite dilating the cervix of some patients one month before admission. A metal catheter has also been introduced with a simple flange 3 cm from the end, and a rounded obdurator to assist movement through the cervical canal. The degree of the curvature can be varied to suit individual patients, and it is used to pass through the cervical canal before removing the obdurator. A fine cannula containing the embryo is then inserted through it. We have had pregnancies using the Bourn and metal catheters, some occurring despite the presence of blood and mucus on the tip of the catheter. Rare failures have forced us to replace the embryo on the following morning under general anaesthesia, using a tenaculum on the cervix.

A new catheter has now been designed by Edwards, called the Wallace catheter. It is made of polyethylene, has a low friction and is so soft and yielding that it follows the curvature of the cervical canal. It has a rounded end, and a side delivery aperture. The diameter is 4 French gauge. The aperture is carefully placed proximal to the end in order to give some protection to the contents of the cannula as it passes through the cervical canal. It has an outer sheath of teflon, which is movable and this can be used to stiffen the polyethylene. In the great majority of cases, the polyethylene slips easily through the cervical canal and into the uterus without resistance, and the replacement is over within a minute or two. In cases of difficulty, the outer sheath can be slid forward gently, adding stability to the inner catheter and helping to pass the internal os. We have had several pregnancies, even though the catheter has only been introduced recently. We now use the metal and Bourn catheters only if there are problems in passing the internal os.

Edwards: Sterile precautions are used during replacement of embryos, with clothing, masks, gloves and shoes. The early catheters were all end-loading. They are simple and quick to load, but they may become plugged with mucus and tissue if difficulties arise in passing the internal os. The Wallace catheter has side-delivery, and it can be loaded without too much difficulty. It is equally important to have a smooth withdrawal as it is to have a smooth entry into the uterus, otherwise dislodged tissue and mucus might cause as much uterine damage as scratching or scraping on entry.

Melbourne — Monash (Leeton): We transfer embryos between the 1-cell and 4-cell stage. The patients are given valium, and the knee–stirrup position is used. We like husbands to be present during the replantation; everybody is then much more relaxed. We do not use strict sterile techniques at all. We try to line up the cervix with the uterus, swab the ectocervix with culture medium, and leave the vagina alone. Our catheters are all made of teflon and different types have hardly influenced the rate of pregnancy. We were using an open-ended catheter, but now we are using a sleeve, with a side aperture. The sleeve is made of teflon, and it has made a great deal of difference to our techniques because it protects the catheter during the entry through the cervical canal. It also helps to provide a guide to the length of the cervix, so that the distance can be judged accurately. The length of the uterine cavity has already been checked by sounding, and we aim to get the tip of the catheter about 1 cm from the fundus.

Last year, we had five difficult replacements but, of the nine pregnancies, seven involved no pain, and were excellent transfers. In the remaining two, some blood and mucus was seen inside the catheter. In two of the pregnant cases, there was some slight brown loss noted 2 or 3 days after the transfer.

Trounson: We had to abandon Portex catheters, because we know they are toxic to mouse embryos. They are all dead within the hour, and this is not the case with any of the other catheters. Teflon has been satisfactory.

Melbourne — Royal Women's Hospital (Johnston): We have replaced embryos in all stages of preimplantation development, mostly 8-cell, but recently most have been 4-cell. Premedication is minimal, and various positions of the patient have been adopted for an easy entrance into the uterus. These include lithotomy, lateral and knee-chest. We have pregnancies in all these positions.

Currently, we believe the position of the uterus is more important than the position of the patient. Lithotomy is used if the uterus is anteverted or anteflexed. The knee–chest position is used when it is retroverted. A large variety of catheters have been tested, including metal cannulae with abdurators, now used very rarely in difficult cases. Only teflon catheters are now used, especially one called the Lopata catheter. The outer sleeve stops 4 cm from the end of the catheter, so the tip of the catheter enters the uterine cavity. An inner catheter, carrying the embryo, emerges from the side. Originally, the larger catheter was passed just through the internal os and the smaller catheter into the cavity. Now, because the fine catheter might damage the endometrium, both catheters are passed close to the fundus and the outer catheter is withdrawn. Serrations on the penetrating end of the catheter must be avoided because they can cause trauma.

Two new prototypes have been introduced. We want a slightly malleable catheter, with a rounded end, to prevent damage to the endometrium. This may be the kind of catheter which will prove to be the most suitable. Another idea is to incorporate an abdurator with a springy wire to hold the catheter in any pre-set shape, the end of the catheter being bent to suit the shape of the cervical canal.

We have always had reservations about using a tenaculum to grasp the cervix and so manipulate the uterus. When trying to pass the catheter through an anteflexed or retroflexed uterus, there can be considerable difficulty until the cervix is lightly grasped with a tenaculum and the uterus straightened by gentle pressure. The catheter then slides directly in. A little traction on the uterus evidently does far less damage than repeated attempts to pass through the internal os.

Edwards: The expelled medium can run back between the inner and outer sheath, carrying the embryo with it. This danger is increased if the tips of the two are close together.

Lopata: It is essential to remove the outer catheter from the uterus before expelling the embryo from the inner catheter.

Norfolk (Jones, H): We use a metal outer catheter, which passes just inside the tip of the cervix. It may be curved, to conform with the shape of the canal. The teflon catheter carrying the embryo is then passed through this outer sleeve into the cavity. A little air is introduced when the catheter is loaded, to break any tension, and help to eject the embryo. The catheter is rotated through 180 °C as it is withdrawn, in the hope of leaving the embryo behind. The uterus is placed in the lowest possible position, in order to assist the expulsion and movement of the embryo into it. The patient is left in the replacement position for 4 hours, and she is given tetracycline 24 hours before and after replacement.

Paris — Sèvres (Cohen): We have only done 4 replacements, with one pregnancy developing to 12 weeks which resulted in a trisomy 22. A second pregnancy was a "biochemical" pregnancy.

Some of our methods differ considerably from other groups. During laparoscopy for oocyte recovery, a cannula is placed in the cervix, and the os is gently dilated to pass through the cannula. The uterus is not entered, the cannula passing as far as the internal os. Besides helping in oocyte recovery, this method also gives a slight dilatation of the os. During the replacement itself, a tenaculum is used to straighten the cervical canal gently, and a catheter is passed through and into the uterine cavity. We believe this method causes less damage than the usual methods, which can give bleeding from the canal or from the cervix. We have not seen any bleeding at all in our four cases.

Paris — Clamart (Frydman): The cervical os is examined at the first consultation. Replacements are done not in theatre, but in the consulting room, and we even use music to relax the patient! Sometimes forceps are placed on the external os, and we have one pregnancy even though there was some difficulty in passing the catheter in this case. The catheter has a side opening, and we have abandoned using a double catheter.

Vienna (Feichtinger): Replacements are usually performed with embryos between 2- and 6-cell stages (36–46 hours after recovery). The patient is placed on the operating table before the vulva is shaved and disinfected with a mercury solution. Previously several positions were tested, mostly lithotomy, once a knee–elbow, but a lateral position now suits best. The patient is covered with sterile towels and then laid on her side. The cervix is fixed with an automatic speculum and rinsed with warm culture medium. A Portex cannula of 4 French gauge with the Luer fitting is marked to show the position in the uterus.

The embryo is withdrawn into the cannula directly from the culture tube. Laminated air flow and masks are not used. The embryo is expelled into the uterus in 0.05 ml of medium and the catheter is suddenly withdrawn. In most cases, a metal sleeve is inserted to the internal os in order to help passing. Unfortunately, the instrument seems traumatic and causes uterine contractions, and a thinner metal sleeve with a 3 French gauge catheter did not improve matters. From 19 replacements, four patients had a transitory elevation of $HCG\beta$ in the serum after about 8–10 days, but then they menstruated a few days later than expected. None of the others showed evidence of implantation.

Of our 19 replacements, leakage was noticed in 9 cases, 3–5 minutes later, even with amounts of medium as low as 0.05 ml. There is probably a high frequency of contractions a few minutes after replacement (Fröhlich, 1974). Metal sleeves may cause this problem, being too traumatic; with smaller catheters made of plastic contractions do not occur and smooth catheters may also prevent this effect.

The progress of growth after replacement is monitored by drawing blood every second day in order to estimate for LH, HCGβ, progesterone and SP$_1$. HCGβ has been elevated in four of our 17 patients between 9 and 12 days after laparoscopy. In one patient, levels of HCGβ decreased more slowly until the 15th day, hence showing slight elevation for about one week. Transient implantation was confirmed in the serum of some of these patients by detecting SP$_1$, the pregnancy-specific β_1-glycoprotein of the syncytiotrophoblast (Enzymeimmunoassay; Behring Werke Ag, West Germany).

HCGβ can be elevated as early as eight days after ovulation (Catt *et al.*, 1975), and brief elevated levels of SP, also occur, e.g. in women using an IUD as a contraceptive (Seppälä *et al.*, 1978). Perhaps a short pregnancy occurs because implantation is similarly disturbed by an endometrial insult resulting in a pseudodecidual reaction.

References

Catt, K. J., Dufau, J. L. & Vaitukaitis, J. L. 1975. Appearance of HCG in pregnancy plasma following the initiation of implantation of the blastocyst. *Journal of Clinical Endocrinology and Metabolism*, **40**, 537.

Fröhlich, H. 1974. Steuermechanismen der Motilität des nicht-graviden Uterus *in situ*. *Wien. Klin. Wschr.*, **86**, Suppl. 24.

Seppälä, M., Rutanen, E. M., Jalanko, H., Lekovita, P., Stenman, V. H. & Engvak, E. 1978. Pregnancy-specific β_1-glycoprotein and chorionic gonadotropin-like immunoreactivity during the later half of the cycle in women using intrauterine contraceptives. *Journal of Clinical Endocrinology and Metabolism*, **47**, 1216.

Index

Page numbers in *italics* indicate Figures or Tables

421

50. ::
G4.

Doctor P. Little

2-8-73